Studies in Economic History

Series Editor

Tetsuji Okazaki, Faculty of Economics, The University of Tokyo, Tokyo, Japan

Aims and Scope

This series from Springer provides a platform for works in economic history that truly integrate economics and history. Books on a wide range of related topics are welcomed and encouraged, including those in macro-economic history, financial history, labor history, industrial history, agricultural history, the history of institutions and organizations, spatial economic history, law and economic history, political economic history, historical demography, and environmental history.

Economic history studies have greatly developed over the past several decades through application of economics and econometrics. Particularly in recent years, a variety of new economic theories and sophisticated econometric techniques—including game theory, spatial economics, and generalized method of moment (GMM)—have been introduced for the great benefit of economic historians and the research community.

At the same time, a good economic history study should contribute more than just an application of economics and econometrics to past data. It raises novel research questions, proposes a new view of history, and/or provides rich documentation. This series is intended to integrate data analysis, close examination of archival works, and application of theoretical frameworks to offer new insights and even provide opportunities to rethink theories.

The purview of this new Springer series is truly global, encompassing all nations and areas of the world as well as all eras from ancient times to the present. The editorial board, who are internationally renowned leaders among economic historians, carefully evaluate and judge each manuscript, referring to reports from expert reviewers. The series publishes contributions by university professors and others well established in the academic community, as well as work deemed to be of equivalent merit.

All books and chapters in the Studies in Economic History book series are indexed in Scopus.

Akio Takahashi

Regime Changes and Socio-economic History of Rural Myanmar, 1986–2019

Springer

Akio Takahashi
Institute for Advanced Studies on Asia
University of Tokyo
Tokyo, Japan

ISSN 2364-1797 ISSN 2364-1800 (electronic)
Studies in Economic History
ISBN 978-981-99-3271-9 ISBN 978-981-99-3272-6 (eBook)
https://doi.org/10.1007/978-981-99-3272-6

Translation from the Japanese language edition: "Myanmar no taisei henkan to nouson no shakai keizaishi: 1986–2019" by Akio Takahashi, © Akio Takahashi 2021. Published by University of Tokyo Press. All Rights Reserved.

This Springer imprint is published by the registered company Springer Nature Singapore Pte Ltd.
The registered company address is: 152 Beach Road, #21-01/04 Gateway East, Singapore 189721, Singapore

Preface

This book is an English translation of *Myanmā no taisei tenkan to nōson no shakaikeizai-shi: 1986–2019 nen* (Regime Change in Myanmar and the Socio-economic History of Its Rural Areas: 1986–2019). The original book was published by the University of Tokyo Press in February 2021. That same month, a military takeover occurred in Myanmar and yet another "Regime Change" took place—from a democracy to a military regime. However, this book covers only the period up to the middle of the democratic regime led by Aung San Suu Kyi. Since the COVID-19 epidemic began in early 2020, no one has conducted a socio-economic survey of rural Myanmar. Neither have I. Thus, I cannot write here much about rural Myanmar after 2021, because I have so far written papers and books only based on what I have actually seen, heard and investigated in the villages. The only thing I know from Japan through Internet news and social networking services is that demonstrations and armed struggles against the military regime are continuing not only in ethnic minority villages, where warfare has continued intermittently since independence, but this time also in ethnic Bamar villages.

What I can then do here, within the limits of my conscience as a researcher, is to let the reader imagine from the contents of this book why these explicit anti-coup resistance movements have arisen and continue. This book is of course not written on such a premise, but it is interspersed throughout with elements that can explain the causes and motivations of the current rural movement and hints for understanding current rural trends. Some of the relevant key words are the three pillars of agricultural policy; enactment and amendment of "Ward or Village Tract Administration Law" (Chap. 1); de-agrarianisation; terms of trade for agriculture (Chap. 2); farmland confiscation; chemicalisation of agriculture; transport infrastructure; information technology; higher education (Chap. 3); dyadic networks; catalysts; "relatives of the place" (Chap. 6); absence of a Japanese-style "village collective" (*kyōdōtai*); and "collective failure" (Chap. 7). From these key words, readers may draw various inferences about the current rural resistance movements and beyond. I will discuss my inferences about the post-coup situation in the epilogue. The main focus of this book is to describe the socio-economic transformation and the unchanging social core of Myanmar villages that I visited from 1986 to 2019.

The people of rural Myanmar have helped me greatly in writing this book. The rapport that was built at the end of the socialist period continues to this day. Not a few of my friends have passed away, but even though the generations have changed, so many people have always treated me with an open heart. In particular, villagers who assisted my research as village mayors and research assistants not only cooperated with my various surveys for a long time after completing their duties, but also provided me with materials and information for writing this book via telephone and social media, when I was unable to enter Myanmar due to the COVID-19 epidemic.

I was satisfied with the publication in Japanese, but it was Ms. Juno Kawakami of Springer who suggested that I publish the book in English. The University of Tokyo Press was very favourable to me regarding a publishing contract in English. Dr. Laur Kiik, Postdoctoral Fellow at Tokyo College, the University of Tokyo, offered suggestions on revising the English language text. Ms. Aya Unno, Secretary to Director of the Institute of Advanced Studies on Asia, assisted in preparing the reference list and index, as she also did when the Japanese book was published.

Acknowledgement should be given to all those who have assisted in publishing this book.

Tokyo, Japan Akio Takahashi

Contents

About the Author

Akio Takahashi is former Director of the Institute of Advanced Studies on Asia and Professor Emeritus of the University of Tokyo. The main subject of his research is the agricultural and rural economy of Myanmar (Burma). He taught Southeast Asian Economy at the Graduate School of Economics, University of Tokyo, from 1996 to 2023. He received his B.A. (1981) and his Doctor of Economics degree (1993) from the Faculty of Economics, Kyoto University. Before teaching at the University of Tokyo, he was Researcher at the Institute of Developing Economies (IDE) from 1981 to 1996. While working for IDE, he was sent to Myanmar twice: first he stayed there as a student in the department of Burmese language at the Institute of Foreign Languages, Yangon, from 1986 to 1988, and then as a Senior Researcher at the Department of Agricultural Planning, Ministry of Agriculture, from 1993 to 1995. He has made numerous village studies in rural Myanmar by means of direct interviews with the villagers since the final years of the Burmese Socialism era. His main interest has been the relationship between political regimes and village economy, including non-farm activities as well as agriculture. He has also studied the change of agricultural policy and the economic history of Myanmar after independence. Recently, he has extended his research perspectives to the social economy of peripheral areas where various minorities reside and to the history of peasant livelihoods in Myanmar. Besides his academic studies, he has stayed in Myanmar for several months a year in 2000–2003 and in 2013–2017 as an expert for the Japan International Cooperation Agency (JICA) and advised both the governments of Myanmar and Japan.

Professor Takahashi's major publications on Myanmar's economic history and socio-economic transformation in rural areas include *Myanmar of the People: A Country in Transition, Seen Through the Life in Rural Villages* (Tokyo: Akashishoten, 2018), *State and People of Myanmar: Toward a Theoretical Comparison of Village Society in Japan and Myanmar* (Tokyo: Akashishoten, 2012), *Myanmar's Village Economy in Transition: Farmers and Non-Farmers Under the Market-oriented Economy* (Tokyo: Tokyo Daigaku Shuppankai, 2000), and *A Rice Village in the Burma Delta: Village Economy under 'Socialism'* (Tokyo: Institute of Developing Economies, 1992).

Chapter 1
Introduction: The History of Myanmar's Political and Economic System, and the Structure of This Book

Women from a rice-planting group planting rice along ropes laid across the paddy field. In the 1980s, the Special High-yielding Rice Production Programme introduced during the late socialist era forced farmers to plant rice in dense, regular rows. This rope-planting practice was discontinued after the transition to a market economy under the SLORC military regime. (Thindaunggyi Village, August 1987)

A. Takahashi, *Regime Changes and Socio-economic History of Rural Myanmar, 1986–2019*, Studies in Economic History,
https://doi.org/10.1007/978-981-99-3272-6_1

My research in rural Myanmar (Burma) began in 1986, at the end of the Burmese socialist era. I continued field research during the two decades of military rule and then a decade of democratisation. I have visited more than 200 villages and interviewed more than 10,000 villagers. The interviews were conducted using questionnaires that I prepared in Burmese language. This book traces the economic history of contemporary Myanmar's agricultural and rural villages, focusing on the socio-economic transformation of the rural communities that I have surveyed for more than 30 years. My research also attempts to understand the core of Myanmar's rural communities, including social characteristics, which have remained largely unchanged, at least during the period of my survey.

The theme of the first half of this book is *de-agrarianisation*.[1] This is a key word in the transformation of rural society. This book adds the author's unique perspective to the existing theories of de-agrarianisation to describe how the social economy of Myanmar villages has changed. In Myanmar now, nearly 70% of the total population of over 50 million people live in rural areas, and nearly 70% of them are engaged in agriculture. However, macro-data analysis and in-depth rural socio-economic surveys have revealed a clear trend toward de-agrarianisation since at least the mid-1980s.

The theme of the book's second half is "*the absence of a village collective*". This is the nature of rural Myanmar, the core that has not been transformed. In spite of the repressive political and economic regimes of socialism and military rule, the villagers of Myanmar have lived surprisingly autonomously, freely and independently. This is because Myanmar villages are not "village collectives" like the villages in Japan. This book explains this using both empirical and theoretical perspectives. It also explains why Burmese socialism did not penetrate to the grassroots, and why village-based projects, such as microcredit, cooperatives, and community forestry, which are designed by international organisations and NGOs, have struggled to succeed.

In this chapter, I will first outline what "regime change" means in Myanmar, how the transitions can be delineated, and what the "regime" was like during the different periods. Since gaining independence from the United Kingdom in 1948, Myanmar (Burma) has undergone major changes in its political and economic system from the period of parliamentary democracy[2] (1948–1962), Burmese Way

[1] De-agrarianisation is a concept proposed by Deborah F. Bryceson in her fieldwork in Africa. It includes four elements: (1) occupational adjustment, (2) income-earning reorientation, (3) social identification, and (4) spatial relocation (Bryceson & Jamal, 1997: 2). Rigg added: (5) spatial interpenetration to these four items (Rigg, 2001: 6). All of these terms describe the villagers' divergence from the peasant way of life. These five terms mean, respectively: (1) a growth of the non-agricultural population, (2) an increase in income from non-agricultural sources within households, (3) an increase in the number of people who have or want to have a sense of social belonging as non-agricultural workers rather than as agricultural workers, (4) rural-to-urban migration and (5) factories and urban residential areas entering even rural areas. I have suggested that this category could also include the decline in the relative value of agricultural land, the rise of non-agricultural workers in the rural economic strata, the seizure of political power by non-agricultural workers, and the urbanisation of the landscape of peasant houses (Takahashi, 2016: 145).

[2] In this book, this period is also referred to as the "post-independence civil administration period". The period from 2011 to 2021 is referred to as the " democratisation period" to distinguish it from the post-independence period, although parliamentary democracy was restored after 2011.

to Socialism period (1962–1988), the period of direct military rule (1988–2011), and the period of partial democratisation (2011–2021) which ended with the recent military takeover.

The changes in the country's official name, both the Burmese and English names, can be summarised as follows:

1948.1.4–1974.1.3 Union of Burma (ပြည်ထောင်စု မြန်မာနိုင်ငံတော်)

1974.1.4–1988.9.22 Socialist Republic of the Union of Burma (ပြည်ထောင်စု ဆိုရှယ်လစ် သမ္မတမြန်မာနိုင်ငံတော်)

1988.9.23–1989.6.17 Union of Burma (ပြည်ထောင်စု မြန်မာနိုင်ငံတော်)

1989.6.18–2010.10.20 Union of Myanmar (ပြည်ထောင်စု မြန်မာနိုင်ငံတော်)

2010.10.21–now Republic of the Union of Myanmar (ပြည်ထောင်စု သမ္မတမြန်မာနိုင်ငံတော်)

As can be seen from the above, the name of the country in the *Burmese* language was unchanged. The name is consistently "Myanmar (မြန်မာ)", while "Bamar (ဗမာ) or Burma" was never used.[3]

Moreover, the change of the political and economic regime did not coincide with the change of the country's name: the regime headed by General Ne Win[4] that came into power by *coup d'état* on March 2, 1962, called itself the "Revolutionary Government (*tohlanyêi asôuyà*)", aiming at socialism in Burma, but did not alter the country's name. This changed in 1974, when Ne Win shed his military uniform, changed his own title from the Chairman of the Revolutionary Council to President, and had the "People's Council" (*pyidhù kaunsi*) —elected in undemocratic elections —organise the government. He retired from the presidency in 1981 but remained the nation's highest authority until 1988. Although the name of the country changed

[3] Regardless of whether the country name in English was changed from Burma to Myanmar after 1988, this book will use "Myanmar" when the referenced literature uses "Myanmar" (မြန်မာ), and will use "Burma" when the referenced literature uses "ဗမာ" or "Burma". However, words that have already been established as historical terms, such as Burmese Socialism and Divisional Burma, are used as they are. From now on, the use of Burmese (Myanmar) script (*myanma sa*) will be kept to a minimum. The Romanisation system devised by Okuhira Ryuji (The Burma Research Group, 1991, p. 18) will be used, while including my own transliterations in some parts. Although "Myanma" is the formal adjective for "Myanmar", the latter is also used.

[4] The Burmese people do not have a surname, so "Ne Win" is a first name, not a family name. Honorifics are based on gender, age or social status. In the case of a man, a person of higher social status or age is addressed with U, a person of similar age with Ko, and a person of lower social status with Maung. For women, a person of higher age or status is addressed with Daw, while a person of the same or lower status is addressed with Ma. These honorific titles depend on the relationship between the person calling and the person being called, so they vary depending on the relationship between the two parties. There are exceptions to this rule, such as the use of the name of the rank of a soldier in active service, and the use of doctor for a Ph.D. holder or physician. When translating the names of public figures such as Ne Win, Than Shwe, and Aung San Suu Kyi into Japanese or English, honorific titles are generally not used.

in 1974 (as can be seen above), the Burma Socialist Programme Party (*myanmà hsousheli lânzin pati*) led the country throughout from 1962 to 1988, with Ne Win leading the party. Thus, this period can be called the Burmese way to socialism period or the Ne Win regime period.

The military junta headed by General Saw Maung, which emerged following a *coup d'état* on September 18, 1988, immediately reverted the country's name back to the one before January 3, 1974, and in June of the following year, changed the official English name from "Burma" to "Myanmar".[5] In 1992, Than Shwe succeeded Saw Maung, and in 1997, the name of the military regime was changed from State Law and Order Restoration Council (SLORC) to State Peace and Development Council (SPDC), but the name of the country did not change.

A new constitution was ratified in 2008 and adopted in 2011. The country's official name was changed to "The Republic of the Union of Myanmar" in 2010, before President Thein Sein was confirmed as the new state leader. In 2016, Thein Sein's government was replaced by the government of the National League for Democracy (NLD).

In addition, it is important to note that, in Myanmar's post-independence history, the political system and the economic system do not necessarily coincide. The military government of Ne Win, which seized power in a *coup d'état* in 1962, rejected parliamentary democracy and pursued more socialist policies through dictatorship, adding socialism to the country's name in 1974. However, the military regimes of Saw Maung in 1988 and Than Shwe, who succeeded him in 1992, rejected socialism and shifted to capitalist economic policies. The same direction was followed during the partial democratisation period ushered in by President Thein Sein in 2011, and the democratically elected Aung San Suu Kyi administration that followed.

After independence, Myanmar leaders had a tacit understanding that the country should seek to establish a socialist economic system. Since becoming a British colony in the nineteenth century, capitalism—based on modern property rights and the free market of goods and services—had developed in earnest in Myanmar. However, *laissez-faire* competition had created a significant disparity between socio-economic groups. Access to economic rights was defined by "race" and ethnicity,[6] leading to the formation of what became known as a "Plural Society" in which several groups were "living side by side but separately" and the social division of labour was structured hierarchically according to "race" (Furnivall, 1957, p. k–r).[7] In this society, Europeans, mainly the British, controlled most of the large corporations, and the upper echelons of the government and military were also in their hands.

---

[5] Not only the English name of the country, but also the English names of many towns and streets were changed. The military government announced that "Myanmar" would be the country name and "Bamar (Burma)" would be the ethnic name, like Shan and Chin. However, historically, "Myanmar" and "Bamar" have been used to mean the same thing, with "Myanmar" used in written language and "Bamar" in spoken language. Since the United Nations uses the English name "Myanmar", this book will use "Myanmar".

[6] In Burmese, both race and ethnicity are called *lumyô*. In this book, *lumyô* is translated mostly as ethnicity, but sometimes as "people" when it is clear from the context.

[7] On Furnivall and "Plural Society", see Takahashi (2008b: 369).

Indians formed the middle class as merchants, moneylenders, lower-ranking officials, landlords, and so on; to a lesser extent the Chinese also belonged to this class. Under such "foreigners," the majority of Myanmar[8] people formed the lowest strata of society as small farmers and agricultural labourers. The nationalism of Myanmar people, which was formed under such an economic system, tended to be anti-colonial and anti-capitalist at the same time. The independence movement and subsequent nation-building tended toward socialism, the opposite of capitalism.

After gaining independence in 1948, Burma sought to become a socialist state gradually, through parliamentary democracy. Farmland had during the colonial period been accumulated in the hands of "foreign"—such as Indian and Chinese—non-resident landlords, as well as Myanmar non-cultivating landowners. Therefore, after the independence, the nationalisation of farmland and its redistribution to Myanmar farmers was considered to be the most important issue in the agricultural sector. In addition, it was decided that the state would be responsible for the trade of rice,[9] the largest export product, which had been in the hands of those considered to be "foreigners". The state purchased paddy from farmers at low prices, exported husked rice to foreign countries, and used the earned foreign currency for economic development. In the industrial sector, the government gradually increased its investment in the three main sectors: rice milling, lumbering, and cotton reeling. These had been the main industries of the colonial period and these large factories were owned by "foreigners" such as Europeans, Indians, and Chinese. At the same time, a nationalisation plan aimed to build factories in 65 types of industry, including steel, fertiliser, and cement. These industrialisation policies were adopted to break away from the colonial monoculture economy that specialised in rice, but the premise of these policies was to obtain foreign currency through rice exports.

---

[8] Article 3 of the Union Citizenship Act, promulgated in 1948 when Myanmar became independent, defines the ethnic groups that have lived in the Union since before 1823—such as the Arakanese, Burmese, Chin, Kachin, Karen, Kayah, Mon and Shan—as "indigenous races of Burma (*tâinyîndhâ*)". In this book, I refer to all these indigenous peoples collectively as Myanmar. I refer to the ethnic group as Bamar. This resembles how John S. Furnivall and Michael Adas separated "Burmese" and "Burman" to avoid confusion in their descriptions. However, Furnivall uses the term "Burmese" for the people whose mother tongue is Burmese, and "Burman" for the general term of the above-mentioned indigenous peoples (Furnivall, 1957: g), while Adas used these terms exactly in reverse (Adas, 1974: 3). The term "foreigner" is used in this book to refer to Europeans, Chinese, Indians, and so on at that time.

[9] The English word "rice" has multiple meanings: rice as a plant; paddy (or husked rice) as fruit of rice plant; husked brown rice; and polished white rice. In this book, "rice" is used for the concept that encompasses all four of these stages, while "husked rice" is used for the latter two stages. However, depending on the context, no strict distinction of these stages is made.

The economic policies of the military government led by Ne Win, who seized power in a *coup d'état* in 1962, generally followed these policies. However, Ne Win's regime rejected parliamentary democracy, pushed socialism to the fore and thoroughly nationalised the economy. A centralised planned economic system was introduced. Foreign investment, foreign aid and even the entry of foreigners were severely restricted. The regime was a military socialist regime that advocated the "Burmese way to socialism",[10] which was completely different from the previous regime.

In the agricultural sector, in return for granting peasants the right to cultivate land, the state required peasants to supply agricultural products to itself at a fixed price determined by the government. Ne Win's government created a system in which the state was the landowner, and the peasants were its tenants. Reforms were implemented so that the distribution, processing, and export of agricultural products, as well as agricultural finance, were handled centrally by the state. In the non-agricultural sector, starting with the nationalisation of the banks in February 1963, major industries such as tobacco manufacturing, timber, oil, and textile processing were nationalised one after another. Thus, during the 1960s, the colonial legacy of the capitalist economic system was largely swept away and replaced by state-owned economic institutions. This economic oligopoly of state-owned and state-controlled enterprises lasted until 1988, and still partly remains even today after three decades of market reforms. The inefficiency of the management of the remaining state-owned enterprises is well known (Thein & Tun, 2019).

The military junta that emerged from the September 1988 *coup d'état* steered the country toward a capitalist economic system, even though its leaders were cadres of the Burmese Socialist Programme Party. However, instead of calling it capitalism, the junta called it "Open-door Policy (*dagâ phwìn wadà*)". This was symbolised by the liberalisation of private import and export operations (excluding rice and teak) announced in October 1988 and the Foreign Investment Law promulgated in November 1988, while the political situation was still uncertain. In 1989, the State Enterprise Law was promulgated, which greatly liberalised the activities of private enterprises, with the exception of certain key spheres, including defence, postal services, and broadcasting. In 1990, the Financial Institutions Law was enacted, which encouraged the creation of private banks. Foreign banks also opened offices. The liberalisation of the export and banking industries, which until then had been monopolised by the state, and the opening of these sectors to foreign investment

[10] This socialism is characterised by the following: socialism is the final stage rather than the preliminary stage for communism; it is not a proletarian dictatorship but is based on a broad social stratum that includes mainly peasants and workers as well as engineers and intellectuals; spiritual life is emphasised rather than material life; and freedom of religion is fully recognised for party members (Takahashi, 2002: 212). The economic management system however, was quite similar to the general socialist system, except that agriculture was not collectivised. In other words, many policies were almost the same as in other socialist countries: the nationalisation of the means of production, the planned economy system and centralised economic management, the control of the distribution system and the state monopoly of trade, the state control of the financial system, and the import-substitution industrialisation by state enterprises (Takahashi, 1999: 303).

marked the abandonment of socialism. As a result of this open-door policy, the exploration and production of crude oil and natural gas by foreign firms was accompanied by similar reforms in other sectors of the economy including tourism, construction, transportation, and other industries. In the mid-1990s, foreign investment in Myanmar's manufacturing, in particular the garment sector, began to rapidly grow. Both domestic and foreign capital invested in Myanmar's manufacturing and real estate sector which began to take off around 1995.

Following the seizure of power by the military in 1988, the country was subjected to increasing sanctions from Western countries on the grounds of human rights abuses. Thus, during the 1990s, much of the foreign investment and trade came from Asian countries such as Thailand and Singapore. The Asian economic crisis of 1997 hit the country, forcing the military government to restrict imports and foreign currency transfers, and the "open economy" came to a halt. To summarise, the country was autonomously "isolated" until 1988, but as soon as it opened up, it was confronted with the same restrictions on markets, aid and investment that it had encountered during the "isolation" period, but this time as a result of the heteronomous economic sanctions imposed by the Western countries (Takahashi, 2013, p. 301).

Myanmar had to wait until the quasi-democratic government[11] of Thein Sein came to office in 2011 before the constraints of sanctions began to be loosened and the move toward a truly open economy could proceed. This government implemented a series of major reforms that were unimaginable under the previous military regime, including the mass release of political prisoners, the abolition of prior censorship of the media, a ceasefire with some ethnic minority armed organisations and a freeze on the construction of the Myitsone Dam, which was being built at enormous cost by China. Most notably, Thein Sein set the stage for the milestone victory of Aung San Suu Kyi and other NLD candidates in the April 2012 round of by-elections.

Thein Sein's progress led to the resumption of EU preferential tariffs, which had been suspended in 1997, the lifting of the ban on new investment by the United States, the waiver of the repayment of 300 billion yen in Japanese loans, and other moves to fully lift most economic sanctions in earnest. The achievements of the Thein Sein administration were to improve relations with the international community, including Europe and the United States, to re-enter the global economy, and to create an international environment in which economic development could be pursued (Kudo, 2015, p. 1).

---

[11] Thein Sein's government cannot be called fully democratic due to many facts: a quarter of the seats in parliament were reserved for members of the national army; Aung San Suu Kyi, a symbol of democracy, was under house arrest; the National League for Democracy (NLD), which she led, boycotted the 2010 elections; and many ministers, including President Thein Sein, were former officers of the military. However, taking into account the fact that free general elections were held in 2015, democratisation progressed under the government of President Thein Sein, and the fact that the next government since 2016 also did not resolve issues such as the constitution and freedom of speech, I will refer to the governments from 2011 to 2021 as "democratising governments" in the sense that they aspired to democracy and as a result democratisation partially progressed.

In parallel with the lifting of these economic sanctions, the Thein Sein government promoted the opening up of the economy by unifying exchange rates under a managed floating exchange rate system,[12] enacting new foreign investment laws, and establishing special economic zones in areas such as Thilawa and Kyaukpyu. In addition, agricultural and labour-related laws were developed to protect the rights of farmers and labourers and to create an environment that helped the entry of foreign capital.

The NLD won an overwhelming victory in the 2015 general election, and Aung San Suu Kyi's government[13] came to power in 2016. Based on the principle of "no economic development without peace," the government gave priority to the peace process and to official efforts at reconciliation with ethnic armed organisations, as well as tried to continue the momentum of the previous administration with regard to the economy. However, the peace process did not progress and the economy gradually lost momentum. In response, the NLD administration shifted its emphasis to the economy and promoted an "Open-door Policy", enacting the first company law in 103 years, allowing 100% foreign investment in the wholesale and retail trade, as well as easing restrictions on domestic lending by foreign banks, establishing a Ministry of International Cooperation, and opening the insurance sector to foreign investment.

Although Myanmar showed significant growth in the economy, it may have remained difficult for the country to continue steady growth unless it improved its infrastructure, including roads and electricity. Other barriers to further economic growth were the outdated legislation and low level of human resource development.

The following table summarises the changes in the post-independence systems outlined above.

	Time period	Political system	Economic system	Country open/closed
Post-independence civil administration	1948–1962	Democracy	Socialism	Open
Burmese way to socialism	1962–1988	Dictatorship	Socialism	Closed (autonomous)
Military regime	1988–2011	Dictatorship	Capitalism	Closed (heteronomous)
Democratisation	2011–2021	Democratising	Capitalism	Open

[12] This started on April 2, 2012. Until then, there were several exchange rates: the official exchange rate (pegged to the Special Drawing Rights (SDR) since 1977, with the exchange rate for one dollar being 5–8 kyats; in March 2012, it was 5.49 kyats per dollar), the government-approved rate (450 kyats per dollar), the market rate (about 800 kyats), the foreign exchange certificate (FEC) market rate, and the bank transfer rate. These complex exchange rates were barriers to trade and investment.

[13] It is appropriate to call it the "Aung San Suu Kyi Government" because Aung San Suu Kyi was appointed as the State Counsellor, stating clearly that she was "above the President" (who is the Head of State), and not only obtained the legal authority to advise all the Ministers, but was also leading in substance.

If we compare each period from the above three perspectives—openness or isolation to the international community; the political system; and the economic system—we find that no two periods follow the same pattern. Furthermore, even when speaking about "socialism", we must consider that the post-independence civil administration period aimed at socialism, but in reality had a mixed economy. In contrast, the socialism of the "Burmese way to socialism" period was a far more rigid blend of socialism and state control of the economy than what had come before during the U Nu period. Likewise, the form of capitalism practiced in Myanmar differs between the military regime period, in which the military took over the legacy of the socialist era and only made the economic system capitalist, and the democratisation period, in which the governments abandoned socialist legacies one after another. The first half of the democratisation period, which began in 2011, was a democracy that came from above in which the military took off their uniforms, but in 2016, the NLD, a civilian political party, came to power, albeit under a system where the NLD did not control key government ministries responsible for defence, border affairs and home affairs.

In this book, Chap. 2 traces the changes in agricultural policies during Myanmar's complex "regime" transitions. The timeline is divided into the post-independence civilian period, the Burmese socialist period, the military regime period, and the democratisation period, according to the left column of the table above, while considering the table's four columns to the right. Rather than surveying all possible agricultural policies, I focus on three policies that characterise Myanmar's agricultural policy from independence in 1948 to the present: the State Farmland system, the Product Procurement system, and the Planned Cultivation system. Chapter 2 describes in detail the historical evolution of these three policies. This will help us understand how Myanmar's agricultural policies have affected farmers and the population at large.[14]

In relation to agriculture, we should specifically consider rural areas. Even today, nearly 70% of Myanmar's total population of over 50 million lives in rural areas, and nearly 70% of that population is engaged in agriculture. The history of *rural* policy is as important as the history of agricultural policy, and the two are intertwined. I will analyse newly discovered documents, including those considered to be restricted or "secret", to illustrate how the regime has struggled to control rural areas. Rural policy is important not only for agriculture, which is the economic foundation of the state, but also for the security of rural areas, where most of the population lives. Therefore, the regime transitions and the policies related to rural areas will also be discussed in Chap. 2.

In Chap. 3, we explore how agriculture and rural areas are positioned in Myanmar's national economy. Using macroeconomic statistics, such as the statistical yearbook, monthly statistical indicators, agricultural statistics, population and housing census, and internal data of the Ministry of Agriculture, I argue that: (1) the position of agriculture in the national accounts has been declining; (2) agricultural income is

---

[14] How the intentions and policies by the state deviated from the reality of agriculture and villages is revealed in the line of argument in this book.

remarkably low; (3) the importance of rice is declining, despite Myanmar being often referred to as a rice-producing country; and (4) there are doubts about the future potential of Myanmar agriculture. In addition, we find that there are surprisingly few farmers in rural Myanmar. These considerations will show the extent of de-agrarianisation at the national economic level.

In Chap. 4, I analyse closely the socio-economic transformation of two villages, which have different ecologies and histories. The villages are located about 500 km apart from each other on the same longitude, with one village in the north and the other in the south of the country. I have been doing research in these two villages since 1986. My analysis will be based on the individual household surveys and interviews that I did in Burmese language while living in these villages. At first, using various academic and local materials, and documents of the colonial government offices, I will discuss the history of the villages, which may date back to as far as the 11th century. This discussion will include the climate, the topography, and the changes in population and ethnic composition over a century. Then, based on the data from my household surveys in 1987, 1994, and 2013, I describe in detail the changes over 26 years in these villages. These changes include occupational structure, land tenure, farming methods, agricultural productivity, price structure, the composition of the non-agricultural sector, and everyday livelihoods. In addition, I share the results from my participant observation research for the period 2013 to 2019, to describe the changes in the social economy of the village, and to clarify the reality of de-agrarianisation.

In Chap. 5, in order to discuss the relationship between Buddhism and village economy in Myanmar, I will focus on a great change that took place in one of the two villages mentioned above, Thindaunggyi Village.[15] This village's *paya*—pagoda or Buddha image—which in 1987 had been like those found in any other village in Myanmar, transformed into a famous *paya*. It is now known to all Buddhists in Myanmar. This change came about partly because of changes in Myanmar's socio-economic situation. I analyse the relationship between religious activities and economic development through the records of my individual household surveys in this village and the accounting books of the *paya*. In addition, I examine the economic ripple effect that the *paya* brought about on the village through a survey of the stores and restaurants in the shopping street that sprang up around the *paya*. This study expands the body of research on how the practice of Buddhism can have an enormous economic effect in Myanmar. It also shows a process of de-agrarianisation of this village, which has changed from a farming village to a shopping district.

[15] In this book, the real names, rather than pseudonyms, of places and villages are given because this information is necessary for other researchers to follow up and verify my findings. The names of deceased persons are also given. On the other hand, for the still-living persons, I used real names for persons who were considered public figures and pseudonyms for others. The same applies to company names.

In Chap. 6, I examine the relationship between regime change and migration. I use my individual household questionnaires from 1987, 1994, and 2013 to analyse population movements at the household level in the other village where I have conducted long-term research—Zeepinwea Village. While population mobility is known to have been very high in the delta region of Myanmar during the colonial period, I have shown that frequent population movements continued also during the socialist period, despite restrictions on people changing their place of residence (Takahashi, 1997, p. 22). This chapter describes how villagers moved under the market-economy system that came about after the demise of the socialist system. I show how migration is another aspect of the process of de-agrarianisation.

In Chaps. 7 and 8, I explore the core of Myanmar villages, in order to understand why villages have not changed their structure despite the regime changes in Myanmar. In Chap. 7, I compare village structures in Japan, Thailand, and Myanmar from the perspective of what kind of "cohesion" the villages have, that is, village communality. First, I survey the academic literature on Japanese and Thai village studies, and organise these studies into the thesis of group or organisation and the thesis of subjective cognition. I apply this logic to the reality of Myanmar's rural villages to construct a theory of Myanmar village society. This is a unique attempt, which has no predecessors. While seeming similar to Japan, the village groups and organisations in Myanmar, as well as the village itself, are generated and function on completely different principles.

In Chap. 8, I explore how Myanmar villages are organised and what the essence of a Myanmar village is. I suggest that a Japanese village is a "collective for production" and a Myanmar village is a "community for living". In Japanese villages, joint production activities—such as agricultural cooperative movements, irrigation management, rice procurement, land consolidation, reduction of rice acreage, and management of common lands—have been conducted by each village as one unit. In Myanmar, however, there are no such organisations for agricultural production, and even if there are, they are either short-lived or converge on administrative or individual management. However, various groups—namely, consumer cooperatives, congratulatory or condolence associations, fire brigades, pagoda committees, and drinking water committees—have been set up in Myanmar villages for purposes of *living* together, in the same way as in Japan. Thus, a village in Myanmar is a community of life, but not a collective of production.

The groups and organisations related to daily life are not necessarily village-wide, and members are relatively free to come and go as they please. In other words, while Japanese village groups and organisations that are formed on a village-wide basis are permanent, and have fixed members, the groups and organisations in Myanmar are formed by the free will of individuals, have little continuity, and have fluid membership. Although Japanese villagers tend to follow village customs and events without complaint, Myanmar villagers follow them when it is convenient for them and when doing so is no longer convenient, they choose not to follow. The strategy of socio-economic development of villages by grouping and organising villagers has been quite successful in Japan, but it does not necessarily work well in Myanmar. The reason is that villages in Myanmar are not village collectives like those in Japan, but mere communities. Villagers are not subjected to group "restraint" and can be freer from collective "surveillance". In other words, the village in Myanmar is a society where there are few "failures of collectives". I see this as a means of unconscious resistance against Burmese socialism and against the coercive rule under successive military regimes. Thus, in Chaps. 7 and 8, I detail the socio-economic characteristics of Myanmar villages by comparing them with Japanese villages and consider their positive significance beyond the argument that Myanmar villagers are economically poor or loosely constructed socially.

Chronology of Burmese politics, economy, agriculture, and rural areas

Year	Politics and economy	Agriculture and village
1044	King Anawrahta establishes the Pagan Dynasty, the first unified dynasty	
1287	The Mongol invasion destroys the Pagan dynasty	
1364	Establishment of the Inwa dynasty (–1526)	
1486	Establishment of the First Taungoo Dynasty (–1599)	
1597	Establishment of the Second Taungoo Dynasty (–1752)	
1752	The Konbaung dynasty established in Shwebo (–1885)	
1824	First Anglo-Burmese War (–1826). Burma cedes Tenasserim and Arakan to Britain	
1852	The Second Anglo-Burmese War. Britain annexes Lower Burma	
1876		Lower Burma Land and Revenue Act
1880		Department of Agriculture is set up
1885	The Third Anglo-Burmese War. Kingdom of Burma falls	
1886	The British Indian Empire annexes the whole Burma	
1889	Enforcement of the Mountain Land Civil Administration Act	The Upper Burma Land and Revenue Regulation
1894		Land Acquisition Act
1904		Department of Cooperatives is set up
1905		Canal Act
1907		Village Act
1930	Anti-Indian riots in Yangon Formation of the *Dobama Asiayone*	Rice prices plunge because of the Great Depression, leading to widespread poverty in rural areas Peasant Revolt known as the Saya San Rebellion begins

(continued)

(continued)

Year	Politics and economy	Agriculture and village
1937	Burma is separated from British India by the Government of Burma Act	
1941	Establishment of the Southern Agency	Agricultural Produce Market Act
1942	Occupation by the Japanese military begins	
1945	Japanese Occupation ends	
1946	Panglong Conference held	Establishment of the State Agricultural Marketing Board (SAMB)
1947	Parliament approves the Constitution of the Union of Burma Assassination of Aung San and his cabinet	
1948	Independence from Great Britain	Land Nationalisation Act of 1948
1950		State Agricultural Marketing Board Act
1953		Land Nationalisation Act of 1953
1956		Cooperative Societies Act of 1956
1958	Ne Win's "Caretaker" Government takes office	
1960	U Nu returns as Prime Minister	Common Fund for Rural Economic Development Act
1962	Military coup Revolutionary Council established	Agricultural Products Purchasing Regulations Act
1963	"New Economic Policy", including nationalisation of industries, announced	The Tenancy Law and the Protection of Farmers' Rights Law
1970		Cooperative Societies Act of 1970
1974	Constitution of the Socialist Republic of the Union of Burma enacted Student demonstrations at U Thant Funeral, the regime closes universities	
1987	The third demonetisation of currency Riots in Yangon	Abolition of the paddy procurement system and shift to a tax-in-kind system
1988	Anti-regime protests and uprising Ne Win resigns Military coup; State Law and Order Restoration Council established, General Saw Maung chairs Foreign Investment Law	The paddy procurement system revived
1990	NLD wins general election	
1992	Than Shwe replaces Saw Maung as head of SLORC	Cooperative Societies Act
1993	Foreign Exchange Certificates (FEC) begin to be issued	Rapid increase in irrigation facilities Spread of two-season cropping

(continued)

(continued)

Year	Politics and economy	Agriculture and village
1997	Myanmar joins ASEAN Asian Economic Crisis	
2003	Bank run Depayin massacre (Aung San Suu Kyi attacked)	The paddy procurement system abolished
2005	Naypyidaw becomes capital	
2007	Intensification of anti-government movement by monks and citizens, armed crackdown	
2008	Referendum A new constitution enacted	Catastrophic death and damage caused by Cyclone Nargis
2010	First general election in 20 years; NLD boycotts	
2011	Thein Sein government inaugurates Myanmar national and state legislatures Labour Organisation Law and Microfinance Law	Liberalisation of rice exports
2012	Mass release of political prisoners NLD wins series of by-election Prior censorship of media abolished Foreign Investment Law	Ward or Village Tract Administration Law enacted; Village Act abolished Farmland Act enacted Vacant, Fallow and Virgin Land Management Act enacted Parliamentary Land Investigation Commission established
2013	Meiktila Incident, anti-Muslim riots intensify across the country Private daily newspapers are allowed to resume	State Agricultural Marketing Board Act abolished The Law of Protection of the Farmer Rights and Enhancement of their Benefits enacted
2014	The Myanmar Special Economic Zone Law Media Law, Printing and Publishing Law National Education Law	Common Fund for Rural Economic Development Act of 1960 abolished
2015	The NLD wins general election	The Agricultural Produce Market Act abolished
2016	The Aung San Suu Kyi government inaugurated State Counsellor Law Myanmar Investment Law	Central Reinvestigation Committee for Confiscated Farmlands and Other Lands established
2017	UN High Commissioner calls the massacre and expulsion of Rohingya people 'ethnic cleansing' Myanmar Companies Law	Embankment Law and Irrigation Law

(continued)

(continued)

Year	Politics and economy	Agriculture and village
2018	The presidential transition from Htin Kyaw to Win Myint The beginning of the fiscal year changed from April 1 to October 1	Land Acquisition, Resettlement and Rehabilitation Law
2019	General Administration Department transferred from under military to civilian control Rohingya issue goes to the International Court of Justice	Rural Development Law

Chapter 2
Agricultural and Rural Policies Amid Regime Changes

A villager polishing rice in her yard. In 1987, at the end of the socialist era, farmers were forbidden from even milling their own rice, so this was "black rice-milling". In the 1990s, the processing and marketing of rice was liberalised. Small rice mills began to run in the village. Foot-milling as seen in this photo is no longer practised. (Zeepinwea village, April 1987)

Introduction

When we talk about agricultural policy or agricultural system, various policies and systems come to mind such as the land system, distribution policy, price policy,

A. Takahashi, *Regime Changes and Socio-economic History of Rural Myanmar, 1986–2019*, Studies in Economic History,
https://doi.org/10.1007/978-981-99-3272-6_2

production policy, agricultural finance, extension policy, taxation system, cooperatives and so on. This chapter does not attempt to cover all of them, but rather looks back at the three key policies that are at the heart of the history of post-independence Myanmar agriculture. I call these the "three pillars of agricultural policy" (Takahashi, 1992: 72): (1) land policy (state ownership of farmland); (2) distribution and price policy (procurement system); and (3) production policy (system of planned cultivation). The system of state ownership of farmland literally means that the state owns all farmland. The system of procurement means that farmers must sell their produce to the state at a fixed price. The system of planned cultivation means that farmers must grow their crops according to the state's plan (Takahashi, 2000: 43).

These three pillars were all in effect by around 1966–1967, some five years after Ne Win's military government took power, and played a central role in the agricultural policy of Burmese socialism (Takahashi, 1992: 85). Myanmar agricultural policy was tightly managed through these three pillars from the mid-1960s until the abolition of the procurement system in 1987. However, these institutions were legislated already shortly after independence and maintained even after the 1988 *coup d'état*. Their residue can be seen in the post-2011 democratisation period.[1] Thus, the Myanmar characteristics of the history of agricultural policy in the seven decades after independence can be clearly depicted by focusing on these three pillars. Let us look at these three pillars one-by-one.

2.1 Agricultural Land Policy

2.1.1 The Period of Post-Independence Civil Administration

After 1886, when the British completed the annexation of Myanmar, the most notable change in the economy was the expansion of rice cultivation and the development of rice-related industries in Lower Myanmar. The key players in the rice industry were Burmese land-owning (owner) farmers, but as time went on, landownership became more concentrated, and the peasantry was differentiated. In 1910, of the total 10.61 million acres[2] of arable land in Myanmar, 1.48 million acres, or only 14%, was held[3] by non-farming landowners. By 1937, however, 6.44 million acres, or about one-third of the total cultivated land of 19.30 million acres, belonged to non-farming landowners. Particularly in Lower Myanmar, more than half of the total arable land of 11.2 million acres, or 5.31 million acres, belonged to non-farming landlords. The population that was working in agriculture in Lower Myanmar in 1931 was as

[1] This period ended at the end of January 2021. This publication covers the period until 2019.

[2] 1 acre = 4047 m^2 = 0.4047 ha.

[3] In this book, "ownership" and "holding" are used interchangeably as follows. Namely, "ownership" means possessing something while reserving the right to use, profit from, and dispose of it freely, while "holding" means having something under one's *de facto* control, regardless of having or not having the above rights. According to this definition, "holding" encompasses "ownership."

follows: 2% were non-farming landowners, 20% were land-owning farmers, 20% were tenant farmers, and the remaining 58% were agricultural labourers who owned no land. In other words, about half of the arable land was controlled by only 2% of non-farming landlords. More than half of this arable land that was held by non-farming landowners was in the hands of Indians and other "foreigners" (Takahashi, 1999: 296). This situation remained unchanged even in 1947, after the Japanese occupation and as the country was on the verge of independence.

Myanmar's first constitution promulgated in September 1947, stipulated that members of Parliament shall be elected by the people (Article 76). With regards to land, the 1947 constitution stipulates that "the State is the ultimate owner of all lands" (Article 30(1)), and that "the State shall have the right to regulate, alter or abolish land tenures or resume possession of any land and distribute the same for collective or co-operative farming or to agricultural tenants" (Article 30(2)). Furthermore, regarding the allocation of resources such as land, the 1947 constitution states that "the State shall direct its policy towards giving material assistance to economic organisations not working for private profit, and that preference shall be given to co-operative and similar economic organisations" (Article 42). As can be inferred from these articles, the post-independence Union of Burma was a democratic state with a socialist orientation.

After independence in January 1948, the 1948 "Land Nationalisation Act" was enacted in accordance with this constitution, with the ultimate aim of creating a modern economic system for collective farming.[4] The law defined "agricultural land (*leyamyei*, လယ်ယာမြေ)" as "land which is occupied, or is ordinarily utilised or has been leased for purposes of agriculture or horticulture or husbandry or for purposes subservient to agriculture, horticulture or husbandry and includes the sites of buildings, dwelling houses and other structures on such land"; but this "does not include land which is within a town or village and is occupied as the site of a dwelling".[5] The definition of "farmer"[6] was derived from this definition of "agricultural land". Namely, "farmer" ("agriculturist" in the Act) means a person who works for the year 1948–49, or who habitually worked prior to that year, any agricultural land, as his principal means of subsistence with his own hands as a land-holder or as a tenant (*thîzâ*), or as an agricultural labourer (*thuyînhgâ lekuli*), or in the case of a person disabled by age or physical defect, under a farmer's personal superintendence, throughout the working periods of the year (Article 2). Only in special conditions did the law recognise the "farmer" as a supervisor of agriculture. In principle, the law

[4] Speech of Thakin Tin, Minister of Agriculture and Forestry, inserted in the first page of the Act.

[5] The Burmese version of the act lists specific land utilisation, such as paddy field (လယ်), upland field (ယာ), *kâin* (ကိုင်း), *cûn* (ကျွန်း) etc. (*Kâin* is an alluvial land that appears on the banks of a river during periods of reduced water flow; when it appears in the middle of a river, it is called *cûn*. However, in some regions, both are called *kâin*, or both are called *cûn*. According to the classification by the Agricultural Administration, both are called *kâincûn* (ကိုင်းကျွန်း).)

[6] The Law's Burmese-language version refers to farmers as "*taundhu ledhamâ* (တောင်သူလယ်သမား)", and the English version as "agriculturists". For the detailed meaning of *taundhu ledhamâ*, see Takahashi (1992: 63–64).

considered only those who cultivate the land themselves as farmers. Finally, a "farm household" ("agriculturist family" in the Act)[7] means a group of persons, related by blood or marriage, living together and depending for maintenance on the earnings of one or more of the group's senior members, who shall be farmer(s).

Under the Land Nationalisation Act of 1948, expropriated farmland was redistributed[8] to farmers, while any exempted farmland was regulated along with all the newly allocated farmland. The Act also defined the tenure of *exempted* farmers—those who were exempted from expropriation—and *allocated* farmers—those who were allocated farmland.[9] According to the Act, exempted farmers were entitled to the "right of possession" (*painhsaingwìn*) (Article 6). The allottees were given the "right of cultivation" (*lou'kaingwìn*) and the "right of profit" (*achôkanzâgwìn*) (Article 12). The "right of cultivation" was not defined in detail in the Act. This might be because the term can be taken as it is and interpreted as 'the right to cultivate agricultural land'. However, the Act defined the content of "possession" clearly. This "possession" did not mean possession in the usual sense, but occupation (*le'shì htâjîn*) of agricultural land. In other words, the Act used the Burmese word "*painsaingyîn*" and the English word "possession" for "ownership", but stated that its content was *le'shì htâgyîn* in Burmese and occupation in English. Thus, the Act did not indicate "ownership" but "occupation" (Takahashi, 1998: 31–33).

The Land Nationalisation Act of 1948 emphasised the ideals of total abolition of private land ownership, the nationalisation of agricultural land and establishment of collective farming. It was met with strong resistance not only from landowners but also from farmers who were opposed to the abolition of private land ownership. Thus, agrarian reform based on this Act was attempted only in a few areas. The following year, in 1949, the law was suspended.

In 1953, a new Land Nationalisation Act was enacted by Parliament, defining key terms quite differently from the 1948 Act. First, the definition of "agricultural land" was expanded to include "uncultivated land which can be cultivated in accordance with the needs of the state". Next, although the definition of farmers was the same—those who work, or who habitually worked prior to that year, any agricultural land, as their principle means of subsistence—a new category of those who use farmland as their main means of livelihood by supervising agriculture during the farming season

[7] The Act's Burmese-language version calls a farm household "*taundhu ledhamâ eindaundâzù*" or "household of farmer(s)" and the English version calls it an "agriculturist family". In Japan, the definitions consider that there are farm households first and then there are farmers, whereas in Myanmar, the definitions are the opposite: first there are farmers and then there are farm households (Takahashi, 2012: 65–66). Burmese language has no word that can be directly translated as "farm household", but for the sake of convenience, I will use the term "farm household" for "*taundhu ledhamâ eindaundâzù*". Families living together but feeding separately shall be regarded as separate families.

[8] The acreage allocated was based on *dadounghton (dadôunhton)*—the area that a nuclear family could cultivate with its own labour and a yoke of draught cattle, and earn a living. For details of *dadounghton*, see Takahashi (1992: 73–74).

[9] For example, in the case of a self-farming farmer who cultivates paddy fields, some 50 acres or less was exempted from expropriation. We call such cases "exempted farmers". In contrast, the farmers who received farmland through the agrarian reform are called "allocated farmers".

was added. The terms "tenants" and "agricultural labourers" were deleted.[10] While tenants were included in the category of those who cultivate their own land, it is highly likely that agricultural labourers were not included in this category. This relates to the low priority given to agricultural labourers in Article 59 of the Land Nationalisation Rules of 1954 (Takahashi, 1992: 73). In addition, under the guise of supervising agriculture, the 1953 Act actually allowed non-farming landowners to continue to exist. As we will see later, the Burmese socialist period wiped out the non-farming landlords, but the farming style in which farmers hired agricultural labourers and only supervised and managed their own farms remained prevalent (Takahashi, 2000: 105–106; 2012: 69–70). This is not unrelated to the addition of the "supervisor of the farming processes" to the definition of "farmer".

The definition of "ownership" also underwent an important change, which may be too often overlooked. Article 3 of the Land Nationalisation Act of 1953 used the word *painsaingyîn* (possession) in Burmese and "possession" in English, as in the 1948 Act. However, it stated that "*painhsaingyîn* (possession)" means: (1) occupation of agricultural land that had been prior to enforcement of this law, acquired by individuals, banks, companies, associations, jointly owned by a Hindi family or religious building, based on the "right of ownership", or (2) after enforcement of this law, possession of the land by prescription of this law (Article 3).[11] In the 1953 Act's Burmese-language version, the "right of cultivation" that was in the Land Nationalisation Act of 1948 receded and the "right of ownership" became stronger. In the English-language versions, the 1948 law only once states ownership in the form of "his own", whereas the 1953 Act uses the verb "to own" at least 10 times and the term "owner" 5 times. I myself have heard in many villages in Myanmar that farmers had the right to "own" farmland until the mid-1960s (Takahashi, 1992: 75–76).

The Land Nationalisation Act of 1953 allowed both exempted and allocated farmers to divide, exchange, and inherit agricultural land. This was despite the Act adopting a policy that severely restricted the private transfer of agricultural land in general by stating that agricultural land shall not be pawned, sold, disposed of by other method, or divided except in conformity with this Act and its by-laws (Article 4). In addition to the above rights, exempted farmers could sell or give their land to farmers or people who had pledged to farm, and they could donate their land to religious organisations. In other words, farmers were granted not only the right to use and profit from farmland, but also the right to dispose of it in a very broad way. More importantly, it was stipulated that not only exempted farmers but also allocated farmers had the same "ownership" as before the promulgation of the law. This gave non-farmers an excuse to "own" farmland by being "agricultural supervisors". Thus,

---

[10] In the English version, tenants and agricultural labourers are included in the category of agriculturist (farmer), and no supervisor clause is found. Post-independence Myanmar laws were written in the Burmese language, and the English versions were merely translations. In other words, the actual implementation of the legislation was carried out according to the Burmese version. Therefore, in this book, I give priority to the laws written in Burmese.

[11] For this definition as well, the 1953 Land Nationalisation Act's English-language version had different nuances from the Burmese version, so I translated it here according to the Burmese version.

this Act was not really a law for the nationalisation of farmland, nor was it intended to abolish landownership (Klimko, 1966: 60–61). From the point of view of farmers' right to farmland, it can be said that the 1953 Act changed the 1948 Land Nationalisation Act's "right to cultivate" to the "right to own", with some restrictions. In any case, the agrarian reform started based on this law, but was suspended in 1958 due to security deteriorating. Until the 1970s, only 3,345,984 acres of agricultural land had been nationalised, exempted from expropriation or redistributed. This was only 17% of the 19,574,471 acres of farmland registered with the Department of Land Records (*myezayîn htanà*)[12] (BaMaKa, 1964: 2).

2.1.2 The Period of the "Burmese Way to Socialism"

After seizing power in a *coup d'état* in March 1962, the national military established a "revolutionary government" (*tohlanyêi asôuyà*) led by General Ne Win. The government of General Ne Win showed a positive attitude towards the resumption of agrarian reform (pyancâyêi htanà, 1964a: 80–85). However, the government gradually became reluctant to redistribute farmland on the grounds that there was insufficient farmland for the number of people working in agriculture and that there would always be complaints about the quality and type of land, cultivated crops, and local conditions when allocating farmland (pyancâyêi htanà, 1964b: 111–112). In March 1964, the government effectively declared that it would not proceed further with the redistribution (MaSaLa, 1985: 105; Takahashi, 1998: 46).

As if to compensate for the failure to redistribute agricultural land, the government promoted the transformation of "right of possession, or ownership" into "right of cultivation". The 1963 Tenancy Law (1963 *kùhni' thîzâ hcàhtâyêi ùbadei*), which was enacted to protect farmers as cultivators, stated that landowners did not have the right to choose tenants, and that the government would select them (Article 3). The payment of farm rent was limited to cash only (Article 4, Paragraph 2). The names of landowners and their tenants, the area of their farmland, and the farm rents were registered in a "tenant registration book (*thîzâ hma' pountin*)" kept by the village agricultural land committee. However, in 1965, the Tenancy Law was amended to stipulate that landlords must not receive farm rents. At first glance, this may appear to be a conversion of tenants into land-owning farmers, but as will be explained later, the state instead used its control of the "right of cultivation" as leverage to collect "farm rent" on behalf of landlords in the form of procurement.

The term "*ûpainpau'kwìn*" was where the state lumped together both the rights granted by the 1953 Land Nationalisation Act to allotted farmers and exempted farmers, as well as the "ownership" of agricultural land by landlords and farmers in non-nationalised areas. The term's literal translation is a "right to declare occupation". Its definition is a right to register one's name at the Settlement and Land Record

[12] It is almost equal to the total acreage of agricultural land which is the sum of the net sown area and current fallow area.

Department as a person who has the right to occupy and cultivate farmland (MaSaLa, 1971b: 265). Then, among those who exercised this right, only those who were cultivating the farmland[13] as their own or as tenants at the time of the implementation of the Tenancy Law were granted "right of cultivation" ("*lou'paingwìn*", renamed from *lou'kaingwìn*). This meant that land-owning farmers would have their farmland registered in their own name, while tenants would have their cultivated farmland registered in the name of the landlords. Yet, those tenants who the state decided fit the principle of *le'shìle'gou*' (currently cultivating the land)[14] became holders of the "right of cultivation",[15] because the landlord had no right to decide who the tenant was. Since there was no farm rent, the distinction between land-owning farmers and tenants remained nominal; there was no longer any real distinction. Myanmar state-owned newspaper the Working People's Daily soon announced that "all agricultural land will belong to the state, and private ownership will be completely dissolved; Farmers would be granted only the cultivation right of farmland, and only those who were actually cultivating the land would be able to use it".[16] However, the situation described by Ne Win as the lack of farmland available for reallocation did not change. Agricultural labourer households—which accounted for half of all rural households—were unable to obtain the cultivation rights even with this "reform". Eventually, the two strata of farmers—farmers with operational farmland and agricultural labourers without land—became fixed, a situation that has not changed some 70 years since the independence.

As for the private disposal of this "right of cultivation", Article 4 of the 1953 Land Nationalisation Act was applied. This article prohibited the pawning, sale, division, and other forms of private disposal of agricultural land. Articles 10 and 12 of the Law grant certain rights of disposal of agricultural land to exempted and allocated farmers, but these were ignored. Instead, all private disposal of agricultural land—including sale, transfer, division, exchange, loan, and pawning—was simply prohibited under Article 4 (MaSaLa, 1971b: 265). Inheritance, however, was ambiguous.[17] It was possible to inherit agricultural land if "*le'shìle'gou*" was applied (Takahashi, 1991: 162–165; 1992: 116).

The penalty for violators of the law was the forfeiture of agricultural land. Even if the cultivator was not at fault, the Central Agricultural Land Committee stipulated

[13] In legal terms, such a farmer is one who *le'shìle'gou' lou'kainneshì* = continues to cultivate at present" (BaMaKa, 1964: 5).

[14] Directive of the Central Agricultural Land Committee dated 13 February 1964 (1/64).

[15] In reality, in both those villages where agrarian reform was implemented and those where it was not, the village agricultural land committees recognised cultivators on the basis of *le'shile'gou*' (BaLaKa, 1973: 8; Takahashi, 1991: 158–159; 1992: 97–102).

[16] Working People's Daily, Editorial, 8 July 1965.

[17] As for the private inheritance of farmland, the revolutionary government admitted the right to inherit farmland (which is thought to mean the aforementioned *ûpainpau'kwìn*) but annotated that the cultivation right was not automatically inheritable (BaMaKa, 1973: 9–11). This shows that the state was trying to thoroughly control the "right to cultivate". However, if a parent's farmland was cultivated together with his or her children or grandchildren before his or her death, it seems that "*le'shile'gou*'" was allowed.

that the state can seize agricultural land free of charge in cases of emergency under the Land Acquisition Act of 1894 (BaMaKa, 1973: 21).[18]

Thus, the Land Nationalisation Act of 1953 was not amended at all, the *de facto* ownership of farmers was denied, peasants had only fragile cultivation rights at the mercy of the state, and the Burmese socialist agrarian system was established. This system was much different from the system of the immediate post-independence civil administration period under U Nu.

2.1.3 Military Period

The military regime that emerged after the 1988 *coup d'état* advocated a market economy but did not amend or repeal the Land Nationalisation Act of 1953, despite its many socialist elements. Indeed, the regime continued to use the Act. The principle of the Act, which was to redistribute nationalised agricultural land to farmers with little agricultural land and to agricultural labourers without agricultural land, was forgotten. Instead, the Land Nationalisation Act of 1953, the Land Acquisition Act of 1894, and various notifications and orders based on these acts during the Burmese socialist period were used as a means to seize agricultural land from farmers who had cultivation rights. Those notifications and orders were used arbitrarily. The compensation paid to the right-holders (farmers) who had their land confiscated was a small amount, equal to the profit from agricultural production for one year. The pretext for such a small compensation was that, during the Burmese socialist period, farmers' cultivation rights were renewed for only one year (Takahashi, 1992: 101). In addition, the compensation was called *ni'najê* (damage) rather than *yojê* (compensation).

The government used such confiscated farmlands for its agricultural projects, industrial parks, infrastructure such as roads and dams, and expansion of urban areas; as well as for expanding the military's bases, training facilities, entertainment and recreational facilities, and army farms; and for private agricultural plantations, factories and commercial sites, and real estate development. Confiscated land also became a target of speculation. Many farmlands seem to have been not used effectively and became underproductive or abandoned.

Even during the post-2010 partially democratic period, it was not clear from government documents how much land had been seized by the military, the government, and corporations. According to findings of the Farmers Affairs Committee in the Upper House of Parliament, as many as two million acres of land across Burma could be considered "confiscated".[19] A considerable amount of farmland was ripped out of the hands of the farmers.

---

[18] In reality, Article 17 of the 1894 Land Acquisition Act only states that there should be no encumbrances, not that there should be no compensation. Here, too, there is a deliberate misreading of the law.

[19] Irrawaddy, 1 July 2016.

2.1.4 Democratisation Period

On 30 March 2012, exactly one year after Thein Sein came to power, the Land Nationalisation Act and the Tenancy Law were abolished and the new Farmland Law (*leyamye ùbadei*) was enacted. The category of "agricultural land" still included paddy fields (*le*), upland fields (*ya*), *kâincûn*, and perennial plant land (*ûyin*), as in the Land Nationalisation Act of 1953, but added were vegetable gardens, nipa palm (*dànì*) planting areas, swidden (*taunya*) and *myenù*.[20] However, the term "livestock breeding land" disappeared. Uncultivated land that could be cultivated according to the needs of the state was also removed from the definition. Livestock breeding was added to the definition of "farmers": those who use agricultural land and engage in agriculture (crop cultivation) or livestock breeding or both by themselves as their main means of livelihood, those who have always done so, or those who constantly supervise them. The new clause can be interpreted to include agricultural capitalists and labourers as farmers (Article 3). Foreigners and foreign companies were allowed to enter the agricultural and livestock industry (Article 9). Thus, the 2012 Farmland Law defined farmers more broadly than the 1953 Act.

In this law, as in the 1953 Act, the ultimate owner of the land is the State, and only the right to cultivate agricultural land (*leya lou'paingwìn*) is granted to farmers. This right is defined as the right to use agricultural land for the development of agriculture in accordance with the Farmland Law, Rules, and regulations promulgated thereunder (Article 3). The holder of this cultivation right not only may use the farmland and enjoy the income from it, but may also sell, mortgage, lend, exchange, inherit, and sell the right (Article 9). This point differs greatly from the Burmese socialist period and the subsequent military period, when the right of disposal was severely restricted. In addition, the 2012 Law stipulates that sufficient compensation should be paid to the owner of cultivation right, so as not to cause damage to the owner (Article 26).[21] In other words, even though the name—the "right of cultivation"—remained the same, it actually became close to a right of ownership.

Still, the law and related laws and regulations put various restrictions on the right of cultivation. There is a mechanism to restrict the cultivation right in the government notifications and directives to be promulgated thereafter. Among the articles of the Law, there are provisions such as: pledging the cultivation right only for agricultural and livestock related businesses and only to the governmental bodies and the banks authorised by the government; not changing the cultivating crops without permission of the authorities; and not abandoning the farmland (Article 12). In case of violation, there are penalties such as fines, imprisonment, and forfeiture of cultivation rights

[20] Agricultural land that is flooded during the rainy season and then emerges after the water has receded, with the quality and shape of the land varying each year.

[21] Under the Land Acquisition, Resettlement and Rehabilitation Law enacted in August 2019, when agricultural land as well as other land are expropriated, not only compensation (*yojê*) is paid for the land and the houses and trees on it, but also damage (*ni 'najê*) is paid for the income lost due to confiscation and various expenses for resettlement. Compensation and damage are paid not only to landholders but also to tenants and labourers. This law finally led to the repeal of the Land Acquisition Act of 1894.

(Article 32). In this sense, there is a residue of the Land Nationalisation Act of 1953, even though it was supposedly repealed by the 2012 Farmland Law.

2.2 Procurement System

In the British colonial era, Burma specialised in rice and teakwood production and export, organised under the British imperial system of the division of labour. Europeans took control of the large rice mills and export trade. Indians and Chinese moved into the domestic distribution process of rice. The Burmese peasants, responsible for production, were subordinated and exploited by these "foreigners".[22] Hence, the Burmanisation of the rice distribution process—restoring the distribution system to the hands of the Burmese people—was an urgent issue after independence, along with agrarian reform. Although Myanmar's post-independence rice exports declined from an average of 3.5 million tonnes per year around 1940 to 1.5–2 million tonnes per year because of the Japanese occupation, they still accounted for around 70% of total exports and were the backbone of the national economy.

The State Agricultural Marketing Board (SAMB),[23] *nainngando kau'pêthîhnan yâunweyêi aphwè* in Burmese, was established in 1946, prior to independence, to handle the rice trade on behalf of "foreign" traders. SAMB had a few purposes: (1) to transfer all agricultural export operations away from the hands of "foreign" exporters to SAMB; (2) to use the foreign exchange earned from rice exports for economic development; (3) to stabilise rice prices and make farmers' livelihood steadier; and (4) to prevent wages from rising due to low consumer rice prices and to promote economic development (Than & Nishizawa, 1990: 92–93). Thus, based on the experience of the colonial era, when excessive rice exports led to domestic hunger and rebellion, the SAMB project was intended not only to promote export but also to stabilise people's livelihoods at the same time.

SAMB's rice purchases were conducted in two ways: (1) milled rice purchasing, utilising the old distribution structure: farmer → paddy broker → miller → SAMB; (2) direct purchasing of paddy from the farmers and agricultural cooperatives, which was introduced in 1951 (Saito, 1963: 9). The government promoted direct purchasing—by using SAMB's newly-taken control over the rice export business as leverage— and attempted to break down the old colonial-era distribution system. Indeed, by the mid-1950s, the direct purchase of paddy constituted the majority of rice purchase by SAMB. However, by the 1960s, the volume of milled rice purchasing had again increased to two to four times of direct purchasing (MaSaLa, 1987: 445). The SAMB era became called the "rice millers' era" (MaSaLa, 1987: 294). The

[22] Ba Maw, who was Prime Minister during the Japanese occupation, stated that "the Burmese were cut off and pushed aside from most of the occupations that should rightfully belong to us" (Ba Maw, 1973: 18).

[23] In addition to rice, SAMB also exported beans, oilseeds, corn, and so on, but these were not important (Sato, 1962: 66–67). The State Agricultural Marketing Board Act was enacted in 1950, after the Independence in 1948 and the establishment of SAMB in 1946.

old structures remained parallel, and their dissolution did not occur until Ne Win's strong-arm politics. SAMB's purchases were limited to rice for export and for the military. The amount of rice it collected accounted for only a little less than half of the country's total production. The remainder was left in the hands of private traders, including "foreigners". In other words, only the export procedure of rice was fully monopolised by SAMB, while the purchase, processing, and storage of paddy and rice for export, as well as the entire distribution process of rice for domestic consumption, were still handled by the traditional distribution system. (Takahashi, 1992: 82)

In January 1963, Ne Win's Revolutionary Council, which had taken full control of the country in the previous year, reorganised SAMB into the Union of Burma Agricultural Marketing Board (UBAMB), known as the *pyidaunzù myanmanainngan kau'pêthîhnan yâunweyêi aphwè*. Through UBAMB, the government promulgated a series of decrees whereby solely the state would conduct all transactions in major agricultural products, including paddy and rice. Eventually, in 1966, a system was established under which only the state could purchase, transport, process, store, sell, and export agricultural products. In the early 1960s, rice crops accounted for 60% of the total area planted and 60% of the total export value (Takahashi, 2012: 42–46). In other words, the Burmese socialist strategy of economic development was to collect inexpensive paddy directly from the farmers by the state, process it in rice mills confiscated or controlled by the state, and supply cheap rice to consumers in order to gain the confidence of the people, as well as to import raw materials, intermediate goods, and capital goods with the foreign currency obtained from exporting rice, to accumulate capital. The procurement system anchored the Burmese socialist line of economic development strategy (Takahashi, 2000: 48).

In the case of exports, only state agencies could handle foreign currency, and they set the exchange rate of the Burmese currency *kyat* abnormally high. Moreover, for domestic rice, the price of paddy was kept low to meet the low rationing price for consumers. Thus, the farmers' willingness to produce naturally declined. The export volume of Myanmar, which had been the world's largest rice exporter until 1962, declined like on a downhill slide (Takahashi, 2008a: 57–61). In 1987, when farmers' dissatisfaction with the unjust way of measuring paddy at the depot finally exploded, this procurement system was abolished.[24] However, farmers had to pay paddy as land tax in kind and were obliged to sell a certain amount of paddy at a low price to cooperatives under the name "*seidana zabâ* (rice of sincerity)" (Takahashi, 1988: 71). In that sense, the procurement system had remained, in a different form.

The military regime, which came into power in 1988, after suppressing the democratisation movement, immediately revived the procurement system. However,

---

[24] The procurement system was abolished on September 1, 1987, when I lived in Myanmar. The order to abolish high-denomination banknotes was issued four days later. During these days, merchants and citizens withdrew their deposits from the banks for speculation and hoarding in anticipation of rising prices, and they suffered enormous losses. Since the failure of the procurement system was evident long before 1987, it is possible that the government used the abolition of the system to demonetise currency four days later. In any case, this series of measures became a fuse for the democratisation movement of the following year (Takahashi, 1992: 3–4).

while during the socialist period, rice was rationed to all citizens (except rice-growing farmers), the new military regime limited the rationing only to civil servants, hospitals, and old-age homes. Thus, the burden on farmers, in terms of the amount of paddy they had to offer to the state, was greatly reduced (Takahashi, 2000: 41, 47). As for the domestic distribution system, registered traders have been allowed to trade paddy and rice since 1987, and since 1995, anyone can trade paddy and rice without registration (Takahashi, 2000: 48). However, the new military regime monopolised the export of rice through the state-run Myanmar Agricultural Produce Trading (MAPT).[25] Moreover, paddy, jute, cotton, sugarcane, and other crops had to be offered to state-owned companies, to secure inexpensive raw materials. Other crops remained as they were when they were liberalised in 1987.

In April 2003, fifteen years after the military regime took power, Myanmar underwent a rapid liberalisation of the country's rice sector. The paddy procurement system was terminated, and the domestic distribution of rice was completely liberalised. The following year, the rationing system was also abolished. At the same time, the ban on exports by private traders was lifted. However, this was a very tightly controlled market liberalisation, with the state strictly controlling the rice exports by way of a licencing system for traders and export quotas.

In 2011, soon after the advent of Thein Sein's government, it became possible for anyone to obtain a licence to export rice, and the export quota was nullified. The export tax on rice was also progressively reduced from 8% to 5% and then to 2% in August of the same year. In 2011, at a time when it was still far from certain how far democratisation and liberalisation reforms would go, rice exports were finally liberalised. In 2013, the regime repealed the State Agricultural Marketing Board (SAMB) Act, which was enacted in 1950 and had served as the basis for state agencies to be involved in the purchase, processing, distribution, and export of rice and other agricultural products. When the Aung San Suu Kyi administration took office in early 2016, they continued to pursue a policy of liberalisation.

2.3 System of Planned Cultivation

Just like the two other pillars of agricultural policy, the system of planned cultivation originated in the civil administration period immediately after independence. The Land Nationalisation Act of 1953 stipulated that the president may deem to apply or ask to apply specific crops or specific means to use on agricultural land respectively (Article 38-1). In addition, the Land Nationalisation Rules of 1954 state that the applications and reports on the use of agricultural land must be submitted to the

[25] UBAMB was repeatedly renamed: to the Trade Corporation No. 1 (*kounthweyêi kopouyêishîn ahma' thi'*) in December 1964, the Agricultural and Farm Produce Trading Corporation (AFPTC), *leyakâincûn hnìn ûyinhcanmyei htwe'kounpi' sî kounthweyêi kopouyêishîn* in Burmese) in April 1976, and finally, Myanmar Agricultural Produce Trading (*myanmà leya htwe' kounpi'sî yâunweyêi*) in April 1989. However, its character as a state institution for trading agricultural products had remained unchanged up to 2003 (Takahashi, 1992:109).

authorities (Article 81). However, as with the agrarian reform, this policy seems to have been largely unimplemented due to political instability and the government's lack of enforcement capacity.

The Burmese socialist regime imposed a series of restrictions on the use of agricultural land based on provisions contained in the 1953 Land Nationalisation Act. A directive was issued in June 1967, stipulating that farmers in areas designated by the government must grow specific crops as directed by the Central Agricultural Land Committee (BaMaKa, 1972: 78–79). The government tried to forcibly spread this system in the countryside. We can learn about this method from a list of regulations on the use of farmland, known as *thîzâ hma' pountin* (tenant registration book) (Takahashi, 1992: 100–102; 1998: 51; 2000: 45–46) which was originally introduced to register landlords and tenants. This list recorded the land number, cultivator's name, acreage, land type, and so on, as well as the name of the crop to be grown on each piece of farmland. The crops designated as "planned crops (*simankêin thîhnan*)" are those that the State deems necessary and wants procured. Twenty-one planned crops were specified in 1966, accounting for most of the crops produced in Myanmar, including rice and pulses. This system continued even after September 1987, when the government loosened its control over domestic trade in major agricultural products such as paddy and pulses, but with a decrease in the number of designated crops. Then, in July 1988, the system was paused for two months as Myanmar experienced a massive political and social upheaval.

In September 1988, the military government revived the planned cultivation system as well as the procurement system. However, many crops were excluded from the procurement system and the amount of paddy demanded was reduced. Thus, the strong link between the planned cultivation system and the procurement system, which had existed during the socialist period, faded away. The total area under planned cultivation decreased significantly. Nonetheless, there were at least two exceptions. The first was rice. The military regime used the planned cultivation system to increase rice production. Particular emphasis was placed on the promotion of double cropping of rice through the expansion of irrigation facilities. Dams, pumps, and tidal irrigation systems were increased without regard to the will of the farmers, and rice cultivation was forced on these irrigated lands. Government authorities also deliberately flooded farmland to prevent farmers from growing beans and vegetables, and took away cultivation rights during the dry season from those who had access to irrigation canals but did not practise dry-season cropping of rice. As a result of such "planned cultivation", the area under rice cultivation increased during the first half of the military period. The second exception was industrial crops such as sugarcane, cotton, and jute. While paddy and rice could be sold to the private sector, which weakened the relationship with government procurement, most of the industrial crops were forced to be planted by planned cultivation policy and the harvests were "procured" to the state-owned enterprises at low prices. The planned cultivation system was used as a means of protecting state-owned enterprises that could not operate if they purchased raw materials at market prices.

Article 43 of the Farmland Act of 2012 saw the repeal of the Land Nationalisation Act of 1953 and with that, the planned cultivation system was eliminated. However, farmers still need *permission* to change what crops they cultivate. With the exception of rice, such permission can be granted by the Region or State Farmland Management Committee (Article 28, Paragraph 2). Since rice is a staple food, the Central Farmland Management Committee must instead make a special investigation and grant permission, so as not to harm the country's self-sufficiency (Article 28, Paragraph 1). Although this is not planned cultivation, farmers still cannot change crops without permission. In addition, converting farmland into non-agricultural land is also subject to the condition that it is in the public interest. The permission of the Region or State authorities is sufficient for land other than paddy fields (Article 30, Paragraph 2), but to convert paddy fields into non-agricultural land requires the permission of the Central Farmland Management Committee (Article 30, Paragraph 1). This special consideration required for rice cultivation can be described as a tradition or unwritten law practised since Myanmar's independence.

2.4 The Three Pillars Amid Changing Politico-Economic Systems

In this chapter, we have surveyed the history of modern Myanmar's agricultural policy from the perspective of how "the three pillars" of the country's agricultural policy have changed. All these three pillars—state ownership of farmland; state procurement system; and planned cultivation system—originate from the country's parliamentary democracy period immediately after independence.

First, the system of *state ownership* of agricultural land has been a consistent national policy of Myanmar since independence, but the policy can be divided into socialist and capitalist forms, according to the way that the farmers were given the right to cultivate their land. The socialist form, in turn, varies between the post-independence civil administration period—during which the right to dispose of cultivation rights was allowed to some extent to farmers, but the orientation was collectivisation—and the Burmese socialist period—during which the right of farmers to dispose of their farmland was denied entirely, but agriculture was not collectivised, and crops were requisitioned from individual farmers in return for their right to cultivate. The capitalist form varies between the post-1988 military period—in which the military government promoted plantation agriculture, while stripping the farmers of cultivation rights and the 2010s' democratisation period—in which the government expanded cultivation rights and brought the rules closer to a system that allows for *de facto* private ownership. The nature of the right to cultivate has changed greatly, but it has remained the basis of agricultural policy, as if it were a national policy.

Similarly, both the state institution in charge of the *procurement system* and the legislation on which it was based were established during the post-independence civil administration period. During the Burmese socialist period, however, the state controlled the entire supply chain from domestic distribution, processing, storage, and export of major agricultural products, such as beans, sesame, maize, and tobacco, in addition to rice. The state's procurement continued with the post-1988 military regime which rejected socialism. The purpose was to guarantee the livelihood of government employees and the survival of state-owned enterprises. During the democratisation period, both the procurement system and its underlying laws were abolished. Everything from distribution to export was liberalised.

Throughout, the *planned cultivation* system regulated agricultural production as the preliminary stage of the procurement. This policy also originated in the post-independence civil administration period, but was materialised effectively during the Burmese socialist period. About 20 crops were designated as "planned", and most of the agricultural land in Myanmar came under this system, except for some ethnic minority areas where the state lacked control. The planned cultivation system was designed to secure the supply of agricultural products, but in the latter half of the Burmese socialist period, this system was also used to spread high-yielding rice varieties, and the quota delivery of agricultural products became more severe as production increased (Takahashi, 1992: 88–89, 102–103). During the post-1988 military period, this system was used as a means of expanding two-season rice cultivation, apart from ensuring the supply of rice. In the case of industrial crops, however, forced cultivation and forced offerings to the state continued. The system of planned cultivation was abolished only after the democratisation period began. However, in the case of rice, although cultivation was not compulsory, comparatively more complicated and time-consuming procedures were still required to switch to other crops or to convert paddy fields to non-agricultural land.

How these three pillars related to each other and how the actual agricultural policy was executed varied from period to period. In the post-independence civil administration period, when the prototypes of the three pillars was established, the Land Nationalisation Act and the State Agricultural Marketing Board Act were enacted as separate laws. Thus, the three pillars were not implemented in unison. Moreover, the nationalisation of farmland was never fully completed, the direct purchase of paddy from farmers was replaced by purchase from rice mills, and the planned cultivation stipulated in the Land Nationalisation Act ended up being a moot point as security deteriorated.

Although the Burmese socialist regime did not change the agriculture-focused laws of the post-independence civilian period, it strongly promoted the three pillars. The symbol of this was the tenant registration book (*thîzâ hma'pountin*). In this book, the name of the planned crop to be planted was written for each farmer's holding (*ûpain*). Sometimes, the amount to be offered was also written in the book. If the farmer failed to fulfil the obligation, the state would take away his or her cultivation right which was annually renewed. Thus, during the socialist period, the system of national ownership of farmland, the system of procurement, and the system of planned cultivation came together and penetrated to every corner of the village.

In the later military period, the system of agrarian nationalisation was used as a means of seizing land for development projects that suited the military business and its cronies. The system of planned cultivation was used for different purposes than in the socialist period, such as for forcibly increasing rice production and for helping state-owned enterprises survive. Nonetheless, the three pillars were maintained, with a reduced system of procurement.

Shortly after the period of democratisation began, the Land Nationalisation Act and the State Agricultural Marketing Board Act, which had served as the basis for the three pillars of agricultural policy since independence, were both repealed, dissolving the three pillars.

2.5 Changes in Rural Village Policy

Having discussed the evolution of agricultural policy, let us now turn to how *rural* Myanmar more broadly has been governed, by examining the village laws and related policies and realities. As the later chapters will show, Myanmar villages are populated not only by farmers but also by a large number of people who do not hold farmland. Moreover, the rate of increase in the number of these non-land-holding people is much higher than that of farmers. As this book's goal is to depict the transformation of Myanmar's rural social economy, I will now first examine the history of rural and village policies.

The Village Act, which was promulgated in 1907 under British rule, has been used by the different post-independence regimes as the basic law for rural governance—immediately after independence. It had been used during the post-independence civil administration period, during the socialist period and during the later military period. This law defines a "village", called "*cêiywa*" or "*ywa*" in Burmese language, as a residential area that does not fall within the area of a town. In many cases, a village is not an administrative unit; instead, a "*cêiywa ou'sù*" or a "village tract" as an aggregation *(ou'sù)* of one or more villages is the smallest administrative unit. These definitions remained the same in the 2012 Ward or Village Tract Administration Law (*ya'kwe' dhòumahou' cêiywa ou'sù ou'chou'yêi ùbadei*). The 1907 Act further defines a "village tract" as "the area under the jurisdiction of the Village Headman, including one or more villages and the land surrounding them".

Since before the 1907 Act came into being, the structure of Myanmar's administration has remained as follows: Nation → State or Division[26] → District (abolished in 1974 but restored during the military regime) → Township (T/S) → Ward or Village Tract. The ward (*ya'kwe*) and village tract are the administrative end. The ward is created by dividing the urban area, and the village tract is created by gathering scattered villages. The head of the village tract has had different titles. The 1907 Village Act called him the Village Headman (*ywadhajî* in Burmese). This remained so during the post-independence civil administration period. However, under the Burmese socialist regime, he was called the chairman (*ou'kàhtà*) of the Village Tract Security and Administration Committee from March 1962 to March 1974, and the chairman of the Village Tract People's Council from March 1974 to September 1988.

[26] The Burmese word "*tâin*" and the English word "Division" were renamed as "*tâindeithàjî*" and "Region" respectively in the 2008 Constitution (Article 9).

During the period of direct military rule, he was called the chairman of the Law and Order Restoration Council of the Village Tract from September 1988 to December 1997, and from January 1998 to March 2011, he was the chairman of the Peace and Development Council of the Village Tract. Since March 30, 2011, during the democratisation period, he was called the village administrator. In this book, we will refer to all of these titles collectively as "mayors of the village tracts" or "mayors" for short, but we will also use the terms "headman", "chairman", and "administrator" in accordance with the time period being described.

The term "*ywagâun*", which is translated literally as "village head," appears in the 1907 Act (Article 15), and there seems to have been one in each village (hamlet) that constituted a village tract. When I was researching villages during the socialist and military periods, the *ywângaung* was called *aphwèwin*, *yaeingâun* or *ywaou'kahtà*. *Aphwèwin* was a "member" of the Village People's Council, the Law and Order Restoration Council, or the Peace and Development Council; *yaeingâun* is the "head of a hundred households," the head of a large group of households; and *ywaou'kahtà* is the "chairman" of the village council. The Ward or Village Tract Administration Law, which was amended for the third time in 2016, includes the term *cêiywa tawunngan*, or "village head". In this book, all of them are uniformly called "village (or hamlet) chiefs". In other words, there are several village chiefs under a mayor.

According to the 1907 Village Act, the headman (mayor) of a village tract was elected by the villagers and was appointed or rejected by the Deputy Commissioner. Not more than four other members of the village committee, chaired by the headman, were also elected. The term of office for the headman and the village committee members was three years, without prejudice to reappointment.

The 1907 Act[27] stipulated the following duties and powers of the village headman:

(1) To inform the relevant authorities about the sale of stolen goods, murder or attempted murder, suspected robbery or dacoity, robbery or dacoity, death, infectious diseases, destruction of Government property, unlicenced possession of firearms, etc. (Article 7)
(2) To search for and arrest criminals and suspected criminals.
3) To stop all unlawful attacks on the village.
(4) To provide food, transportation, directions, etc. to officials who visit the village tract on official business.
(5) To collect land tax on the land within the village tract.
(6) To record demographic information such as births and deaths.
(7) To prevent public nuisance, infectious diseases of humans and animals, and fire.
(8) To maintain the sanitation of the village.
(9) To ensure discipline with regard to slaughtering cattle, horses, sheep, pigs, etc.
(10) To notify villagers of notices and announcements from government agencies.
(11) If a person brings a machete, mallet, knife, saw, whip, etc. to a festival, it shall be confiscated. (Article 8, Sect. 2.1 above)

[27] The following is an extract from the Act, not verbatim.

(12) Local police officers must fulfil the same public duties as the headman described above. (Article 8, Sect. 2.2)

In turn, the duties and prohibitions of the villagers included:

(1) To report to the headman about the above-mentioned crimes and violence that the headman polices.
(2) To report births and deaths to the headman.
(3) To prevent nuisances, infectious diseases of humans and animals, and fires, and to pay attention to general hygiene. (Article 11)
(4) To pay a fine for the failure to perform a public duty. (Article 12)
(5) No new village or cluster of houses shall be established without the permission of the Deputy Commissioner. (Article 18)
(6) No festival shall be held without the permission of the Deputy Commissioner. (Article 21).

There were rules even for people who were not residents of the village:

a. If any person comes into a village-tract of which he is not a resident, he or the person, if any, in whose house he is living shall, within four hours of his arrival, report to the headman, and must also report it when he leaves the village. (Article 15)
b. Violators shall be fined or imprisoned, or both. (Article 16)
c. A person who is not a resident of a village-tract shall not build any house, hut or enclosure, or take up his residence in the village-tract without the permission of the village committee (Article 17)

In addition, the Rules issued under Sect. 29 of the Act contained further duties of the head of the village tract:

a. There must be at least one cemetery in the village area. The cemetery must be at least 100 feet (1 foot is about 30 cm) away from any pond, waterway, or dwelling. (Article 13)
b. A drinking well or pond shall be constructed in each village within the village tract. Within 20 yards (yard = about 91 cm) of the well or pond, bathing, washing, dumping of garbage and trespassing of livestock shall be prohibited. (Article 16)
c. A garbage dump shall be set up near the village area where garbage shall be burned or buried. (Article 20)

The further rules for the villagers were:

a. A corpse must not be left unattended for more than 48 h (72 h in the cool season). (Article 2)
b. Latrines shall be located not less than twenty feet from any dwelling and sixty feet from any well (Sect. 2.5).
c. When a house is built in the village, it shall be separated from other houses by a distance of twenty feet in front and rear and six feet on each side. (Article 6).

d. When rearing livestock, care must be taken not to cause nuisance to others and not to pollute rivers, waterways, wells, ponds, etc. (Article 11)

As can be seen from the above items, the colonial government focused on the maintenance of security and sanitation in the villages. The fundamental idea for controlling the village was that the village should not disrupt the security of the colonial state or become a source of contagious diseases. The village must be obedient to the government without disturbing state security, as symbolised by the clause that the village must provide various services to the officials visiting the village. In addition, many of the clauses stipulated the vertical relationship between the village headman and individual villagers, establishing the headman's authority over the villagers. There were no clauses that would strengthen the horizontal relationship among villagers. Likely, the aim was to prevent villages from uniting against the colonial government.

The 1907 Village Act was amended at least twelve times during the colonial period and twice during the post-independence civil administration period, but the law continued to function as the basic law for village governance. However, during the post-independence civil administration period, the enforcement of the Village Act was limited due to the continuing resistance of landlords against agrarian reform, as well as the rebellions by communist parties and ethnic minority armies in rural areas (Hagiwara et al., 1973: 112–130; Taylor, 1987: 229–249).

The "revolutionary government" headed by General Ne Win, which came into power in 1962 under the guise of quelling the country's turmoil by military force, set up the Security and Administration Committee (*lounjounyêi hnìn ou'chou'yêi komiti*) as an administrative organ of the Revolutionary Council. As the name implies, it aimed to restore state security and stabilise the administration from the centre to the village level. The Village Tract Security and Administration Committee consisted of 13 members: a chairperson and a general secretary appointed by the government, three members of the Burmese Socialist Programme Party, five representatives of the farmers, and three representatives of the workers. Among them, the chairperson, general secretary, a BSPP member representative, a farmer representative and a worker representative organised the Village Tract Executive Committee. The chairperson, the secretary general, and the BSPP representative actually controlled the administration of the village tract. Under the Security and Administration Committee, the Law Committee, the Planning Committee, the Economic Committee, and the Agricultural Land Committee were organised (BaLaKa, 1973: 3–11). The most important law that the Security and Administration Committee should base their activities on was the Village Act, followed by the Penal Code, the Forest Act, the Fisheries Act, the 1963 Tenancy Law, and the Land Nationalisation Act of 1953.

Ne Win's government was trying to control every move of the village and its people, in order to maintain security and spread socialism. The duties and powers of the above committees, taken together, included almost all the provisions of the 1907 Village Act on the responsibilities of the village headmen. In addition, a long list of provisions were added: issuing permission for the use of loudspeakers; disbanding unauthorised gatherings; scrutinising the applications by villagers to expand village land; prohibiting fishing, fisheries, salt production, forestry, and so on without a permit; punishing violators of the Canal Act; capturing cattle and buffaloes entering protected forests; organising cooperative societies; determining the tenants of agricultural land in the village; bringing to justice those who violate the Land Nationalisation Act by selling, pawning or otherwise transferring agricultural land for private use; providing guidance on the planting of planned crops; and confiscating agricultural land that does not comply with the rules. (BaLaKa, 1973: 10–13)

More than a decade after coming to power in a coup that suspended Myanmar's original constitution, Ne Win promulgated a new constitution in 1974, whereby, under the one-party dictatorship of the Burmese Socialist Programme Party (Article 11 of the constitution), elections for the People's Councils (*phyithù kaunsi*) were held in the village tracts. Between 10 and 30 councillors (*aphwèwin*) were elected in each village tract, depending on its population size (Law on the Election of the First People's Assembly and People's Council in 1973, Article 8, Paragraph 1). From among them, three to five members were elected to become the executive committee (Article 7, paragraph 3 of the Rule on the People's Council Law). In accordance with the new Constitution, the Village Tract People's Councils were subject to the leadership of the village tract Burma Socialist Programme Party Committee.

The People's Councils Law detailed the responsibilities and powers of the councils. Article 133, concerned with the economy, stipulates that the councils should formulate and implement village plans in accordance with the economic plans of the higher people's councils, such as the state, division, and township councils; investigate and report to higher authorities on any problems related to taxes; develop people-owned[28] or state-owned economic activities; supervise the supply of consumer goods to villagers, implement development programmes while preserving the natural environment, and develop the planned cultivation and new farmland in accordance with the state's agricultural land administration. The term "plan (*siman*)" was frequently used to promote a socialist planned economy in rural areas through the village tract people's council. Article 134, related to social policy, included fostering intellectually, physically, and morally sound youth by promoting education and sports, taking care of villagers' health and hygiene, preserving ethnic culture, and preventing wind and flood damage. Article 135, related to planning and public security, included maintaining security and law and order in accordance with the plans of the higher people's councils; following the principles and rules for the organisation of people's militias (*pyidhù si'*); cracking down on those who disturb security and national unity; protecting people's and state property; preparing and maintaining a "guest list" (*èzayîn*) for those who stay in the village; monitoring foreigners; building houses and other structures in accordance with the law; cooperating in collecting taxes and distributing social benefits; collecting and maintaining statistics on social, economic, planning and security matters; cooperating in the activities of civil servants in the village; reporting to higher authorities immediately when problems occur that cannot be solved by the village tract council. In this way, the law had detailed instructions

[28] When I asked the villagers about this term in 1987, they said that this "people's ownership (*pyidhùbain*)" was completely synonymous with "state ownership (*nainnganbain*)".

on how to enforce the Burmese socialist programme and maintain public order. Although the People's Councils Law did not explicitly mention the Village Act, the above three articles (Articles 133, 134, and 135) stated that the Law was subject to the relevant laws and rules, which naturally included the Village Act. The new rules contained stricter and more detailed security provisions than the Village Act, giving the appearance of a police state.

However, whether or not these strict plans and regulations were followed was another matter entirely. In fact, these apparently strict systems were not fully enforced in the villages, but were transformed by *nalehmu*. "*Nalehmu (nâlehmù)*" can be translated as "tacit understanding" or "doing things in an easy way". In this book, it refers to various compromises and tacit approvals between the government officials and the villagers (Takahashi, 1992: 104–105; 2000: 132; 2012: 79–82).

The military regime that begun in 1988 abolished the People's Councils and replaced them with Law and Order Restoration Councils, from the state to the village tract levels. The legislation and guidance that had established and maintained the Burmese socialist system that since 1962 disappeared from the villages. However, security and sanitation remained the key principles of village governance. According to a booklet, written in Burmese, entitled "*cêiywaou'sù nyeinwu'pipyâhmù tihsau'yêiaphwèmyâ ì lou'ngântawunmyâ hnìn lou'ngân hsaunywe'hmùsani*' (The Responsibilities and Practices of the Village Tract Law and Order Restoration Council Activities)", the Village Tract Law and Order Restoration Council consisted of four members: three people whom the villagers trusted and respected, and a village secretary who was a civil servant of the General Administration Department of the Ministry of Home Affairs. A chairperson was chosen by the Township Law and Order Restoration Council from among the three other than the secretary. Not even merely formal elections were held anymore.

The authority of the Village Tract Law and Order Restoration Council was described in "*myòu hnìn cêiywa e'ùbadei le'swêsaun* (Instructions for Town and Village Act)", issued in 1995 by the General Administration Department (GAD), a powerful branch of the Ministry of Home Affairs. Firstly, it stipulated that all powers are granted under the Villages Act of 1907. It presumed that all pre-1988 decrees and regulations based on other than the Village Act had been repealed. While the original 1907 Act was in English, the Instructions were written in Burmese. It contained excerpts from Articles 12 to 21 and the Rules issued under Article 29 of the 1907 Act in no particular order. It can be said that the village administration of the military regime focused on the maintenance of security, sanitation and subordination to the government by eliminating socialist plannings and cooperations and returning to the 1907 Village Act of the colonial period. Some of the villages that I visited during this period had itemised village codes, most of whose provisions corresponded to the provisions of the Instructions. The village codes were written to make state control more effective, rather than to resist outside powers as was, for example, the case with medieval Japan's *Muraokite* (village rules governing local behaviour).

The 1907 Village Act, which was enacted during the colonial period and remained effective for 105 years during the post-independence, socialist and military rule periods, was finally abolished in February 2012 with the partial democratisation of Myanmar politics. The new Town and Village Tract Administration Law, promulgated in 2012, set up new rules for the village.

Firstly, the system of electing village administrators (mayors) was democratised, and the procedure was specified. In the first step of the election, the head of a household or an adult representative of a household elected a candidate by secret ballot among a ten-household group.[29] The candidate had to meet the qualifications for a candidate stipulated in the Law and be suitable to be a village tract administrator. Next, the representatives selected in this way elected a candidate from among themselves to become the village tract administrator. In the final step, the supervisory committee under the township administrator confirmed once again that the candidate is from parents who are both Myanmar citizens, is over 25 years old, meets the conditions to fulfil the tasks of the village administrator, in terms of education, economic background and health, and is not a civil servant. After the Law's third amendment in 2016, the village administrator became elected by secret ballot by representatives of each household in the village.

Secondly, some provisions were added on how to manage resources within the village tract area. The responsibilities of the village tract administrators included permitting the construction of houses on village land, pastureland, forest land, and cemeteries; managing irrigation and drainage channels, ponds, wells, pumping facilities, and springs in the village; controlling poaching in lakes and fishponds; and guarding signs and stone monuments that mark the boundaries of the village.

Thirdly, new regulations were added in line with the times. It was added that the villagers must: obtain the village tract administrator's permission when using large speakers; go through the village tract administrator to get the permission of the authority in charge when running billiards and other mass entertainment facilities; cooperate with the policy for poverty reduction; prepare the guest list (*èzayîn*); and notify the authority when foreigners came to the village, even if they did not stay overnight. The duties of administrators and villagers in maintaining village security and hygiene did not change, still including the prevention of wind, flood, and fire, deterrence and prosecution of crime, control of intrusion of outsiders, including foreigners, quarantine against infectious diseases of humans and animals, and reporting. However, the village tract administrator was democratically elected and given a proper budget and salary. The role of resource management was added in the 2012 Law.

The basic concerns of the central government in village governance remained security and sanitation. Because the Law encouraged the democratic election of mayors and the community activities of village tracts, village autonomy could have developed further in future. However, a village tract remained an aggregation of villages. It is necessary to keep in mind in the following chapters that, in reality, it

---

[29] The ten-household group is a group of households mentioned in the 1907 Village Act. Ten households form a group based on the neighbourhood. The head of the group, *hseeingâun* (also known as *hseeinghmù*), is supposed to play an assistant role to the village committee. In some cases, the number of households is less than 10, and in other cases, the number of households is 20 or 30.

is the village (*ywa*), not the village tract (*cêiywa ou'sù*), that unifies the landscape and serves as the daily living area of people. Moreover, as we will see later, this village (*ywa*) is not like a Japanese "common (or natural) village" (*Shizen-son*) in the sociological sense, or like the Japanese old villages (*kyuson*) or hamlets (*buraku*).

In the following chapters, I will examine Myanmar's agriculture and rural areas from the perspectives of how agricultural performance has changed, how rural society has changed, and what has remained unchanged despite changes in the politico-economic and agricultural systems.

Chapter 3
Agriculture and Rural Villages in the National Economy

Agricultural labourers heading home after finishing their work. The labourers had been weeding the onion field behind them since the morning. As with the rice-transplanting groups (shown on the photo in the Introduction), a group head organises the weeding group and brings the group to work for the owner of an onion field. (In Thindaunggyi Village, January 2014)

A. Takahashi, *Regime Changes and Socio-economic History of Rural Myanmar, 1986–2019*, Studies in Economic History,
https://doi.org/10.1007/978-981-99-3272-6_3

Introduction

In this chapter, I discuss the position and the role of agriculture and rural villages in the Myanmar national economy. What counts as "agriculture"? In Myanmar, the word for "agriculture"—*sai'pyôuyêi* refers to crop farming only and does not include livestock farming (*mwêimyuyêi*). Therefore, statistics on agriculture and livestock farming are always listed separately. However, the term for agricultural land or farmland—*myeiya*—refers not only to land for crop farming (that is, "agriculture") but also to land for animal husbandry. Officially, according to Myanmar policy, land that is defined as part of towns and villages cannot be agricultural land. Agricultural land must be outside of towns and villages. Thus, land that is considered residential land cannot be agricultural land. Therefore, growing vegetables or harvesting mangoes on residential land within a town or village is not included in Myanmar agricultural statistics. In contrast, cattle and pigs are often raised in residential areas, and village administration officials keep track of the numbers of these animals, so they are included in local and national statistics. I have also heard of counting the number of mangos, palms, papayas, and so on in a residential area and putting them into the gross domestic product, so it is likely that such agriculture may be included in national statistics.

Next, what is a "rural village"? As mentioned in the previous chapter, Myanmar law defines a "village" as a residential area that is not a "town". The Towns Act of 1907 provides that the President of the Union may, by notification, declare any local area to be a town (Article 4). The Ward and Village Tract Administration Law of 2012 stipulates that "town" means a region where a boundary is stipulated and formed under this Law by collecting the relevant wards together, and that "village" means a region where a boundary is stipulated and formed under this Law in such estate which is not included within the relevant town boundary. Neither law contains provisions on population size or population density.[1]

Villages could be classified as agricultural, fishing, and mountain villages, for example, but Myanmar does not often classify villages in this way. The "rural villages" described in this book are effectively "agricultural villages", their main industry being, or having been, agriculture. However, in Myanmar, as in Japan, the relationship between village and agriculture is becoming more estranged. I will clarify this throughout this book.

Based on the above, let us first review the history of Myanmar agriculture, which has been inseparable from rural areas, by investigating macroeconomic statistics at the national level. I will begin with how different types of land have increased or decreased across Myanmar, then review the evolution of land utilisation and crop production, and finally consider how the position of agriculture has changed in the national economy. Large-scale macro statistics do not always correspond exactly

[1] Although not defining a "town", the UN Statistics Division defines "urban" areas in Myanmar as areas classified by the General Administration Department as wards, which generally have an increased density of building structures, population and better infrastructure development (United Nations 2022: 125). Again, there is no mention of population size or population density, which are included in the definition of urban areas in many other countries.

with the reality on the ground. This is especially true in Myanmar due to its years of dictatorship, propaganda, and a general mistrust of government officials, who moreover may not have the requisite skills for such studies. Nonetheless, by looking at these figures, we can capture some overall trends.

Secondly, I would like to consider how many "farmers" in Myanmar hold "farmland" or "the right to cultivate". As mentioned in Chapter 2, agrarian reform was conducted in post-independence Myanmar similarly to post-war Japan, but it was not as successful as in Japan in terms of distributing farmland equitably. Saito Teruko and I have pointed out that Myanmar continued to have many landless people in rural areas just after the land reform and even during the socialist period (Saito, 1980: 79–81; 1982: 235–238; Takahashi, 1992: 63–67; 1995: 55–56). As I have since 1986 surveyed rural villages in various parts of Myanmar, including the delta, the central dry zone, and deep in the mountains of Shan State and Chin State, I have confirmed that there have been many "non-farm households"[2] (Takahashi, 2000: 116–120; 2004: 339–342; 2007: 409–410). However, it has not been clear how many farm households and how many non-farm households there were in the country, and what their regional distribution was. I happened to obtain the results of a preliminary household survey in rural areas conducted in 2009 (prior to the 2010 Census of Agriculture), at the then Settlement and Land Record Department, Ministry of Agriculture and Irrigation. I will use this as a basis for discussing the spread of "farm households" and of "non-farm households".

Third, I will use a few statistical data to consider the socio-economic situation of Myanmar's "rural" areas. Rural Myanmar has a large number of non-farmers who do not hold cultivation rights of agricultural land. Thus, rural Myanmar cannot be described only in terms of "agriculture". Fortunately, I can to an extent use the results of the 2014 Population and Housing Census, the first in 31 years, to examine socioeconomic changes in rural areas in comparison to urban areas. Mainly, I will examine the total population, sex ratio, household size, literacy rate, education, religion, ethnicity, and so on, but also labour force and employment rates, and the composition of rural employment.

Finally, moving away from population censuses, we will compare the consumption structure of rural and urban households, referencing the household expenditure surveys done by Myanmar's Central Statistical Organisation (CSO).

However, such macroeconomic data provide only a partial glimpse of rural society. The surveys include only a limited number of survey items. Moreover, because the surveys must be conducted uniformly for the whole country, they do not consider regional contexts. Long-term, continuous, and detailed surveys would be necessary

[2] In this book, I define "non-farm households" as households that do not fit Chap. 2's definition of a "farm household". Thus, a "non-farm household" would be a household where none of its members have "cultivation right". Such non-farm households can be divided into: 1) "agricultural labourer households", whose livelihood comes mainly from members who are employed in agricultural hired labour; and 2) "non-agricultural households", whose principal livelihood earners are not employed in agriculture, neither as self-employed farmers nor as agricultural labourers. Incidentally, all persons who are engaged in agriculture, whether as self-employed farmers or as hired labour, would be termed as "agricultural workers".

to describe the transformation of rural society in more detailed terms, such as multiple employment (in which individuals and households work in multiple sectors), socioeconomic stratification, labour relations (including labour exchange and cooperation), population movement and remittances, power relations within villages, and the reality of rural "modernisation". I will discuss these issues in the following chapters.

3.1 Trends in Agriculture Amid Regime Changes

3.1.1 Land Utilisation

Economists call land, capital, and labour the three factors of production. In the industrial and commercial sectors, dealing with capital and labour is usually sufficient. However, in the agricultural sector, land becomes important. Thus, the study of agricultural economy emphasises land issues much more than the study of other sectors. In this book, too, in discussing the economic problems of Myanmar's agriculture, I will start with land.

Table 3.1 shows the shares of agricultural land and forest in Myanmar's total land area. Agricultural land is the total of net sown area and fallow land. Currently, about 125,000 km^2 (about 30.94 million acres) of Myanmar's 676,600 km^2 (about 167.19 million acres) is farmland. That is about 18.5% of Myanmar's land. Looking at the trends in the same table, we can see that for the 20 years from 1971/72[3] to 1991/92, farmland area remained around 25 million acres and did not expand at all, but it increased by more than 5 million acres in the following 20 years.

Thus, farmland in Myanmar increased significantly during the two-decade period of military rule. This was due to the reclamation of so-called barren land, as indicated in Table 3.1 by the decrease in cultivable wasteland. However, the increase in farmland stopped during the democratisation period. This is because many of the players in the reclamation of cultivable wasteland during the military rule were the national army and its affiliated companies, as well as small and large entrepreneurs called "cronies" who emerged during the military rule. There were many cases in which the junta judged land to be wasteland, despite it having holders. The military government often evicted farmers who were actually cultivating the land, and continually suppressed their voices. After Thein Sein's regime came to power in 2011, it launched the "Investigation Commission for the Prevention of Public Disenfranchisements Connected to the Confiscation of Farmland and Other Lands" to investigate land seizures by the military and corporations during the previous two decades. The commission was tasked with finding solutions, including returning seized land to the original holders. As mentioned in the previous chapter, the seized lands are

[3] From 1948 to 1973, Myanmar's fiscal year was from October to September. From 1974 to 2018, it was from April to March. From 2018 to 2021, the fiscal year was October to September. During the colonial period, the fiscal year was from October to September until the 1870s, and from April to March until independence in 1948.

Table 3.1 Myanmar's land area classified by type of land

(Unit: %)

Year	1961/62	1971/72	1981/82	1991/92	2001/02	2011/12	2017/18
Net area sown	11.8	11.7	12.2	12.0	14.8	17.6	17.8
Current fallows	4.8	3.1	2.7	2.8	0.9	0.5	0.7
Cultivable waste	15.5	12.7	12.6	12.2	9.8	7.9	8.2
Reserved forest	12.8	14.0	14.7	15.0	20.7	24.5	27.9
Other woodland	55.1	33.6	32.8	32.8	28.6	25.1	21.4
Other		24.9	25.0	25.2	25.2	24.4	24.0
Total area (thousands of acres)	150,551	167,186	167,186	167,186	167,186	167,186	167,186

Note 1 One acre is approximately 4047 m^2
Note 2 The statistics for 1961/62 do not cover the whole country
Source Agricultural Statistics annual editions; values for 2017/18 are from Statistical Yearbook 2018

a huge area. In other words, the new policy favoured farmers' rights, discouraging the national army and the cronies from reclamation. The NLD government also pledged to focus on the return of these confiscated farmlands. This policy saw some farmland returned to smallholders and may have slowed down the pace of farmland expansion.

18% of Myanmar's land area consists of agricultural land—this is a relatively low figure. It is larger than Japan's 12%. However, it is lower than in developed countries such as in the United States of America, the European Union countries or Australia, where the share of agricultural land in the national land area is over 40% or 50%, but also in other ASEAN countries such as Thailand, the Philippines and Vietnam, where the share is over 30%, and Cambodia and Malaysia, where the share is over 20%. If more cultivable wastelands are not developed, Myanmar will not reach the same level of agricultural land composition as in Cambodia and Malaysia.

In contrast, forest land occupies half of the country, indicating that Myanmar is a very mountainous country. Although the area of protected forests has increased under the military regime, it is highly doubtful whether the forests are being "protected" as stated in government reports. Forestry in Myanmar has long been in decline because of illegal logging under the military regime, whether in protected forests or not.

3.1.2 Six Categories of Agricultural Land

Table 3.2 shows the forms in which agricultural land is used. In Myanmar, farmland is classified into six types: *le* (paddy fields), *ya* (upland fields), *kâin* (farmland that is in the riverbed during the rainy season but comes out in the dry season), *ûyin* (garden

Table 3.2 Acreage of each land category (upper panel) and the category's composition ratio to the net area sown (lower panel)

(Unit: Thousand Acres)

Year	1970/71	1980/81	1990/91	2000/01	2010/11	2017/18
Le (paddy)	12,599	12,977	12,582	14,358	15,997	15,673
Ya (upland)	4,399	4,692	5,033	7,615	10,476	10,331
Kaing (alluvial)	827	964	1,008	1,265	1,403	1,365
Uyin (garden)	950	1,135	1,281	2,041	4,944	5,063
Dani (nipa)	77	85	93	108	123	117
Taungya (swidden)	660	699	571	500	1,028	548
Net area sown	19,512	20,552	20,568	25,887	33,971	33,097

(Unit: %)

Year	1970/71	1980/81	1990/91	2000/01	2010/11	2017/18
Le (paddy)	64.6	63.1	61.2	55.5	47.1	47.4
Ya (upland)	22.5	22.8	24.5	29.4	30.8	31.2
Kaing (alluvial)	4.2	4.7	4.9	4.9	4.1	4.1
Uyin (garden)	4.9	5.5	6.2	7.9	14.6	15.3
Dani (nipa)	0.4	0.4	0.5	0.4	0.4	0.4
Taungya (swidden)	3.4	3.4	2.8	1.9	3.0	1.7
Total	100.0	100.0	100.0	100.0	100.0	100.0

Note The sum of the given percentages does not necessarily equal exactly 100, because the composition ratio is rounded to one decimal place. The same applies to other tables
Source Same as Table 3.1

or perennial crops land), *dànì* (nipa palm land), and *taunya* (swidden).[4] In *le*, rice is grown as the main crop, while beans and vegetables are cultivated as second crops. In *ya*, beans, maize, cotton, cereals, and vegetables are grown. In *kâin*, rice, beans and vegetables are grown. In *ûyin*, perennial crops such as mango, banana and citrus fruits are grown. In *taunya*, cereals and beans are grown. Finally, in *dànì*, nipa palm is grown exclusively.

The upper part of Table 3.2 shows the overall area of each land category. The lower part shows each land category as a percentage of Myanmar's net area sown (net area sown is the area obtained by subtracting the area sown with *multiple* crops from the total area sown). The largest percentage by far is paddy fields. Their area was stagnant at around 12 million acres during the socialist period, but expanded during the later military regime.[5] However, the paddy field area decreased slightly during

[4] In English-style spelling, *kâin* is spelt *kaing*, *ûyin* is *uyin*, *dànì* is *dani*, and *taunya* is *taungya*.

[5] As mentioned, the socialist period was from March 1962 to September 1988, the military period then lasted until March 2011. Tables 3.1, 3.2, 3.3, 3.4 and 3.5 in this chapter show the data in 10-year increments starting from 1961/62. They do not include the data for 1988/89, when the transition from the socialist period to the military period took place. There are two reasons for this: (1) it is

the democratic period. In terms of percentage, paddy fields have been on a consistent downward trend since the 1970s: Whereas previously paddy fields used to account for more than 60% of farmland, they now account for less than half. Although the area under cultivation increased during the military period, the ratio of paddy field area was still in the 50% range. During the democratisation period, it seems to have recovered slightly, but has not exceeded 50%.

In contrast, the area of upland fields and gardens increased significantly during the military period. For example, during the two decades from 1970/71 to 1990/91, upland and garden areas increased only by 14% and 35%, respectively, but during the following two decades, upland areas more than doubled and garden areas nearly quadrupled. These figures suggest that the conversion of cultivable wasteland into farmland was progressing, but that it was more likely to be in the form of upland farms and gardens than in the form of paddy fields, where development costs are high to secure water. While the expansion of upland areas has stagnated since the beginning of the democratisation period, the expansion of garden areas has continued. In fact, the reclamation of "wastelands" for rubber and palm oil plantations has been proceeding rapidly, with momentum not stopping even after the return of some confiscated farmland to smallholders began. In this way, a different form of agriculture from the peasant agriculture of the past is emerging. In combination with the development of contract farming, it has the potential to significantly change the future agricultural and rural landscapes and social relations in Myanmar.

3.1.3 Sown Area of Major Crops

Various crops are grown on farmlands. Table 3.3 shows the main crops. Rice is by far the largest crop in terms of area. As a matter of course, the area under rice cultivation has been trending alongside the area of paddy fields described above. The area of rice had remained almost unchanged for 30 years, from 11.56 million acres in 1961/62 (the year before the Burmese socialist regime began) to 11.93 million acres in 1991/92. Thereafter, it increased to 18.76 million acres during the following military regime. However, if we look at what percentage of the total cropped area is planted with rice, we can see that in 1961/62, rice accounted for 60% of the total sown area, but it gradually declined to less than half at the end of the Burmese socialist regime. The percentage of rice continued to decline during the SLORC/SPDC military regime period, accounting for only about a third by the end of this period. During the democratisation period, both the area of rice cultivation and its ratio slightly recovered, but this is due to the new Farmland Law's restriction on

---

easier to compare the figures at equal intervals if the years are divided into 10-year increments, and (2) the reliability of the 1988/89 figures is questionable because of the political and administrative turmoil. Therefore, we consider the period from 1961/62 to 1991/92 as the socialist period, and the period from 1991/92 to 2011/12 as the military period. The period from 2011/12 to 2017/18 is regarded as the democratisation period. For Table 3.2, I could not find the data for the 1960s, so the table starts with data from the financial year 1970/71.

Table 3.3 Composition ratios of major crops

(Unit: %)

Year	1961/62	1971/72	1981/82	1991/92	2001/02	2011/12	2017/18
Paddy	60.8	54.2	50.2	46.9	40.7	33.8	35.5
Wheat	0.5	0.7	1.0	1.5	0.5	0.4	0.3
Maize	1.1	1.1	1.5	1.4	1.6	1.8	2.5
Millet	2.4	1.7	1.8	1.9	1.5	1.0	N/A
Sesame	8.0	10.1	13.5	12.5	8.2	7.1	7.3
Groundnut	7.3	7.4	5.9	5.0	3.6	1.8	5.1
Matpe	0.6	0.8	0.9	2.9	4.5	4.8	4.8
Green gram	0.4	0.4	0.4	1.7	4.7	4.9	6.1
Pigeon pea	0.9	0.9	0.7	1.1	3.1	2.9	3.2
Chickpea	1.5	2.0	2.1	1.8	1.2	1.5	1.8
Other beans	3.8	4.1	3.7	3.7	5.3	2.3	5.8
Cotton	2.5	2.4	2.2	1.7	1.9	1.4	1.1
Rubber	0.8	0.9	0.8	0.7	1.2	2.4	3.2
Jute	0.1	1.0	0.5	0.4	0.3	0.0	0.0
Sugarcane	0.5	1.2	1.1	0.5	1.0	0.7	0.8
Other crops	8.7	11.1	13.6	16.4	20.8	33.3	22.6
Total sown area (thousands of acres)	19,013	22,702	25,123	25,426	39,153	55,589	50,526

Source Agricultural abstract of Burma for 1961/62; Statistical Yearbook for other years

changing crops and the lack of other crops to be planted in the paddy fields. Thus, this trend does not mean that farmers were willingly increasing their rice cultivation. Rice is still the most important agricultural crop in Myanmar, but its importance is declining year by year.

The most important crops after rice are sesame and groundnut. These two crops are not usually eaten directly but are mainly processed into cooking oil. Rice, cooking oil, and *ngapi* (fish paste) are said to be essential to the traditional Myanmar diet. Thus, the oil crops are also essential to Myanmar agriculture. During the socialist period, planting of groundnut remained unchanged, but sesame planting increased, so that the total area and ratio of both crops increased. During the SLORC/SPDC military period, however, the growth of both sesame and groundnut plantings stagnated, and the ratio of both groundnut and sesame decreased, as Myanmar's total planting area increased. This does not mean that there was an oversupply of oil crops, but that Myanmar started importing cheap palm oil. During the democratisation period, the planting of groundnut increased—not for making edible oil but for directly eating it.

In place of the above traditional major crops, cultivation of legumes has been increasing, including groundnut (which also belongs among the group of edible oil crops above),[6] matpe (black gram), green gram, pigeon pea and chickpea. The total sown area for these crops increased at an annual rate of 1.3%—from about 2.8 million acres to 4.1 million acres—during the 30-year period from 1961/62 to 1991/92 (socialist period). However, it increased at an astonishing rate of 4.6% per year during the following 20 years from 1991/92 to 2011/12, exceeding 10 million acres at the end of the military period. During the socialist period, legumes accounted for around 15% of the total sown area, but during the later military period, as one of the most important exports to replace rice, the area planted with legumes increased rapidly, and in the 2017/18 fiscal year, legumes accounted for 26.8%, or more than a quarter of the total sowed area.

Another crop that grew rapidly in area during the military regime was rubber. Planted on less than 200,000 acres during the socialist period and accounting for less than 1% of the total sown area, it increased to 1.34 million acres during the SLORC/SPDC military regime and continued to grow during the democratisation period to 1.62 million acres in FY 2017/18, accounting for 3.2% of the total sown area. This is due to strong demand from China and the reclamation of cultivable wastelands, mentioned earlier. In contrast, industrial crops such as cotton, sugarcane, and jute, for each of which state-owned corporations were set up, have declined with stagnant growth in cultivated area. This is probably because a state-enforced procurement system was in place for these crops, just as for rice—which led to a decrease in production.

3.1.4 Positioning of Agriculture in the National Economy

Let us explore changes in the share of the agricultural sector in gross domestic product in terms of *constant* prices (real prices), removing the effects of price fluctuations (Table 3.4). During the socialist period, the agricultural sector accounted for less than 30% of the gross domestic product. Thereafter, in the 1990s, it reached nearly 40%. However, in the latter half of the 2000s, the share began to decline again and returned to the level of the 1960s. During the democratisation period, the agricultural sector's share of GDP declined further to an unprecedented level of 17.7% in FY2017/18. The forestry sector, which had been Myanmar's means of earning foreign currency along with agriculture, has been shrinking since the 1980s, while the fisheries sector has been expanding in its place. While the agricultural sector has declined, the manufacturing sector has risen significantly. Compared to the socialist period, the manufacturing sector doubled its share of GDP in the 2000s and continued to grow during the democratisation period.

The rise and fall of the agricultural sector are more clearly shown by the change in the GDP composition ratio when measured by *current* (or nominal) prices (Table 3.5). The ratio of agriculture to GDP, measured in current prices, increased in the

[6] Groundnut is also added to the category of "legumes" here because it belongs among *Faboideae* (subfamily) *Arachis* (genus), despite also belonging among oil crops.

Table 3.4 Composition of gross domestic product (GDP) by sector (constant producers' prices)

(Unit: %)

Year	1961/62	1971/72	1981/82	1991/92	2001/02	2011/12	2017/18
Agriculture	26.0	27.8	28.9	37.5	33.6	25.8	17.7
Livestock and fishery	5.6	7.7	6.6	7.6	8.3	8.6	8.0
Forestry	2.9	2.6	2.2	1.9	0.9	0.4	0.1
Manufacturing	10.5	10.4	10.2	8.8	10.1	20.7	23.6
Construction	1.9	1.9	2.7	2.9	2.1	4.7	5.6
Transport	5.8	5.7	5.1	4.0	6.2	12.8	12.9
Social and administrative services	7.4	8.5	10.0	7.2	6.0	1.9	2.6
Commerce and trade	29.3	24.4	21.3	22.2	20.9	19.9	18.5
Others	10.6	11.0	13.0	7.9	11.9	5.2	11.0
GDP (million kyats)	7,798	10,641	16,717	49,933	100,275	42,228,504	63,827,919

Note For fiscal years 1961/62 to 1981/82, the 1969/70 base year price; for fiscal years 1991/92, the 1985/86 base year price; for fiscal years 2001/02, the 2000/01 base year price; for fiscal years 2011/12 and 2017/18, the 2010/11 base year price

Source Report to the Pyithu Hluttaw, 1998/99 and later editions of the Statistical Yearbook

Table 3.5 Composition of gross domestic product by sector (current producers' prices)

(Unit: %)

Year	1961/62	1971/72	1981/82	1991/92	2001/02	2011/12	2017/18
Agriculture	22.9	18.9	39.1	48.4	49.0	24.0	15.4
Livestock and fishery	4.4	5.7	6.8	8.8	7.5	8.1	7.8
Forestry	4.8	2.7	1.5	1.6	0.5	0.4	0.1
Manufacturing	14.7	29.0	9.3	7.0	7.8	19.7	23.9
Construction	3.0	3.6	1.6	2.1	2.2	4.7	6.3
Transport	3.7	5.6	3.5	2.3	5.1	11.9	11.1
Social and administrative services	8.9	8.6	4.7	3.4	1.3	2.1	3.2
Commerce and trade	26.1	17.8	25.0	22.3	24.2	19.3	20.8
Others	11.5	8.1	8.5	4.1	2.4	9.8	11.4
GDP (million kyats)	7,706	18,531	42,879	186,802	3,548,472	46,307,888	90,450,949

Source Same as Table 3.4

latter half of the socialist period and further increased in the following military period, reaching more than 50% after 1992/93. Agriculture's share of GDP was larger when measured in current prices rather than in constant prices, because agricultural prices, which had been controlled during the socialist period, were liberalised at once in the beginning of the following military period, and agriculture's terms of trade improved relative to the manufacturing sector and the commercial and service sectors. In other words, the figures in Table 3.5 show that farmers became relatively wealthier in the first half of the military period. However, the situation reversed during the second half of the post-socialist military rule. By the end of this military rule period, the agricultural GDP ratio in current prices had fallen to the level of the socialist period when agricultural prices were low and under state control. During the democratisation period, the ratio fell further, below 20%. In fiscal year 2017/18, the ratio was 15.4%, lower than the real GDP composition ratio.

In conclusion, after the collapse of Ne Win's socialist system, the transition to a market economy in Myanmar initially had a positive impact on farmers, but it did not necessarily increase agricultural productivity or the income from agriculture relative to other economic activities. During the democratisation period, the manufacturing sector overtook agriculture in terms of GDP composition in both real and nominal terms. However, since the working and dependent population is much larger in the agricultural sector than in other sectors, it remains the most important industry in Myanmar. Thus, for the time being, economic policies are likely to focus on this sector.

3.2 Cultivation Rights and Landless Households

Rural areas or villages are not only inhabited by farmers and farm households. Thus, we should ask, how many are farming? Let us estimate the number of farm households in rural areas from a household survey conducted in 2009, prior to the 2010 Census of Agriculture. As shown in Table 3.6, out of 6.36 million households[7] in Myanmar's rural villages, about 3.21 million possess farmland (they have cultivation rights), about 1.16 million do not but are employed by those who do, and about 1.99 million do not engage in agriculture. As discussed above, in Myanmar, farmland ultimately belongs to the state, while farmers can only have the cultivation rights. This has not been changed by the Farmland Law promulgated in 2012. "Owning" or "holding" farmland means having merely this cultivation right, and only households which have such individuals are farm households (*taundhu ledhamâ eindaundâzù*).

[7] This figure is considerably less than the 2014 Population and Housing Census figure of about 7.83 million households. The reason for this is not that the number of rural households has suddenly increased in the last five years, but that the 2009 survey does not include peri-urban rural areas and remote rural areas.

Table 3.6 Number of households by cultivation right holdings (2009)

State/region	Households employed in agriculture			Households *not* employed in agriculture	Total household numbers	Percentage of landless households (%)	Percentage of agricultural labourer households (%)	Percentage of households employed in agriculture (%)
	Cultivation right holder	Non-holder of cultivation right	Total					
Kachin	99,093	19,935	119,028	36,973	156,001	36.5	12.8	76.3
Kayah	19,691	2,423	22,114	8,992	31,106	36.7	7.8	71.1
Karen	37,723	21,783	59,506	45,166	104,672	64.0	20.8	56.8
Chin	66,036	3,504	69,540	3,893	73,433	10.1	4.8	94.7
Sagaing	484,228	116,700	600,928	219,574	820,502	41.0	14.2	73.2
Tanintharyi	67,458	13,316	80,774	53,487	134,261	49.8	9.9	60.2
Bago East	156,221	91,440	247,661	124,453	372,114	58.0	24.6	66.6
Bago West	176,263	104,003	280,266	117,326	397,592	55.7	26.2	70.5
Magway	415,515	110,373	525,888	200,125	726,013	42.8	15.2	72.4
Mandalay	460,039	144,302	604,341	254,774	859,115	46.5	16.8	70.3
Mon	88,290	39,651	127,941	132,463	260,404	66.1	15.2	49.1
Rakhine	195,879	111,732	307,611	160,063	467,674	58.1	23.9	65.8
Yangon	107,545	77,739	185,284	130,029	315,313	65.9	24.7	58.8
Shan South	160,631	10,412	171,043	31,441	202,484	20.7	5.1	84.5
Shan North	180,195	7,220	187,415	37,105	224,520	19.7	3.2	83.5
Shan East	38,969	5,528	44,497	4,961	49,458	21.2	11.2	90.0
Ayeyarwady	459,864	278,261	738,125	428,763	1,166,888	60.6	23.8	63.3
Total	3,213,640	1,158,322	4,371,962	1,989,588	6,361,550	49.5	18.2	68.7

Note 1 Among "households employed in agriculture," the category "cultivation right holder" refers to farm households and the "non-holder of cultivation right" refers to agricultural labourer households

Note 2 (Number of landless households) = (number of agricultural labourer households) + (number of households not employed in agriculture)

Source Settlement and Land Record Department, internal document, 2011

Table 3.6 shows that farm households account for only half of the total number of rural households. However, we should add to this the agricultural labourer households—households in which members work in agriculture even though they do not hold farmland. Then, the total number of households employed in agriculture is about 4.37 million. This is 68.7%, or about two-thirds, of the 6.36 million rural households.

The proportion of "landless households" varies across Myanmar. It is low in the mountainous ethnic-minority states of Kachin, Karenni (Kayah), Chin, and Shan. In these states, the proportion of households engaged in agriculture is also high, indicating that there are few job opportunities other than agriculture in the village. In addition, the number of households with landless agricultural labourers is extremely small. It can be imagined that it is difficult to make a living without farmland in the mountains. On the contrary, the ratio of landless households is high in the delta areas, which have many ethnic Bamars, such as the East and West Bago, Yangon, and Ayeyarwady regions, and in ethnic-minority states such as Mon, Karen[8], and Rakhine. All of them are rice-growing areas where paddy rice cultivation is flourishing in the plains. In these states and regions, the number of landless agricultural labourer households exceeds 20%. (The only exception is Mon State, where it is less than 20%.) In other words, agriculture in these wet-rice-growing areas is carried out not only by farmers but also by many landless agricultural labourers. Nevertheless, the ratio of households engaged in agriculture in these parts of Myanmar is also lower than the national average. (An exception is the western part of Bago Region.) This implies that people in these regions have many employment opportunities other than agriculture, even if they do not hold farmland.

According to statistics, Myanmar's total area of farmland in 2009/10 was about 30.19 million acres (CSO Statistical Yearbook 2012). If we divide this figure by the number of households that have farmland, the average size of cultivation is 9.4 acres, or 3.7 hectares, per household, which is three times that of Japan. However, this figure is cut in half if rural landless households are included. Moreover, the disparity in farmland size among the households that have farmland is also very large. The same kind of agrarian reform that Japan undertook after World War II was also attempted in Myanmar at about the same time, just after independence. Yet, in Myanmar, half of the households do not have farmland and more than 30% of households do not engage in agriculture. This is quite different from the structure of rural areas in Japan right after its agrarian reform.

[8] It has already been mentioned that the English name of the country was changed from Burma to Myanmar in 1989, and the English names of provinces, towns and ethnic groups were also changed. In the same way, the English names of regions, towns, and ethnic groups were also revised. Karen was changed to Kayin, but since the Karen people continue to use the name Karen, the name Karen is used in this book as it was before the change.

3.3 Village Social Economy from the Viewpoint of Employment and Consumption

3.3.1 First Population and Housing Census in 31 Years

At the end of March 2014, Myanmar conducted a national population and housing census, the first such census since 1983. Before discussing the social economy of rural villages using this census, let us first compare the two census results of 1983 and 2014 to give an overview of the changes over the three decades in between.

As shown in Table 3.7, Myanmar's population increased from about 34.12 million to about 50.28 million. The average annual population growth rate was 1.26%. This is far below the 1.8 to 2% growth rate that the authorities had expected when preparing their annual statistics. The population is much smaller than the 60 million population estimate used by the government and UN agencies prior to the 2014 census. The total fertility rate fell from 4.73 in 1983 to 2.26 in 2014, and the earlier estimates seem to have failed to anticipate this sharp decline. The two population censuses include about 1.2 million people residing in conflict and contested parts of minority states such as Kachin and Karen, which could not be fully surveyed because of what officials called "security reasons".

The 2014 sex ratio, that is, males per 100 females, is 93.0, which is much lower than the 98.6 in the previous population census in 1983 and the lowest among ASEAN countries. The ratio of males at birth is 102–105, but 90 for people in their 40s and a mere 80 for people in their 60s. Because men have a higher mortality rate than women, the ratio of female heads of households has increased.

Calculations from Table 3.8 show that the average annual population growth rate in urban areas was 1.84%, higher than the 1.04% in rural areas, resulting in an increase in the urbanisation rate: from 24.8% to 29.6%. Nevertheless, Myanmar's urbanisation rate is still the second lowest among Southeast Asian countries, after Cambodia. As a result of this urbanisation, the agricultural population has also changed: in 1983, agriculture, forestry and fisheries workers accounted for 64.6% of all workers, but by 2014, they had declined to 52.4%. The ratio of the agricultural population has declined faster than the urbanisation rate has grown because, in rural areas, de-agrarianisation is also progressing.

The size of the household, that is, the average number of members in a household, decreased from 5.19 to 4.41. In urban areas, the decline is from 5.17 to 4.54, while in rural areas the decline is greater, from 5.20 to 4.35 (Table 3.8). As a result, rural households became on average smaller than urban households. The number of households has increased mainly due to the custom of *oekhwe (ôkhwêi),* whereby children build a separate house to form a new household after marriage. If the number of children is large and the parents tend to live long, the number of households increases exponentially. However, when the birth rates of the separately living children fall, the population does not increase as fast as the number of households. In other words, the household size becomes ever smaller. Both censuses include information on the households' kinship relations, estimating that about 80% of households are nuclear

Table 3.7 Summary of population censuses (comparison of 1983 and 2014)

Item	1983	2014
Total population	34,120,000	50,280,000
Total fertility rate (persons)	4.73	2.26
Ratio of men to women (%)	98.6	93.0
Urban population ratio (%)	24.8	29.6
Average size of household (persons)	5.2	4.4
Juvenile population: 0–14 years old (%)	38.6	28.6
Working-age population: 15–64 years old (%)	57.5	65.6
Elderly population: 65+ years old (%)	3.9	5.8
Ageing index	10.2	20.1
Labour force participation rate of 15–64 year olds (%)	57.2	67.0
Labour force participation rate of 10–14 year olds (%)	10.8	12.1
Population employed in agriculture, forestry, fisheries (%)	64.6	52.4
Literacy rate (age 5+) (%)	76.6	88.8
Population with a high school education or more (%)	5.1	10.2
No education (age 5+) (%)	48.4	20.2
Ratio of single-family households (%)	0.8	4.6
Ratio of female heads of household (%)	16.0	23.7
Percentage of Buddhist population (%)	89.4	89.8
Percentage of ethnic Bamar (%)	68.9	(Unpublished)

Source 1983 Burma Population Census. The 2014 Myanmar Population and Housing Census

families. Therefore, stereotypes about rural areas having larger families do not apply to Myanmar.

The ratio of the working-age population increased from 57.5% to 65.6%. The age dependency ratio—which indicates the number of young people (under 15 years of age) and elderly (65 years of age or older) who are supported by 100 working-age people—decreased from 73.9% to 52.5%, indicating that Myanmar is in a full-fledged "demographic bonus" period. However, it should not be overlooked that the ageing index has doubled from 10.2% to 20.1%.

The labour force participation rate—the labour force as a percentage of the working-age population (15–64 years)—also increased: from 57.2% in 1983 to 67.0% in 2014. Evidently, the rate of participation in the labour market increased as the economy shifted from socialism to a market economy. However, very concerning is the labour force participation rate of the younger population aged 10–14. It increased slightly from 10.8% in 1983 to 12.1% in 2014. These child labour problems, which were somewhat less apparent during the Burmese socialist period, were often identified by the UN and NGOs as areas for improvement in democratising Myanmar.

Table 3.8 Comparison of urban and rural populations

	1983	2014
Population (total)	34,124,908	50,279,900
Male	16,939,593	24,228,714
Female	17,185,315	26,051,186
Sex ratio (%)	98.6	93.0
Urban	8,466,292	14,877,943
Male	4,214,463	7,114,224
Female	4,251,829	7,763,719
Sex ratio (%)	99.1	91.6
Rural	25,658,616	35,401,957
Male	12,725,130	17,114,490
Female	12,933,486	18,287,467
Sex ratio (%)	98.4	93.6
Number of conventional households	6,497,632	10,877,832
Urban	1,601,354	3,049,433
Rural	4,896,278	7,828,399
Population within conventional households	33,714,816	47,929,999
Urban	8,274,965	13,839,853
Rural	25,439,851	34,090,146
Mean household size	5.19	4.41
Urban	5.17	4.54
Rural	5.20	4.35

Source Same as Table 3.7

Early employment is also associated with educational background: the number of those aged 5 years and above with no schooling decreased from 48.4% to 20.2%. However, as of 2014, the proportion of the total population aged 25 years and above with no education was 7% in urban areas compared to 20% in rural areas. In addition, 30% of the population in urban areas and 52% in rural areas had only primary school (five-year) or lower education. The proportion of the population with a high school education doubled in those three decades, but was still only about an eigth.

In contrast to this low level of education, Myanmar's literacy rate has remained high, partly due to the spread of monastic education. However, in order to catch up with the economic development of other ASEAN countries, a high literacy rate is insufficient. There is an urgent need, firstly, to make basic education more accessible, and then, to enhance middle and high school education.

The results of the survey on the population by religion were not released until more than a year later than the rest of the data, on 21 July 2016. The census was overshadowed by a serious religious conflict. The more than one million Rohingya Muslims living in the border areas with Bangladesh were not included in the 2014 Population and Housing Census, while Buddhist nationalist groups have been leading radical anti-Muslim movements and calling the "growing" Muslim population a "major problem" for the state. For the sake of social "stability," publication of the religious population data was delayed, and the Muslim population was likely underestimated.

The data on ethnicity, which was supposed to be released at the same time as the data on religion has not been released yet. It is said that the reason for this is that the future of the peace talks and the fighting between the Myanmar national army and ethnic minority armies was unclear. A population census is an act by which the state arbitrarily classifies, simplifies, and makes visible its citizens, or creates them (Scott 1998: 32). It is natural for people who do not agree with the state to resist a population census in various ways.

3.3.2 Employment and Unemployment Rates in Urban and Rural Areas

As noted earlier, the labour force as a percentage of the working-age population (ages 15–64) increased from 57.2% in 1983 to 67.0% in 2014 (Tables 3.9 and 3.10). In urban areas, the increase was from 54.5% to 62.6%, and in rural areas, from 58.1% to 69.1%. The employment rate of the working-age population increased from 56.3% in 1983 to 64.4% in 2014. It increased from 52.5% to 59.6% in urban areas and from 57.6% to 66.6% in rural areas. The rise in the employment rate in urban areas may be due to the increase in the number of private firms in the market economy and the increase in the labour force employed there. It is not clear whether the increase in rural areas was from agricultural employment incentivised by the liberalised price of agricultural products or from non-agricultural employment in and outside rural areas that has accompanied the market economy. I consider the latter hypothesis more plausible (Takahashi, 2016: 138–142).

Changes in the employment rate also vary across age groups. The employment rate for people aged 65 and over fell substantially: from 38.4% in 1983 to 21.9% in 2014. It fell from 27.7% to 14.5% in urban areas and from 41.8% to 25.2% in rural areas. Thus, the withdrawal of older workers from the labour market became more pronounced over these three decades in both urban and rural areas. In contrast to the sharp decline in the employment rate of older people, the employment rate of young people, or children, between the ages of 10 and 14 has increased. In 1983, 3.4% of the population in this age group in urban areas was employed, while in rural areas 12.8% was. By 2014, this figure had increased substantially to 6.5% in urban areas and remained virtually unchanged at 12.1% in rural areas. This reflects the fact that child labour such as harvesting, caring for livestock and domestic help in other

Table 3.9 Labour force statistics (1983)

Nationwide								
Age range	Population	Labour force	Employed	Unemployed	Not in labour force	Unemployment rate (%)	Labour force participation rate (%)	Employment rate (%)
10–14 years old	4,268,670	462,911	446,248	16,663	3,805,759	3.6	10.8	10.5
15–64 years old	19,625,065	11,222,470	11,040,187	182,283	8,402,595	1.6	57.2	56.3
Over 65 years old	1,340,198	514,598	514,136	462	825,600	0.1	38.4	38.4
Total over 10 years old	25,233,933	12,199,979	12,000,571	199,408	13,033,954	1.6	48.3	47.6
Total population	34,124,908	Male	16,939,593	Female	17,185,315			
Urban								
Age range	Population	Labour force	Employed	Unemployed	Not in labour force	Unemployment rate (%)	Labour force participation rate (%)	Employment rate (%)
10–14 years old	1,065,952	41,315	35,873	5,442	1,024,637	13.2	3.9	3.4
15–64 years old	5,121,646	2,792,645	2,689,350	103,295	2,329,001	3.7	54.5	52.5
Over 65 years old	325,057	90,281	90,147	134	234,776	0.1	27.8	27.7
Total over 10 years old	6,512,655	2,924,241	2,815,370	108,871	3,588,414	3.7	44.9	43.2
Total population	8,466,292	Male	4,214,463	Female	4,251,829			
Rural								
Age range	Population	Labour force	Employed	Unemployed	Not in labour force	Unemployment rate (%)	Labour force participation rate (%)	Employment rate (%)
10–14 years old	3,202,718	421,596	410,375	11,221	2,781,122	2.7	13.2	12.8
15–64 years old	14,503,419	8,429,825	8,350,837	78,988	6,073,594	0.9	58.1	57.6
Over 65 years old	1,015,141	424,317	423,989	328	590,824	0.1	41.8	41.8
Total over 10 years old	18,721,278	9,275,738	9,185,201	90,537	9,445,540	1.0	49.5	49.1
Total population	25,658,616	Male	12,725,130	Female	12,933,486			

Source 1983 Burma Population Census

Table 3.10 Labour force statistics (2014)

Nationwide								
Age range	Population	Labour force	Employed	Unemployed	Not in labour force	Unemployment rate (%)	Labour force participation rate (%)	Employment rate (%)
10–14 years old	5,108,362	620,322	543,040	77,282	4,488,040	12.5	12.1	10.6
15–64 years old	32,982,768	22,110,882	21,237,454	873,428	10,871,886	4.0	67.0	64.4
Over 65 years old	2,897,563	638,881	635,085	3,796	2,258,682	0.6	22.0	21.9
Total over 10 years old	40,988,693	23,370,085	22,415,579	954,506	17,618,608	4.1	57.0	54.7
Total population	50,279,900	Male	24,228,714	Female	26,051,186			
Urban								
Age range	Population	Labour force	Employed	Unemployed	Not in labour force	Unemployment rate (%)	Labour force participation rate (%)	Employment rate (%)
10–14 years old	1,355,792	102,365	87,768	14,597	1,253,427	14.3	7.6	6.5
15–64 years old	10,406,599	6,517,588	6,203,728	313,860	3,889,011	4.8	62.6	59.6
Over 65 years old	887,548	129,376	128,461	915	758,172	0.7	14.6	14.5
Total over 10 years old	12,649,939	6,749,329	6,419,957	329,372	5,900,610	4.9	53.4	50.8
Total population	14,877,943	Male	7,114,224	Female	7,763,719			
Rural								
Age range	Population	Labour force	Employed	Unemployed	Not in labour force	Unemployment rate (%)	Labour force participation rate (%)	Employment rate (%)
10–14 years old	3,752,570	517,957	455,272	62,685	3,234,613	12.1	13.8	12.1
15–64 years old	22,576,169	15,593,294	15,033,726	559,568	6,982,875	3.6	69.1	66.6
Over 65 years old	2,010,015	509,505	506,624	2881	1,500,510	0.6	25.3	25.2
Total over 10 years old	28,338,754	16,620,756	15,995,622	625,134	11,717,998	3.8	58.7	56.4
Total population	35,401,957	Male	17,114,490	Female	18,287,467			

Source The 2014 Myanmar Population and Housing Census

households is still common in rural areas, while child labour in small-scale domestic factories and restaurants is increasing in urban areas.

The *unemployment* rate for people aged 10 and over supposedly increased from 1.6% in 1983 to 4.1% in 2014. However, the 1983 population census is not very reliable because it assumes that there is no unemployment under socialism. Looking at the 2014 census, urban areas had a higher rate of 4.9% and rural areas had 3.8%. Rural areas have a large number of "disguised unemployment", such as daily agricultural labourers, so it is not possible to make a general statement. However, going to the city, too, does not necessarily mean that one will be blessed with employment opportunities.

3.3.3 Rural Economy Viewed by Employment Structure

Tables 3.11 and 3.12 show the number (upper panel) and composition (lower panel) of workers by industry for people who live in conventional households (other than "institutional households"). In 1983, agriculture, forestry, and fisheries workers accounted for 64.6% of all workers, but in 2014, they decreased to 52.4%. Assuming that 96% of the "agriculture, forestry, and fisheries" workers are employed in agriculture,[9] we can divide the annual GDP ratio of the agricultural sector by the ratio of agricultural workers,[10] getting a value of 63.5% in 1983 and 39.2% in 2014. These values are equal to the ratio of the GDP per capita among agricultural sector workers to the GDP per capita among all sector workers, or to a close approximation, the ratio of the income per capita in the agricultural sector to the income per capita in the overall national economy. In other words, already in 1983, the average income of agricultural sector workers was only about two-thirds of the average income of all workers, and by 2014 it had fallen to about two-fifths. In the transition away from socialism, the terms of trade for agriculture temporarily improved, but with the development of the market economy, agriculture is no longer a lucrative job. Thus, from such GDP statistics and population censuses, we can infer *the macroeconomic incentives* for *de-agrarianisation*.

Let us examine the number of people working in agriculture, forestry, and fisheries in rural areas. In 1983, the number of people employed in agriculture, forestry and fisheries in rural areas was about 7.38 million, accounting for 80.4% of the total working population in rural areas. Of these, about 4 million were farmers who held cultivation rights, 3.09 million were agricultural labourers who did not hold the right and were employed by farmers, and the remaining 0.29 million were forestry or

---

[9] In the 1983 census, 96.1% of the workers in agriculture, and fisheries were employed in the agricultural sector, and only a small number in forestry and fisheries. 2014 census does not disclose such detail, but we assume that it is almost the same.

[10] The 1983 and 2014 Population Census reflect the population and households at midnight on March 31 and March 30, respectively. Therefore, the values for 1982/83 and 2013/14 were used for GDP; the agricultural sector accounted for 39.4% of GDP in 1982/83 and 19.7 % in 2013/14 (Takahashi 2016: 120).

Table 3.11 Employment by industry, 1983 (based on 20% sample survey) (10 years and over)

(Unit: Person)

Industries	National	Urban	Rural
Agriculture, forestry and fisheries	7,756,106	372,716	7,383,390
Mining	69,994	16,486	53,508
Manufacturing	1,105,340	509,612	595,728
Construction	156,802	92,406	64,396
Electricity, gas, water, etc.	20,917	15,613	5,304
Commerce, tourism	1,362,253	908,432	453,821
Transportation, warehouse	345,130	260,179	84,951
Public and private service	806,383	548,995	257,388
Others	377,646	90,931	286,715
Total	12,000,571	2,815,370	9,185,201

(Unit: %)

Industries	National	Urban	Rural
Agriculture, forestry and fisheries	64.6	13.2	80.4
Mining	0.6	0.6	0.6
Manufacturing	9.2	18.1	6.5
Construction	1.3	3.3	0.7
Electricity, gas, water, etc.	0.2	0.6	0.1
Commerce, tourism	11.4	32.3	4.9
Transportation, warehouse	2.9	9.2	0.9
Public and private service	6.7	19.5	2.8
Others	3.1	3.2	3.1
Total	100.0	100.0	100.0

Source 1983 Burma Population Census

fisheries workers. In 2014, the number of people working in agriculture, forestry and fisheries in rural areas was about 10.48 million, and the ratio to the total rural working population had decreased to 68.7%. The report of the 2014 census does not include the breakdown of agriculture, forestry, and fisheries workers, unlike that of 1983. My surveys in various villages and the analysis in Table 3.6 show that the ratio of agricultural labourers to farmers has likely increased.

From the above, we can conclude that, in 1983, 75.2% of Myanmar's total population lived in rural areas, and 80.4% of their labour force was engaged in agriculture, forestry, and fisheries, but by 2014, the rural population had decreased to 70.4% of the total population, and the proportion of the rural population employed in agriculture, forestry, and fisheries had decreased to 68.7%. Although there is no significant margin of error if we consider the population employed in agriculture, forestry, and fisheries as the population employed in agriculture, we should not forget that the

Table 3.12 Employment by industry, 2014 (based on 20% sample survey) (10 years and over)

(Unit: Person)

Industries	National	Urban	Rural
Agriculture, forestry and fisheries	11,026,852	548,724	10,478,128
Mining	168,103	30,203	137,900
Manufacturing	1,431,134	686,436	744,698
Construction	956,613	496,359	460,254
Electricity, gas, water, etc.	71,116	52,401	18,715
Commerce, tourism	2,930,062	1,803,426	1,126,636
Transportation, warehouse	813,048	539,865	273,183
Public and private service	2,035,948	1,158,298	877,650
Others	1,627,655	503,665	1,123,990
Total	21,060,531	5,819,377	15,241,154

(Unit: %)

Industries	National	Urban	Rural
Agriculture, forestry and fisheries	52.4	9.4	68.7
Mining	0.8	0.5	0.9
Manufacturing	6.8	11.8	4.9
Construction	4.5	8.5	3.0
Electricity, gas, water, etc.	0.3	0.9	0.1
Commerce, tourism	13.9	31.0	7.4
Transportation, warehouse	3.9	9.3	1.8
Public and private service	9.7	19.9	5.8
Others	7.7	8.7	7.4
Total	100.0	100.0	100.0

Source The 2014 Myanmar Population and Housing Census

agricultural working population includes not only farmers but also many landless agricultural labourers.

3.3.4 Consumption Structure of Rural Households

Table 3.13 compares the breakdown of the average monthly household consumption expenditure in urban and in rural areas. The first similarity between urban and rural areas is the very high Engel's coefficient, that is, the share of food costs in household expenditure, exceeding 60%, which is the highest among Southeast Asian countries, as well as much higher than Japan's 25%. Second, food expenditure on rice is the highest. Rice is the dominant staple food almost everywhere in Myanmar. Third, the report lists the expenditure on donations and ceremonies as a special item. This

Table 3.13 Household Consumption Expenditure (2012) (monthly average)

Items	Urban		Rural		Rural–Urban ratio
	kyat	%	kyat	%	
Rice	23,811	11.8	26,073	17.2	1.10
Other cereals	6,159	3.1	3874	2.6	0.63
Meat	16,594	8.2	12,484	8.2	0.75
Fish and shellfish (fresh and dried)	18,449	9.1	12,343	8.1	0.67
Fresh vegetables and legumes	13,886	6.9	13,542	8.9	0.98
Fruit	6,139	3.0	4,370	2.9	0.71
Beverages	5,189	2.6	3,475	2.3	0.67
Eggs and dairy products	5,145	2.6	3,515	2.3	0.68
Fats, oils and seasonings	12,867	6.4	12,765	8.4	0.99
Eating out	13,604	6.7	7,013	4.6	0.52
Food total	121,843	60.3	99,456	65.4	0.82
House rent and repairs	5,921	2.9	2,938	1.9	0.50
Fuel and light	14,552	7.2	11,807	7.8	0.81
Furniture and housewares	13,659	6.8	5,497	3.6	0.40
Clothing and personal use goods	9,022	4.5	7,228	4.8	0.80
Medical care	4,247	2.1	2,818	1.9	0.66
Transportation and communication	12,616	6.2	8,143	5.4	0.65
Education	6,475	3.2	3,510	2.3	0.54
Donations and ceremonies	7128	3.5	6,496	4.3	0.91
Culture and entertainment	334	0.2	258	0.2	0.77
Other consumption expenditure	6,358	3.2	3,859	2.5	0.61
Non-food total	80,312	39.7	52,555	34.6	0.65
Total expenditure	202,155	100	152,011	100	0.75

Source Statistical Yearbook 2015

is probably because daily rituals, such as offering morning meals for monks, and donating for ceremonial rituals for various occasions are commonplace.

Let us compare urban and rural areas in more detail. The bottom line of the table shows that the total consumption expenditure of rural households is only two-thirds of that of urban households. Even if rural households have a self-sufficiency that is not calculated here, this disparity reflects the lower income in rural areas. As a result, rice is the only food on which rural areas spend more than urban areas do. We can infer the importance of rice as a source of nutrition in rural areas with low incomes. The only other consumption items for which there is little difference between rural and urban areas are fresh vegetables and beans, and fats, oils, and seasonings. This reflects Myanmar's three major nutrient supply patterns: rice for carbohydrates, beans and *ngapi* for protein, and cooking oil for fat. Expenditures on other items such as meat, fish and fruits are much lower in rural areas than in urban areas. Other than food expenditure, the gap between rural and urban areas is large in terms of expenditure on housing, furniture and household goods, and education. In the case of housing, it is natural that land prices are higher in urban areas. Moreover, one can imagine the interior of a rural house with less furniture and furnishings. Low spending on education is directly related to low school attendance and illiteracy. Indeed, according to the 2014 Census, the proportion of the total population aged 25 and above who have never received education is 7% in urban areas, while it is 20% in rural areas. The literacy rate of 15 years and over is also high at 95.2% in urban areas, but only 87.0% in rural areas. Rural women in particular are at a considerably lower rate, at 83.8% (Takahashi, 2018: 27). In addition to the child labour mentioned above, the issue of education in rural areas is an important issue for the future.

Chapter 4
A Socio-economic History of Two Villages

A. Takahashi, *Regime Changes and Socio-economic History of Rural Myanmar, 1986–2019*, Studies in Economic History,
https://doi.org/10.1007/978-981-99-3272-6_4

Rice harvesting in Zeepinwea Village (Photo taken in November 1987) and a combine harvester in front of the Village Tract office (Photo taken in January 2013). Rice had long been harvested by hand with a crescent-shaped sickle, but in the 2010s, combine harvesters were suddenly introduced, after leapfrogging the stage of reapers or binders.

Introduction

In July 1986, I visited Zeepinwea (*Zîpinwê*) Village through the muddy paths of the rainy season. This village became the starting point for my subsequent visits to more than 200 villages. In those days, permission from the authorities was required to go more than 50 miles (about 80 km) from Yangon, and another permission was required to stay overnight. So, I chose a village in Yangon Region's Hlegu (*Hlêgû)* Township, about 50 km northeast of Yangon city. I took the bus to the village twice a month, and from February to April of the following year, 1987, I went there almost every day to conduct a survey on the economic activities of all households in the village.[1] The village was accessible only on foot from the Hlegu Town where the township government of Hlegu is located. None of the households in the village had electricity.

I did a second survey in 1994. At that time, there was an unpaved road to the village that was passable by cars. I loaded my car with luggage and entered the

[1] At that time, the total number of households in the village was 138, and I visited all of them, but I could not survey two households. However, I knew that their occupations were daily labourers in agriculture, so these two households are included in the tables and texts dealing with their occupations.

village, stayed at the house of the chairman of the Village Tract Law and Order Restoration Council and conducted a complete survey of all 170 households in the village. In those days, only eight households had electricity, but not at the chairman's house. Only for those times when I was staying in the house was an electricity line connected directly from a nearby electricity pole.

In January 2014, when I did a third survey, the total number of households in the village had increased to 316.[2] I decided that a comprehensive survey was not feasible due to time constraints, so I randomly selected a total of 56 households from the households that I had surveyed in 1987 and 1994, selecting them by residential area and the holding acreage of cultivation right. In addition, I selected and interviewed 15 households that had started living in the village after 1994. As I was not allowed to live in the village at that time, I commuted to the village by motorcycle from a hotel in Hlegu Town, located about 1.5 km away. A concrete paved road had been built from the town to the middle of the village. Electrification had also progressed considerably.

The second village that I have long been visiting is Thindaunggyi (*Thindaunjî*), about 4 km northwards from Kyaukse (*Cau'hse*) Town and about 50 km south of the ancient capital Mandalay. I arrived at this village in July 1987 by horse cart. The village was about 500 m east in a straight line from the then National Highway No. 1 connecting Yangon and Mandalay, but at that time, the only way to enter the village was to detour about one kilometre along a sandy dirt road. Electricity was available to only four households. I was invited to stay in a corner of a barn belonging to an influential man in the village named U Chit Myaing,[3] and began my economic survey of all 126 households in the village. After interviewing 50 households, I had to return to Yangon. A villager who served as my assistant surveyed a further 52 households, but 24 households could not be surveyed.[4]

In 1994, I was driven to this village by a four-wheel drive vehicle along the same dirt road to conduct a second survey. Around that time, U Chit Myaing was the village tract mayor and I was accommodated in a converted onion-storage room, in a corner of his large brick house, known in Burmese as a *taik* or *tai'*.[5] 27 households, including his house, had electricity. At that point, the total number of households in the village was 156, and I was able to survey all households. Just as I was conducting this research, an almost straight paved road from the main road into the village was completed, thanks to the work of many villagers and people from neighbouring towns and villages.

---

[2] The third village survey was conducted in January 2014, but all data such as population, number of households, occupation, and farmland area are those of 2013.

[3] For more on who U Chit Myaing was and what his life was like, see Takahashi (2018: 97–100).

[4] Since the occupations and farmland holdings of these missing 24 households were known, their occupations were added to the tables and texts dealing with the occupations of households in Thindaunggyi village in 1987.

[5] The term "*taik*" refers to houses made mainly of bricks, plaster, stone or concrete. It is distinguished from houses made of wood or bamboo. Even if only the roof is made of tin, it is called "*taik*". Since its cost of construction was much higher than that of wood or bamboo houses, it has been regarded as a symbol of wealth in Myanmar villages.

During a third survey in August 2013,[6] I was not allowed to stay in the village, but stayed in a hotel in Kyaukse Town and commuted to the village by motorcycle. I selected a total of 54 households randomly from among the households that I had surveyed in 1987 and 1994, as in Zeepinwea Village, according to the area of cultivation right. I visited each individually.

All of the above surveys were conducted by using questionnaires that I prepared in Burmese language. Each household survey was conducted with no assistant other than a villager, and interviews were conducted one-on-one between myself and the respondent. I interviewed the villagers in Burmese, including any *ad hoc* questions that came up on the spot. I wrote their answers in Burmese on the questionnaires.

4.1 The Origins of the Villages

4.1.1 Zeepinwea (Zîpinwê) Village

According to the villagers, ethnic Bamar (Burmese) people began to live in the present Zeepinwea Village in the late eighteenth century. This was when King Alaungpaya, who established the Konbaung Dynasty, conquered Lower Myanmar. Before that, Zeepinwea was a village of the Mon people. It is said that the Mon people established a village here around the 13th or 14th century, but the exact date and the name of the village at that time are not clear. The origin of the village's present name is also not clear, but it is certain that the name was derived from the Myanmar word for the *zîdhî pin* trees (*Ziziphus mauritiana*) found here and there in the village and from the "*wea (wê)*"—swirl, whirlpool—of the Ngamoeyeik (*Ngàmôyei'*) River. Just as the Bamar people who migrated to Lower Myanmar during the Konbaung era changed the name of Dagon to Yangon while expelling or assimilating the indigenous Mon people, the names of these small villages must have been changed to Burmese.

There is another story about the origin of the village. It is said that during the British colonial period, there was a small river port called *Zîpin zei'* near the bridge where the Yangon–Mandalay Road crossed the Ngamoeyeik River. The town of Hlegu developed around this port. Based on this story, some elders (*lugyi* or *lujî*)[7] say that Zeepinwea village was named after this landing port. If so, the name of Zeepinwea did not appear until 1852, when Lower Myanmar was colonised (Takahashi, 1992: 45–46).

---

[6] The third survey was conducted from late July to late August 2013 in Thindaunggyi Village and from early January to late January 2014 in Zeepinwea Village. Since all the data for both villages are from 2013, I will refer to the survey records for both villages as "as of 2013". The surveys were only five months apart, and there were no major political or economic changes during this period. They are also in the same financial year in Myanmar.

[7] If you look up *lujî* (elder or doyen) in a Burmese dictionary, you will find that it means not only "elder" but also "community leader", "important person", and "respected person".

4.1.2 *Thindaunggyi (*Thindaunjî*) Village*

It is said that Kyaukse, now a district in central Myanmar's Mandalay Region, was the first place where the Bamar people, driven by the Nanzhao dynasty, descended from the Shan mountains to the plains (Luce, 1959b: 78–80). Legend has it that King Anawrahta (reigned 1044–1077), the founder of the Pagan dynasty—the first unified dynasty of the Bamar people, established in the mid-eleventh century—built weirs and irrigation canals in Kyaukse and settled farmers to establish "eleven villages (*ledwìn hsèti'ywa*)". The irrigated rice agriculture that began here spread across the central plains and supported the economies of successive dynasties. In this sense, Kyaukse can be said to be the original place of Myanmar's paddy agriculture.[8]

Thindaunggyi Village, which I have been studying since 1987, is reported to be one of King Anawratha's "eleven villages". According to the epigrapher Gordon Luce, an inscription dated 1198 found at the Danmayazika (*Danmà Yazìkà*) Paya (*phayâ*)[9] in northern Bagan, includes the name of Thindaung (without "*gyi*") (Fig. 4.1) as one of the "eleven villages" named *Sañtoń* in the Old Burmese (Luce, 1969: 30). According to the Burma Gazetteer (Kyaukse District), which was written in the colonial period based on historical books, this Thindaung was located 3 miles north of the town of Kyaukse (Stewart, 1925: 14). Luce agreed with this statement (Luce, 1959a: 42). The distance from Kyaukse to Thindaung Village is about 2.5 miles, so the error is small. In another paper, however, Luce stated that Thindaung was located north of Kyaukse Town, west of the Zawgyi River and very close to the Myitnge River (Luce, 1959b: 83), which is more than 15 miles away from Kyaukse Town.

At the entrance to the village of Thindaunggyi, there is the Shwetheindaw Paya. It is said to have been built by King Anawrahta. It is not only an object of worship for the local people, but also attracts visitors from all over Myanmar, as will be described below. According to a book describing the history of this paya, Thindaung, one of the "Eleven villages", was located about 0.5 miles east of the present Thindaunggyi, in a natural fortress surrounded by a swampy area called "*in*". Thus, the only way for the Thindaung villagers to visit the paya was to take a small boat or walk through the water (Nyunt, 2002: 2–3). According to Luce, the word "*rwā* (village)" in the

---

[8] However, it seems that the Mon people had been engaged in irrigated agriculture here before the Burmese (Bamars) descended to Kyaukse (Luce, 1959b: 81).

[9] The Myanmar word "*phayâ*" is often translated as "pagoda," but the two are not synonymous. Pagoda, in a narrow sense, refers to a stupa, and in a broader sense, to a Buddhist temple complex in East and Southeast Asia (Encyclopaedia Britannica online). In the case of the famous Shwedagon Paya in Yangon, the object of worship is the pagoda (or, more precisely, the *zedi*), so it is acceptable to say Shwedagon Pagoda. However, since the object of worship at the Mahamuni Paya in Mandalay and the Shwetheindaw Paya in Thindaunggyi village is a Buddha image, we must hesitate to translate them as pagodas.

Usually, a collection of religious buildings centring on a pagoda or a Buddha image is called a *paya*. If such a commentary is added, it may be translated as a pagoda. However, a paya is not a temple or monastery in any sense of the word. This is because there are no monks living in a paya, and the management and administration of the paya is done entirely by lay believers, without the involvement of monks. Monks often act as advisors in paya management. Sometimes, a paya is built within a monastery.

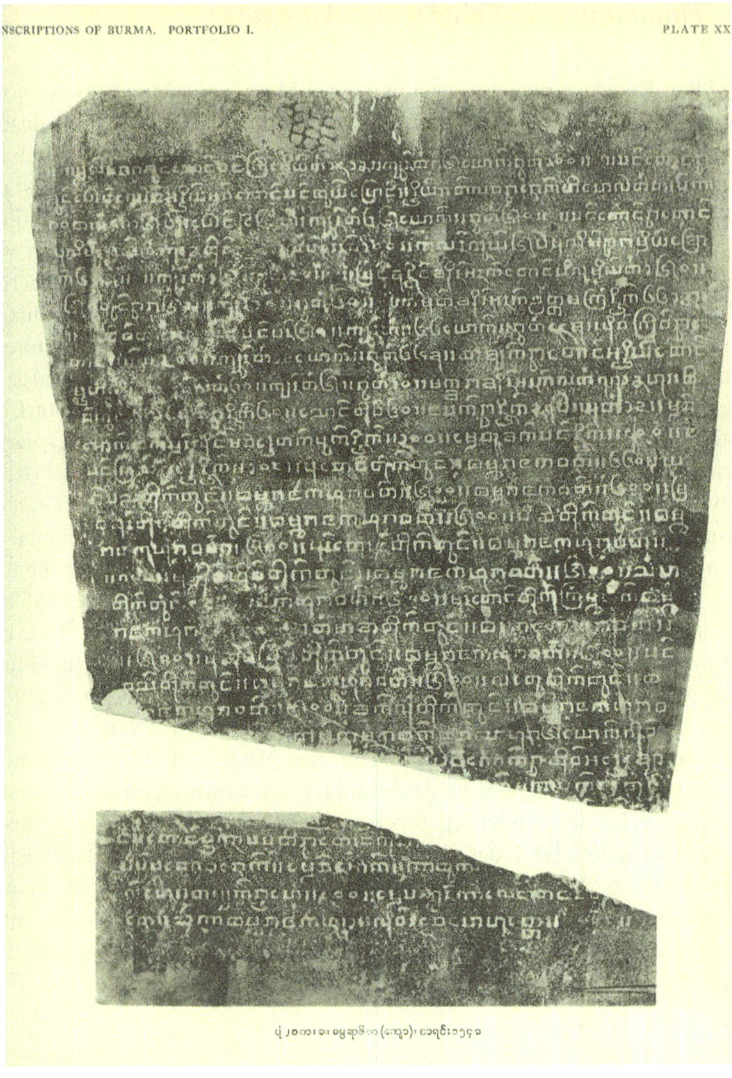

Fig. 4.1 Dammayazika inscription. *Note* The word "Thindaung" can be seen on the first and third lines of the inscription. *Source* Inscriptions of Burma, Portfolio I, Plate XX a and b

"eleven villages" means "world" and is synonymous with *kharuin* or "political and economic centre" (Luce, 1959a: 40–41). A *kharuin* was usually surrounded by walls and moats, but in the case of Thindaung, the "*în* (lake or swamp)" was a natural fortress (Nyunt, 2002: 21). Later (period unknown), the village was moved across the swamp to the side of Shwetheindaw Paya. Finally, the "*in*" was drained and turned into paddy fields during the British colonial period (Nyunt, 2002: 3). This story implies that old Thindaung is just 3 miles from Kyaukse Town, and the present

Thindaunggyi Village is one of the "eleven villages" established by King Anawrahta in the eleventh century.

However, there is one more village that claims to be the Thindaung of Anawrahta. The name of that village is Thindaungnge. It is in Sintgaing Township, north of Kyaukse Township. This village is near the Thindaung of Luce's other paper, mentioned above. The above-mentioned history book of Shwetheindaw Paya argues that the village of Thindaungnge has no walls, no moat and no ancient paya, whereas Thindaunggyi needed no walls or moats thanks to the presence of the "*in*", a natural fortress. Moreover, Thindaunggyi has a traditional paya associated with *kharuin,* called Shwegugyi Paya, in addition to the venerable Shwetheindaw Paya. Finally, the ruins of an old town called Myo Hsoung Koung (*Myôzôungôun*) are located to the east of the village. Thus, the history book's author asserts that "the village of Thindaunggyi is the ancient Thindaung" (Nyunt, 2002: 9). Furthermore, she describes that '*gyi* (*jî*)' in the name of Thindaunggyi Village means "big", while '*nge*' in the name of Thindaungnge Village means "small". In Myanmar, it is common knowledge that '*gyi*' existed before '*nge*' (Nyunt, 2002: 19–20). However, there is no proof that the ancient town at Myo Hsoung Koung or the Shwegugyi Paya existed in the time of King Anawrahta. Nonetheless, the Minye (*Mînyê*) canal that runs between the village and the main road has been dated to the reign of King Narapatisithu (1174–1211), the seventh king of the Pagan dynasty (Stewart, 1925: 15). The history of the village, together with the history of Shwetheindaw Paya, seems to date back to *at least* the late twelfth century, if not the eleventh century of King Anawrahta.

4.2 Climate and Topography

4.2.1 Zeepinwea Village

Zeepinwea Village is located in Yangon Region, at 17°5′ N, 96°14′ E. The average monthly temperature and monthly precipitation in Yangon Region's Hlegu Township, where the village is located, are shown in Fig. 4.2. The average annual precipitation for the 10 years from 2004 to 2013 was 2724 mm, not significantly different from the 2639 mm from 1987 to 1996. The rainfall is concentrated in the rainy season (*môu yadhi*) from May to October, which is followed by the dry season from November to May. As can be seen from the line graph of the monthly mean temperature, the first half of the dry season, from November to mid-February, is relatively cool, while the second half, from mid-February to the beginning of the rainy season, is the hottest season of the year. The former is called the cool season (*hsâun yadhi*) and the latter is called the hot season (*nwei yadhi*). Thus, the dry season is divided into two phases and one year in Myanmar is sorted into three seasons. In the rainy season, the temperature drops to the extent that the sunlight decreases, but the hot and humid days continue.

Zeepinwea Village Tract is uncommonly composed of one village but is divided into three parts. The map in Fig. 4.3 shows these three settlements: Paukkoung (*Pau'*

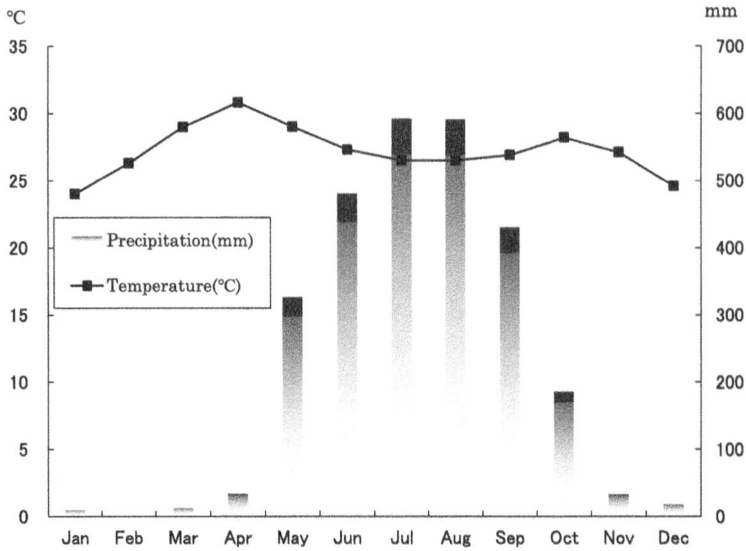

Fig. 4.2 Average monthly temperature and monthly precipitation in Hlegu township (2004–13). *Source* Hlegu Township Office, Ministry of National Planning and Economic Development

kôun) (I) is in the upper left corner, surrounded by a pentagon; Ywalay (*Ywalêi*) (III) is in the lower right corner; and Ywagyi (*Ywajî*) (II) is a large settlement between the two. The northern entrance of Ywagyi is located about one kilometre from Hlegu Town. Its houses are arranged in rows on the natural levee of the right bank of the Ngamoeyeik River, a tributary of the Yangon River. In Fig. 4.3, the Ngamoeyeik River seems to be far away from the houses, but it used to flow close to Ywagyi before its course was changed. It has now become the Ngamoeyeik Oxbow Lake.

At the southeastern edge of Ywagyi, the houses run out and Ywalay appears about 400 m ahead. The houses of this village still stand in rows on the natural bank of the Ngamoeyeik River. In other words, Ywagyi and Ywalay are linear villages on the riverbank, the kinds of which can be found all over the delta. Their elevation is only about 10 m. In contrast, Paukkoung hamlet is a compact village, located upstream of a brook that flows into Ngamoeyeik River. Its elevation is a few metres higher than Ywagyi. Paukkoung is a hamlet of the Sgaw Karen (Kayin) ethnic group. All the land in the hamlet used to be common land (Takahashi, 1992: 134–135), but was divided into individual residential areas by the government soon after the start of the post-socialist military regime.

In the south and west of Zeepinwea Village, there is a vast paddy field area which is part of the Bago Delta. From Fig. 4.3, it can be seen that the back swamp behind the natural levee has become paddy fields. During my 1987 and 1994 surveys, all of these paddy fields were full of paddy rice in the rainy season, but in the dry season, the paddy fields harden to a greyish-white colour, so groundnut was grown only in a small number of sandy loam fields where residual soil water was available. However,

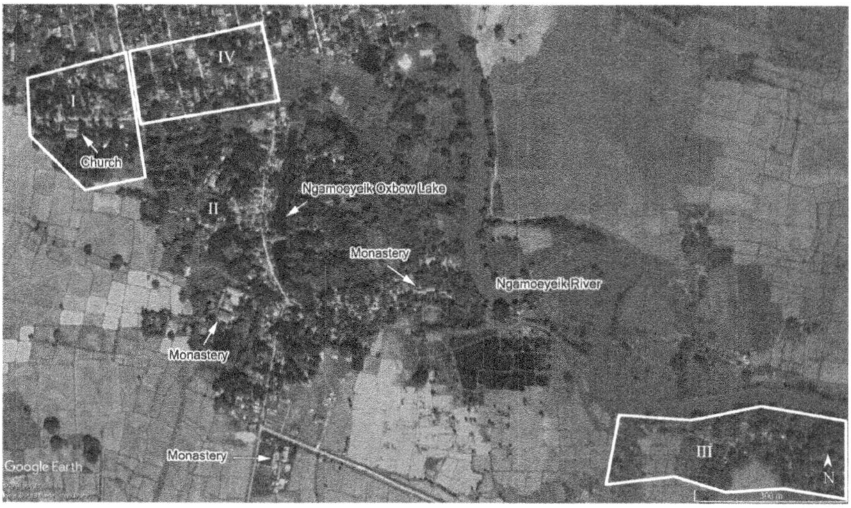

Fig. 4.3 Zeepinwea Village. *Note* The photo was modified by the author. *Source* 2018 Google Earth

in 1995, a dam was built upstream of the Ngamoeyeik River, and some of the paddy fields became irrigated, allowing rice cultivation even in the dry season.

The Ngamoeyeik River meanders through the delta, joining the Yangon River about 70 km downstream and flowing into the Andaman Sea about 40 km further down. This is a tidal river—which are found here and there in the delta. During the rainy season, the rainfall from the sky combines with a large amount of water from the Ngamoeyeik River and other small rivers meandering through the delta. As the sea water blocks the mouth of the Yangon River at high tide, large quantities of water lose their outlets and flood over river embankments, inundating residential areas. In contrast, during high tide in the dry season, the flow of the river is sometimes reversed. This phenomenon can be observed in Ngamoeyeik River near Zeepinwea village, 100 km from the mouth of the Yangon River. The area is dotted with villages named after the whirlpools (*wea*) created by the reverse flow of the river.

4.2.2 Thindaunggyi Village

Thindaunggyi Village is located in Mandalay Region, at 21°39′ N, 96°8′ E. It is about 507 km due north of Zeepinwea Village in a straight line. The average monthly temperature and monthly precipitation in Kyaukse Township, to which the village belongs, are shown in Fig. 4.4. The average annual precipitation for the 10 years from 2003 to 2012 was 807 mm, which was less than one third of that in Hlegu Township. The average annual precipitation from 1969 to 1981 was 786 mm. From

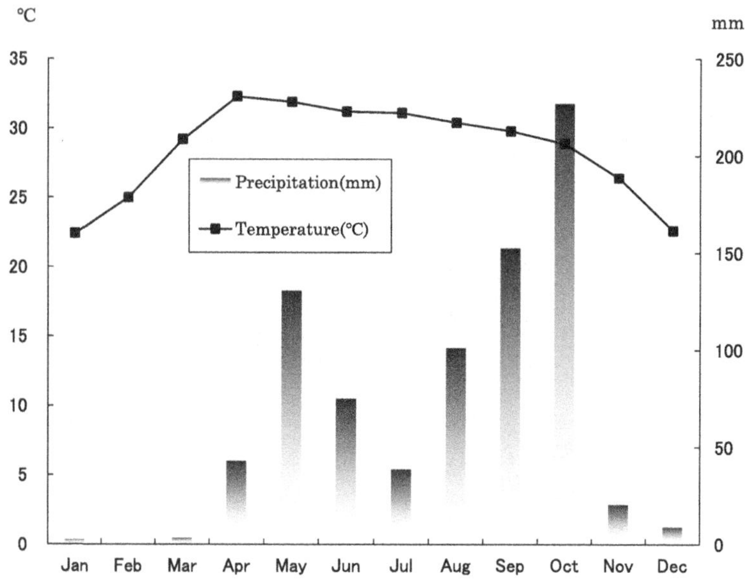

Fig. 4.4 Average monthly temperature and monthly precipitation in Kyaukse township, 2003–12. *Source* Kyaukse District Office, Ministry of National Planning and Economic Development

1981 to 1992, it was 693 mm (Takahashi, 1993: 35–36). Thus, there seems to be a little more rainfall since the beginning of the twenty-first century.

The three seasons are the same as in Hlegu Township, but the patterns of precipitation and temperature are different. In Kyaukse Township, the rainy season is from May to October, but it also rains in April. Rainfall is low in June, July and August, when the peak of the rainy season is observed in Hlegu Township, but high in September and October. The rainy season is hotter with less rainfall and with days above 30 °C. After the end of the rainy season, the temperature starts to decrease, especially from the end of November. In early February, there are many cool days when the temperature drops to 25 °C or below. However, this season is characterised by the large daily variations that exemplify inland areas. The temperature drops below 20 °C in the morning and evening, but exceeds 30 °C in the daytime. The heat is unbearable until the rainy season arrives. Even during the rainy season, the temperature does not drop as much as in Zeepinwea Village .

The topography of Kyaukse Township can be divided into two parts: plains in the central and western parts and mountains in the east. In the township's eastern part, bordering on Shan State, there is a steep mountain range, which is the western edge of the Shan Plateau. It occupies half of the township. The western part of the township is an alluvial plain created by the Panlaung and Zawgyi Rivers, which flow northwards into the Ayeyarwady (Irrawaddy) River. A number of canals derived from these rivers stretch across this plain. Isolated rocky hills protrude from the plain. Near the hilltops are scattered payas (pagodas), decorated with white lime from the eastern mountains. Thindaunggyi village is located at the southern foot of Mount Shweitaunhtî, one of

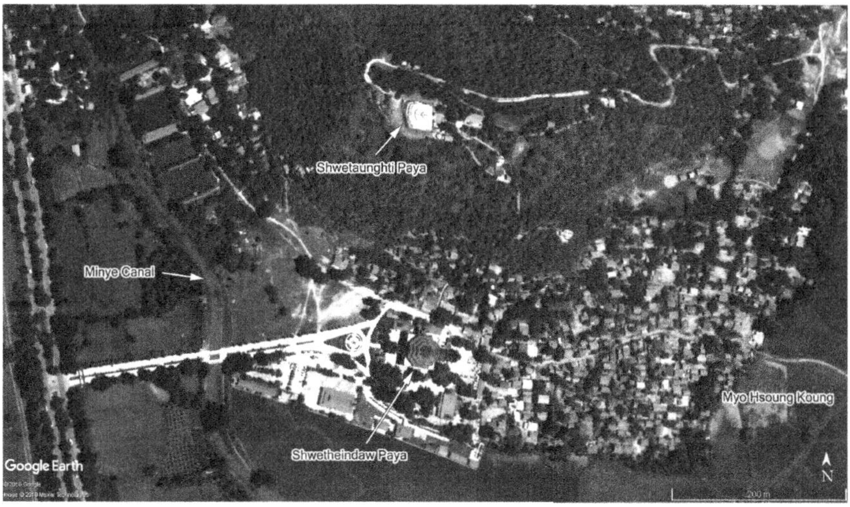

Fig. 4.5 Thindaunggyi Village. *Note* The photo was modified by the author. *Source* 2018 Google Earth

those isolated rocky hills. The elevation of this hill is about 150 m. In 1987, the village was located between 90 and 100 m above sea level (see Fig. 4.5). However, with the number of households rapidly increasing, the existing settlements became full, and the residential areas spread from the foot of the mountain towards the top, with houses rising up to 115 m as of 2018.

Thindaunggyi Village, where I have surveyed since 1987, and Taunghlwe Village, on the other side of Mount Shweitaunhtî, form one village tract, the Thindaung Village Tract. However, the two villages are clearly different. Thindaunggyi Village is surrounded by hedgerows and is separated from the other villages as a single unit. Until about 2000, the roads leading into the village were gated and closed at night. There is also a small shrine, dedicated to the village's guardian spirit or numen (*ywazâun na'*) and a Buddhist monastery, separate from Taunghlwe Village. Villages, in which houses are irregularly clustered to form a lumpy flat shape, are called agglomerated villages, and are ubiquitous in the central arid region of the Ayeyarwady River's mid-basin, or what has long been called Upper Myanmar. In contrast, linear villages—where houses are arranged in rows along small rivers or roads—are common in the Ayeyarwady and Sittang River's delta region known as Lower Myanmar. Thus, my two studied villages are fairly typical: Zeepinwea Village is a linear village in Lower Myanmar; Thindaunggyi Village is an agglomerated village in Upper Myanmar.

As can be seen from the aforementioned rainfall, in Kyaukse Township, paddy rice cannot be grown without irrigation even during the rainy season. Therefore, irrigation has been developed for more than 1000 years to ensure a stable harvest of paddy rice during the rainy season. Moreover, double cropping of paddy rice has been practised in the dry season where irrigation water is available. In a paddy field area known as the Thindaung Kwin (Circle), which stretches to the south and east of Thindaunggyi Village, three water courses—Chanwin, Kalaletpwe and Taunggatu—branch off from the Minye Canal (Takahashi, 1993: 51–52). In the village, dry-season cropping—called *mojoe* (*môujou*) or "before the rainy season"—and wet-season cropping—called *kaukkyi* (*kau'cî*) or "big or long rice"—have been practised for a long time. In paddy fields where sufficient water is not available in the dry season, onion, garlic, pepper and sesame have been cultivated (Takahashi, 1991: 168–171). In contrast to Zeepinwea Village, where only paddy monoculture was practised, double cropping has been done in the paddy fields of Thindaunggyi since ancient times.

4.3 Population History

4.3.1 Zeepinwea Village

The name of Zeepinwea Village first appeared in the Colonial Administration's report on the Census of 1891 (see Table 4.1). The Census did not consider Zeepinwea as one single village, but listed four villages: East Zeepinwea, West Zeepinwea, North Zeepinwea, and Paukkoung. The total number of households and population in each of these four villages was considerably larger than that of Zeepinwea today, suggesting that the population began to migrate to this area long before 1891. East Zeepinwea, West Zeepinwea and Paukkoung are today's Ywalay, Ywagyi and Paukkoung hamlets. On Fig. 4.3, North Zeepinwea Village is the settlement in the rectangle numbered "IV". It is bordered by a stream flowing into Ngamoeyeik Oxbow Lake. Although on the map it appears that it would be more natural to include this settlement in Zeepinwea Village, it is now included in Hlegu Town. When I surveyed the village in 1987, the boundary between Hlegu Town and former North Zeepinwea village was clear, with a paddy field with no houses. However, the boundary between the former North Zeepinwea hamlet and the current Zeepinwea Village is extremely difficult to identify for outsiders. From these facts, we can infer that Zeepinwea was in 1891 divided into three villages for administrative convenience at that time, while the people of Zeepinwea considered the three villages as one "Zeepinwea Village" from the time the village was established. The village of North Zeepinwea was not included in the 1901 census. It was probably annexed to the town of Hlegu between 1891 and 1901. In 1908, the "Village Tract" system was established, and East and West Zeepinwea were merged to form Zeepinwea Village Tract. However, Paukkoung village was listed as an independent village tract in the 1911 census, and had not yet been annexed to Zeepinwea Village Tract in 1921. The number of households and the population size of these two villages at that time were the same as several decades later, in 1987. Therefore, it can be assumed that the original form of the present Zeepinwea village was established in the 1910s. The elders of Zeepinwea village that I met in 1986 said that Paukkoung settlement had always been a part of Zeepinwea village. It did not seem to belong to the same administrative unit throughout the colonial period, but in the agrarian reform of 1957, Paukkoung was treated as part of Zeepinwea village (Takahashi, 1992: 97–100). It was probably annexed to the Zeepinwea Village Tract after independence in 1948.

Looking at the changes in the number of households in the village, it was 187 in 1901, 161 in 1911, further decreased to 137 in 1921, and only increased by one to 138 in 1987. Thus, it seems that the size of the village did not change much between 1921 and 1987, including during the struggle for independence. Of course, there may have been fluctuations in the number of households coming and going and the total number of households during these 66 years. The overall population showed similar decline between 1901 and 1921, but increased slightly between 1921 and 1987, because the average number of people per household increased from 5.26 to 5.43. Over the next seven years until 1994, the total number of households increased at an average annual rate of 3% to 170. Over the following 19 years it increased at an average annual rate of 3.3% to 316 in 2013. The population, on the other hand, grew at an average annual rate of only 1.5% from 1987 to 1994, and 2.8% from 1987 to 2013. As a result, the average number of persons per household or the mean household decreased from 4.88 in 1994 to 4.45 in 2013. As discussed in the previous chapter, this reduction in household size appears to have been caused by a combination of three factors: the practice of *oekhwe* (*ôkhwêi*), a decline in the birth rate, and the outflow of single persons.

As shown in Table 4.1, the ethnic composition of Paukkoung Village in the 1891 census was almost equally Karen (Christian) and Bamar (Buddhist). In 1901, there were more Bamars than Karens, while in 1911, the Karens were more numerous, but there is no doubt that the two ethnic groups lived together in Paukkoung village. However, in 1921, the ethnic Bamars (Burmese) suddenly disappeared, and the number of Paukkoung households was almost halved from 37 to 19. It is clear that there was an exodus of Bamars from Paukkoung to other villages and towns between 1911 and 1921, because the population of Zeepinwea Village did not increase by that amount. Unfortunately, the villagers have no memory of such an exodus, and the reasons for the migration are unknown. In any case, these historical circumstances led to a segregation of the two ethnic groups in Zeepinwea and Paukkoung villages. After independence, Paukkoung Village was annexed to Zeepinwea, and a new Zeepinwea Village was formed. It is not clear why the name of Paukkoung Village disappeared, and the two villages became a single village, rather than two villages forming one village tract, as in the case of Thindaung Village Tract. The villagers told me that one village and one village tract are the same thing. Nonetheless, it seems that this annexation relates to the extremely small number of households in Paukkoung village and the fact that the village was burned down during the civil war between the Myanmar and Karen armies that took place immediately after independence, when many Karen villagers fled to Ywagyi and Ywalay. At the time of the 1987 survey, only ethnic Sgaw Karen lived in Paukkoung, and only ethnic Bamars lived in the former Zeepinwea villages (Ywagyi and Ywalay). However, at the time of the 1994 survey, one Bamar man and one Bamar woman, each married to a Karen person, lived in Paukkoung settlement, and in 2013, two Karen women, each married to a Bamar man, and one Karen couple lived in Ywagyi. In addition, an ethnic Chin

Table 4.1 Changes in the number of households, the population, and the population by religion in Zeepinwea Village

Year, name of village/ hamlet	Number of households	Population	Mean household size	Population by religion		
				Buddhism	Christianity	Hinduism
1891						
East Zeepinwea village	182	888	4.88	881	6	1
West Zeepinwea village						
North Zeepinwea village						
Paukkoung	39	221	5.67	106	115	
Total	221	1,109	5.02	987	121	1
1901						
East Zeepinwea	34	150	4.41	150		
West Zeepinwea	130	649	4.99	648	1	
Paukkoung	23	171	7.43	100	71	
Total	187	970	5.19	898	72	0
1911						
Zeepinwea	124	592	4.77	576		16
Paukkoung	37	194	5.24	70	124	
Total	161	786	4.88	646	124	16
1921						
Zeepinwea	118	623	5.28	549		24
Paukkoung	19	97	5.11	1	86	10
Total	137	720	5.26	550	86	34
1987						
Ywalay hamlet	24	146	6.08	149		
Ywagyi hamlet	93	494	5.31	494		
Paukkoung hamlet	21	110	5.24		110	
Total	138	750	5.43	643	110	0
1994						

(continued)

Table 4.1 (continued)

Year, name of village/hamlet	Number of households	Population	Mean household size	Population by religion		
				Buddhism	Christianity	Hinduism
Ywalay hamlet	40	180	4.50	180		
Ywagyi hamlet	104	516	4.96	516		
Paukkoung hamlet	26	134	5.15	2	132	
Total	170	830	4.88	698	132	0
2013						
Ywalay hamlet	45	179	3.98	179		
Ywagyi hamlet	235	1,047	4.46	1,043	4	
Paukkoung hamlet	36	180	5.00	2	178	
Total	316	1,406	4.45	1,224	182	0

Source Figures up to 1987 are from Takahashi (1992, p. 46) and figures for 1994 and 2013 are from my surveys

man started farming in Paukkoung and several Mon households moved into Ywagyi. Consequently, Zeepinwea Village Tract is being transformed into a more multi-ethnic co-residential village.

Table 4.1 also shows that there were Hindus in the village. They were Indians who came to Myanmar during the colonial period. 16 Indians lived in Zeepinwea Village in 1911, and a total of 34 Indians lived in Zeepinwea and Paukkoung Village in 1921. According to the villagers, they were tenants of the Chettiars (Tamil moneylenders). In contrast to the increase of Indian population, the population of ethnic Bamar in Zeepinwea village (including Paukkoung village) decreased from 1901 to 1921. While the decrease in the Bamar population was larger than the increase in the Indian population, it seems that Indians entered the village in such a way as to displace the Bamar farmers and agricultural labourers. The trends in the Bamar and Indian populations, especially between 1911 and 1921, suggest so. The probability of this assumption is increased by the fact that a Chettiar was the absentee landlord of the farmland in Zeepinwea village at that time (Takahashi, 1992: 99). While Indian landlords preferred Indian peasants, tenancy contracts were often for one year and not renewed (Furnivall, 1957: 65–67), and a landlord could easily change tenants. It is unclear when, after independence, Indians disappeared from Zeepinwea Village. The farmland owned by the Chettiars was distributed to Bamars and Karens through land reform.

Table 4.2 Changes in number of households and population in Thindaung Village Tract

Year	Number of households	Population	Mean household size
1911	203	822	4.05
1921	195	640	3.28
1987	361	1,902	5.27
(in Thindaunggyi Village)	(126)	(660)	(5.24)
1994	394	2,154	5.47
(in Thindaunggyi Village)	(156)	(786)	(5.04)
2013	610	2,722	4.46
(in Thindaunggyi Village)	(236)	(1,024)	(4.34)

Note The population by religion is not listed since only Buddhist Burmese have lived in Thindaung Village Tract
Source Census of India, Burma, 1911, 1921. Figures for 1987, 1994, 2013 are based on author's research

4.3.2 Thindaunggyi Village

The colonial period census shows the number of households, the population, and the population by religion[10] only for the broader Thindaung Village Tract, but not specifically for Thindaunggyi Village. Although, it is known from the census data and my interviews that Indian Muslims from Letpan Village owned the agricultural land in this village during the colonial period, it can be said that only ethnic Bamars lived in Thindaunggyi Village. Only ethnic Bamars live there now, too. However, because it is an old village that is estimated to have existed since the 11th or 12th century, other ethnic groups may have inhabited it before the twentieth century. As shown in Table 4.2, in contrast to Zeepinwea Village, both the number of households and the population of Thindaung Village Tract increased significantly during the 66 years from 1921 to 1987. During this period, the number of households increased by a factor of 1.85, from 195 to 361, and the population increased by a factor of 2.97, from 640 to 1902. Population growth outpaced household growth, with the average number of people per household increasing from 3.28 to 5.27.

For the period after 1987, let us look at the changes in Thindaunggyi Village based on my fieldwork. In the seven years from 1987 to 1994, the total number of

[10] In the 1911 census report, it is stated that there were 52 Muslims (listed as Mahomedans) and 4 Hindus in Thindaung Village Tract, but both populations were zero in 1921. At the same time, the population of Muslims and Hindus in the neighbouring Indain Village Tract was zero in 1911, but 68 Muslims and 28 Hindus were noted in 1921. It seems that in the 1911 census report, the number of Muslims and Hindus who should be listed in Indain Village Tract was shifted downwards to Thindaung Village Tract, because Muslims still live in Indain Village Tract now.

households increased by an average of 3.5% per year to 156. In the following 19 years, the total number of households increased at an average annual rate of 2.2% to 236. In contrast, the population grew at an average annual rate of only 2.4% from 1987 to 1994 and only 1.5% from 1987 to 2013. Thus, similarly to Zeepinwea Village, the average number of persons per household decreased—from 5.24 in 1987 to 5.04 in 1994 and 4.34 in 2013. The reasons for the reduction in household size were the same as in Zeepinwea Village.

4.4 Transformation of Occupational Structure

The Myanmar Population Census defines a household as the unit of consumption, at least in relation to food and housing: "a family-based group that lives under the same roof and eats from the same pot". In addition, most of the household expenditures, such as clothing, fuel, education, and religious expenses, are paid from household accounts. Thus, the household is a unit of consumption expenditure. As for agricultural production, the allocation of farmland at the time of agrarian reform was done on the basis of households. Members of a *farm* household are aware that they are a farm household, and most household members, including children and the elderly, are self-employed in agriculture in some way. The household can be considered as a unit of production and income not only for farms, but also for shops and rice mills. However, the household is not the unit of production for agricultural workers, civil servants, carpenters, plasterers, and so on, where each household member works separately to earn income. In such cases, it is better to divide household members according to their sources of income for a more accurate analysis of household economic activities. Yet even in such cases, the income of the husband and wife is included in the household accounts, and the income of the children, as long as they live together with their parents, is almost entirely included in the household budget. In addition, as long as the household members live together in the same house, the house, compound, livestock, fruit trees, and so on are the life and management resources of the household as a whole, even though each member has his or her own share. Therefore, even if each member of the household has a different occupation, the household can be considered as a unit of income. The members' different occupations could be regarded as a strategy for diversifying the sources of income of the household, similar to a company that has various business units. From this point of view, this book assumes that the household is the basic economic unit and that the economic activities of individual household members are included in it. Of course, this approach does not mean that the economic activities of individual household members are ignored; on the contrary, a closer look at the economic activities of individual members often reveals the economy of the household.

In Burmese, the head of a household is usually called *eindaun ûsî*. *Eindaun* means "household" and *ûsî* means "leader". The *eindaun ûsî* is the equivalent of "the head of a household" on the Japanese resident's card[11] and is nominal. In contrast, the member who is the main livelihood supporter of the household is called *eindaundhâzù acîakê*. I translate *eindaundhâzù acîakê* as a "householder" in this book. The occupation in which the householder spends the most time a year is defined as the "main occupation of the household" or "household occupation" in this book. However, in Myanmar, both in administration and in statistics, the primary classification of village household occupation is based on whether or not the household has the right to cultivate the farmland (cultivation right) and engage in their own farming. Considering this fact, for households engaged in their own farming, that is, farm households, agriculture shall be the main occupation of the household, even if a person other than the householder is self-employed in it. In this book, when the main occupation of a household is agriculture, "self-employment subsidiary occupation" is defined as work performed by members of the farm household alongside their own farming, which is not wage labour, while "labour subsidiary occupation" is defined as wage in which the household members sell labour force directly. Similarly, if a household's main occupation is other than agriculture, the occupations in which the householder is secondarily engaged or the occupations other than the "main occupation of the household" engaged in by other members of the household, which are not wage labour, are defined as "self-employment subsidiary occupation", while wage labour is defined as "labour subsidiary occupation". The two are collectively called "subsidiary occupation" or "side job". In this section, I only describe the main occupations. I will discuss subsidiary occupations later.

4.4.1 Zeepinwea Village

Table 4.3 shows the main occupations of Zeepinwea Village households by the number of households in each occupation.[12] Households with own farming as their main occupation are farm households in the sense defined in Chap. 3. In Japanese statistics, a farm household is defined, first of all, as a household with a certain amount of cultivated land under management and a certain amount of agricultural product sales, and only secondly, the family members engaged in agriculture are counted as farmers. Thus, a household (*Ie*) is the first and an individual is the second. In Myanmar, in contrast, if an individual holds the right to cultivate land, whether by ownership, borrowing, or pledging, and cultivates or supervises the process of cultivation, he or she is a "farmer" regardless of the size of the area or the value of sales. Any households of which such individual is a member are defined as "farm households". The individual is the first priority.

[11] In Myanmar, there is a similar kind of resident's card called *eindaundhâzù sayîn*. It means "household members list". The village tract mayor is supposed to manage it.

[12] For the 56 sample households surveyed in 2013, the household occupations back in 1987 were: 33 farmers, 8 *sayinngas*, 5 *kyabans*, 4 civil servants, 1 side-car driver, 1 bus conductor (spare), 1 peddler, 1 vegetable gardener, 1 canteen waiter and 1 unemployed.

Table 4.3 Changes in the composition of household occupations in Zeepinwea Village

Occupation	1987	1994	2013
Own farming	64	66	55
Agricultural labourer	(46)	(52)	(100)
Sayinnga	30	29	25
Kyaban	16	23	75
Vegetable gardening	3	8	3
Carpenter, plasterer	3	10	5
Small shop owner		2	11
Peddler, street vendor	3	5	53
Side-car driver	1	2	13
Motorcycle taxi driver			13
Car driver/assistant	2	3	11
Cargo handling			9
Public servant, company employee	7	9	10
Factory worker			11
Other jobs	8	8	5
Without an occupation	1	5	17
Total number of households	138	170	316
Total population	753	830	1,406

Note The occupation in which the householder works the longest in a year is defined as the "main occupation of the household" or "household occupation". However, the household occupation is listed as "own farming", if at least one member of the household engages in one's own farming.
Source According to the author's survey

"Agricultural (hired) labour" means working for a farmer. The households that engage in this type of labour as household occupation are landless households without farmland. Agricultural hired labourers can be divided into two types: *sayinnga* (*sayînngâ*), who is employed for a relatively long period of time as annual or seasonal labourer; and *kyaban* (*càbân*), who is employed on a daily or percentage basis (Takahashi, 1992: 169). The word "*kyaban (càbân)*" means "in time or irregularly", and is an abbreviation of a *càbân alou'thmâ* which means a worker who does any job at random. He or she often engages not only in agriculture but also in non-agricultural work such as handling cargo, working at road construction, assisting carpenters and plasterers, and so on.

As explained in Chap. 3, vegetable gardening is the cultivation of fruits and vegetables on a small area of land in the village that is indistinguishable from residential land and does not fall into one of Myanmar's six categories of agricultural land. In the 1987 and 1994 surveys, such gardening was not recognised as agriculture. However, some people were turning paddy fields into vegetable gardens. The 2012

Farmland Law recognises small vegetable gardens for growing fruits and vegetables as agricultural land, so it may be classified as agriculture after 2012.

As the table shows, the change from the end of Burmese socialism in 1987 to the later military rule in 1994 was not so pronounced. This is partly because of the short period. There was only an increase in the number of *kyabans* and carpenters. It is worth noting, however, that only half of the households in the village hold agricultural land (cultivation right)—even during the socialist era when equality was the main objective.

The changes in the following 19 years were more remarkable. First, the number of farm households decreased. In the first half of the military period, the liquidation of farmland had not yet occurred, but in the second half, the sale of farmland gradually increased. Possible reasons for the decline in the number of farm households include the purchase and accumulation of farmland by some farmers in the village and the sale of farmland to residents outside the village. In Zeepinwea village, selling to outsiders is by far the most common reason. Even though the sale and purchase of farmland was illegal until the 2012 Farmland Law came into effect, the village farmland was sold to Hlegu townspeople and Yangon citizens to anticipate legalisation. Thus, while the number of farm households decreased by 11 households from 66 in 1994 to 55 in 2013, the number of non-farm households increased significantly, from 104 to 261, a two-and-a-half-fold increase. In 1987, farm households accounted for 46.4% of the total number of households in the village, but this had fallen to 38.8% by 1994 and to only 17.4% by 2013. Looking only at this, Zeepinwea is no longer a "farming village". Nevertheless, if we add the number of landless households with agricultural employment (100 households with agricultural hired labourers, plus 3 households with vegetable gardeners), we can say that half of the households in the village were engaged in agriculture in 2013. Still, compared to 1987, when 80% of the households in the village were engaged in agriculture, the ratio has decreased significantly.

Second, from 1987 to 2013, the number of households sustained by agricultural labourers and peddlers increased significantly, accounting for half of the total number of households in the village. Among agricultural hired labourers, the number of households with stable employment (*sayinnga* households) decreased slightly, while the number of households with daily or percentage-based agricultural labour (*kyaban* households) tripled between 1994 and 2013. *Kyabans* are more likely to be men, but most peddlers and street vendors are women. The village has long had women who peddle vegetables and boiled beans on their heads early in the morning. However, the 2000s saw a dramatic increase in the number of women who bought not only vegetables and milk from the village, but also fruits and other goods from the town and surrounding villages, and sold them on the roadsides around the central market in Hlegu Town. The number of peddlers and street vendors increased more than tenfold: from five households in 1994 to 53 households in 2013. Only four or five peddlers sold boiled beans and the rest were street vendors. Most of the households whose main occupation was hawking and street vending did not have farmland, and their livelihoods were sustained by female vendors or peddlers. Wives or widows had to work for the household economy because their husbands died, their husbands could not work due to illness or old age, or their husbands did not work due to alcoholism.

The daily income of both *kyaban* and street vendors was unstable and small. It would not be an exaggeration to say that all households that made their living mainly by these means were poor households.

Third, new types of jobs have emerged. In 1987, the village did not have a single shop selling food and daily necessities; in 1994, the village had two, and in 2013, eleven. Not only small shops with palm-leaf roofs and bamboo enclosures, but also large general stores made of concrete and brick, liquor stores that were busy during the day, shops selling fertiliser and seeds, and shops equipped with large refrigerators that sell ice cream and frozen foods newly appeared. These stores often sell commodity on credit, regardless of whether the customer is rich or poor. The longer the payments are deferred and the larger the number of repayments is, the more popular the stores are.

In 1987, there was only one household whose main business was driving a bicycle taxi, called a *sai'kâ* (side-car)—a bicycle with a seat for people to sit on next to the rider—but by 2013, the number had increased to 13 households. This probably relates to the introduction of paved roads to the village. These "side-cars" were replaced by motorcycle taxis, which carry people and goods on motorcycles. However, this did not mean that motorcycle taxis were a growing industry. The rapid increase in the number of villagers' self-owned motorbikes meant that there was already excessive competition.

The number of factory workers is likely to continue to increase. Korean and Chinese sewing factories have been built around the expanding city of Greater Yangon, and factory buses come to pick up workers near the village. The number of young people working in these factories is increasing. Working as car drivers or their assistants (called "spare") have also become new employment opportunities for adult males. There were eight people who supported their households as drivers or assistants on the cargo service between Yangon and Muse, a town on the Chinese border. One person carried the load in a vehicle called a *tawlaji* with a rear-car-like loading platform behind the motorcycle. The rest were drivers of rice husk transport trucks. "Cargo handlers" are men hired as labourers to collect and transport rice husks for the village-tract administrator's business of collecting rice husks from the surrounding rice mills and delivering them as fuel to the famous Yum Yum noodle factory. The village-tract administrator owns three trucks for transporting rice husks and one four-wheel drive vehicle. He is a businessman who enjoys playing golf on holidays.

4.4.2 Thindaunggyi Village

Table 4.4 shows the changes in the occupational structure in Thindaunggyi village. In 1987, the number of households that possessed cultivation rights (that is, farm households) was 68, which was just over half of the total number of households in the village. As in Zeepinwea, the most common main occupation of landless households

Table 4.4 Changes in the composition of household occupations in Thindaunggyi Village

Occupation	1987	1994	2013
Own farming	68	73	76
Agricultural labourer	25	33	41
Plasterer	18	24	60
Carpenter	2	4	10
Shops and restaurants		3	27
Public servant	4	5	2
Coachman	2	3	
Tawlaji owner			3
Other jobs	7	11	17
Total number of households	126	156	236
Total population	660	786	1,024

Source Same as Table 4.3.

was agricultural hired labour.[13] In Thindaunggyi village, however, there have been very few stable forms of agricultural labour employment (*sayinnga*), with almost all agricultural labourers being employed only on a daily basis or on a percentage basis. If we include the 25 households hired by farmers to do farm work, 73.8% of village households in 1987 were engaged in agriculture. By 1994, the structure had remained almost the same, with farmers accounting for half of the total households in the village. Combined with 33 agricultural labourer households, there were 106 households engaged in agriculture, accounting for 67.9% of all households in the village. Thindaunggyi Village was still a "farming village". By 2013, however, farmers accounted for less than one-third of the 236 households in the village (only 76 households), and even together with the 41 agricultural labourer households, they accounted for less than half of the total number of households.

In inverse proportion to this, the number of plasterers and shop owners increased. There is a legend that plastering was designated as Thindaunggyi's"village occupation" by an imperial decree in the dynastic period (Takahashi, 1995: 66–68). Plastering declined during the British colonial period, but recovered after independence, gradually increasing the number of people employed in it. In 1987, 18 households (14.3% of all households in the village), and in 1994, 24 households (15.4% of all households), were plasterers. By the time of my 2013 survey, 60 households, or more than a quarter of all households in the village, were plasterers. They overtook the number of agricultural labourers around the turn of the century and became the largest source of employment for those who do not have the right to cultivate agricultural land. Every day, the plasterers leave their villages early in the morning with

[13] For the 54 sample households surveyed in 2013, the household occupations back in 1987 were: own farming (farmer) 33, agricultural hired labour 10, plasterer 7, a carpenter, a clerk, a civil servant, and a bicycle repairer.

their lunch boxes. Some go as far as Yangon or the towns of Muse and Mongla on the Chinese border to work.

Another rapidly growing sector is shops and restaurants. Until the 1990s, the village had only a few shops and restaurants in small huts, selling miscellaneous goods. Others set up stalls and tables on the roadside and sold betel[14] and/or mohinga.[15] Their income was not much different from that of agricultural labourers. With the development of Shwetheindaw Paya, which I will discuss below, the number of relatively large shops, previously absent from the village, increased. They began selling offerings called *gadawbwe* and serving tea and meals around the paya, earning dozens of times the daily wage of agricultural labourers. These shops and restaurants were new occupations that have emerged in the 2000s. Another, albeit lesser, new occupation emerged around the same time. In Upper Myanmar, horse-drawn carts have long been used as an important means of transportation in many villages.Thindaunggyi Village, too, always had two or three households whose main occupation was a coachman. These families sold their horses to buy a *tawlaji*, which was used in the same way as a horse-drawn carriage to carry children to school in Kyaukse Town and women to the market for shopping. Soon, the horse-drawn carriages disappeared because *tawlaji*s could transport larger quantities more quickly.

What both villages have in common is that the proportion of households that make their living mainly from agriculture is decreasing, while non-agricultural employment is increasing rapidly. Rural villages are no longer necessarily "agricultural or farming villages". Foreigners, as well as the Myanmar people living in cities, tend to assume that rural areas are inhabited by people who are engaged in agriculture, but the current situation is moving in a direction that negates such preconceptions.

4.5 Changes in Farmland Holdings

As mentioned earlier, both Zeepinwea and Thindaunggyi were "farming villages" when I surveyed them in 1987, with farmers and agricultural labourers accounting for 70–80% of all households in the villages. Despite the fact that farming has decreased since then, agriculture is still a major industry in both villages, and in order to understand the trend of de-agrarianisation, it is first necessary to examine the change in the size of farmland holdings (that is, possession of cultivation right).

[14] A chewing delicacy called *kônya* in Myanmar. A thin slice of dried betel nut is wrapped around a betel leaf coated with lime dissolved in water, which is then placed in the mouth and chewed.

[15] Myanmar national dish of noodles made from fermented rice flour and served in a broth made from catfish and other fish.

4.5.1 Zeepinwea Village

Out of the 138 households in Zeepinwea Village in 1987, there were 65 households with cultivation rights (Takahashi, 1992: 115). Of these, 13 households had an area of 14 acres or more, 33 households had between 10 and 14 acres, and 19 households had less than 10 acres. One household leased all of its cultivation rights.

In 2013, I randomly selected a total of 33 households from each of the above three stratums—7 households with more than 14 acres, 16 with 10–14 acres, and 10 with less than 10 acres. I included only those households that I had also surveyed in 1994 and that were still living in Zeepinwea Village in 2013. I targeted for 50% of each stratum, and ensured a balance between the three hamlets.[16] In addition, I added six households that did not have cultivation rights in 1987 but had acquired it by 1994 or by 2013 to the less-than-10-acres stratum. I singled out farmers with holdings between 10 and 14 acres because 12 acres of farmland is the *dadounghton* of the village (see footnote 8 in Chap. 2), to which I included about 2 acres above and below. This is considered to be the area where a farm household could make a living purely from agriculture, and a very large number of farmers owned this acreage in 1987.

As shown in Table 4.5, from 1987 to 1994, one of the seven households in the 14+ acres group increased their farmland holdings, while five households decreased their farmland holdings. The reason for the one increase was that the farmer took over the right to cultivate the paddy fields that his uncle had stopped cultivating. The decreases were due to inheritance[17] (2 cases), gift (2 cases), and sale (1 case). In both of the gift cases, the gifts were made to a nephew by a holder, who then temporarily held the cultivation rights because an elder or younger brother had died, and returned it to their nephews when they came of age. The reason for the one sale was that the farmland was too large to secure the labour force. In the 10–14 acres group, three households increased their farmland holdings, while seven households decreased their holdings. All three increases were due to the expansion of farmland by purchase. The reasons for the decreases were 5 sales and 2 gifts to nephews. One household sold their farmland to buy draught cattle; two households sold their farmland to buy a paddy field near their village because the paddy field they were currently cultivating was too far away; and two households sold their farmland because the paddy field was too far away to cultivate. All of these cases were due to circumstances related to cultivation. In the less-than-10-acres group, four households increased and four decreased their farmland. The increase was due to purchases in three cases and inheritance in one case. These four households had been landless before that. The decreases were due to

[16] For the non-farm households that do not own farmland, I selected 23 households based on the same criteria and interviewed them individually. In other words, the total number of sampled households is 56.

[17] Farmers do not distinguish between inheritance after an ancestor's death and gift before an ancestor's death, always referring to the transfer of farmland cultivation rights to children or grandchildren as "inheritance". When farmers do refer to a "gift", they mean a free transfer of rights to relatives or acquaintances who are more than three degrees of kinship apart (Takahashi, 1992: 116; 2018: 180–185).

Table 4.5 Changes in agricultural land holdings in Zeepinwea Village

Strata by holding area in 1987 (acres)	1987 → 1994 (number of households)			1994 → 2013 (number of households)			1987 → 2013 (number of households)			Average size of holdings (acres)			Number of households sampled	Average annual rate of change (%)		
	+	Same	–	+	Same	–	+	Same	–	1987	1994	2013		1987–1994	1994–2013	1987–2013
14+	1	1	5	0	0	7	0	0	7	20.7	16.6	5.7	7	– 3.14	– 5.45	– 4.83
10–14	3	6	7	3	4	9	2	2	12	11.9	9.9	5.8	16	– 2.59	– 2.75	– 2.70
0–10	4	8	4	3	5	8	7	1	8	4.3	6.3	4.8	16	5.59	– 1.38	0.45
Total	8	15	16	6	9	24	9	3	27	10.25	9.61	5.38	39	– 0.92	– 3.01	– 2.45

Note 1 The "0–10" category includes six households that did not have farmland in 1987 but obtained the right to cultivate after

Note 2 "+" means "increase" and "–" means "decrease"

Source According to the author's survey

the sale of land in three cases and the gift of land in one case. One of these households became landless.

Between 1994 and 2013, all the households that were in the 14+ acres group in 1987 had their farmland reduced. Six were by sale and one was confiscated for free to build an irrigation canal. In three of the six sales cases, the buyers were residents of Yangon, while until 1994 all buyers had always been fellow farmers in the village. In all six cases, the purpose of the sale was to obtain large sums of money at one time for the treatment of serious illnesses. The 10–14 acres group increased their farmland by purchase in one case and by inheritance in two cases, and decreased it by sale in seven and by inheritance in two cases. Among the seven sales, two were to farmers in the village, two to Yangon citizens, and three to farmers in Khayan (*khàyân*) Township, about 50 km from the village across the Bago River. The reasons for the sale were to treat illness in four cases, to repay debts in one case, to build a new house in one case, and to buy another paddy field in one case. In the less-than-10-acres group, increases in the area of farmland were due to one purchase and two inheritances. In these inheritance cases, two households changed from non-farmers to farmers through inheritance. At the same time, another two households had gone from non-farmers to farmers in the 1990s, but later became non-farmers again. In eight households, farmland decreased: one by confiscation for irrigation canals, one by inheritance, and the rest by sale. In five cases, the land was sold to treat diseases. In one case, the land was sold to build a new brick and plaster house—a *taik* (*tai'*). In Myanmar villages, the *taik* is considered to be one of the symbols of wealth, and this was the second *taik* built after the village tract administrator's house, mentioned above. The farmland was sold in one case to a sister in the village, in three cases to Khayan farmers, and in one case to a Chin youth who moved to the village from Yangon.

The above discussion has described the changes in the size of agricultural land holdings from 1987 to 1994 through to 2013, while dividing the land holdings into three layers. In the 14+ acres group, all sample households reduced their farmland size to the extent that there was a total collapse. One household held 18 acres in 1987 but was landless in 2013. In the 10–14 acres group, two households increased their farmland, while 12 households decreased their farmland. Five of them went from farmers to landless non-farmers. The difference is smaller for the less-than-10-acres group, with 8 households reducing their farmland and 7 households increasing their farmland. Among them were 6 households that were landless in 1987, but later acquired farmland. 3 of these households became landless again, so that only 3 households remained farmland holders in 2013. There were five households that turned from being farmers to being landless.

Let us follow the changes in the average size of holdings by strata among the sample households. Between 1987 and 1994, holdings declined 3.1% per year for the 14+ acres group and 2.6% per year for the 10–14 acres group. In contrast, holdings increased 5.6% per year for the less-than-10-acres group. Between 1994 and 2013, the rates of annual decline for the three groups were 5.5%, 2.8%, and 1.4%, respectively. Thus, altogether, between 1987 and 2013, the 14+ acres group lost 4.8% of land per year, the 10–14 acres group lost 2.7% per year, and only the less-than-10-acres group increased their holdings by an average of 0.5% per year. As a result, the overall acreage holdings became relatively more equal, which is the opposite of peasant differentiation. The average acreage of all 39 sample households declined by nearly half, from 10.25 acres in 1987 to 5.38 acres in 2013, suggesting that the collapse of the largest holdings led to a downwards levelling off. In the 26 years since 1987, there were only three households whose holding area remained the same.

The most common method of agricultural land transfer in Zeepinwea has been buying and selling. In my 1987 survey, the number of households that acquired farmland through purchase or lost farmland through sale was very small, but it became conspicuous in the later military period. Compared to the socialist period—when the low price paddy procurement system weighed heavily on the peasants—the new military regime's reduction of the procurement burden and the liberalisation of paddy and rice sales led to the widespread sale and purchase of paddy fields, despite the prohibition by the Land Nationalisation Act. Even so, until around 1995 or 1996, most of the sales were among the Zeepinwea villagers themselves. After that, sales to people outside the village started to be noticeable. In the sample households alone, there were 19 sales for every 2 purchases, and 17 of these sales were to people outside the village. Not only the farmers from Khayan Township, mentioned above, but also farmers from nearby Thongwa (*Thôungwà*) and Kawa (*Kàwà*), as well as farmers from far-away Mon State, bought farmland in the village. 30 new households moved in. People of the Shan, Karen, and Chin ethnic groups living in Yangon also bought farmland in Zeepinwea. They built payas, created vegetable gardens, and rented out farmland for tenants living in Zeepinwea. In the beginning, the migrants' purpose was farming, but in time, with the expansion of Yangon City and the planning of the Hanthawaddy International Airport, there seems to have been an increase in purchases for speculative purposes. The speculators did not migrate to the village. In addition to sales and purchases, transfers of farmland cultivation rights by inheritance and gifts were the second most common type of transfers, increasing slightly from six in 1987–1994 to seven in 1994–2013, but actually decreasing if we consider the length of the period. In particular, gifts were not found after 1995. The number of transfers of agricultural land by inheritance and gift was one half of the number of sales in 1987–1994, but became less than one third in 1994–2013. Two households in the sample and five households in the whole Zeepinwea Village had their farmland confiscated free of charge in 1998 for the construction of the Ngamoeyeik Canal.

In the period 1987–1994, most of the reasons for selling were related to agriculture, such as buying farmland elsewhere, buying cattle, and the paddy fields being too far away or too large to secure labour. However, between 1994 and 2013, 14 out of 19 cases of sale were to finance the treatment of diseases. It is likely that the seven-year period from 1987 to 1994 was too short for the sale of farmland for disease treatment, but it is also possible that there was no hope of curing these serious diseases even if farmland was sold. In any case, the overwhelmingly leading cause of farmland sales in the twenty-first century was to finance the treatment of serious diseases.

There were also cases where the cultivation right was temporarily rented out or borrowed. This was also illegal until 2012, so there was only one such case in Zeepinwea Village in 1987. However, by 1994 there was a sporadic increase in the lending and borrowing of cultivation rights: of the 65 farmland-holding households, seven rented out their farmland to tenants, and four of them rented out all their farmland. At the same time, 13 households paid rent as tenants, and five of them were landless households who did not have cultivation rights. Therefore, the number of farm households in 1994 was 66 (see Table 4.3). These tenancy contracts were still mostly mutual support based on parent–child relationships. Tenancy contracts based on economic calculations were still in their embryonic stages (Takahashi, 2000: 123). In 2013, of the 33 farmland-holding households that I discussed above, 13 households became landless, while, conversely, three households that were landless acquired cultivation rights, leaving 23 households with cultivation rights. Eight of these households rented out their farmland to tenants, and four of them rented all their farmland. At the same time, seven households paid rent as tenants, and three of them were landless households. Even in this period, most of the tenancy contracts were between relatives. I counted the number of households that owned cultivation rights (that is, farmers), and found that only 22 households were farmers in the sample as of the 2013 survey. 33 households, half the number of farmers in 1987, were surveyed, but the number of farmers had decreased considerably.

4.5.2 *Thindaunggyi Village*

Let me now turn to Thindaunggyi Village, 507 km almost due north from Zeepinwea. The villagers of Thindaunggyi told me that they had never even heard of *dadounghton* when I first visited them in 1987. However, the area of farmland that a farm household with a yoke of draught cattle could live on farming alone, that is, the area of farmland corresponding to *dadounghton*, was between 6 and 8 acres in Thindaunggyi, according to my survey (Takahashi, 1991: 159–160). Of the 102 households for which we were able to collect questionnaires in 1987, 23 had more than 8 acres of farmland (comparable to farmers with more than 14 acres in Zeepinwea Village), 21 had between 4 and 8 acres (comparable to Zeepinwea farmers with 10–14 acres), and 19 had less than 4 acres (comparable to Zeepinwea farmers with less than 10 acres). As in Zeepinwea Village, in my 2013 survey, I randomly selected, respectively, 12, 11 and 10 households from each stratum in 1987, with a target of 50% from each stratum. I visited these households individually.[18] Data from these households were of course also included in my 1994 survey questionnaire of 156 households.

As shown in Table 4.6, from 1987 to 1994, five of the 12 households in the group with more than 8 acres of farmland increased their farmland holdings, while five decreased their farmland holdings. Inheritance (one case) and purchase (four cases)

[18] For the non-farm households, I randomly selected a quarter of the 56 households that remained in the village between 1987, 1994, and 2013. I also conducted individual interview surveys with two households that could not be surveyed in 1987 but were surveyed in 1994, with three households that split up (*oekhwe*) and became independent households between 1987 and 1994, and with two households that moved into the village after 1995. Thus, a total of 54 households were surveyed in 2013, including 33 households that were farm households in 1987.

Table 4.6 Changes in agricultural land holdings in Thindaunggyi Village

Strata by holding area in 1987 (acres)	1987 → 1994 (number of households)			1994 → 2013 (number of households)			1987 → 2013 (number of households)			Average size of holdings (acres)			Number of households sampled	Average annual rate of change (%)		
	+	Same	–	+	Same	–	+	Same	–	1987	1994	2013		1987–1994	1994–2013	1987–2013
8+	5	2	5	3	1	8	3	0	9	14.4	14.0	10.2	12	– 0.39	– 1.63	– 1.33
4–8	4	1	6	5	0	6	3	2	6	7.0	7.2	6.7	11	0.39	– 0.38	– 0.17
0–4	6	3	4	5	2	6	8	0	5	2.0	2.8	3.1	13	4.41	0.60	1.61
Total	15	6	15	13	3	20	14	2	20	7.67	7.86	6.55	36	0.35	– 0.96	– 0.61

Note The "0" category includes three households that did not have farmland in 1987 but obtained the right to cultivate later

Source According to the author's survey

were the reasons for the increase, while all the decreases were due to inheritance (including as gift before an ancestor's death, as already mentioned). In the group of 4–8 acres, four households increased their farmland holdings, while six households decreased their holdings. While one household increased their holdings by inheritance and three households by purchase, two households decreased their holdings by inheritance and four decreased them by sale. In the less-than-4-acres group, six increased their farmland holdings. Three of these households did not have cultivation rights in 1987. Four households decreased their holdings. Among them, three households reduced their farmland holdings by selling them, while the remaining one household became landless after their farmland was confiscated free of charge as a golf course site for the Myanmar military. None of the (relatively) large households with more than 8 acres sold their farmland. Instead, it was the small and medium farmers with 8 acres or less that sold their farmland. Reasons for sale included buying cattle (two cases), repairing houses (two cases), paddy fields being too far away, lack of labour, and donation to monks. There was no sale for the reason of disease treatment.

Between 1994 and 2013, in the group of households with more than 8 acres, three households increased their farmland area and eight households decreased their farmland. The increase was due to inheritance (one case) and purchase (two cases), while the decrease was due to inheritance (three cases) and sale (four cases), as well as donation as paya land. In the 4–8 acres group, five households increased their farmland and six households decreased their farmland. All increases were due to purchases, but the reasons for the decreases were more complex. Namely, one household had a part of its farmland confiscated for an army golf course site and sold the remaining. Another householder gave a part of farmland to a son as inheritance and sold another part to a daughter. The other reasons for decrease were inheritance during life (one case), sale (two cases), and, again, confiscation by the national military for a golf course (one case). Two households stated that their reason for selling was to send their children to university, one to pay off their son's debts[19] and one for medical treatment. In the less-than-4-acres group, three households increased their farmland through purchase and two through inheritance, while six households decreased their farmland through sale. The reasons for selling were diverse: house extension, building a new house, disease treatment, distance to paddy fields, debt repayment, and purchase of farm machinery.

---

[19] The former mayor of Thindaunggyi Village Tract sold 4 acres of paddy for 1.5 million kyats in 1995 to pay off debts incurred by his eldest son through land speculation and sold 2 acres of paddy for 2.5 million kyats in 2006 to pay off his second son's debts after his second son lost a lot of money in paddy trading. Furthermore, his third son was in the business of selling a private wealth lottery called *khye* (*chê*), and when its winnings were so large that he could no longer pay, the former mayor sold an acre of paddy field for 18.5 million kyats in 2012 to pay for this. These paddy fields were adjacent to each other, so we can imagine how the land price skyrocketed between 1995 and 2012. The buyers were not villagers, but merchants from Kyaukse and Mandalay. Incidentally, the daily wage of a day labourer in the village in 2012 was 4000 kyats, and the monthly salary of a new civil servant just after graduation from university was 100,000 kyats.

The former mayor had sold all of his farmland to help his sons, but he said that he was just happy to have in this way "inherited" the farmland to them in his lifetime before he died.

Having measured agricultural land movement in Thindaunggyi Village in terms of the number of households, let us now look at it in terms of acreage. The average area of land held by the upper-class farmers with more than 8 acres of land remained almost the same from 1987 to 1994, and then decreased from 1994 to 2013. However, the average annual decrease over the latter 19 years was only 1.7%, much lower than the 5.5% decrease in Zeepinwea Village. Thus, the decrease from 1987 to 2013 was only 1.3% in Thindaunggyi, compared to the 4.8% in Zeepinwea. The decline over the same period for farmers with 4–8 acres was even lower at 0.2%, much smaller than the 2.76% in Zeepinwea. For small-scale farmers in both villages—those with less than 4 acres in Thindaunggyi and those with less than 10 acres in Zeepinwea—the average size of holdings increased dramatically between 1987 and 1994. This is because households that did not have farmland before became landholding households. After that, the average size of small-scale farmers' landholdings decreased in Zeepinwea Village, leading the average size of landholdings to increase by only 0.5% from 1987 to 2013. In Thindaunggyi Village, the average size of small-scale farmers' landholdings increased by 1.6% from 1987 to 2013.

This comparison shows that in Thindaunggyi Village, there was no significant change in the average acreage of holding for any strata. The reason for this small variation is that the farmland in Thindaunggyi Village has long been irrigated, allowing for double cropping, so farmland prices have been much higher than in Zeepinwea village, which was non-irrigated and paddy-rice monoculture. Moreover, in Thindaunggyi, the area of land inherited or sold at one time was usually smaller. However, a detailed comparison of each stratum shows that the area of the upper-class farmers decreased, the area of the middle-class farmers remained almost the same, and the area of the lower-class farmers increased. In other words, the standardisation into a medium-size farmer progressed in Thindaunggyi Village during the 26 years since 1987.

Some households in Thindaunggyi Village sold their farmland for treatment of diseases, but their number was much smaller than in Zeepinwea. This relates to the fact that the custom of "pawn tenancy" exists in Thindaunggyi but not in Zeepinwea. Pawn tenancy means that the pawner transfers his or her cultivation rights to the pawnee in exchange for money for a certain period of time (often three years). In this case, a lump sum of cash for three years is paid in advance. In Zeepinwea Village, the tenant rent in 2013 ranged from 50,000 to 100,000 kyats for a monocropping paddy field per acre, and twice that for a double cropping, and was paid after harvest, measured by the price of paddy. In Thindaunggyi Village, the pawn price was 1,000,000–1,500,000 kyats per acre, paid in advance. With such a large amount of cash, people could cover the cost of treatment for serious illnesses. The price of farmland in Thindaunggyi was 10 times higher than that in Zeepinwea, although it varies from year to year and from place to place. Thus, it is unlikely that a farmer above the middle class be left landless after selling all their farmland due to illness.

In Thindaunggyi Village, the sale and purchase of farmland was active since the socialist era, but there were few rentals (Takahashi, 2000: 124). However, the number of rentals began to increase due to the policy of a market economy during the military regime. In my 1994 survey, of the 75 households that held the right to cultivate farmland, four pawned part of their farmland and 10 were the pawnees of other people's farmland, in addition to one woman who temporarily asked her brother to work as a tenant due to the sudden death of her husband. There were three cases of households renting or pawning all their farmland and one case of pawn tenancy by a household with no cultivation rights at all, so the total number of farm households in the village at the time of the 1994 survey was 73. In 2013, of the 33 households sampled based on their farmland tenure in 1987, only three had lost all of their farmland. At the same time, three formerly landless households had acquired farmland. There was no significant change in the number of cultivation right holders, as in Zeepinwea Village. Of the 33 farm households surveyed in 2013, two pawned part of their farmland and two pawned all of their farmland to pay for medical treatment, while three landless households took others' farmland as pawn for cultivation. Consequently, the number of farm households in the sample households was 34. Despite the active buying and selling of cultivation rights for agricultural land, the number of farmers who become non-farmers was much lower than in Zeepinwea Village. This may be due to the high price of farmland, which allows for cut and sell, the existence of pawn tenancy, and the fact that there were many other employment opportunities in addition to farming.

There was an incident when such expensive farmland was seized for free. This was due to a garrison of the Myanmar military. As far as we could find in the village, four households had their farmland confiscated by the military in 1984 for rice cultivation in paddy fields, and seven households had their farmland confiscated from 1993 to 1996. The former were not compensated, but some farmers received some amount of cash for the latter confiscation. In 2015, these households filed a complaint with the relevant authorities to reclaim their farmland.

We have described in detail the changes in agricultural landholding in these two villages. Let us consider this in conjunction with the increase in the proportion of non-farmers observed in the change in the occupational composition, that is, with *de-agrarianisation* in the occupational structure. In Zeepinwea Village, many households lost their farmland and became non-farmers (see Table 4.3), thereby the number of farm households decreased. In contrast, in Thindaunggyi Village, the number of farm households did not decrease but increased slightly, both among the sample households and in the village as a whole. The number of non-farmers increased in Thindaunggyi Village because the children of farmers who divided households by splitting from their parents' households through *oekhwe* inherited farmland that had already been greatly shrunk by their parents' generation. Moreover, the children of non-farm households also became independent through *oekhwe*. In the case of Zeepinwea village, the increase in the number of non-farm households due to these factors was much larger than due to the fall of farm households, and this was compounded by the influx of non-farm households from other villages.

4.6 Transformation of Agricultural Production

4.6.1 Zeepinwea Village

The agricultural production pattern of Zeepinwea Village was a monoculture of rainfed rice, as has been common in the delta region of Myanmar. In 1996, water from the Ngamoeyeik Canal began to flow into the paddy fields where some villagers grow rice, and some of the rice fields became irrigated, allowing for double cropping. Irrigated "summer paddy" (dry-season rice) cultivation, which spread rapidly in the 1990s during the military regime, was also introduced here and there in the delta region.

Before this, from 1987 to 1994, there was no change in the farming methods in Zeepinwea. Traditional rice monoculture had been carried out since before the country's independence. In what follows, I will first describe this situation, and then describe the later changes in farming methods, to explore the overall history over the quarter century after 1987.

In the village of Zeepinwea, when the rainy season arrived, usually in late May, the villagers repaired the ridges between rice fields and began ploughing and puddling paddy fields filled with rainwater. Two bullocks or water buffaloes[20] were connected at the neck with a wooden yoke, and a wooden beam was connected directly to the centre of this yoke to pull the plough or harrow. The man who steered the cattle controlled the yoke with a handle. In the central plains and deltas, where many ethnic Bamar people live, this Indian-type yoke plough was used widely (Takahashi, 2000: 77). Walking tractors[21] began to spread around 2004. In January 2014, eight of the 55 farmers in the village owned one. In the case of draught cattle, rentals had been rare, but walking tractors were frequently rented. Even so, not all rice field preparation was completed using only walking tractors. All the eight households who owned walking tractors also raised oxen or bullocks.

Concurrently with preparing the main paddy field, nurseries were made, and paddy seeds were sown. In 1987, all farmers were still forced to transplant rice seedlings by the state, but in 1994, 40.1% (295 acres) of the 735 acres of rice planted by farmers in the village were directly sown with germinated paddy seeds. In 2013,[22] sampled households had a total of 162 acres of rainy-season paddy fields, of which 72 acres, or 44.4%, were directly sown. The tendency for farmers with larger holdings to do direct seeding was the same in 1994 and 2013. However, in most of the direct-sown paddy fields, supplementary planting was done where germination was poor.

---

[20] Bullocks over four years old, as well as male and female buffaloes over three years old, were used. They are collectively called draught cattle.

[21] In Burmese, it is called *le'tûnhtunze'*, that is, "hand-operated tractor".

[22] In my 1987 survey, Zeepinwea interviews covered agricultural activities done from April 1986 to March 1987; in the 1994 survey, interviews covered agriculture done from April 1993 to March 1994; and in the 2014 survey, interviews covered agriculture from January 2013 to December 2013. For Thindaunggyi Village, the same was done in 1987 and 1994, while the 2013 survey covered agricultural activities from April 2012 to March 2013.

While direct sowing and uprooting of seedlings were done by men, transplanting and supplementary planting of rice were done by women. In transplanting, seedlings were usually planted by holding them directly by hand, but in rice fields with deep water and where manual planting was difficult, seedlings were thrust into the soil by holding them between a split-ended bamboo stick called *hkayin* (fork). Although there was no difference between direct sowing and transplanting in terms of seed varieties, many farmers planted more than one variety in order to equalise the farming season and avoid risks. When the sown area was divided into local varieties and high-yielding varieties, the latter was compulsorily transplanted since 1981 (Takahashi, 1992: 102). The proportion of local varieties increased from only 16.4% in the 1987 survey to 54.4% in 1994, indicating a return to local varieties. In addition, 95.7% of the paddy fields in the 2013 rainy-season crop were planted with glutinous rice and a local variety called *taungbyang*, while high-yielding varieties were almost absent. The number of local varieties started to increase around 2003 simply because of their high market price. It was as if the equalisation of the farming season and risk aversion had been forgotten.

After the rice had been planted, supplementary planting was done if the rice that was transplanted or direct sown did not germinate and grow well. In addition, the villagers fertilised the field with urea and control insect numbers by collecting insects in burnt kerosene. However, they rarely did weeding and water management, which are typical of fertility management, because the paddy fields rapidly increase their water depth during the rainy season, making water control impossible. Yet, this increase in water levels reduces weed growth, so some yield can be expected without weeding. In 2013, kerosene ignition was not used to kill insects, and the rice plants were left in the paddy fields without herbicides or insecticides.

After 120–130 days for high-yielding varieties and 140–180 days for local varieties, the rice would be ready for harvest. All rice harvesting was done with a sickle called a *dazin*. Local rice varieties were reaped about 30 cm from the root, while high-yielding varieties were cut from the root. The reason was that the cattle did not get enough food if the high-yielding varieties are cut too high. However, in the 1990s, some villagers began to re-cut the stubble because the cultivation of *kau'yô hmou*, or paddy straw mushrooms, began to flourish. The growers began to hire labourers to cut the stubble. In 1998, paddy straw mushrooms were no longer cultivated due to the outbreak of fungi. The traditional high cutting method was temporarily revived due to the increase in the number of local rice varieties.

The harvested ears of paddy were taken to the threshing floor called *talîn*. To prepare this floor, people sprinkled water on the ground in paddy fields or gardens, and then a yoke of cattle pulled a log called an *jândôun* over that ground to level the soil and to dry it to make it crunchy. The ears laid out on the *talîn* was trampled by several oxen and ox carts, and threshing proceeded. The threshed paddy, which was full of rubbish, was placed in baskets hung under the apex of a *sinn*—which was made up of several metres of wood or bamboo in the shape of a triangular pyramid—and was winnowed by waiting for the wind to blow. Threshing machines began to be used in the threshing process around 2003, and by 2007, *talîn* disappeared from the paddy fields around Zeepinwea Village. In 2013, there were 6 households in the village that owned a thresher. The wind-winnowing system was also replaced by the Chinese winnower (*yàha'*). Thus, the triangular turreted *sinn*, which could be seen from a distance, disappeared. Finally, harvesting by combine harvesters started to increase around 2016, making threshers and winnowers useless.

The introduction of walking tractors and threshers was not for saving labour but for the summer paddy cultivation that started in 1996. Ploughing and levelling in summer paddy cultivation is done from late December to late January. Thus, it is impossible for oxen or buffaloes to plough the paddy fields that have begun to harden in the dry season, and to dig up the stubble that is still fresh and firmly rooted in the soil, even if the fields are still wet. It is also impossible for cattle to complete tillage and land preparation work in a short period of time after harvesting the monsoon (rainy season) paddy. In the beginning, farmers borrowed used walking tractors from the Department of Agricultural Mechanisation under the Ministry of Agriculture and Irrigation, but eventually, they began taking out loans to buy new walking tractors. They ploughed not only their own paddy fields but also those of others, thus repaying the loans in three years. Threshing machines, too, were indispensable for summer paddy cultivation. The harvest season for summer paddy is in May when the rainy season is just around the corner, so there is no time for threshing leisurely in *talîn*. If the paddy is not threshed quickly with a thresher, the paddy becomes wet, and the quality and yield of the paddy are reduced. Combine harvesters can complete this process even faster. However, farmers did not have enough money to buy combine harvesters, thus these machines came from outside the village with drivers. Mechanisation began with the need for summer paddy cultivation, but of course these machines were also used in monsoon paddy cultivation.

In the dry season of 2013, 13 of the 22 sampled farm households were engaged in summer paddy cultivation. Although it is common sense that summer paddy is non-photosensitive, high-yielding modern varieties, out of the total 56.5 acres of summer paddy cultivated by these households, 25 acres were local and traditional varieties of glutinous rice. It was said that glutinous rice varieties needed less chemical fertiliser and could be sold at high prices for brewing.

Long before summer paddy cultivation began, groundnut was grown in the dry season as an after-crop to paddy rice. However, groundnut was planted on less than one tenth of the area of monsoon paddy cultivation, and it was only cultivated sparingly for oil subsistence. Land preparation for groundnut began in mid-November, when the harvest of early and medium-maturing paddy was over and the soil was still moist. The ploughing with a plough and pressuring with a log called *jândôun* were repeated four or five times. The sowing process was completed by sowing seeds and pressuring again. No fertilisers or pesticides were used, and no weeding or ploughing was carried out. The harvest season arrived in four or five months. Because of this coarse cultivation method, yield was less than half of the yield around Magway in central Myanmar.

Green gram (*Vigna radiata*), called *pêdhisêin* in Burmese, came to the village around 1996, when the irrigation canal flowed onto the paddy fields. In the beginning, it was cultivated in the same way as groundnut, but the method was changed to ploughing once with a walking tractor, sowing and ploughing again with a walking tractor, and then applying pressure with a *jândôun* log drawn by a cattle yoke to prevent transpiration of moisture. As in the case of groundnut, no fertiliser was applied, but a large amount of nutrients and insecticides were used, and sometimes fungicides were also used. Unlike groundnut, green gram is a commercial crop. At one time, its area sown was close to one third of the monsoon paddy area. When I talked to a farmer in 2008, he said that if he could harvest 10 baskets[23] per acre and sell it at 15,000 kyats per basket, he could make his money back, but farmgate prices were actually much higher than that and continued to rise. Since green gram farming brought incomparably higher benefits to farmers than paddy rice did, its cultivation should have become more and more popular. However, in the dry season of 2013, only four of the 22 sample farmers planted green gram; by 2017, none of the farmers in the village were growing the crop. No amount of pesticides could prevent the spread of pests and fungus. Even if they did plant green gram, it would only cost them more and they could not expect to get 10 baskets, so they stopped growing it. Thus, groundnut was revived. With the introduction of new varieties, the productivity of groundnut increased, and some farmers began to sell the extracted oil. In addition, some farmers turned their paddy fields into vegetable gardens and began to grow seasonal vegetables and fruits all year round.

4.6.2 Thindaunggyi Village

Thindaunggyi Village is located in the central arid region of Upper Myanmar, where rainfall is so low that it is impossible to cultivate rice with rainwater alone. However, irrigation from the Minye Canal, which is one of the irrigation canals from the Zawgyi River that flows from the Shan Plateau, has been used for double cropping of rice and for various patterns of other double cropping.[24]

Two types of rice are grown in the village. One type is *mojoe* (*môujou*) rice, which is sown in the nursery in late March, transplanted from mid-April to mid-May, before the rainy season, using irrigation water, and harvested from early July to early August, during the rainy season. *Mojoe* rice has been classified as "summer paddy" since the early 1990s—when the Ministry of Agriculture named dry-season rice the "summer paddy" and started its extension—but this rice has been grown for much longer time. The other type is *kaukkyi* (*kau'cî*) rice, which is sown in the nursery in early July, after the start of the rainy season, transplanted in early August, and harvested from mid-November to late December, after the rainy season. In rainy-season cropping, some years have no rainfall during the planting season and thus irrigation water

[23] One basket (*tîn* in Burmese) is a unit of volume in Myanmar and is equal to 9 English gallons (about 40.9 litres). During the colonial period, paddy and rice were measured in this volume, but after the start of the paddy procurement during the socialist period, one basket (one *tîn*) was instead defined as 20.8 kg of paddy with a moisture content of 15%. In the case of green gram, one basket is 32.7 kg.

[24] For the agricultural calendar of Thindaunggyi Village, see Takahashi (2000: 78). For the irrigation system and management in the village, see Takahashi (1993: 51–62).

is immediately required, while in other years the rainy season ends early and thus irrigation is required after the rainy season.

Mojoe (*môujou*) means "before (*cou* = *jou*) the rainy season (*môu*)" and is a general term for crops sown before the rainy season. The *mojoe* rice varieties included in this category are all non-photosensitive high-yielding and early-maturing varieties with a growing period of 110–120 days. The introduction of high-yielding varieties in the early 1980s led to a rapid increase in *mojoe* cultivation in Thindaunggyi and the broader Kyaukse district. The socialist government encouraged *mojoe* cultivation because it is harvested during the period of short supply in the middle of the rainy season. However, under the paddy procurement system, the advantage of being harvested at a time of scarcity was not valued in terms of price.

On the other hand, any crops cultivated during the rainy season and usually harvested in the dry season are called *kaukkyi* in this region. Monsoon paddy is also called *kaukkyi*. The term "*kaukkyi*" means "long rice" and is a generic term for local late-maturing, long-stemmed rice varieties with a long growing period of 150–160 days. In my 1987 survey, all rice varieties grown as monsoon paddy were local *kaukkyi*. In other words, the name of the rice variety and the name of the cropping season were the same. However, in the 1990s, high-yielding varieties became gradually used in the rainy season. The same rice variety became called "*mojoe*" if it was sown before the rainy season and "*kaukkyi*" if it was planted during the rainy season. In contrast to the return to local varieties in Zeepinwea village, by 2013, any paddy cultivated in the rainy season in Thindaunggyi had changed to high-yielding varieties. In Lower Myanmar, where Zeepinwea is located, it is customary to entertain the guests with local rice varieties called *po san* (*taungbyan* is one of them) or *ngakywê pyu*, and even now, *po san* is the most expensive rice. In Thindaunggyi, which is located in Upper Myanmar, as in the villages in Lower Myanmar, people disliked the taste of high-yielding rice varieties that were forced into the village in the 1980s, and used local varieties for home-cooked rice and feasts. However, in the 1990s, a new high-yielding variety of rice called "*ayeyarmin* (*eyamîn*)",[25] with a medium maturing period (140 days), was introduced for *kaukkyi* to the village. Thereafter, farmers gradually accepted this variery as rice for home consumption and it eventually replaced the local varieties. Thus, the local long-stemmed and late-maturing variety of *kaukkyi* disappeared from the paddy fields, leaving only the name of the cropping season.

The process of paddy rice cultivation was almost the same in both *mojoe* and *kaukkyi*. Stable manure was added to paddy fields in January and February during the dry season, and ploughing and harrowing were done in March for *mojoe* and in August for *kaukkyi* by a yoke of cattle. There are no buffaloes in the villages of Upper Myanmar because it is too hot and water is scarce. Nowadays, most Thindaunggyi farmers who hold cultivation rights for more than 4 acres of farmland own walking tractors, unlike in Zeepinwea Village. Even so, they still use oxen for the final levelling work before transplanting. Many farmers still keep oxen for this purpose. After the

[25] Ayeyarmin is a gamma-irradiated mutant of *machando*, imported from Malaysia in 1977. Not an IR strain but classified as a high-yielding variety. It is especially popular in Kyaukse District.

preparation of the main field was completed, the women transplanted the seedlings. In Thindaunggyi Village, direct sowing is not practised as in Zeepinwea, because weeds grow faster than rice plants there due to low rainfall and the slow increase in water depth. In addition, weeding is done, which is also different from the villages in Lower Myanmar. This is probably because weeds cannot there be suppressed by water. This weeding work was also done by women, and all weeding in the paddy fields had long been done by hand. However, herbicides have also been used since the turn of the century. At the time of my 2013 survey, of the 34 farmers sampled, five households used herbicides during the dry season and three used herbicides during the rainy season. Herbicide spraying was a men's job.

Subsequent rice harvesting was done in Thindaunggyi in the same way as in Zeepinwea. Threshing was not done in a *talîn* in the paddy field, but the bundles of rice plants were carried to the house lot and threshed by cattle. Winnowing machines had been used since the socialist era, instead of *sinns*. In 2008, there was only one thresher in the village, so the threshing fee was 4 baskets per 100 baskets of paddy, but the following year, the fee was reduced to 3 baskets due to the increase in the number of machines. However, after harvesting by combine harvesters started to spread around 2016, threshers were no longer hired. The same was true in Zeepinwea, where the rice-harvesting labour charge and the rent for combine harvesters were almost the same, while the combine harvesters were cheaper for threshing and winnowing. In Thindaunggyi, as in Zeepinwea, the farmers suddenly began to hire combine harvesters without going through the reaper and binder stages. This is an example of the phenomenon of leapfrogging, similar to when mobile phones began spreading without fixed-line telephones having spread before. The harvested rice plants and threshed paddy used to be transported to the village and dried in the sun, but now the rice millers and brokers buy the wet paddy directly from the paddy fields.

Sesame seeds are generally grown during the rainy season in Myanmar, but in Thindaunggyi village, they were harvested at the beginning of the rainy season. In Kyaukse region, this kind of sesame is called *mojoe* ("before rainy season") sesame. Ploughing started around the full moon day of the month of *Tabaung* (mid to late March), using irrigation water to sow sesame. Sesame was rarely cultivated as a single crop, and was usually double-cropped with *kaukkyi* rice, onions or garlic.

Chilli pepper was prepared for production in November and grown in gardens and some paddy fields. Transplanting began in mid-January when irrigation water was drawn into the fields, after which it grew using irrigation water and was harvested several times from May to July. Chilli pepper was usually grown after *kaukkyi* rice in irrigated fields, but some farmers grew it after *mojoe*.

Onion and garlic are both called "*chetton* (*ce'thon*)" in Burmese, with the red one being onion (*ce'thon ni*) and the white one being garlic (*ce'thon hpyu*). Not only are the names the same, but the cropping season and cultivation method were also almost the same. The plants were planted around the end of November and irrigated immediately. They required water for less than a month. They were harvested in March, after being irrigated once in mid-January and again a month later. Although they did not require much water, irrigation was essential.

Around Thindaunggyi Village, the paddy fields for onion and garlic are called "*chetton* fields", and those for summer paddy are called "*mojoe* fields". The "*chetton* fields" are located at the end of the canal, so they are poorly irrigated and cannot be used to grow *mojoe* rice. In some years, there was no irrigation water at all in these *chetton* fields, so water had to be drawn up from the drainage canal by a pump with a diesel engine.

In 1994, I surveyed all 73 farm households in the village on what they grow and how much. 52 households planted an average of 3.27 acres of *mojoe* rice, 68 households planted an average of 4.35 acres of *kaukkyi* rice, 40 households planted an average of 3.02 acres of sesame, 15 households planted an average of 0.96 acres of chilli, 26 households planted an average of 1.80 acres of onion, and 21 households planted an average of 1.32 acres of garlic (Takahashi, 2000: 209). In 2013, I surveyed a sample of 34 farm households. 20 households planted an average of 3.47 acres of *mojoe* rice, 32 households planted an average of 3.88 acres of *kaukkyi* rice, 8 households planted an average of 1.43 acres of sesame, 3 households planted an average of 0.70 acres of chilli, and 22 households planted an average of 3.35 acres of onion. No household grew garlic. Because of the difference in sample size between 1994 and 2013, I will compare the ratio of the number of farmers planting each crop to the total number of farmers and the average area of each crop. This comparison shows that the number of farmers planting *mojoe* rice decreased but the average area of *mojoe* rice increased slightly, while *kaukkyi* rice was grown by most farmers in both years but the average area decreased slightly. It can be said that neither changed significantly. As for other crops, the number of households growing sesame, chilli, and garlic decreased sharply, while the number of households growing onions and the area planted with onion per household increased dramatically. The reason for the large increase in onion cultivation is that its export expanded, and the price increased. Sesame and pepper decreased because their harvesting season coincides with the harvesting season of the *mojoe* and the transplanting season of the *kaukkyi*, making it difficult to secure labour. The price of garlic did not rise as much as that of onions, despite the large capital investment needed, so only onions were planted in the *chetton* fields.

In the past, there were diverse cropping patterns in Thindaunggyi Village. If *kaukkyi* rice cultivation was the main season crop, there were five patterns of *double* cropping, combining *mojoe* rice, sesame, chilli, onion and garlic as the second crop. There were also cropping patterns such as sesame to garlic or onion, a double cropping that did not include rice cropping, and mono-cropping of *mojoe* rice or *kaukkyi* rice. However, in response to the development of the market economy, people's rational choice to grow what is profitable resulted in cropping patterns with a significant loss of varieties. The current remaining cropping patterns are double cropping of *mojoe* rice and *kaukkyi* rice, *kaukkyi* rice and onion, or a monoculture of these two crops. Even so, paddy rice cultivation, which is not highly profitable, is still prioritised. This is because of the strong recognition that rice is Myanmar's staple food, the relatively stable rice price due to the minimum price guarantee system (even though all rice is traded on the market), and the policy guidance, including the Farmland Law, that treats only rice specially. On the other hand, the introduction of irrigation into the paddy monoculture fields in Zeepinwea Village allowed for double cropping, and narrowed the gap in agricultural income between Zeepinwea and Thindaunggyi villages.

4.7 Fertiliser Input and Yield

As a continuation of the changes in agricultural technology, let us review the changes in fertiliser inputs and yield per acre.

4.7.1 Zeepinwea Village

Table 4.7 shows the fertiliser input, yield and their average annual changes in Zeepinwea village. Stable manure, which is made by mixing cattle manure with straw and fallen leaves, is put into the paddy field during the dry season (February–March) and ploughed into the field to become the basal application. The amount of manure input increased from 1987 to 1994, but this was because some farmers used stable manure as a substitute for phosphatic fertiliser. The decrease in the number of inputs from 1994 to 2013 was because the number of cattle and buffaloes had decreased. Cattle are indispensable for ploughing and levelling paddy fields and threshing paddy, but with the introduction of walking tractors and threshers, they have become less needed. Once combine harvesters come in, it will be more difficult to secure straw, so the number of cattle will decrease and the amount of stable manure input will also decline.

As for chemical fertilisers, the input of urea increased slightly between 1987 and 1994 and then rose at an annual rate of 2.9% between 1987 and 2013. As will be discussed below, the price of urea fertiliser soared between 1987 and 1994, but farmers bought it even though it was expensive. In return, they gave up buying triple super phosphate (TSP), the price of which did not rise as much as urea. Farmers chose urea, which is the most important nutrient for paddy rice, regardless of its relative price. The input of TSP appears to have fluctuated greatly: it was not used around 1994, but returned to being normal in 2013. As for potash fertiliser,[26] it was rarely used after the beginning of the post-socialist military regime. However, since the compound fertiliser, which started to be used around 2017, includes potassium, the input amount has been returning to the socialist period.

A comparison between the rate of increase in fertiliser input and the rate of increase in the yield of monsoon paddy shows that the increase in yield was larger from 1987 to 1994 and smaller from 1994 to 2013. This may be due to the return

[26] In Myanmar, potassium chloride, potassium nitrate and potassium sulphate are used as potash fertilisers.

Table 4.7 Fertiliser input and yield in Zeepinwea Village

Year	Inputs and yields per acre							Average annual rate of increase (%)			
	1987		1994		2013			1987–1994		1994–2013	
Crop	Monsoon Paddy	Groundnut	Monsoon Paddy	Groundnut	Monsoon Paddy	Groundnut	Summer Paddy	Monsoon Paddy	Groundnut	Monsoon Paddy	Groundnut
Stable manure (cart)	0.70		0.96		0.27			4.50		− 6.41	
Urea (kg)	19.39		20.14		34.90		66.40	0.54		2.93	
TSP (kg)	8.92		0.01		15.30		31.00	− 62.11		47.09	
Potash (kg)	4.62		0.01		None		None	− 58.37			
Pesticide use	None	None	None	None	None	None	Use				
Yield (basket)	31.90	18.10	37.50	15.70	48.10	31.00	73.50	2.32	− 2.01	1.33	3.65

Note 1 TSP is triple super phosphate

Note 2 A basket (*tin* in Burmese) is the Myanmar unit of volume, with one basket or one *tin* equal to nine British gallons

Source According to the author's survey

to local varieties with low adaptability for heavy maturing and fertiliser efficiency, rather than the diminishing effect of increased fertiliser inputs.

The yield of monsoon paddy in Zeepinwea was the lowest in 1987, when the proportion of high-yielding varieties was the highest, and increased by 1994, when the proportion of high-yielding varieties decreased to about half of the total area sown. The yield increased further in 2013 when most of the high-yielding varieties disappeared. The reason for this is not that the yields of local varieties are better, but that the yields of high-yielding varieties, which are usually 70–80 baskets per acre, were significantly lower in this village. High-yielding varieties are susceptible to diseases and insects, and in Zeepinwea, frequent outbreaks of rice stem borer and brown spot have hindered the increase in yield. It was difficult for the farmers, who did not use pesticides, to eradicate these diseases. However, this was not the case in the introduction of summer paddy cultivation in 1996, which had a high yield of 73.5 baskets per acre. This is because pesticides were used when pests were present.

Despite no fertilisers or pesticides being used, the yield of groundnut increased at an annual rate of 3.7% from 1994 to 2013. This is because varieties with higher yields became popular. However, only a small number of farmers were growing groundnut, on a very small scale. It is difficult to predict whether it will be planted by many farmers, as it was during the socialist period, or whether commercial production will develop over a large area, as it did in the case of green gram. If I dare to speculate, even if commercial production were to take place, it is unlikely that Zeepinwea would be able to compete with groundnut farmers in the Magway area. Even if groundnut continues to be grown, it would most likely remain in semi-subsistence production on a very small scale.

4.7.2 Thindaunggyi Village

The fertiliser inputs were higher in Thindaunggyi Village than in Zeepinwea Village, both in terms of stable manure and chemical fertiliser, as shown in Table 4.8. This is probably because the village has a lot of double-cropped fields, which require more fertiliser. Stable manure is ploughed into the paddy fields before the summer paddy (*mojoe*) cultivation in February and March. The applied amount of stable manure decreased at a fairly rapid rate, averaging 8.7% per year from 1987 to 1994 and 6.0% from 1994 to 2013. This is because the number of cattle declined, including not only draught cattle but also cows and calves.

More chemical fertiliser is used in summer paddy cultivation than in monsoon paddy cultivation. As for summer paddy, urea input declined from 1987 to 1994 because its price had soared too much. The input of triple super phosphate (TSP) decreased much more than the input of urea (12.7% *versus* 4.5% per year), even though TSP's price did not increase as much as urea's price and its relative price to urea fell substantially. This is probably because, as in Zeepinwea, priority was given to urea, which for paddy crop is most important, and thus the purchase of TSP was

Table 4.8 Fertiliser input and yield in Thindaunggyi Village

Year	Inputs and yields per acre									Average annual rate of increase (%)					
	1987			1994			2013			1987–1994			1994–2013		
Crop	Summer Paddy	Monsoon Paddy	Onion	Summer Paddy	Monsoon Paddy	Onion	Summer Paddy	Monsoon Paddy	Onion	Summer Paddy	Monsoon Paddy	Onion	Summer Paddy	Monsoon Paddy	Onion
Stable manure (cart)	3.02			1.61			0.50			– 8.65			– 5.96		
Urea (kg)	78.51	29.74	9.52	57.03	40.95	2.06	61.69	50.10	53.39	– 4.46	4.67	– 19.65	0.41	1.07	18.69
TSP (kg)	22.98	23.66	11.36	8.91	37.25	19.80	57.72	42.94	41.87	– 12.66	6.70	8.26	10.33	0.75	4.02
Potash (kg)	9.53	1.29						(7.54)							
Pesticide use	None	None	None	None	None	Use	Use	Use	Use						
Yield (basket or viss)	68.80	35.10	692.62	66.80	46.00	786.32	93.25	58.99	1,159.89	– 0.41	3.94	1.83	1.77	1.31	2.07

Note 1 The unit of measurement for paddy is basket, and for onion is viss (*pei'tha*)
Note 2 Viss or p*ei'tha* is a traditional unit of weight in Myanmar. 1 viss was set at 3.6 pounds (approximately 1.63 kg) during the colonial period
Source According to the author's survey

reduced. The amount of TSP input to summer paddy cultivation in 1994 was much smaller than during rainy-season cultivation.

As for fertiliser inputs in monsoon paddy, inputs increased consistently. From 1987 to 1994, urea input grew at an annual rate of 4.7%, despite high prices, and TSP input grew at an annual rate of 6.7% when relative prices declined. Between 1994 and 2013, the rate of increase decreased dramatically, but both urea and TSP input still increased gradually. The reason for this decrease in the rate of increase was that more farmers used compound fertiliser. Incidentally, there were no farmers using compound fertiliser for summer paddy cultivation.

Potash fertiliser was rationed in 1987, during the socialist period, but was subsequently disused since it was available neither by rationing nor in the market. However, the use of compound fertiliser, which contained potassium, started around 2010. The intersection of the 2013 column and the potash fertiliser in the table shows the input per acre of compound fertiliser, not potash alone, for reference.

Chemical fertilisers were not rationed for onions during the socialist period, so farmers kept the fertiliser that had been rationed for monsoon paddy farming and instead applied it to onions. Although this was a dangerous practice that, if known to the authorities, could have resulted in the forfeiture of cultivation rights, it seems that as long as the procurement quotas were met, there was a patronage by *nalehmu*. Similar illegal diversions were taking place wherever double cropping was possible at the time. In 1994, urea was freely available in the market, but because of its high price, TSP was applied more than usual. The use of pesticides, which was not present in 1987, was confirmed in 1994. The amount of fertiliser applied to onions increased significantly from 1994 to 2013. This is exports to neighbouring countries led to a dramatic rise in onion prices. Productivity per acre also increased at an annual rate of 2.1%—though not as much as the increase in fertiliser inputs—to 1.5 times higher in 2013 than in 1994.

The relationship between the rate of change in paddy yields and fertiliser inputs shows that the amount of fertiliser applied to summer paddy (*mojoe*) decreased significantly from 1987 to 1994, but the yield did not decrease so much. This is because the rice variety was changed from *sin thiri* to *manawthukha*, which is a higher yielding variety. During this period, the yield increase of monsoon paddy (*kaukkyi*) was 3.9% per year, which was not as high as the rate of increase in fertiliser input, but the effect of increased fertiliser inputs was substantial. The increase in the TSP input to summer paddy from 1994 to 2013 was as high as 10.3% per annum, but this was due to abnormally low inputs in 1994, and if it had been applied normally in 1994, the annual growth rate would have been only about 1%, as high as for urea and TSP inputs for monsoon paddy. This means that fertiliser inputs to both summer and monsoon paddy increased steadily from 1994 to 2013, although the rate of increase was low. It is also possible to say that the yield of both crops increased more than the rate of increase in fertiliser input. In Thindaunggyi Village, despite the fact that only high-yielding varieties were cultivated in both the rainy season and the dry season, paddy rice was harvested steadily, without the spread of diseases that troubled Zeepinwea village.

4.8 Changes in Agricultural Prices

Changes in agricultural technology interrelate with the prices of agricultural inputs and agricultural products. Therefore, let us review how the prices have changed for farmland, for inputs such as cattle, ox carts, fertiliser, and labour, and for products such as paddy and onions at the farm gates in the two villages. Since prices in Myanmar have risen substantially over the past quarter century, let us also include price changes in US dollar terms, as well as in kyats in the supplementary table.

The results are shown in Tables 4.9 and 4.10. However, as mentioned earlier, until 2012, Myanmar had several exchange rates. In this book, we use the *market* rate that farmers could use in 1994 and 2013, but in 1987, we use the official rate at the time when one US dollar was 6.12 kyats, because the prices of fertiliser, paddy, and other important commodities were linked to this official rate.[27]

4.8.1 Zeepinwea Village

As shown in Table 4.9, the price of paddy, the main crop in Zeepinwea Village, increased at an average annual rate of 49.8% from 1987 to 1994. However, the sharp rise in domestic rice prices did not affect export prices, as rice prices fell slightly in dollar terms. In 1987, the price of paddy was kept low under the procurement system. After procurement, only about as much rice as was needed for home consumption was left, and even if more rice was left, it had to be sold at the official low price. In 1994, the procurement system was still in place, but it had been relaxed considerably. 28.4% of the paddy produced by village farmers was sold to the government agency, Myanmar Agricultural Produce Trading (MAPT), while 13.2% was sold freely. The paddy prices in the table are calculated by taking this into account. Only urea fertiliser price increased at a higher rate than the paddy price. Urea prices increased in dollar terms from 1987 to 1994, because chemical fertilisers had been supplied cheaply by Japanese economic aid during the socialist period, but prices soared after this aid stopped.

At the time of my survey in 1994, the government's fertiliser ration was maintained, but the price was 600 kyats per bag (50 kg) and the supply was insufficient. Accordingly, farmers were forced to buy urea even at the market price of 1000 kyat. The prices in the table consider this market purchase. Comparing the paddy–fertiliser price ratio—that is, how many kilograms of chemical fertiliser could be bought with 1 kg of paddy—between 1987 and 1994, we can see that the urea ratio fell significantly and, conversely, TSP rose. However, at that time, only one out of 66 households applied the latter to its paddy fields, while urea was used by all farmers. Despite the relative price of urea increasing, farmers decided to use urea in order to maintain paddy production, even reducing the input of TSP, the relative price of which had

[27] Until the demonetisation in September 1987, I myself lived in Yangon by exchanging one US dollar at the official rate of about 6 kyats.

Table 4.9 Variation of prices related to agricultural production in Zeepinwea Village

	Price (kyats)			Average annual growth rate (%)		U.S. dollar equivalent ($)		
Year	1987	1994	2013	1987–1994	1994–2013	1987	1994	2013
Paddy fields (kyats/acre)								
lowest price	300	3,000	500,000	38.9	30.9	49	27	513
highest price	400	4,000	2,500,000	38.9	40.3	65	35	2,564
One bullock	3,000	15,000	500,000	25.8	20.3	490	133	513
One cattle cart	3,000	20,000	200,000	31.1	12.9	490	177	205
Urea (kyats/50 kg)	18	746	20,000	70.2	18.9	2.9	6.6	20.5
TSP (kyats/50 kg)	60	400	22,000	31.1	23.5	9.8	3.5	22.6
Potash	35			–100.0		5.7		
Farm gate price								
Summer paddy (kyats/basket)	–	–	3,804					3.9
Monsoon paddy (kyats/basket)	9.55	162	4,575	49.8	19.2	1.6	1.4	4.7
Goundnut (kyats/basket)	56	250	8,000	23.8	20.0	9.2	2.2	8.2
Agricultural labour wage (kyats/day)								
Male	7	70	3,000	38.9	21.9	1.1	0.6	3.1
Female	5	50	2,000	38.9	21.4	0.8	0.4	2.1
Exchange rate (per US$1)	6.12 (30)	113	975	51.7	12.0			
Paddy–Fertiliser price ratio (summer paddy)								
Urea			0.46					
TSP			0.42					

(continued)

Table 4.9 (continued)

	Price (kyats)			Average annual growth rate (%)		U.S. dollar equivalent ($)		
Year	1987	1994	2013	1987–1994	1994–2013	1987	1994	2013
Paddy–Fertiliser price ratio (monsoon paddy)								
Urea	1.28	0.52	0.55	– 12.0	0.3			
TSP	0.38	0.97	0.50	14.3	– 3.4			

Note 1 In 1994, there were two prices for urea: a low government ration price and a high market price. 746 kyats is a weighted average of the two prices, weighted by the quantity purchased by farmers

Note 2 In 1994, paddy was both procured to the government (MAPT) and sold freely in the market. 162 kyats is the weighted average of both prices by sales volume

Note 3 In 2013–14, there was no procurement system and all paddy could be sold freely in the market. Since the price of paddy differs depending on the variety and quality, I weighted the farmgate prices of each farmer by the quantity sold

Note 4 Agricultural labour wages include the cost of meals

Note 5 (Paddy–fertiliser price ratio) = (price of 1 kg of paddy) / (price of 1 kg of fertiliser), that is, the weight (kg) of fertiliser that can be bought with 1 kg of paddy

Source According to the author's survey

Table 4.10 Variation of prices related to agricultural production in Thindaunggyi Village

	Price (kyats)			Average annual growth rate (%)		U.S. dollar equivalent ($)		
Year	1987	1994	2013	1987–1994	1994–2013	1987	1994	2013
Paddy fields (kyats/acre)								
lowest price	3,000	30,000	1,000,000	39.0	20.3	490	265	1,026
highest price	5,000	150,000	7,000,000	62.6	22.4	817	1,327	7,179
One bullock	3,500	15,000	500,000	23.1	20.3	572	133	513
One cattle cart	2,500	15,000	180,000	29.2	14.0	408	133	185
Urea (kyats / 50 kg)	22	780	22,000	66.5	19.2	3.6	6.9	22.6
TSP (kyats / 50 kg)	70	738	20,000	40.0	19.0	11.4	6.5	20.5
Compound fertiliser (kyats / 50kg)			17,000–40,000					
Farm gate price								
Summer paddy (kyats/basket)	9.55	211	4,863	55.6	18.0	1.6	1.9	5.0
Monsoon paddy (kyats/basket)	9.55	223	5,174	56.9	18.0	1.6	2.0	5.3
Onion (kyats/viss)	3	7	392	12.9	23.6	0.5	0.1	0.4
Agricultural labour wage (kyats/day)								
Male	8	90	4,000	41.3	22.1	1.3	0.8	4.1
Female	5	70	3,000	45.8	21.9	0.8	0.6	3.1
Exchange rate (per US$1)	6.12 (30)	113	975	51.7	12.0			
Paddy–Fertiliser price ratio (summer paddy)								
Urea	1.04	0.65	0.53	− 6.6	− 1.0			
TSP	0.33	0.69	0.58	11.2	− 0.8			

(continued)

Table 4.10 (continued)

	Price (kyats)			Average annual growth rate (%)		U.S. dollar equivalent ($)		
Year	1987	1994	2013	1987–1994	1994–2013	1987	1994	2013
Paddy–Fertiliser price ratio (monsoon paddy)								
Urea	1.04	0.69	0.57	– 5.8	– 1.0			
TSP	0.33	0.73	0.62	12.0	– 0.8			
Onion–Fertiliser price ratio								
Urea	4.18	0.28	0.55	– 32.2	3.7			
TSP	1.31	0.29	0.60	– 19.4	3.9			

Note 1 In 1994, the prices of urea and TSP included a low government ration price and a high market price. 780 and 738 kyats are weighted averages of these prices by the quantity purchased by farmers

Note 2 In 1994, there were three sales channels for paddy: government (MAPT), cooperative, and free sale in the market. 211 and 223 kyats are weighted averages of the three types of prices by sales volume

Note 3 In 2013, there was no procurement system and all paddy could be sold freely in the market. Since the price of paddy differs depending on the variety and quality, I weighted the farmgate prices of each farmer by the quantity sold. The same applies to onion

Note 4 For others, the same as in Table 4.9

Source According to the author's survey

fallen. As it turned out, the farmers made the right choice. This is because fertiliser costs, including urea, even when purchased at high prices, only account for about 5% of production costs, while labour costs account for 75%. The average annual increase in labour wages over the seven years from 1987 to 1994 was 38.9% for both men and women, less than the increase in the price of paddy. There was no significant change in the production cost structure during this period, and despite some insect damage, the yield increased slightly, suggesting that the liberalisation of agricultural distribution increased the revenue from rice production and raised the income of farmers in villages where rice is the main crop.

By 2013, there was already no procurement system, and any paddy could be sold freely in the market. However, since the paddy price differed depending on the variety and quality, the farmgate price of each farmer is weighted and averaged by the sales volume in the Table. From 1994 to 2013, the paddy–fertiliser price ratios remained stable, with the urea ratio remaining almost the same and TSP decreasing slightly. Yield grew at an annual rate of 1.33% (Table 4.7) and paddy price soared at 19.2%. This means that gross income per acre increased at an annual rate of 20.8%. On the other hand, agricultural labour wages skyrocketed by 21.9% for men and 21.4% for women per annum. Cattle prices increased by 20.3% per annum. In 2013, as in 1994, the labour-intensive cost structure of production remained almost unchanged. Although farmers claimed that higher wages made farming more difficult, the figures shows that gross income per acre increased at the same rate. This implies that the profitability of paddy farming did not actually decline as much as the farmers felt. However, non-agricultural work opportunities were emerging in the village, where wages for both men and women were 500–1000 kyats/day higher than agricultural wages as of 2013. Consequently, as for rice transplanting, which required the most labour, farmers were forced to call in a large number of female transplanters from outside the village.

In a phenomenon observed in many parts of Myanmar, farmland prices soared in Zeepinwea village since the transition to a market economy during the post-socialist military regime. In dollar terms, too, the prices rose considerably. In 1987, the Land Nationalisation Act strongly prohibited the sale and purchase of cultivation rights, among various transfers, and even if they were secretly sold in *nalehmu*, the land prices were very low due to the low-price paddy procurement system. From 1987 to 1994, both the highest and the lowest paddy field prices increased at an average rate of 38.9% per year, but the price of paddy increased at a rate of 49.8%, which led some farmers to purchase farmland for paddy rice cultivation (Takahashi, 2000: 137). However, from 1994 to 2013, the land prices rose 30.9% per year at the lowest level and 40.3% at the highest level, much higher than the paddy price rise of 19.2%. Nevertheless, the farmland price at the turn of the century was about 20,000–40,000 kyats per acre, and as mentioned earlier, many farmers, including villagers from distant areas, purchased farmland in Zeepinwea and moved into the village. In those days, the land price was low, compared with the profit of 200,000 kyats per acre if the planting of green gram was successful. Since 2008, green gram cultivation often resulted in losses and was no longer a profitable crop, but the land price continued to rise. This is because people began to purchase farmland for speculative purposes, regardless of the agricultural productivity of the land. Namely, the speculators expected that Yangon city and Hlegu town would be expanding and that a new transportation network would be built to connect Yangon with the long-postponed Hanthawaddy International Airport. In this way, farmland in Zeepinwea Village was sold one after another to outsiders, causing a huge outflow of farmland from the village to the outside. The new owners did not cultivate the land themselves, but farmers in Zeepinwea and its vicinity cultivated it as tenants. This was a revival of the absentee landlords who were supposed to have disappeared in the early 1960s. However, the new rent was very low, because the absentee landlords were only interested in speculation and not in making money from farming.

It is also important to consider the relative prices of paddy and oxen. As can be seen from Table 4.9, at the time of the 1987 survey, one ox was worth the same as 7.5–10 acres of paddy field. In other words, the price of 10–12 acres of paddy fields, which is equivalent to *dadounghton*, was slightly higher than the price of one ox. The reason why farmland was inherited undivided in spite of the custom of partitioning inheritance (Takahashi, 1992: 120–126) is that the children who did not get the farmland were satisfied if they got an ox, sometimes with a calf attached to it, as their inheritance property instead of a *dadounghton* farmland. A bullock cart was also acceptable. By 1994, the relative price of farmland had risen to the point where one ox was worth only 4–5 acres. Even so, the number of oxen equivalent to the price of 10 acres of paddy fields was two to three, and it was still possible to make oxen an inheritance property equivalent to *dadounghton* without dividing the farmland. In 2013, the land price per acre ranged from one ox in the cheapest paddy field to five oxen in the most expensive paddy field. 10 acres (*dadounghton*) became equivalent to 10–50 oxen. There was not a single farmer in the village who kept such a large number of cattle, with the number of cattle declining. For farmers who did not have sufficient savings of gold, silver, jewellery, cash, and so on, it became necessary to divide the cultivation right of farmland at the time of inheritance. Thus, *dadounghton* gradually collapsed. Those who inherited only a small amount of farmland could not make a living by farming alone, so they either sold their land or started a second business. In Zeepinwea village, both of these options have increased.

4.8.2 Thindaunggyi Village

In Thindaunggyi Village in 1994, the paddy was sold to a mixture of three channels: to the MAPT, to the cooperative, and to the free market. The prices of summer and monsoon paddy in Table 4.10 are the weighted averages of prices for each of these three sales channels, weighted by their respective sales volumes. The reason why the prices of summer paddy and monsoon paddy were higher in Thindaunggyi than in Zeepinwea is that the higher yield allowed more paddy to be sold in the market, that is, the weighting of higher market prices over official prices was greater when weighted. In 2013, there were no procurements to MAPT or cooperatives, and all rice could be sold freely in the market. Yet the prices of different types of paddy differed, so the Thindaunggyi farmgate prices were calculated using the same method as in Zeepinwea.

In Thindaunggyi, the urea price shot up and the paddy–fertiliser price ratio lessened from 1987 to 1994, but the decline was not as great as in Zeepinwea because of the higher farmgate price of paddy. Nevertheless, in summer paddy cultivation in 1994, farmers chose to reduce TSP input to secure urea input, as in Zeepinwea Village, but the amount of urea input was also lower than in 1987. As for the fertiliser input for monsoon paddy, both urea and TSP input increased since the income from summer paddy could be used to purchase fertilisers. Unlike in Zeepinwea Village, the fertiliser cost accounts for 20% of the production cost in both the wet and dry seasons, so the increase in the price of urea was a serious problem, but more important was the labour cost, which accounts for nearly 60% of the production cost. The average annual increase in agricultural labour wages for men and women from 1987 to 1994 was 41.3 and 45.8%, respectively, while the price of paddy rose 55.6% for summer paddy and 56.9% for monsoon paddy per annum. The yield of summer paddy decreased by 0.4% per year, while that of monsoon paddy increased by 3.95% per year. Cattle prices, which affect draught animal costs, accounting for 10% of production costs, increased at a rate of 23.1% per year. In general, it can be said that the farmers' income from rice cultivation increased due to the reduced burden of selling paddy at official prices.

From 1994 to 2013, the paddy–fertiliser price ratios of urea and TSP declined by 1.0 and 0.8% per year, respectively. This was almost the same for summer and monsoon paddy, with fertiliser prices slightly higher relative to paddy prices. In contrast, the input per acre increased by about 1% per year for both fertilisers, as described earlier. And the annual yield increased by 1.8% in summer paddy and by 1.3% in monsoon paddy. The decrease in the paddy–fertiliser price ratio was almost offset by the increase in the yield, which exceeded the increase in the fertiliser input.

Rice cultivation in Thindaunggyi Village always requires transplanting rice seedlings in both the wet and dry seasons. It is not possible to use direct sowing in some parts of the paddy fields when labour wages rise, as one could in Zeepinwea Village. In 2013, combine harvesters had not yet been introduced, so harvesting was still done by hand. Some farmers used herbicides to save weeding labour, but they were few. In other words, the amount of labour input into paddy rice cultivation was almost the same as in 1994. With this in mind, if we follow the trends in paddy prices and labour wages in Table 4.10, the paddy price increased by 18% per year for both the summer and monsoon paddy, while the labour wages increased by 22% for both men and women. Since yields grew by 1.77% per annum for summer paddy and 1.31% for monsoon paddy, even if agricultural labour costs increased production costs, it does not follow that they reduced profitability. However, it is clear that agricultural labour wages rose relative to the price of paddy, and it is not difficult to imagine that this led to the application of herbicides and the introduction of combine harvesters. Agricultural wages in Thindaunggyi were higher than in Zeepinwea because, as will be explained later, the great prosperity of the Shwetheindaw Paya in this village led to the emergence of various occupations that offered higher wages than agricultural wages.

Onion is not grown in the delta region where Zeepinwea village is located but is a product of the central arid region where Thindaunggyi village is. 3 kyats per viss was the price of onion in 1987. In 1994, it was 7 kyats. The average annual increase was 12.9%, which was significantly less than the price increase of paddy. As mentioned earlier, sesame was the most popular second crop with a large number of households, planted on a large area. It was followed by onion, but the number of onion growers and their acreage were much smaller. However, by the time of my 2013 survey, both the area under cultivation and the number of households growing onion had increased significantly, and it could be said that everything other than rice cultivation was devoted to onion. This was because exports to Malaysia and Indonesia expanded rapidly from about 1998 onwards, followed by Singapore, Bangladesh, India and China, as prices soared. Looking at the price changes from 1994 to 2013, the farmgate price rose at an annual rate of 23.6%, which was a higher rate of increase than for paddy. The amount of fertiliser that could be purchased for one kilogram of onion (onion–fertiliser price ratio) doubled since 1994, suggesting that the onion crop became much more profitable. However, onion cultivation is more labour-intensive than rice cultivation and is more affected by rising agricultural wages. In addition, the use and price of pesticides increased dramatically. According to farmers, the production cost of onion cultivation was around 400,000 kyats per acre, and the price of 400 kyats per viss was a profitable line. 2013 was not a profitable year for onion cultivation, but before that, it sometimes reached 800 kyats, and after the survey, it reached 1200 kyats in 2015 and 1600 kyats in 2016. Some splendid *tait*s, which could be called "onion palaces", were built in the village.

Exports of onions are restricted when domestic prices rise or when the production declines sharply due to disasters, or when exports are suddenly halted due to circumstances in the importing country. Each time this happens, prices fluctuate greatly. Thindaunggyi farmers are well aware of this and have nevertheless increased their onion production. According to the farmers, the production cost for rice was about 200,000 kyats per acre in both the dry and rainy seasons, and since the yield and price were stable, a certain level of profit could be expected every year.[28] On the other hand, they told me that although the price of onion crop was unstable, one acre of onion crop could be as profitable as 3 acres of paddy rice crop. The farmers seem to be trying to secure a certain level of profit from rice cultivation, which has a low risk of price fluctuation, and then further improve their livelihood through onion cultivation, which has a high risk.

To finish our discussion of agricultural price fluctuations in Thindaunggyi Village, let us overview farmland and cattle. In 1987 in Thindaunggyi, unlike in Zeepinwea, the price of one cow was already about the same as the price of one acre of farmland. This is because double cropping was possible, and the second crop could be sold at a higher price in the market without being subject to the procurement system.

[28] From Tables 4.8 and 4.10, it can be estimated that the net revenue per acre of summer paddy is about 250,000 kyats and that of monsoon paddy is about 100,000 kyats in 2013.

Therefore, children did not inherit 8 acres of paddy fields, which is equivalent to *dadounghton*, in a lump sum, and it was common to divide and inherit fields. Some of the children expanded their farmland again, either by combining farmland inherited by their spouses or by buying new paddy fields, and some took up other occupations without giving up their farmland. A few sold all their farmland, as mentioned above. The trend in agricultural land prices between 1987 and 1994 shows that the lowest land prices rose by 39.0% per annum and the highest by 62.6% per annum. The purpose of the buyers was to farm. In paddy fields where double cropping was possible, sufficient returns on investment could be expected in the wake of the liberalisation of agricultural commodity prices.

In the period 1994–2013, paddy fields in the lower price range were purchased for agricultural purposes such as onion cultivation, while those in the middle and higher price ranges were purchased for different purposes. The paddy fields in this category are located along the old National Highway No. 1 and the road leading to Shwetheindaw Paya, and thus can be used for restaurants and gas stations. Some of the paddy fields in these locations were worth not only 7 million kyats per acre, as given in Table 4.10, but even 100 million kyats in 2016. The agricultural revenue from these paddy fields was estimated to be about 500,000 kyats per year at most, which means that the land price was equivalent to 200 years of revenue.

4.9 Expansion of the Non-agricultural Sector

So far, I have discussed how agriculture in these two villages, located over five hundred kilometres apart, changed over a quarter century. Next, I will discuss why these two villages can no longer necessarily be described as "agricultural villages". The main occupations of the householders in the villages have already been reviewed (Tables 4.3 and 4.4). In both villages as a whole, the number of non-farm households, including income, increased significantly. By 2013, the ratio of farm households in the village had fallen significantly compared to 1987 (during the socialist period), to just under 20% in Zeepinwea Village and just over 30% in Thindaunggyi Village. I have already noted that the number of non-farm households increased mainly due to many new households not owning farmland as a result of the practice of dividing households, known as *oekhwe*.

The above discussion is based on assigning one occupation to one household, but it is possible that some household members are employed in other occupations, or that one person is concurrently employed in multiple occupations. Therefore, I will examine the changes in the employment status of each villager rather than each household. However, since this is a sample survey of households who were in the village already in 1987, it does not directly reflect the trend in the village as a whole, where the number of new households that do not own farmland increased due to the *oekhwe* (household division). The sample size is 56 households in Zeepinwea Village and 54 households in Thindaunggyi Village.

Tables 4.11 and 4.12 show the changes in the employment of these household members, divided into three categories: (self-employed) own farming, agricultural labour, non-agricultural employment. In the case where a household member was engaged in multiple occupational categories, I will consider the occupation in which the household member was engaged for the longest period of the year as their occupation. I will describe the case of one person concurrently working in more than one occupational category later. In both villages, the total number of workers in 2013 decreased sharply compared to 1987 and 1994. This is not only because of the village-wide phenomenon of shrinking the size of the household mentioned earlier, but also because the sample households had special reasons, including some householders being too old to work and being supported by their children who split up the household, or still having only few working-age offspring in the households of the offspring who succeeded the original household, which was surveyed in 1994, after the death of their parents.

In Zeepinwea Village, there was no significant change in the number of workers by occupation between 1987 and 1994, but there was a large change from 1994 to 2013.

First, the number of people who were engaged in their own farming—that is, farmers—decreased significantly. The main reason for this is that 13 Zeepinwea households disposed of all their farmland by sale or inheritance, as described above. Although some households had become farm households by purchasing cultivation rights of farmland and some farmed as tenants, the overall decline in the number of farmers and the number of farm households was significant (Table 4.3).

Secondly, the number of women employed in agricultural labour decreased dramatically. As a result, it became difficult to secure transplanters, and they had to be called in from other villages, or some of the paddy fields had to be direct sown. Where did the female transplanters go? As mentioned earlier, they became street vendors selling vegetables and miscellaneous goods on the roadsides around the central market of Hlegu Town. The daily income of a street vendor is lower than that of a rice transplanter, but rice transplanting offers only one month of employment opportunity a year, while street vendors have five days a week all year round, and the labour intensity is lower. The only work in the village for young women with less than a primary school education used to be rice planting and harvesting, but by the 2000s this had completely shifted to street vending. On the other hand, some of the women who graduated from high school or university began to work as seamstresses or clerks in foreign-owned garment factories. Among the 49 female workers in the non-agricultural sector shown in Table 4.11, nine worked as such, and three of the university graduates worked as teachers in or near Zeepinwea Village. In addition, many Karen women worked as housemaids in the homes of foreigners in Yangon, and in recent years, some of them started to work in Singapore in the same occupation.

Third, regarding male workers, there was also a decrease in the number of agricultural hired labourers as well as self-employed owner-farmers, with a contrasting increase in the number of non-agricultural workers. This means that male members of households that had lost their farmland chose to work in the non-agricultural sector

Table 4.11 Number of workers by occupation in Zeepinwea Village

Type of occupation	Own farming			Agricultural labour			Non-agricultural occupation			Total number of workers		
Sex	Male	Female	Total	Male	Female	Total	Male	Female	Total	Male	Female	Total
Number of workers												
1987	46	37	83	20	18	38	23	17	40	89	72	161
1994	45	34	79	23	23	46	19	21	40	87	78	165
2013	22	14	36	12	6	18	36	49	85	70	69	139
Composition ratio: %												
1987	51.7	51.4	51.6	22.5	25.0	23.6	25.8	23.6	24.8			
1994	51.7	43.6	47.9	26.4	29.5	27.9	21.8	26.9	24.2			
2013	31.4	20.3	25.9	17.1	8.7	12.9	51.4	71.0	61.2			

Note 1 "Worker" refers to those who were employed in some occupation during the year up to the time of the survey, including self-employment
Note 2 Each worker is classified according to the occupation in which he or she worked the longest in a year. Therefore, a person is not counted twice
Note 3 "Composition ratio" refers to the ratio of the number of workers in each occupation to the total number of workers (male, female, and total) in each occupational category
Source According to the author's survey

Table 4.12 Number of workers by occupation in Thindaunggyi Village

Type of occupation	Own farming			Agricultural labour			Non-agricultural occupation			Total number of workers		
Sex	Male	Female	Total	Male	Female	Total	Male	Female	Total	Male	Female	Total
Number of workers												
1987	59	45	104	18	33	51	23	8	31	100	86	186
1994	55	41	96	12	24	36	28	17	45	95	82	177
2013	28	24	52	7	20	27	46	26	72	81	70	151
Composition ratio: %												
1987	59.0	52.3	55.9	18.0	38.4	27.4	23.0	9.3	16.7			
1994	57.9	50.0	54.2	12.6	29.3	20.3	29.5	20.7	25.4			
2013	34.6	34.3	34.4	8.6	28.6	17.9	56.8	37.1	47.7			

Note Same as Table 4.11
Source Same as Table 4.11

instead of agricultural employment, and at the same time, the former hired agricultural labourers made the same choice. Motorcycle taxi driver was the most common new job among the younger male population, followed by long-distance cargo driver and assistant, and, among the middle-aged and older age groups, side-car bicycle driver. Some young people began to attach sidecars or rear cars to their motorcycles to carry more persons and goods. Many of the male non-agricultural workers seem to have chosen the transport sector. These are jobs for the relatively less educated. The number of high school and university-educated men was also increasing in the village, although not as much as high school and university-educated women. Such young men worked in foreign-owned factories and offices, four out of 36 in the table.

Among the occupations of Zeepinwea households in Table 4.3, *kyaban*, which is classified as agricultural hired labour, was very common, but only five *kyaban*s were included in my sample households. This is because *kyaban*s were overwhelmingly found in new households that had separated from their parents' households by the *oekhwe*, as well as in households that had migrated from other villages. Such households had not been included in my sample from the beginning.

Unlike Zeepinwea, Thindaunggyi Village saw slight changes already between 1987 and 1994. As shown in Table 4.12, the number of female workers in the non-agricultural sector increased significantly, while the number of female agricultural hired labourers decreased. This is because the female labour force started to engage in plastering, the village occupation. However, women ould not become skilled plasterers, because they worked only as auxiliary, low-paid labourers, mixing plaster and carrying materials.

With regard to changes between 1994 and 2013, Thindaunggyi Village again differs from Zeepinwea in some respects. First, while in Zeepinwea the number of farm households decreased significantly, it remained almost the same in Thindaunggyi. Nevertheless, as in Zeepinwea Village, the number of Thindaunggyi men and women engaged in their own farming decreased significantly. The number of farm households in the sample was 34 in both years, but the number of people engaged in their own farming decreased from 96 to 52, or almost by half from 2.8 to 1.5 people per household. People went to the non-agricultural sector. Parents continued to farm, but their children stopped doing so. Most of the male labour force became plasterers and carpenters in Myanmar's construction boom, while the female labour force became salesclerks for the shops that sprang up around Shwetheindaw Paya. They were the children of small and middle scale farmers who could not keep up with the increase in cash expenditure on agriculture alone. In contrast, the children of rich farmers with large land holdings became shopkeepers, university educated teachers, civil servants, and engineers, and some university educated women became clerical workers in the Paya. However, there were no factory workers, in contrast to Zeepinwea Village. This is *not* because people could not go to the foreign-funded factories, but because better employment opportunities related to the Paya were so readily available in the village.

Second, while the number of female agricultural labourers decreased drastically in Zeepinwea Village, it did not drop much in Thindaunggyi. This is because, as mentioned earlier, double cropping is common in Thindaunggyi, and there are almost uninterrupted employment opportunities for the agricultural labour force, especially female labour, throughout the year (Takahashi, 2000: 251). In contrast, the ratio of male agricultural labourers decreased considerably, because the sons of agricultural labourer households were more likely to work as plasterers.

Third, while the number of non-agricultural workers increased sharply in both villages, the ratio of non-agricultural workers to the total number of workers increased less sharply in Thindaunggyi. While in Zeepinwea it grew from 24.2% to a whopping 61.2%, the increase in Thindaunggyi was from 25.4 to 47.7%. This is because the number of farmers in Zeepinwea Village decreased and the female agricultural labour force shifted to the non-agricultural sector in large numbers, while this did not happen in Thindaunggyi Village. Again, this is because double cropping has long been practised in Thindaunggyi Village, and employment opportunities for agricultural labourers are stable throughout the year. Moreover, since Thindaunggyi land prices are high due to the high productivity of agriculture, farmers can cope with sudden shocks, such as treatment for a serious illness, without having to sell all of their farmland. In any case, de-agrarianisation is clearly progressing in both villages.

Having examined the main occupations, let us now examine the side jobs or occupational multiplicity of households and individuals. Table 4.13 shows how the number of households (upper rows) and individuals (lower rows) in different occupational categories changed in Zeepinwea Village. In 1987, 35 out of 56 sampled households were dual-income households. We can see that a large number—16—of these dual-income households engaged in both their own farming and in non-agricultural activities.

Eight of these 16 households had a male householder or a son who was a civil servant. Because of the socialist regime at that time, the only people who received a monthly salary were civil servants, including teachers. The common pattern was for sons of wealthy farmers to become civil servants; no household had yet a daughter who had become a civil servant.

Another eight of these 16 households were engaged in thatching roofs with palm leaves called *danoung* (*Calamus arborescens*) and in weaving this roofing material during the dry season after their own farming work finished. The weaving is a job for women and the roofing for men. Until 1996, the paddy fields in Zeepinwea were not irrigated, so, except for small-scale groundnut cultivation, farming was only possible during the rainy season. The paddy fields were far from the village, and the men had to devote themselves to farming because it required long hours of male labour to plough and harrow the large paddy fields with oxen and buffaloes. Thus, most of what they could do in the non-agricultural sector was during the dry season when there was no farming activity. In the dry season, not only *kyaban*s but also *sayinnga*s worked as roofers, road construction workers, rice mill navvies, and firewood collectors (Takahashi, 1992: 169). In other words, since agriculture was a rainy season job and non-agriculture was a dry season job, dual employment of agriculture and non-agriculture were compatible. Until 1994, such dual employment was found in significant numbers at both household and individual levels. Some women did both agricultural employment and non-agricultural work, planting rice in

Table 4.13 Number of households and workers with side jobs in Zeepinwea Village

Occupational category	Own farming + agricultural labour			Own farming + non-agriculture			Agricultural labour + non-agriculture			Own farming + agricultural labour + non-agriculture			Total number of households and workers with side jobs		
Sex	Male	Female	Total	Male	Female	Total	Male	Female	Total	Male	Female	Total	Male	Female	Total
Number of households															
1987			5			16			14			0			35
1994			8			3			20			9			40
2013			0			12			4			0			16
Number of workers															
1987	3	7	10	2	5	7	12	5	17	0	0	0	17	17	34
1994	7	15	22	0	1	1	18	21	39	0	0	0	25	37	62
2013	0	0	0	2	2	4	1	1	2	0	0	0	3	3	6

Note "Non-agriculture" means "Non-agricultural Occupation"
Source According to the author's survey

the rainy season and weaving bamboo baskets and *danoung* in the dry season, while others did both rice planting and peddling in the rainy season.

In 1994, some Zeepinwea households were engaged in all three occupational categories (own farming, hired agricultural labour, and non-agriculture) during the year. This is because young persons from households that had in 1987 been doing their own farming plus non-agricultural work began engaging for short periods in agricultural wage labour: women in planting rice and men in uprooting seedlings. This change is also reflected in the increase in the number of *individuals* who combine their own farming and agricultural hired labour in 1994. This change seems to be due to a shift in farming methods: from slower, time-consuming rice planting to a tendency for large groups of people to complete rice planting in one go. In 1994, the number of men and women who were engaged both in agricultural wage labour and in non-agricultural work increased because roads were being expanded and new roads being built in the vicinity of Hlegu Town. Many villagers went to work as wage labourers during the dry season.

In 2013, however, the number of dual or triple jobs decreased sharply at both the household and the individual levels, and the shift to full-time employment progressed. This is due to the emergence of stable jobs with monthly wages in the private sector, beyond government offices. In farm households, both daughters and sons began to work not only in government offices and schools, but also in private factories and shops. Eight of the 12 households in Table 4.13 that had both their own farming and non-agricultural employment were such households. The rest were two households in which the son worked both as a farmer and as a motorcycle taxi driver, and two households in which the householders' wife worked both as a farmer and as a street vendor. In four households that combined agricultural labour with non-agricultural work, one person worked as a motorbike taxi driver and one as a street vendor, while two households had a daughter who worked as a salesclerk in Hlegu Town. It is important to note that these statistical results indicating the increase of full-time employment are based on simply dividing the occupations into three categories, but there are various kinds of jobs within the non-agricultural employment category. For example, in some families, the householder is a carpenter, his wife a street vendor, his son a motorcycle taxi driver, and his daughter a factory worker.

If we classify the occupations more finely, we can say that the development of the market economy increased the number of non-agricultural jobs available to villagers, and the trend towards multiple jobs within households advanced. However, since the seasonality of the past disappeared and villagers could work all year round, the number of multiple occupations at the individual level declined. This expansion of non-agricultural employment opportunities led to many cases where the loss of farmland did not affect livelihoods. For example, U Nyan Tun held 12 acres of cultivation right for paddy field in 1987, but sold 4 acres to pay for his children's education, leaving him with 8 acres in 1994, and then sold all of his farmland to pay for medical treatment for himself and his wife. Nevertheless, two of his daughters became teachers, two of his sons became workers in a foreign garment factory and two sons became goldsmiths, and with their help he built a new brick house (*taik*) and lived a comfortable life. In the twentieth century, the loss of farmland was directly linked to poverty in Zeepinwea, but this is no longer necessarily the case in the twenty-first century.

Let us now analyse how households and individuals in Thindaunggyi Village have embraced multiple employment. We will use the 54 sample households surveyed since 1987, using the same method as in Zeepinwea. As already mentioned, although Thindaunggyi Village saw a slight increase in the number of farm households from 1987 to 2013, the ratio of farm households decreased from more than half in 1987 to just over 30% in 2013. This was mainly due to an increase in the number of non-farm households as a result of *oekhwe* (Table 4.4).

In 1987, those households in Table 4.14 that were engaged in both their own farming and agricultural hired labour had only small amounts of holdings. The men were engaged in percentage-based wage labour for uprooting seedlings and the women in daily wage labour for transplanting rice in the intervals between their own farming. The double cropping of rice provided many employment opportunities. There were also second crops of onions, garlic, and peppers, so there were abundant employment opportunities for women all year round. At the individual level, there were 12 male and 21 female members of small-scale farm households who were engaged in both their own farming and agricultural hired labour. As for own farming plus non-agricultural labour, the farm households with relatively large land holdings had wives and children who were civil servants. In contrast, in small-scale farm households, either the householder or a son doubled as a plasterer, or the wife of the householder worked as a peddler. Households that had both agricultural labour employment and non-agricultural work usually had at least one member working as a plasterer. Plasterers work more days in the dry season than in the rainy season, but there is work in the rainy season, too, because the rainfall around the village is low. In general, including plasterers, the seasonality of non-agricultural job opportunities, as observed in Zeepinwea Village, was not remarkable in Thindaunggyi. The situation was almost the same in 1994. Only the number of households that worked concurrently in their own farming, in agricultural labour, *and* in plastering went from three to zero.

The changes from 1994 to 2013 were quite large in Thindaunggyi, same as in Zeepinwea. In farm households, there was no significant change in the number of women who also worked as agricultural wage labourers, but men's side-jobs shifted to plastering. A major change was the dramatic increase in the number of households concurrently engaged in all three categories of employment: own farming, agricultural hired labour, *and* non-agricultural work. Although the number of households that engaged only in their own farming and in agricultural labour decreased to only one, the number of households that engaged in non-agricultural work in addition to their own farming and agricultural labour increased from zero to ten. While most men's non-agricultural occupation remained plastering, new jobs were created for women, in addition to agricultural hired labour, such as cleaning the area of the Shwetheindaw Paya and keeping shops around the Paya. There was also a substantial increase in the number of farm households who combined their own farming and non-agricultural activities without doing agricultural hired labour. Of the 20 such households, 10 had children who graduated from university and were

Table 4.14 Number of households and workers with side jobs in Thindaunggyi Village

Occupational category	Own farming + agricultural labour			Own farming + non-agriculture			Agricultural labour + non-agriculture			Own farming + agricultural labour + non-agriculture			Total number of households and workers with side jobs		
Sex	Male	Female	Total	Male	Female	Total	Male	Female	Total	Male	Female	Total	Male	Female	Total
Number of households															
1987			7			5			6			3			21
1994			9			7			8			0			24
2013			1			20			4			10			35
Number of workers															
1987	12	21	33	3	2	5	3	0	3	0	0	0	18	23	41
1994	8	15	23	5	2	7	3	2	5	0	0	0	16	19	35
2013	3	11	14	5	0	5	2	1	3	0	0	0	10	12	22

Note Same as Table 4.13
Source Same as Table 4.13

civil servants, including teachers or office workers. Some of them became associate professors or architects. They were born in households of current or former rich farmers who owned or had owned the cultivation rights of relatively large farmlands. The remaining ten such households were small-scale farmers, with men working as plasterers and women earning income as Paya workers. In Thindaunggyi Village, multiple employment at the household level was evident even when we simply divide occupations into three categories. If the non-agricultural sector is subdivided, there was further employment multiplicity at the household level: that is, husband as plasterer, wife as peddler, daughter as shopkeeper and son as night watchman in the Paya. However, as in Zeepinwea Village, the number of *individuals* who engaged in multiple occupations decreased—many people continued to work in the same occupation throughout the year. In both villages, the number of household-level dual and further multiple occupations increased, while at the individual level, young people were working year-round in the non-agricultural sector. In both villages, de-agrarianisation progressed in this way.

4.10 Transformation of the Village Life

Above, I have described the economic transformation of two villages from the perspective of production, including aspects such as farmland, cattle, agricultural input, farm equipment, labour, and agricultural produce prices. In the last part of this chapter, I will trace the changes over three decades from the perspective of villagers' consumption and livelihood. We begin with the infrastructure of daily life, including transportation, electricity, water, and information, and then move on to houses, consumer durables, education, and religious life.

4.10.1 Transportation Infrastructure

In 1987, the only way to enter Zeepinwea Village was to walk about one kilometre from the bus stop near the central market in Hlegu Town, where the then National Highway No. 1 ran, or to take a *sai'kâ* (side-car, meaning a bicycle taxi). The only means of transport owned by villagers, apart from ox carts, was bicycles, but even the farmer with the largest paddy holdings in the village owned only one bicycle. In 1994, the road was widened, albeit unpaved, to allow cars to enter the village. Yet no one owned a motorcycle, let alone a private car, and only 14 of the 170 households owned a bicycle. When going out, villagers basically walked, or if they were tired or had luggage, they used ox carts. The number of motorcycle owners began to increase around the time that the road from Hlegu Town to the village entrance was paved in 2008. By 2013, 44 of the 316 households in the village owned motorcycles. All of them were made in China. In addition, as mentioned earlier, only the village administrator owned a private car.

In 1987, Thindaunggyi Village also had no paved road to enter the village from the old National Highway No. 1. Cars could drive to the village if the sandy road was not muddy, but the main means of transportation for villagers were horse carts, ox carts and bicycles. The difference from Zeepinwea was that Thindaunggyi had horse-drawn transport and 84 out of its 126 households owned bicycles, including households owning more than one.

In 1994, when I stayed and conducted my second individual household survey in Thindaunggyi, 142 of the 156 households owned bicycles, 2 owned motorcycles, and 4 owned cars. During my stay in the village, a paved road from the then National Highway No. 1 to the village by the Shwetheindaw Paya was completed.[29] According to my survey at that time, the motorcycles were used vehicles made in Japan, and the cars were all used Japanese pickup trucks with roofs used to carry passengers as "buses". These "buses" did not come into the village but were used for business between Kyaukse and Mandalay.

However, from the beginning of the twenty-first century, the number of motorcycles began to increase. By 2013, 166 of the 236 Thindaunggyi households owned a motorcycle. The main reason was not only the increase of cash income but also the nationwide spread of Chinese motorcycles, which were much cheaper than their Japanese counterparts. Incidentally, the number of cars did not increase at all, remaining 4, but the pickup-truck "buses" disappeared, and all cars were instead for private use. By 2018, the number of private car owners was 10.

As mentioned earlier, there were many plasterers in the village, and their number was increasing rapidly. They could travel farther by motorcycle to work on day trips. Thus, their market area expanded considerably, which made it possible for the number of plasterers also to increase rapidly. Moreover, motorcycles carrying a variety of goods such as bananas, instant noodles, toys, and popsicles began to come and go. Village products such as rice, onions, sesame, and peppers left the village on *tawlajis*, the four-wheeled attachments moored to the back of a motorcycle. *Tawlajis* were also used when the shopkeepers of village general stores went out to stock up in town and when children went to school. The number of cars did not increase rapidly because the *tawlaji* replaced the horse-drawn wagons that had transported goods. Only recently did small trucks begin to replace these *tawlajis*.

4.10.2 Electrification

Next, let us talk about electrification. In Myanmar, when an electricity metre is attached to the wall of a house and electricity becomes available, it is called "*mî yàde*" or "I have got electricity". Electricity is supplied by state agencies, but individual households have to pay for the wires, electricity metres, metre boxes, and so on, which bring electricity to their households, as well as labour costs. In 1987, Zeepinwea Village had no household with an electricity metre. Night-time light was obtained

[29] As for how funds and labour were raised to build this road, see Takahashi (2018: 68–69).

from candles or kerosene lamps, and a few households closer to Hlegu Town used car batteries charged in the town for both radios and lighting. In 1988, the first household to have a watt-hour metre was the household with the third largest farmland and the largest number of buffaloes in the village. After that, households with relatively large farmlands installed electricity metres at a rate of about one per year, and by the time of my second survey in 1994, seven of the 170 households had electricity. The number of households using candles or kerosene for light decreased to 55, while 108 households were using batteries as a power source. In addition, 28 households used large batteries to listen to radios and tape recorders, though the main purpose was to obtain light. Among the electrified households, only one household owned a black-and-white TV.

By 2013, 114 out of 316 Zeepinwea households had had electricity metres installed, but 202 households, including all 48 in Ywalay, still did not have electricity. Of the 56 households sampled, 35 had electricity metres, and six households were illegally wired by these metre-owning households to share electricity with them. One household in Ywalay hamlet purchased a generator and made electricity by itself. The remaining 11 households were using batteries; three households were still using kerosene lamps. When I asked the 35 households with electricity metres when they had installed them, I found: 1 household had installed a metre in 1990, 1 in 1992, 1 in 1995, 4 in 1998, 2 in 1999, 2 in 2000, 3 in 2003, 2 in 2005, 1 in 2006, 2 in 2008, 3 in 2009, 3 in 2010, 1 in 2011, 3 in 2012, and 6 in 2013. Thus, the electrification of the village did not occur in all households at once, but gradually progressed in a haphazard pattern each year, and many were still left behind.

All of the 41 Zeepinwea households in the sample that had electricity in 2013 had a television and a VCR. Until around 2000, all households cooked with firewood. If there were many trees in the compound, the villagers used branches from them. Otherwise they had to spend a few days going to the Bago Yoma (Mountains) to collect firewood, or buy it. Around the turn of the century, some households began to cook with electric rice cookers and pots. By 2013, 20 of the 56 sample households had switched to this method of cooking. Seven households owned refrigerators. Three of them had large freezers and refrigerators for business use in their general merchandise stores, in front of their residences, selling ice and ice cream.

In contrast, 4 out of the 126 Thindaunggyi Village households in 1987 had electricity metres. Namely, three farm households that owned a large amount of cultivation rights and earned money from second-cropping onions and garlics, as well as one household of a grand master plasterer, enjoyed electricity. However, the power outages were frequent and long, and I had electricity only three days during my two-week stay in the village. About half of the households used batteries and the other half used candles for lighting at night. Fuel for cooking was firewood, except for about 20 households that used charcoal. By 1994, the number of households with electricity metres had increased to 27 out of 156 households. The number of households using batteries had also increased to 83, and the number of poor households using candles decreased to 46. Some households had also started to have appliances other than lighting, with five households owning a TV and two owning a refrigerator. Only one household owned a VCR and built a video theatre on its premises to show movies to the villagers for a fee. However, no electricity was used for cooking: ten households purchased charcoal, 55 purchased firewood, and the remaining 91 households collected firewood from the forests at the foot of the Shan plateau, east of the village.

By 2013, 70% of the 236 households in Thindaunggyi, or 165 households, had electricity metres, and 90% of the households were electrified, including those that were illegally connected to the grid. Of the 54 households in the sample, 45 households had regular electricity, six households got electricity from households with electricity metres, two households were battery-dependent, and only one household relied on candles. Television and VCRs were available to 40 households, and two households had refrigerators. The electrification of cooking utensils advanced, with 37 households cooking with electric rice cookers, electric stoves, and electric pots. However, due to the unstable electricity supply, all households also kept charcoal or firewood available at all times. Ten households cooked only with charcoal and seven only with firewood. I asked 45 households about their electrification history: 2 households got electricity before 1987, 2 in 1990, 2 in 1991, 1 in 1992, 3 in 1993, 2 in 1994, 1 in 1995, 1 in 1996, 2 in 1998, 3 in 1999, 2 in 2000, 2 in 2003, 3 in 2005, 3 in 2006, 1 in 2008, 4 in 2009, 3 in 2010, 2 in 2011, 3 in 2012, and 3 in 2013. Thus, in this village, too, electrification did not occur simultaneously in many households, but progressed intermittently in a few households each year. The electrification of Myanmar villages does not happen all at once, but gradually progresses according to the economic situation of each household. The reason for this is that, in addition to the large economic disparity within the village, the individual burden required to install a watt-hour metre is quite heavy.

4.10.3 Water for Domestic Use

The third infrastructure is water. In 1987, there were eight ponds for drinking water in Zeepinwea Village. Bathing in these ponds and keeping livestock in or around these ponds were strictly prohibited (Takahashi, 1992: 44). Villagers drew water from these ponds for drinking, cooking, and bathing. They also used water from Ngamoeyeik River and its Oxbow Lake for bathing, and rainwater—stored in unglazed jars during the rainy season—for drinking. By 1994, 18 households had dug artesian wells in their compound and used hand pumps to draw water for bathing and cooking. However, because people disliked the metallic smell of the well water, they preferred the pond water or rainwater instead when drinking raw. Villagers in Myanmar have the custom of boiling water and drinking green tea, but they also prefer raw water and are not satisfied with simply boiling well-water. In 2013, 38 of the 56 sampled households had artesian wells, and 22 of them used electric pumps to draw water from them. It is not clear whether the new vinyl chloride pipes had eliminated the metallic smell or people had become accustomed to it, but the well water was drunk raw now, and those who did not like it drank bottled water. In Ywalay and Paukkoung hamlets, many villagers still used the old ponds, but in Ywagyi hamlet the banks of the three village-owned ponds had begun to collapse as few people used them. The three ponds owned by the West Monastery, the East Monastery, and a private individual had become fish-breeding ponds.

In Thindaunggyi, where rainfall is only a third of that in Zeepinwea, it is not possible to store water in ponds all year round, so Thindaunggyi has instead long had public artesian wells. In 1987, the village had three village-owned wells, one paya-owned well and three privately owned wells. Everyone in the village could use these wells without asking. The villagers threw buckets with ropes into the wells and skillfully drew up water. They carried the water to their homes in buckets of various sizes or in drums on cattle carts. This water was used for drinking by people and livestock, and for cooking, while bathing and washing were done around wells or in the irrigation channels running through paddy fields. By 1994, the number of privately owned wells had increased to 11, but both public and private wells were being used in the same way as in 1987. By 2013, 27 households, half of the 54 sampled households, had dug and owned their own wells, and 25 of them used electric motors to pump the well water. Households without wells could no longer use other people's wells without permission because of the cost of electricity. They were thus forced to choose between using other households' wells—normally for a fee, but free of charge if the families were close—or using public wells or irrigation channels. In both Zeepinwea and Thindaunggyi villages, individuals could now dig their own wells and no longer had to travel far to fetch water, but those without the financial means to dig wells and install electric motors were forced to continue using public ponds and wells. Even though the wells were village-owned, the burden of management and repair had to be borne by the poor who used them. Thus, the fewer the number of the poor, the more difficult it would be to maintain the public wells and ponds, and the more the burden would fall on the remaining poor. Many of the newly dug wells were not suitable for drinking, and in such cases, some turned to drinking bottled water, but for the poor, bottled water was out of reach.

4.10.4 Information

In Myanmar villages, the only information medium accessible to most villagers until near the turn of the century was the radio, with few newspaper subscribers and, as mentioned above, with very few households owning a television set. Under the oppressive regimes of socialism and military rule, the villagers listened secretly to the British Broadcasting Corporation (BBC) Burmese-language broadcasting from the radio. In the twenty-first century, television began to spread rapidly. The villagers invariably bought a VCR as well, in order to watch national and international films on video, produced outside of military-state controls, rather than the TV programmes, which were mainly official news and propaganda. After the democratisation in 2011, satellite broadcasting began to reach the villages, and people could watch Radio Free Asia and Mizzima, which were critical of the regime. However, foreign football programmes such as Premier League and Serie A were the most popular among men, while women preferred Korean and Chinese dramas.

A landline telephone was installed at the Shwetheindaw Paya in Thindaunggyi village around 2002. A mobile phone was purchased by the Paya office in 2009. In Zeepinwea Village, a mobile phone was purchased in 2008 by the village tract mayor who ran the rice-husk collection business mentioned above. At that time, SIM cards were very expensive, costing 200,000–300,000 kyats (200–300 US dollars at the exchange rate at that time), so they did not spread any further. Mobile phones started to spread across Myanmar only in 2013 when the price of a SIM card dropped to 1500 kyats (about one dollar), less than a hundredth of the previous price. Inexpensive smartphones made in China soon began to spread. Smartphones suddenly spread to villagers who had never had landlines, let alone mobile phones. By around 2017, even the poorest daily agricultural labourers and street vendors had smartphones. In both Thindaunggyi and Zeepinwea, smartphones reached most people aged from 15 to 60 years old. Farmers could now obtain price information instantly and were no longer cheated by middlemen. Plasterers could easily receive orders from far away. Merchants could choose where to order their goods.

However, gambling also became easier. Illegal betting and lotteries have long been rampant in Myanmar. In particular, illegal "bookies" who dealt in *chê* (the last three digits of a Thai lottery ticket) and *hnalôun* (the last two digits of a Myanmar lottery ticket) have been everywhere, from government offices and shopping districts to farming villages. This was now done via SMS on smartphones, and became more widespread. The gambling also became more diverse, including gambling on the football wins and losses seen on TV (Takahashi, 2018: 72).

4.10.5 Houses

Above, I have described changes in the ownership and use of infrastructure in the two villages over a quarter century. It has become clear that there has been a large disparity in access to electricity, water, and transportation, that is, in the ownership of electricity metres, electric motors for pumping water, and private cars. It is in these modern assets that the improvement of livelihoods and the gap between rich and poor are explicitly recognised in Myanmar villages. Another symbol is the house, especially the roofing materials (Takahashi, 1997: 19; 2007: 410).

In Zeepinwea village, the leaves of various palm plants such as *Danoung* (*Calamus arborescens*), *Taungdang* (*Livistona speciosa*), *Salu* (*Licuala peltata*), and *Dani* (*Nypa fruticans*) have traditionally been used as roofing materials. And as mentioned earlier, job opportunities were provided for women to weave these roofing materials and for men to thatch the roofs in the dry season. In 1987, as shown in Table 4.15, only five of the 138 households had zinc roofs, and the other 133 had palm roofs rethatched annually. The owners of the zinc-roofed houses were all farmers with large cultivation right holdings. By 1994, 39 out of 170 households had zinc roofs. 31 of these were farm households. By 2013, only two households among the 56 sample households had nipa palm roofs, while the other 54 had zinc roofs. Two among the zinc-roofed houses were *taiks*. A zinc roof was no longer an expression of economic disparity, and like the smartphone, it had become a popular product for rich and poor alike. Thus, the *taik* replaced the zinc roof as a symbol of wealth. Various palm roofing materials have lost their weavers and thatchers, and the poor have no choice but to buy zinc roofs.

Upper Myanmar, where Thindaunggyi Village is located, has many roofs made of *wakat* (*waka'*)—small rectangular sheets of bamboo flattened and stacked like tiles—which are not found in Lower Myanmar, where Zeepinwea Village is located. Palm-leaf and thatched roofs need to be rethatched every year, but *wakat* is durable for seven or eight years. Three of the 102 households in Thindaunggyi Village surveyed lived in *taiks* in 1987 (see Table 4.16), one of which was a colonial-era *taik*. Three households had zinc roofs, 15 households had *wakat* roofs, and the remaining 81 households had thatched roofs made of cogon grass (*Imperata cylindrica*; called *thekke* (*the'ke*) in Burmese). The households living in the *taiks* were the household of the grand master plasterer, mentioned above, and two large farm households, while all the households living under zinc or *wakat* roofs were farmers who had cultivation rights.

Older types of *taik* were rectangular and had brick, stucco or concrete roofs, while *taiks* with zinc roofs have become more common since the 1990s. Therefore, the term "zinc-roofed house" here refers to houses with wooden or bamboo walls and concrete or wooden boards for floors, while houses with the same zinc roof but brick or concrete walls and floors are distinguished as "*taik*". In 1994, of the 156 Thindaunggyi households, 9 had *taiks*, 10 had zinc roofs, 41 had *wakat* roofs, 92 had cogon grass roofs, and the remaining 4 were poor households that roofed their houses

Table 4.15 Roofing material classification by households' occupational categories in Zeepinwea Village

Roofing material	Own farming	Agricultural labour	Non-agriculture	Total	Composition ratio (%)
(1987)				(138)	
Galvanised iron	5	0	0	5	3.6
Palmae	59	46	28	133	96.4
(1994)				(170)	
Galvanised iron	31	3	5	39	22.9
Palmae	35	49	47	131	77.1
(2013)				(56)	
Taik	1	0	1	2	3.6
Galvanised iron	19	5	28	52	92.8
Palmae	2	0	0	2	3.6

Note "*Taik*" refers to the structure of the house, not the roofing material
Source According to the author's survey

Table 4.16 Roofing material classification by households' occupational categories in Thindaunggyi Village

Roofing material	Own farming	Agricultural labour	Plasterer	Other non-agriculture	Total	Composition ratio (%)
(1987)					(102)	
Taik	2	0	1	0	3	2.9
Galvanised iron	3	0	0	0	3	2.9
Wakat	15	0	0	0	15	14.8
Cogon	40	20	12	9	81	79.4
(1994)					(156)	
Taik	8	0	1	0	9	5.8
Galvanised iron	9	0	0	1	10	6.4
Wakat	27	0	5	9	41	26.3
Cogon	29	31	17	15	92	59.0
Rice straw	0	2	1	1	4	2.5
(2013)					(54)	
Taik	10	0	0	1	11	20.4
Galvanised iron	13	3	1	4	21	38.9
Wakat	10	3	2	5	20	37.0
Cogon	0	1	0	1	2	3.7

Note Same as Table 4.15
Source Same as Table 4.15

with rice straw. The owners of the *taik*s, except for the master plasterer mentioned above, were all middle- or upper-scale farmers. The owners of zinc roofs were also farmers, except for the households engaged in gold embroidery. The households of *wakat* roofs were of 27 farmers, 5 plasterers, 3 carpenters, 4 teachers and civil servants, and 2 shopkeepers, but again, these households did not include agricultural labourer households. The majority still lived in thatched roof houses, although their share of the total number of households in the village had decreased from 79% in 1987 to 62%. Among them were not only all the agricultural labourer households, but also many farmers, plasterers, and households that engaged in peddling, dairy farming, and coach driving.

By 2013, 11 households, or 20% of the sample Thindaunggyi households, were living in a *taik*. Ten of these households were farmers, and the remaining one was a farmer until he sold his farmland in 2012. In the whole village, I counted 25 *taik*s, including the house of the aforesaid master plasterer who was not included in the sample households. These 25 included two plasterer households, two shopkeeper households, and one household with children who were civil servants, while all the rest were farm households. Farmers had benefited from irrigation, which allowed double cropping, and had invested their agricultural income into assets, including *taiks*. Onion cultivation had contributed to this, especially since 2008. The prosperity of Shwetheindaw Paya is also relevant, but this will be discussed in the next chapter. While the number of *taiks* had increased, the thatched roof houses had almost disappeared, leaving only the very poor. In both Zeepinwea and Thindaunggyi villages, roofs made of leaves or grasses were on the verge of disappearing. In Thindaunggyi Village, however, not all houses were zinc-roofed as in Zeepinwea. Instead, the number of *wakat*-roofed houses was almost the same as the number of zinc-roofed houses, each accounting for nearly 40% of the total. Although zinc roofs do not need to be replaced, the interior temperature tends to rise during the hot season, and the sound of rain is noisy during the rainy season. In Upper Myanmar, where the heat is intense in the hot season, *wakat* roofs with high thermal protection tend to be preferred. However, in Myanmar these days, the prices of natural resources such as wood and bamboo rise faster than the prices of artificial materials such as brick and galvanised iron. Thus, *taiks* and zinc-roofed houses are becoming relatively cheaper than wooden and *wakat*-roofed houses, and thus coming to replace earlier forms of housing.

4.10.6 Education

Next, I will discuss education, focusing on the most significant change in the last quarter of a century—enrolment in universities. In Zeepinwea Village, none of the villagers or anyone born in the village were university graduates or students in 1987 or in 1994. However, by 2013, among the 56 sample households alone, there were 6 men and 16 women who had graduated from universities. In Thindaunggyi village in 1987, there were two men who had graduated from Mandalay university. In 1994, there were still no other university graduates except for these two men. By 2013, however, there were 8 male and 20 female university graduates in the 54 sample households. In both villages, the number of university graduates would be certain to increase further if we included those who left the sample households after graduating from universities and established separate households in the village, as well as those who left the village, and the household members outside the sample.

The reason for this dramatic increase in the number of university graduates from almost zero is that the number of universities swelled throughout Myanmar during this period. During the socialist era, Myanmar had only about ten universities, including the three universities of arts and sciences in Yangon, Mandalay, and Mawlamyine, as well as specialised institutes such as of medicine, engineering, agriculture, and economics. By 2011, however, the number of universities increased to more than 160. All of them were national universities. Dagon University was established in 1993 within easy reach of Zeepinwea village by motorcycle or bus. 17 of the 22 Zeepinwea university graduates mentioned above were graduates of this university. The other graduates were two women who were commuting from

Zeepinwea to a foreign-owned factory and obtained a degree from a distance (correspondence) university, two women who graduated from Yangon University, and a man who graduated from the Defence Services Technological Academy in the distant city of Pyin Oo Lwin and became a technical officer. Thindaunggyi Village has three universities within commuting distance: Kyaukse University, Kyaukse Technological University, and Computer University, which were all established in the end of 1990s. Of the 28 people mentioned above, 20 were graduates of Kyaukse University and five were graduates of Kyaukse Technological University. Moreover, there was one woman each who obtained a degree from Meiktila University of Economics, University of Pharmacy (Mandalay), and Yezin Agricultural University, all of which are not commutable from the village.

The five male university graduates in Zeepinwea village included three factory workers, one taxi driver, and one migrant worker to Malaysia, besides the mentioned technical officer. Of the 16 women, eight became teachers in primary and secondary schools, three worked as clerks in private companies in Yangon, three worked in foreign-owned factories, and two managed their own shops. Of the 20 university-educated women in Thindaunggyi village, one each became a pharmacist, a university lecturer, and an employee of a bank in Yangon, four became teachers in primary and secondary schools, three became clerical workers in Paya, and the remaining ten were engaged in running their own shops or agriculture. The breakdown of the eight men was as follows: one was a judge, one was an associate professor at a university, one was a Paya staff member, two were teachers at primary and secondary schools, two ran their own shops, and one was a farmer.

Examining the relationship between being a farmer and having a university degree as of 2013, in Zeepinwea village, 2 out of 6 male and 13 out of 16 female university graduates' households were non-farm households. However, all of the households were originally farmers with cultivation rights or the parents of these university graduates were farmers. None of the households sold their farmland in order to send their children to universities, but many of the graduates became able to work in the non-agricultural sector with stable incomes and thus enabled their natal households to live as well or better than when they were farm households, even after disposing of their farmland. In contrast, in Thindaunggyi Village, only two out of eight men and two out of 20 women were children of non-farm households. Of these, one man and two women were the children of a rich man who owned a gold embroidery business, and one man was the son of a former farmer. In this village, too, being a child of a farmer was a prerequisite for attending university, but unlike in Zeepinwea, parents continued to farm. The university-educated children inherited a small amount of farmland after *oekhwe* and continued farming by making their spouses or agricultural hired labourers do the farming work. Only a few university graduates (three men and two women) were engaged in farming after being once employed in companies or government offices.

The rapid increase in the number of universities in Myanmar led to problems with the level of teaching staff and students, but for the villagers, it became much easier to enter universities than it had been during the socialist era, and they gained a much wider choice of occupations. As a result, de-agrarianisation progressed at the household level in Zeepinwea Village and at the individual level in Thindaunggyi Village.

4.10.7 Religion

Let us then consider the economic aspects of religious practice in the villages. Between my second survey in 1994 and my third survey in 2013, big changes related to Buddhism occurred in both villages.

In Zeepinwea Village, the Karen people of Paukkoung hamlet, mentioned above, are Christians, while the people of Ywagyi and Ywalay hamlets are Buddhists of Bamar ethnicity, the latter comprising 87% of the total population of the village. The two monasteries, West Monastery (*anau' câun*) and East Monastery (*ashèi câun*), were established in the 1890s and 1910s, respectively. The villagers who lived in the western half of Ywagyi were the main supporters (*daga*) of the West Monastery, and the villagers in the eastern half of Ywagyi and in Ywalay were the main supporters of East Monastery (Takahashi, 1992: 42–44; 2000: 63). The East Monastery was famous for its secret medicine for the treatment of cancer, and cancer patients came not only from Yangon but also from as far away as Bago and Mawlamyine to receive injections of the secret medicine, while the West Monastery used to be an ordinary monastery that preached to the villagers. However, the long-lasting equilibrium between the two monasteries began to break down at the end of the twentieth century. This is because new monasteries were established one after another in the paddy fields to the south of Ywagyi. In 1996, Yangon-based donors rebuilt Shwekyayan Monastery by inviting monks to the old monastery that had originally been located there. In 2005, Dhammagoun Monastery was built, and in 2012, Mingalazeyang Monastery was established. The faith and the donations of some villagers shifted to these new monasteries. Shwekyayan Monastery, with contributions from Yangon companies and rich people, transformed an old *zedi* (stupa) into a large, ornate one in 2004. The chief monk of Dhammagoun Monastery is a Kachin, famous for his meditation. He is a high monk who is frequently invited to travel by overseas Myanmar people. Mingalazeyang Monastery is a teaching and learning monastery, donated entirely by a merchant living in Daikoo Township, 100 km northeast of Zeepinwea village, with which she had no connection. This monastery is led by an outstanding young monk who has passed a difficult national examination and has educated young novices.

Such new monasteries with strong brands forced the West Monastery, just an ordinary monastery, to reform. The chief monk of the monastery came up with the idea of educating ethnic minorities. The monastery began inviting poor ethnic Pa-O boys from deep in the mountains of Shan State to stay at the monastery, first teaching them Burmese language and the doctrines of Theravada Buddhism, then giving them regular education such as arithmetic and history, and allowing the best to go on to universities in Yangon. The school's achievements were soon recognised. A splendid new school building was built on the monastery compound, with the help of Japan's Grant Assistance for Grassroots Human Security. In addition, a wealthy Taiwanese doctor donated for the school building. The school was approved by the

Ministry of Education as a regular school, not just a monastery school, and the chief monk became a major figure in the religious and educational circles of Hlegu Township (Takahashi, 2018: 127–128). After graduating from university, the young Pa-O people scattered to Japan, Thailand, Vietnam, and Malaysia, and with their remittances, the monastery's main hall was rebuilt into a large, three-story *taik*. It could be said that the village monastery, which had been living together with the daily lives and annual events of the villagers, was suddenly thrown into a competition. Yet, the laypeople always tend to make offerings and donations to monks whom they think worthy of their faith, so it is only natural for them to shift their attention to monks whom they respect more, if such monks appear geographically closer to them. The impression that the village as a whole supports the monastery is due to economic circumstances, such as the villagers being too poor to maintain only one or two monasteries at most, or the lack of transport infrastructure that prevents the villagers from making offerings and donations to monasteries outside the village. In such cases, the monastery appears to be the centre of the village's cohesion, which is not the truth. As the economic situation of the village improves and transportation becomes better, the number of monasteries accessible to villagers increases, and the relationship between the village and the monastery diminishes. This is because monasteries are supported by individuals, not by the village. There is no such thing as village-community Buddhism[30] in Myanmar.

Thindaunggyi Village has two monasteries: Tandaw (*htândô*) Monastery and Myotha (*myòtha*) Monastery. Moreover, Taunghle Village, which forms one village tract together with Thindaunggyi, also has two monasteries: Kyaunggyi (*câunjî*) and Masoeyein (*masôyein*). It is said that Tandaw Monastery was established around 1918, followed by Myotha and Kyaunggyi, and the most recent, Masoeyein Monastery, was built around 1925. Thindaunggyi Village has groups providing food offerings for monasteries, called *nei'panso aphwè* in Burmese. Relatively wealthy households send food not only to the two monasteries in the village but also to the monasteries in Taunghle and in Kyaukse Town. In the lower strata, the number of monasteries that a household is able to donate to decreases to two or one. There are some poor people who cannot afford to join any food-offering group. In each monastery, there is a chart with the names of the villagers who are in charge of providing the food offering on a daily basis. Food offering groups are organised within the village, but the donations and offerings easily cross village boundaries. There was a villager who built a monastery in Mandalay and donated it to one monk, his nephew. Others donated huge sums to monasteries in Kyaukse Town. Since my second survey of individual households in 1994, as Shwetheindaw Paya prospered, more and more of the Thindaunggyi villagers' contributions by way of labour and money have been directed towards this Paya. The monasteries in the village also seem to be trying to expand their congregations to Kyaukse and Mandalay. The organiser

[30] Kuramoto states that "Myanmar Buddhism can be expected to have a fixed and stable relationship with village collectives" (Kuramoto, 2014: 127), but from the above discussion it can be said that such an expectation is not necessarily possible. In the first place, villages in Myanmar are not even "village collectives". This will be discussed later.

of the two donation events at Myotha Monastery that I attended was a merchant from Mandalay. In both Thindaunggyi and Zeepinwea villages, parents and children in the same household often follow different monks, indicating that Buddhism is a personal faith.

4.10.8 Social Expenditure

At the end of my questionnaire is a section on expenditure on weddings, funerals and religion. Since the people in Thindaunggyi Village give donations and gifts both inside and outside the village so frequently, many of them could not recall how much they had spent in a year. It was difficult for them to fill in even an approximate amount of social expenditure. Expenditure on weddings, funerals, and ceremonies is called *luhmùyêi athôunzayei'*, or social expenditure. In the village, there are two organisations: a "congratulation and condolence association" called "*luhmùyêi athîn*", and a "social service association with sincerity" called "*seidanashin luhmù kuniyêi athîn*". The former is an organisation that rents out crockery and tables for weddings and funerals free of charge, while the latter, a new association created in 2012, charges a monthly membership fee of 1000 kyats and provides a hearse service for funerals (Takahashi, 2018: 186–187). The villagers could accurately answer me only about the monthly dues to this funeral association. Thanks to these associations, the villagers are expected to be able to reduce their expenditures on celebrations and condolences. However, considering the extensive religious offering and donation activities of the villagers, one can imagine that the religious expenditure is much larger than the social expenditure.

In contrast, Zeepinwea village has no congratulatory or condolence association and the villagers' religious expenditures are almost exclusively related to the five monasteries mentioned above. Therefore, although not precise, the villagers gave me the amounts of their religious and social expenditures in a year. Since I asked for such amounts, some villagers even recorded their expenses throughout a year. Eventually, they found that the amounts were 1.5 times larger than what they had expected. In other words, the amount that the villagers answered was only rough. Therefore, I will compare the magnitudes of religious and social expenditures, rather than the specific amounts. In 1994, out of 144 Buddhist households in Ywagyi and Ywalay hamlets, the amount of religious expenditure was less than the amount of social expenditure in 96 households, the same in 34 households, and greater in 14 households. In 2013, these numbers were 30, 6, and 13, respectively, out of the 49 sample households in Ywagyi and Ywalay. When we go to the village early in the morning, we can see people putting rice in the monks' alms bowls and hear the sutras from the monastery, and we can feel the devotion of the villagers to Buddhism. Surprisingly, however, more households said that they spent more on social-related expenditure than on religious-related expenditure. The large expenditure on congratulations and condolences must be related to the fact that there was no congratulation or condolence association in this village. Among the Christians in Paukkoung hamlet, in 1994, out of 26 households, 3 households had less religious expenditure than social expenditure, 17 had the same amount, and 6 had more religious expenditure. In 2013, however, all seven surveyed households in Paukkoung had higher social expenditures than religious expenditures. This may be because the transportation and information means and economic conditions had improved in the village, allowing for villagers to expand and deepen their interactions with Karen ethnic communities in Hlegu Township and Yangon City.

Chapter 5
Revitalising a Village Through Buddhism: Thindaunggyi Village and Shwetheindaw Paya

"Prayer agent" U Base is seen from his back in the centre of the photo. He is the old man with shaved head, in white shirt. He is chanting in front of offerings (*gadawbwe*) that are lined up around the Paya. Among the 14 local prayer agents, he got the highest income. (June 2018, Thindaunggyi Village)

A. Takahashi, *Regime Changes and Socio-economic History of Rural Myanmar, 1986–2019*, Studies in Economic History,
https://doi.org/10.1007/978-981-99-3272-6_5

Introduction

From 1987 to 2019, when I did my research, the economy of Thindaunggyi Village made a great leap forward. The village, which used to be a rural village like anywhere else in Myanmar, transformed into a temple town that attracts worshippers from all over the country. However, in this village, the object of worship is neither a shrine nor a temple, but the Paya, which I often mentioned in the previous chapter. It is called "*shweitheindo mya'swa phayâ*", or Shwetheindaw Paya for short. The main deity of this Paya is a small statue of Buddha, less than one metre high. When I first visited the Paya in 1987, the main hall (Buddha Hall), where the main deity was enshrined, was a brick building not much different from the main halls of *paya*s in the surrounding villages. Behind this building stood a 14-metre-high golden stupa (*zeidi*), also called Shwetheindaw Paya. Until 2013, this stupa was outdoors and surrounded by palm trees, so, it could not be seen from the national highway. In the same year, a huge new sanctum called *gandàkùdì câunhsaunjî* or *gandakudi*[1] was completed. 30 m by 30 m (900 m^2) and 32 m high, it covered both the main hall and the stupa. The soaring crimson roof of the *gandakudi* can be seen from the national highway. Prior to the construction of the *gandakudi*, the *danmayoung* (*danmàyoun*, large lecture hall) was built, and next to it, the *zayat* (*zaya'*), a resting place for worshippers, was also constructed in 2008. All these buildings collectively are also referred to as Shwetheindaw Paya. In addition, flowerbeds, circular roads, motorcycle and car parking lots, shopping areas, and so on have been developed around the *gandakudi*. The total construction cost is said to have exceeded 5 billion kyats (one US dollar was about 980 kyats in 2013). Why was a rural village where agricultural labourers and plasterers earned only 4000–6000 kyats per day[2] able to undertake such a huge project? And what has this project brought to the village?

In this chapter, I first describe the background of Shwetheindaw Paya and its development, based on interviews with villagers and on books about the Paya. Second, I analyse the structure of the Paya's fund-raising, including donations from worshippers, by scrutinising the Paya's account books and bank books, and interviewing the members of the Paya's Board of Trustees (*gôpàkà apwè*, or *gawpaka*). Thirdly, by tracing the expenditures, we can get a closer look at the actual development of the Paya's business. Fourth, I will estimate the economic impact of the Paya through interviews with the Paya officials and other stakeholders, ranging from surrounding shopkeepers to peddlers and beggars. In this way, we can understand how the merits of the Buddhists were embodied, what kind of blessings they brought to the village, and how the village society was changed.

---

[1] *Gandakudi* is a Pali word meaning "fragment hut", or "Buddha's cabin". "*Câunhsaun*" means "monks' living quarter" and *jî* means "big" in Burmese. In the case of the Shwetheindaw Paya, it is obviously not a monk's quarter, but if we regard Buddha images and stupas as the Buddha, we can say that it is a "*gandakudi*" in the sense that Buddha lives there.

[2] The wages of agricultural labourers include the cost of lunches and snacks provided by their employers. Plasterers are not provided with such meals.

5.1 History of the Development of Shwetheindaw Paya

As mentioned above, both Thindaunggyi Village and Shwetheindaw Paya are said to have been built by the first king of the ethnic Bamar, King Anawrahta (reigned 1044–1077 A.D.) (Sandàthìrì, 1956: 26–28). However, the Paya was neglected and covered with thorns for a long time, and no one knew about it. Naturally, there was no one to offer food, flowers, water, or lanterns. Time passed. During 1915–1918, smallpox, measles, cholera, and other epidemics struck the village (Sandàthìrì, 1956: 29). The villagers temporarily abandoned the village and dispersed. Later, the elders gathered the villagers who had taken refuge and they all returned to the village in groups to clear the jungle around the Paya and remove the thorns that clung to it. The Shwetheindaw Paya regained its former grandeur, and the villagers began to devote themselves to its maintenance and worship (Nyunt, 2002: 45). Looking again at Thindaunggyi Village's population dynamics, discussed in the previous chapter (Table 4.2), we can see that the population decreased from 1911 to 1921. This decrease seems to be due to the epidemic. However, the decrease was not so great because the epidemic came to an end in 1918, and the villagers returned to their homes. As mentioned in the previous chapter, the four monasteries in Thindaunggyi and Taunghle were built between 1918 and 1925. This also coincides with the return from the evacuation due to the epidemic.

After the villagers had returned, the work of clearing the bushes around the Paya continued, and a place of worship made of cogon grass (*the'ke*) was built on the east side of the main hall. In 1938, this place of worship was demolished to make an ordination hall (*thein*), and the broken brick walls of the main hall were repaired (Nyunt, 2002: 46). At the end of the Second World War, machine gun fire from British bombers targeting the defeated Japanese army once hit this wall and a *taik* next to the Paya, but both were not seriously destroyed, and the latter is still used as a residence. In 1952, soon after Myanmar gained independence, a seedling of the Bodhi tree brought back from Sri Lanka by a monk in Mandalay was planted in the Paya precinct (Nyunt, 2002: 50). Thanks to the care of the villagers, it has now grown into a huge tree. When I visited this village for the first time in 1987, I saw a small main hall with the small Buddha statue (main deity) enshrined, a stupa with peeling gold leaf, and this Bodhi tree. Because it was the rainy season, the area around the hall and stupa were filled with mud, and cow dung was scattered in the mud. I sometimes encountered poisonous snakes such as pit vipers and cobras not only around the hall but also inside.

Although the Paya has a long history, the prosperity of the Paya and this small village began with the end of Burmese socialism and the arrival of the new military regime. In 1989, a year after the military regime came into power, U Khin Thaung, a merchant in Mandalay city, was put on trial for fraud in connection with a cooperative. In his time of distress, he asked the Thindaunggyi village elder, U Bat Chit, to offer prayers and an offering (*gadawbwe*) to the Buddha statue of Shwetheindaw Paya. The following year, in 1990, the court was burnt down and the evidence was burnt, so he was spared from the trial. Thereafter, the merchant brought the junta's Minister of

Industry and the Minister of Border Affairs to worship at the Paya many times. It is not certain whether this story told by the villagers was true or false, but the reputation of this paya as a place of great economic success spread. The wealthy merchants of Mandalay came to donate to it.

In 1993, Daw Kyaing Kyaing—the wife of then head-of-state, Senior General Than Shwe—who was born in Kyaukse District, heard about this good reputation and visited the Paya. At that time, there was no roadway leading to the Paya, so she arrived by horse cart and was covered in dust. The commander of the Mandalay Military Division accompanied her, and when U Chit Myaing, then mayor of the village tract, proposed to build a paved road from the national highway to the Paya, it was immediately approved. The villagers who received the endorsement collected donations by the side of the national highway, while other large contributions were received from military officers and high-ranking officials. In 1994, when I was living in the village for the second survey, the paved roadway was completed by the "labour service" (*lou'âpêi*) of the military, government, and people. As a result, many wealthy ministers, bureaucrats, and merchants who could drive their own cars directly to the Paya began to visit it frequently, and the amount of donations soared.

Shwetheindaw Paya is not only venerable for being built by the first king of Myanmar, but it has also flourished by using its history to attract military politicians and *nouveaux* riche businesspeople during the military period. Former Minister of Science and Technology, a retired military officer, donated 400 million kyats for the construction of *gandakudi*. Similarly, ministers under the military government donated not only cash but also gold leaf, cement, generators, ponds, and so on. Sein Moe, a condensed milk company, also donated 300 million kyats for the *gandakudi*. Sein Moe had once been a cottage industry in Kyaukse District but developed into a national brand and manufacturer of canned condensed milk during the military regime. Another company, MSU, donated 200 million kyats for *zayat*. MSU is also a company founded in Kyaukse. It started as a transportation business when border trade with China was legalised in the 1990s but made a fortune by expanding its business to include gas stations and hotel management. A cement company in Mandalay donated 250 million kyats to build a circular road around *gandakudi*. Brewers and financiers in Mandalay also donated hundreds of millions of kyats.[3] Although it was possible during the Burmese socialist era to operate condensed milk production as a cottage industry or to operate as very small-scale innkeepers and transporters, all of the above industries were basically state-run, and it was impossible for the private sector to enter or expand them. In other words, these companies were the ones that had come of age in line with the economic liberalisation and market economy of the post-socialist military period. There are no grounds for concluding that they are cronies, but we cannot help but imagine so when we see some of them worshipping at Shwetheindaw Paya with active or retired military officers and ministers. And without "donations" from business owners to the military officers and ministers, it

---

[3] The donation amounts listed here are based on interviews with *gawpaka* and village elders and are approximate estimates.

would not be possible for the military officers and ministers to offer such large sums of money to the Paya.

In Myanmar, it is said that praying to Buddha is for happiness in the next world, but this Paya is famous for bringing success in the present life, especially social and economic miracles. Thus, this paya seems to have been in line with post-socialist Myanmar's economic liberalisation.

A leaflet entitled "Praying for Vow" was distributed free of charge to each worshipper, and this "Prayer Guide" contained instructions on how to pray for various requests. For example, regarding the economy, a person should pray: "May my planned such and such business be realised and successful" or "May my current such and such business develop successfully". As for career, "May I hold the desired position". Regarding the family, "May all be healthy and happy, united and cooperative, and work well". Regarding education, "May I receive an exceptionally good score and a high level of education." And so on. All of these are prayers for this world, and behind the prayers a lowly social and economic status is apparent. I have noted that Myanmar Buddhists have tended to maximise utility not only in this life but also in the next (Takahashi, 2012: 124). I should add that this is because, under socialism and military rule, people had no hope in this life. However, if a desire could be realised in this world, it would be natural to first try to maximise utility on this shore rather than on the other shore. In proportion to the fact that post-socialist Myanmar's economic liberalisation increased the probability that one's wishes could be realised in this life, the number of Buddhists who desired benefits in this life rather than the fulfilment of their prayers in the uncertain next world also grew.[4] Shwetheindaw Paya's "Prayer Guide" cleverly responded to this growing demand.

An additional sentence was attached to the "Prayer Guide": "I pray with an offering (*gadawbwe*) of vows". *Gadawbwe* is an offering made of banana, coconut, and flowers. Worshippers should not bring these by themselves but must buy ones at the offering shops that line the perimeter of the Paya. Thus, the spiritual experience of the Paya is combined with the purchase of offerings. Moreover, worshippers who believe that simply following the handbook and praying is not enough to make their wishes come true can hire a "prayer agent" called a *hsùtâunpêidhu* or *pwèhlûdhu*. These agents offer long prayers that are not in the handbook, while the worshippers hang their heads, with their hands on the offering that is placed in front of the Buddha statue. Originally, all offerings were placed in front of the statue, but the number of worshippers became so large that offerings could no longer fit in the main hall. Nowadays, the placement of offerings is usually restricted to the area around the stupa, and only special persons are allowed to place offerings in front of the Buddha statue to pray.[5] When the prayers are over, the worshippers hand over some cash,

[4] It is possible, of course, to interpret this as meaning that if we become wealthy in this life, we will be able to accumulate more merit and virtue for the next life, which will ultimately lead to the maximisation of utility in the next life. However, it is also true that with the advent of the market economy, there is a growing tendency to maximise utility in this life, without giving up on the next.

[5] When I visited the Shwetheindaw Paya on 11 December 2018, the Director General of Myanmar Police Force came to pray, but he was praying not in front of the Buddha statue but in front of the

sometimes a lot, to the prayer agent as a sign of their sincerity. These offerings and prayer agents have also brought new earnings to the Paya. I will discuss this later.

The *gawpaka* committee (*gôpàkà aphwè*) oversees the overall management and administration of the Paya, including the planning of new buildings and extensions, the production and distribution of the "Prayer Guide", the appointment of prayer agents, and the establishment of offering shops. The term *gawpaka* is often translated as "the trustees of the stupa", but since *gawpaka*s also exist for the management of Buddhist statues or monasteries, we may include statues and monasteries in the definition. In this book, let us call it "Gawpaka Committee" or "Board of Trustees". Having a *gawpaka* is common at any town or village paya. The Shwetheindaw Paya Board of Trustees has 11 membres: a Chairman, a Vice-Chairman, a Secretary General, a Deputy Secretary General, a Treasurer, and six ordinary members. The day-to-day management of the Paya is carried out by the Secretary General and the Treasurer, while major construction and repairs, large expenditures for festivals and feasts, and the approval of stores around the Paya are decided by the Board collectively. In the following, I will describe the rise of the Shwetheindaw Paya, focusing on the activities of this Board and the economic effects that this rise brought about.

5.2 Revenue Structure of Shwetheindaw Paya

The prosperity of Shwetheindaw Paya can be clearly seen from the crowds on Saturdays, Sundays, and Sabbath Days, as well as from the huge new buildings that have been constructed one after another. However, there are no data on the number of worshippers or the changes in the size of the buildings, so I will try to describe the prosperity of the Paya by examining the amount of donations and the increase in cash assets.

Other than the aforementioned huge donations in kind, such as for buildings and roads, ordinary visitors make monetary contributions to the Paya in one of two ways: either by throwing cash directly into a transparent glass offertory-box called a *hmanboun*, or by handing the cash to a money collector at the Paya office and receiving a receipt. The purpose of the donation is stated not only on each offertory-box but also on each receipt. The purposes are divided into four categories: general facilities and repairs, electricity bills, gilding, and fund. Thus, general donors usually have eight options for how to donate. Donated money other than the fund are managed in a single bank account as contributions that can be paid in and out at any time for the management of the Paya. Therefore, the three types of donation money other than the "fund" are collectively called donations for "miscellaneous expenses". Four to five per cent of the total donations for miscellaneous expenses are made for electricity, 15–20% are for gilding the stupa and the statue, and the remaining 75–80% are for

stupa with an offering. He said that the visit was to thank the Paya for his promotion from Deputy Director General to Director General, shortly after he had previously prayed here.

general facilities and repairs. Each donation is to be used in accordance with the purpose for which it was given, but the Secretary General explains that all donations can be added up and managed in a single account because the amount donated exceeds the amount spent. The "fund" is described in the Paya's accounting books as *htawàrà ngweibadethabin*, or "the tree that grows money forever," and is deposited in a bank account separate from miscellaneous expenses. It is basically money that must not be withdrawn. The interest rate is around eight per cent. The Treasurer of the Board of Trustees goes to the bank in Kyaukse Town every day with two bank books and cash. I have accompanied him on this trip.

The earnings of the Paya are not limited to donations of money. Another earning is the aforementioned *gadawbwe*s (offerings), which are offered by worshippers with their prayer. In the evening, a small portion of the offerings overflowing around the stupa is donated by the Board of Trustees to the monasteries and the Sangha in Kyaukse Township. All the rest is sold to those who dispose of them, and the next day they are sold in their original forms as bananas or coconuts in other towns and villages. However, the disposal price does not include coconuts, which are free, and thus the price of bananas alone determines the disposal price. The proceeds from disposing and selling the offerings are all income for the Paya.

Another earning is business revenue. The Board of Trustees sells photographs, figures, and history books of the Paya, prepares motorcycle parking lots[6] and receives fees for parking motorcycles, builds flush toilets and collects fees for using them, and collects fees from the shops and street stalls around the Paya, all to generate earnings for the Paya. Both the offering sales revenue and the business revenue are used in a specific way, as described below, while the remaining balance is to be credited to the bank account for "miscellaneous expenses".

Table 5.1 shows the amount of money donated by general visitors to Shwetheindaw Paya, as well as the balances of the above-described two bank accounts from 2008 to 2018. The total amount of donations in each year fluctuated between 140 and 150 million kyats from 2008 to 2011, and then rapidly increased from 2012 to 2014, tripling in three years. 2015 saw a slight decrease, followed by a reversal in 2016, a sharp increase in 2017, and a slight increase in 2018. The decrease in 2015 might be related to the general election, but it is only a guess. The composition of donations shows that the ratio of the fund was very low from 2008 to 2011, but it started to increase in 2012 and was boosted significantly in 2015, eventually remaining stable at 7–8% since then. This is probably because the Board of Trustees induced worshippers to make contributions to the fund, as the most recent expenditure was significantly reduced after major new construction and renovation work had been completed by 2014. The average annual increases in donated money over the 10-year period from 2008 to 2018 were 17.7% for miscellaneous expenses, 38.6% for the fund, and 18.5% for the total, with the growth rate of donations to the fund much larger than to miscellaneous expenses.

---

[6] In addition to motorcycle parking, a large parking lot was constructed in 2016, and car parking fees are now included in the revenue of the Paya.

Table 5.1 Donations and savings of Shwetheindaw Paya, and offerings income

(Unit: thousand kyats)

Year	Donation amount				Bank balance				Sales of offerings
	For expense	For fund	Total	Rate of increase (%)	For expense	For fund	Total	Rate of increase (%)	
2008	146,855	2,425	149,280		285,409	8,360	293,769		
2009	137,889	3,477	141,366	−5.3	438,059	14,416	452,475	54.0	
2010	140,490	4,162	144,652	2.3	622,346	18,405	640,751	41.6	
2011	149,075	2,924	151,999	5.1	772,759	16,116	788,875	23.1	
2012	178,206	9,614	187,820	23.6	739,730	31,908	771,638	−2.2	
2013	286,424	21,751	308,175	64.1	803,886	53,754	857,640	11.1	125,435
2014	454,742	25,593	480,335	55.9	1,305,227	80,775	1,386,002	61.6	172,870
2015	420,479	40,739	461,218	−4.0	1,808,287	127,716	1,936,003	39.7	206,664
2016	506,062	37,829	543,891	17.9	2,737,461	206,215	2,943,676	52.0	205,473
2017	728,547	60,283	788,830	45.0	3,845,073	278,613	4,123,686	40.1	210,774
2018	752,038	63,347	815,385	3.4	4,748,779	347,923	5,096,702	23.6	243,000
Year	%	%			%	%			
2008	98.4	1.6			97.2	2.8			
2009	97.5	2.5			96.8	3.2			
2010	97.1	2.9			97.1	2.9			
2011	98.1	1.9			98.0	2.0			
2012	94.9	5.1			95.9	4.1			
2013	92.9	7.1			93.7	6.3			
2014	94.7	5.3			94.2	5.8			

(continued)

Table 5.1 (continued)

(Unit: thousand kyats)

Year	Donation amount				Bank balance				Sales of offerings
	For expense	For fund	Total	Rate of increase (%)	For expense	For fund	Total	Rate of increase (%)	
2015	91.2	8.8			93.4	6.6			
2016	93.0	7.0			93.0	7.0			
2017	92.4	7.6			93.2	6.8			
2018	92.2	7.8			93.2	6.8			

Note "Bank balance" is the balance of the bank account at the end of December each year
Source Accounting books of Shwetheindaw Paya

Figure 5.1 is a graph showing the variation in the amount of donated money by month. Compared with other months, the amount of donations is much larger in April. This is because April has a series of holidays, from the water festival (*thînjan*) to the first day of the Myanmar calendar. The number of worshippers at the Paya is much larger on Saturdays, Sundays, and Sabbath Days, when schools, companies, and markets are closed, compared to other weekdays. In April, the number of visitors increases due to the large number of holidays, and the amount of donations increases proportionally. In Myanmar, where there is a rainy season and a dry season, the number of worshippers at payas usually increases in the dry season, but as mentioned in Chap. 4, it does not rain so much even in the rainy season in Kyaukse (Fig. 4.4). This is why worshippers are almost constant throughout the year. There is no particular increase in the amount of donations in the months when important Buddhist rituals are held, such as July with *wazouthingân* and November with *kàhtein*. This may be because these two events do not affect this Paya, which is basically unrelated to monks, since these events are to make donations to monks. However, the Shwetheindaw Paya precinct does have a hall, called *sûnzâhsaun*, where monks are offered food. Food-offering ceremonies are frequently held there.

Turning to the *savings* balances in Table 5.1, we can see that there has been a steady increase. Only 2012 saw a decrease from the previous year, and the balance at the end of 2013 was also less than the balance at the end of the previous year, considering the donated money and *gadawbwe* (offerings) income. This is because from the end of 2011 to 2013, a large amount of cash was withdrawn from the savings account for "miscellaneous expenses". According to the Paya's account books, the amount of money withdrawn for the construction of *gandakudi* between October 2011 and September 2013 amounted to 598.58 million kyats. This money was added to the

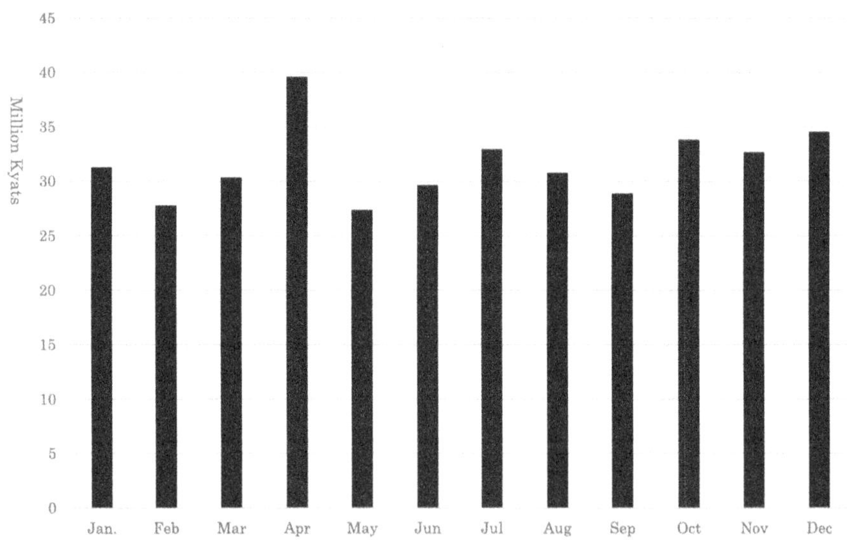

Fig. 5.1 Average monthly donations to Paya (2008–18). *Source* Same as Table 5.1

large contributions from the military officers, lawmakers, and most importantly, the burgeoning private sector. I noted above that the amount of donated money from the general worshippers increased dramatically since the start of *gandakudi* construction. The balance of savings for the fund, which is maintained in a separate bank account, declined in 2011 when it was withdrawn for the *gandakudi* construction, but has increased steadily since then, accounting for about 7% of the total savings.

The rightmost column of Table 5.1 shows the annual revenue from disposing the *gadawbwe*s (offerings) in 2013–18. This revenue was also present in 2008–12, but I could not find any record of it. It seems that it was not recorded in the accounting books. However, the *gawpaka* members told me that the money that remained after deducting the appropriate amount of expenditure was deposited in the account of "miscellaneous expenses". Comparing the annual total amount of donations from worshippers with the annual revenue from the sale of offerings, the latter was 0.41 times the former in 2013, 0.44 times in 2015, and then decreased to 0.30 times in 2018, while the annual revenue from *gadawbwe* disposal increased except in 2016, doubling in six years. Thus, the offerings dedicated by worshippers and kept around the stupa during the daytime can bring in an revenue equivalent to 30–40% of the total amount donated. This *gadawbwe* disposal system, which is rarely seen in the more well-known payas of Yangon and Mandalay, is a significant contribution to the finances of the Shwetheindaw Paya. In addition, this system has brought a new source of income to the villagers, which I will discuss later.

After the donated money and the offerings revenue, the third source of revenue for the Paya is the business revenue. While I have already described the outline of this revenue, I will examine it in detail here by looking at the 2016 business revenue and expenditure table shown in Table 5.2. The sold photographs are of the Shwetheindaw Paya or of the main Buddha statue. The history book is Nyunt 2002, which I referred to above to trace the history of the Paya. These photographs and book are sold in the office at the entrance of the Paya, where you will see them when you donate money and get your receipt. Motorcycle parking and car parking lots are maintained by the Board of Trustees, as mentioned above, and full-time staff in uniform collect the fees. The revenue from the car parking lot, which was built mainly using the offerings revenue and opened in 2016, amounted to a considerable amount of 13.44 million kyats, as shown in Table 5.2. Larger than the above sales revenue and parking revenue were the store registration and rental fees. The above-mentioned prayer agents pay a portion of the prayer fee received from worshippers who offer *gadawbwe*s. The *gadawbwe* disposers pay a fee for the right to enter this business. As can be seen in Table 5.2, the amount paid by merely 14 prayer agents overshadowed most other revenues. 10 *gadawbwe* shops and 25 souvenir shops and restaurants paid monthly shop fees, after having put down a large deposit with the Board. In 2016, the lump-sum store opening deposit was 1.5 million kyats per shop for *gadawbwe* shops and 1 million kyats for other shops. The deposit for opening a store is supposed to be returned when the business ceases, but in the meantime, it is deposited in a bank and earns interest of about 8% a year, which is the revenue of the Paya. *Gadawbwe* disposers do not have shops, so they did not need to pay deposits, but they had to pay 50,000 kyats per person per year to the Board of Trustees to

Table 5.2 Business revenues and expenses in 2016

Items	(thousand kyats)
Photograph sales	2,838
Historical book sales	2,292
Motorcycle parking fee	9,000
Car parking fee	13,440
From prayer agents (14)	16,800
From souvenir shops and restaurants (25)	4,500
From offering shops (10)	2,952
From flower vendor girls (8)	900
From food stalls, etc. (30)	3,240
From offering dispositioner (20)	1,000
Total Revenue	*56,962*
Paya staff salaries (18)	22,752
Gawpaka Committee salaries (2)	2,400
Administrative and miscellaneous expenses	4,800
Total Expenditures	*29,952*
Balance	**27,010**

Note Figures in parentheses indicate the number of persons
Source Same as Table 5.1

remain as dispensers. In addition to the permanent shops, the Board also collected rents from the girls peddling flowers, the farmers selling vegetables on plastic sheets, and the young men pulling carts and selling fried food. For an agricultural labourer, the daily wage at that time was 3500–4000 kyats for a woman and 4000–5000 kyats for a man. The above rents were six to nine per cent of such a labourer wage. Even after paying this rent to the Paya, the worker's net income was both more stable and higher than that of agricultural labourers. Thus, more and more young people were becoming stallholders or street vendors instead of agricultural labourers.

5.3 Expenditure Structure of Shwetheindaw Paya

As discussed above, the Shwetheindaw Paya's sources of revenue can be roughly divided into three categories: donated money, *gadawbwe* sale and disposal, and various businesses. The donated money, from the general worshippers, is intended for four purposes: general facilities and repairs, payment of electricity bills, gilding, and the fund, as described above. The donations are disbursed in accordance with the four "donor intentions" set by the Board of Trustees. The electricity bill is paid every month for the previous month, but there is always a surplus of donations over payments.

For the gilding of Buddha statues and pagodas, 36.73 million kyats was spent in 2013, 32 million kyats in 2014, 118.45 million kyats in 2016, 3.24 million kyats in 2017, and 433.02 million kyats in 2018. All the donated money for gilding purpose is used for that purpose. However, it is often unclear whether the entire amount has already been spent. Unlike at Mahamuni Paya in Mandalay and Paung Daw Oo Paya in Inle Lake, the Shwetheindaw Paya does not permit worshippers to gild the Buddha statue by themselves. Instead, the Board of Trustees applies gold leaves as necessary, so donations are not immediately converted into gold leaf.

The donations for general equipment and repair, which make up the bulk of the donated money, are used for building the temple complexes of the Paya (such as the *gandakudi*, *danmayoung*, and *zayat*), improving the Paya grounds environmentally, buying equipment such as generators and pumps, and repairing buildings and equipment. For example, in 2008, 83.98 million kyats was spent on building the *danmayoung*. In 2009, 66.6 million kyats was spent on flowerbeds and roads. In 2011–2013, 598.58 million kyats was spent on building the *gandakudi*. However, these are so-called matching funds for huge donations by individuals and companies: when individual donations are insufficient for the construction of buildings and roads, donated money from general worshippers is used to make up the shortfall. In other words, the above expenditure is only compensation for the shortfall, and the actual construction cost is much larger than this. All major construction projects were completed by 2014, so since then, the donations for general equipment and repair have been used only for repairing the walls and floors of the *gandakudi* and the *danmayoung*, and for improving the roads and flowerbeds in the precincts. Most of the donations have been accumulated in the bank account.

The revenue and expenditure from the sale and disposal of *gadawbwe*s have been booked separately from donations since at least 2013. Table 5.3 shows the revenue from the sale and disposal of *gadawbwe*s for the year 2014 and how it was spent. In addition to the building of the shopping arcade, the construction of the *sûnzâhsaun* (meal offering hall), the maintenance of car parks and precincts, the installation of water purifiers, repairs, and environmental improvements overlap with the use of the money that the general worshippers donated for general equipment and repairs. This is why the balance of the *gadawbwe* account is managed together with the "miscellaneous expenses" account. However, the construction of the shopping arcade seems to have been financed only from the *gadawbwe* budget since at least 2013. *Gadawbwe* shops, souvenir shops, restaurants, and so on are all planned and built by the Board of Trustees, and they all become the property of the Paya. The shopkeepers pay a deposit for opening their shops and pay monthly rental fees to the Board. As far as the *gadawbwe* shops are concerned, even the price of a *gadawbwe* is decided by the Board. As a result of the development plans by the Board, the number of *gadawbwe* shops increased from 10 to 40, restaurants from 7 to 30, souvenir shops from 16 to 50, and lottery shops from 2 to 5 from 2016 to 2019, and something like a gateway town was formed.

Table 5.4 shows *gadawbwe* disposal revenue and its expenditure in July 2017. In the table, the maintenance and repair expenses correspond to the aforementioned repairs and environmental maintenance. Wage payments are the wages paid to the

Table 5.3 Revenue and expenditure on sale (disposal) of *gadawbwe* (offerings) in 2014

(Unit: thousand kyats)

	Jan	Feb	Mar	Apr	May	Jun	Jul	Aug	Sep	Oct	Nov	Dec	Total
(Revenue)													
Sale of offerings	12,056	11,350	15,166	13,496	14,100	14,448	13,786	16,947	13,936	15,811	15,959	15,815	172,869
(Expenditure)													
Construction of shopping arcade	8,633			278	1,000						380	6,578	16,869
Construction of meal offering hall	3,495	5,048	2,500	3,136	6,070	8,585	2,105	4,891	3,373	331			39,534
Parking lot maintenance		1,329	3,720	801	812	495	2,184	400	7	670	370		10,788
Maintenance of the precinct		3,901	999	321	255		280	573	1,422	710	300		8,761
Water purifier installation					228	82							310
Various repairs	73					838					379		1,290
Environmental maintenance									846	182		1,434	2,462
Total expenditure	12,201	10,278	7,219	4,535	8,365	10,000	4,569	5,864	5,649	1,893	1,429	8,012	80,013
Balance	−145	1,072	7,948	8,960	5,735	4,449	9,217	11,083	8,287	13,918	14,531	7,803	92,856

Note 1 Maintenance of the precinct: Tiling of the floor in Gandakudi and lecture hall, installation of doors, maintenance of the office, installation of donation boxes
Note 2 Various repairs: repair of statues, doors, signboads, floors, etc.
Note 3 Environmental maintenance: Repair of roads around the paya, maintenance of flower beds, repair of electric poles, installation and repair of signboards, etc.
Note 4 The numerals in the table are rounded to the nearest 1000 kyats
Source Same as Table 5.1

Table 5.4 Gadawbwe (Offerings) account for July 2017

	(Unit: thousand kyats)
(Revenue) Sale of offerings	30,825
(Expenditure) Donations to religious education	5,000
Fuel	50
Maintenance and repair costs	1,778
Miscellaneous expenses	1,174
Payment of wages	1,131
Social and travel expenses	115
Invitation of a troupe	3,000
Total expenditures	12,248
Balance	18,577

Source Same as Table 5.1

day labourers hired for maintenance and repairs. Travel expenses refer to the travel-related expenses of the Board members and staff. Social expenses mean the expenses for entertaining VIPs such as ministers and military officers who visited the Paya. It is noteworthy that the Board spent a large amount of money on donations for religious education and on inviting theatre troupes. Shwetheindaw Paya has directly contributed to the development of Buddhist education not only in the village but also in broader Kyaukse District. By inviting theatre troupes, the Paya is giving a part of its profits back to the society.

Business revenue has been mainly used to pay salaries, as shown in the lower part of Table 5.2. As of 2016, the Paya's staff consisted of four administrative staff, two motorcycle and car parking management staff, two security staff, and ten cleaning staff, with a monthly salary of 150,000 kyats for administrative staff and 90,000 kyats for other full-time staff. The administrative staff consisted of one man and three women, all of whom had university degrees, while other staff were educated only to primary or secondary school level. Their salaries reflected this educational background. In 2013, four members of the Board of Trustees were paid 90,000 kyats each: the Chairman, the Vice Chairman, the Secretary General, and the Treasurer. This would be a post allowance, so to speak. However, in 2016, the system was changed to pay 100,000 kyats per month only to the Secretary General and the Treasurer, who have heavy workloads. They were paid according to the content of their work, not their position. Even so, they were paid less per month than the administrative staff, who had lower positions and less work. Ostensibly, this was done on the principle that those who are closer to the Paya should be more modest, but it appears that there were also unrevealed gifts from *gadawbwe* shops, *gadawbwe* disposers, and souvenir shops and restaurants.

The contents of "administrative and miscellaneous expenses" vary. They are used to purchase office supplies, to pay for gasoline and entertainment for the Board members and staff, and to pay the wages of day labourers who help the Board with their work, while being also used to make papers for donation receipts.

As mentioned above, the uses of donated money, revenue from *gadawbwe* sale and disposal, and business revenue are not fungible. In other words, each revenue has specific use. Of course, there have been occasions such as some overlaps in administrative and miscellaneous expenses. Proceeds from *gadawbwe* sale and disposal were used to pay for building the *sûnzâhsaun*, which was to be built with the donated money. Nevertheless, just as there are basically three categories of revenue, there are also categories of specific use for each of them. Donations made by general worshippers to the Paya are used only for four purposes—general facilities and repairs, gilding of Buddha statue and pagoda, payment of electricity bills, and the fund—but are not used to pay the salaries of the Board members and staff or to maintain the shopping arcade. The business revenue is mainly used to pay the salaries of the trustees and staff, and to purchase photographs of the Buddha statue for sale, but it is not used to pay the electricity bills or to invite theatrical troupes. Revenue from the disposal sale of *gadawbwe*s overlaps partly with donations for the construction and repair of the Paya facilities, and partly with business revenue for the payment of wages to day labourers, but is used exclusively for one-time expenses such as donations for religious, festival-related expenses, and road repairs, and not for gilding or the payment of salaries to Board members and staff. By nature, money is fungible, that is, it can be used in any way, and expenditure items are not limited by the type of revenue. It is unlikely that a confectionery company spends its revenue from the sale of chewing gum only on its production, or that an individual with multiple sources of revenue divides his expenditures according to the sources of his revenue. In this sense, Shwetheindaw Paya's use of money is unique.[7] This is probably because the act of donating money created a situation in which the use of money was written on banknotes. This system extended to other revenue as well, probably because the Paya had abundant money and never needed to move money earmarked for a specific use beyond the boundaries of its purpose-specific expenditures. The use of donated money in accordance with the donor's intentions ensures confidence in the Paya and leads to an increase in donations. The believers always pay attention to the responsibility and competence of the Board of Trustees.

[7] Myanmar has other episodes that do not allow for fungibility. One such example is the crop-based agricultural loan system. For example, if a farmer grows rice, he can get a low-interest loan according to the acreage of rice cultivation. There was also a system under which a certain amount of fertiliser was provided at low cost if a farmer planted sugarcane. However, since both the loans and the fertilisers were fungible, the money for rice was often used to grow other crops, to pay for children's education, or to pay for alcohol. Fertiliser for sugarcane was also used for onions and chillies, which had better market prices, and did not increase the productivity of sugarcane. These crop-based agricultural loan schemes were introduced in many countries, but gradually fell into disuse due to the difficulty of monitoring their use. In Myanmar, however, this type of loan is still provided in increasing amounts, and the farmers expect them. There are some similarities with the tacit understanding that donated money to the Paya is used for specific purposes.

5.4 Economic Ripple Effects of Shwetheindaw Paya

To conclude this chapter, I would like to examine the economic impact of the prosperity of Shwetheindaw Paya on the Thindaunggyi villagers. In order to quantitatively calculate the economic ripple effect, an input–output table is necessary.[8] However, there is no such table in Myanmar at either the national or regional level. In addition, since almost all the actors who enjoy the economic effects of the Paya are doing so through *new* occupations, the analysis in this book itself is a process of creating a new part of the input–output table. As for specific figures such as the number of people and the value added, I will focus on the data of 2016, when I was able to obtain the Paya's detailed account book and conduct an interview survey.

As a backward linkage effect of the construction of Shwetheindaw Paya, the procurement of materials such as concrete and steel bars can be assumed. Electric lights and brass ornaments are unique to the Paya. In addition, expensive gold leaves are also indispensable for the Paya. The economic effects are then passed on to the manufacturers of these various materials and the contractors who install them. However, except for the plasterers who can be called the "village occupation" of Thindaunggyi, all the other traders and technicians are from Mandalay city and Kyaukse town. The plasterers in the village participate in plastering the walls and tiling the floors of the Paya as an act of donation to the Paya, even though there is plenty of demand outside the village. They do this for free or at lower wages than usual because of the nature of the act. In other words, as far as the plasterers in the village are concerned, the construction and renovation projects of the Paya have not brought positive economic spillover effects, at least in terms of monetary revenue. In other words, we do not need to consider the backward linkage effect of the Paya on the village economy.

In contrast to the backward linkage effect that goes out of the village, the forward linkage effect of the Paya on the village economy is enormous. However, when we consider the forward linkage effect of the Paya, it is not the usual forward linkage where goods and services are supplied to downstream industries to increase the output of those industries. Nonetheless, if we consider that the Paya provides the "service" of attracting worshippers, then, as in Japan, it can be seen as part of the tourism industry, with shrines and temples as tourism resources. The construction and maintenance of the Paya and related facilities increases the number of worshippers and the amount of donations to the Paya, increasing the revenue of the Paya and swelling the income of villagers who provide various goods and services to worshippers. This income of villagers in turn spills over to the village in secondary and tertiary ways. This is the forward linkage effect of the Paya. Here, we will mostly consider only the spill-over effects "within the village", while discussing the secondary and tertiary forward linkage effects that go out of the village only supplementarily.

It is mostly the newly created occupations that benefit from the forward linkage effects of the Paya. In particular, the first-order (direct) spillover effects reach all the

[8] The strength of forward and backward linkages among economic agents and sectors can be calculated using the inverse matrices of Ghosh and Leontief in the input–output table, respectively.

occupations that were not in the village before 1990, except for the Board of Trustees. In the following, I will introduce the new occupations created by the prosperity of the Paya and describe the economic effects of the Paya.

The money donated by the worshippers to the Paya is used for construction, repair, gilding, electricity, and so on, so there is no direct ripple effect on the village. However, the Board of Trustees, which has the authority to decide how the donations are spent, receives revenue from the disposal sale of *gadawbwe*s and from various businesses. The labour cost part of the expenditure items brings in salary income for villagers and creates new jobs through the construction of the shopping arcade. In 2016, two of the trustees are paid 100,000 kyats per month each, or 2.4 million kyats per year for the two of them, and the 18 full-time employees are paid 22.75 million kyats per year.[9] Before the Paya came to prominence, the Board members were unpaid and contributed their own money to maintain and manage the Paya, as in many other villages. Some of the Board members were from outside the village. As the Paya became more famous, outsiders were excluded, and only villagers were allowed to serve on the Board. A new notion of "village interest" was born. It was not until around 2008, when some of the Board members were paid, that paid staff were hired. Even then, only local villagers were employed. Both the paid Board members and the paid full-time staff can be regarded as newly created positions. The primary spillover effect in the form of salaries paid to them will have a secondary and tertiary spillover effect through their consumption in the village. However, the villagers buy most of their consumer goods in Kyaukse town, so the effect is very small.

In addition to the payment of salaries and the construction of the shopping arcade, if we take the net revenue of the Board of Trustees in 2016—after deducting the cost of repairing and gilding the Paya, maintenance of the surrounding areas such as parking lots, electricity charges, and temporary labourers—to be the increase in their savings balance from 1.94 billion kyats in 2015 to 2.94 billion kyats in 2016, as shown in Table 5.1, then the amount was a billion kyats. General worshippers' donations accounted for a little more than half of this amount, which together with large special donations constituted the direct economic impact of the Paya, but secondary economic impacts such as proceeds from the disposal sale of *gadawbwe*s and revenues from various businesses also accounted for a large part of the revenue. The rents for place paid to the Board by the prayer agents, *gadawbwe* shops, souvenir shops, and flower sellers also entered the Board's revenue as secondary economic effects. In other words, the revenue of the Board is the sum of the direct effect and the secondary ripple effect.

Along with the prosperity of Shwetheindaw Paya, various new occupations related to the *gadawbwe*s (offerings) have gradually emerged since around 1997. These new types of jobs are the most diversified and bring the most value added to the village.

[9] See Table 5.2. In 2013, four of the eleven trustees, including the chairman and secretary general, received a monthly salary of 90,000 kyats. Two of them started to earn more money as prayer agents and gave up their salaries as trustees. At that time, four administrative and cleaning staffs were employed, and their monthly salary was 80,000 kyats. As mentioned above, in 2016, the salary of administrative staff was 150,000 kyats, which was much higher than that of Board members and other staff.

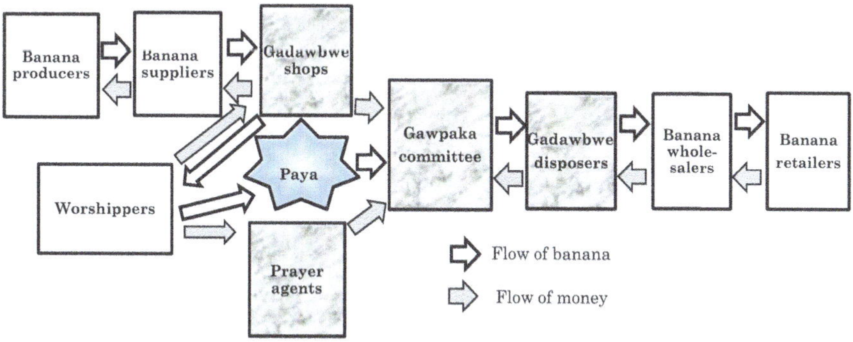

Fig. 5.2 Flow of traditional offerings (banana) and money around the Paya.
Note 1 Offering shops' keepers, Paya trustees (*gawpaka*), prayer agents and offering disposers are all villagers. In contrast, banana producers, suppliers, wholesalers and retailers are all from outside the village.
Note 2: The flow of money that comes into the Paya Gawpaka Committee from worshippers' money donations to the Paya has been omitted because it has nothing to do with these offerings. *Source* According to the author's survey

With reference to Fig. 5.2, I will now describe how the *gadawbwe*s, their material—banana—and the money paid for them flow among the various occupations and how much value added is created.

As mentioned above, the "Prayer Guide" states that "I pray with a *gadawbwe* of vows", and it is half-compulsory to offer a *gadawbwe*. Worshippers are not allowed to bring *gadawbwe*s along with them to the Paya, but must buy ones at the shops that rent the facilities built by the Board of Trustees. The number of banana bunches that make up a *gadawbwe* is fixed, and there are four types of *gadawbwe*: 3, 5, 9 and 108 bunches of bananas, with one coconut and a flower decoration. Since each *gadawbwe* is sold at a fixed price, there is no price competition. However, each shop tries to attract customers by adding chilled bottled water, fruit, tea leaves salad (*laphe'thou'*), or a picture of the Buddha statue to make worshippers buy the more expensive *gadawbwe*s with more banana bunches.[10] Worshippers wishing to offer a *gadawbwe* buy these and the shop employees carry them to the side of the stupa, so that the worshippers do not touch the *gadawbwe*s at this stage. When the *gadawbwe* is placed in its place, the worshipper touches it and recites a prayer. Some prayers are recited by themselves according to the "Prayer Guide", but those who want to have their wishes fulfilled more strongly request a prayer agent to pray for them. The fee for this service is not fixed, but can be freely decided by the worshipper, depending on the degree of the worshipper's desire, the wealth of the worshipper, the skill of the prayer agent, and the success stories associated with him. The income of the prayer

[10] Banana prices soared from around the summer of 2019, with a 3-bunch *gadawbwe* going from 3500 kyats in 2016 to 5000 kyats. Therefore, instead of selling at a fixed price, each *gadawbwe* shop had to compete in price. In this chapter, however, we focus on the situation in 2016, when the most data are available. In addition, coconuts, which had previously been disposed of for free, started to be priced around 2018.

agent is positively correlated with the number of worshippers, as is the case with the *gadawbwe* shops. The Paya is overflowing with worshippers on Sabbath Days and weekends, while it is quiet on other days. Only villagers can be prayer agents, but not all villagers can. Oral permission from the Board of Trustees is required. Until 2015, there were only seven agents, but in 2016, the number doubled to 14. On weekdays, there were two shifts of seven agents each, and on Sabbath Days and weekends, when there were many worshippers, all 14 agents could perform prayers. Initially, up to seven people could become prayer agents on a first-come, first-served basis, but as the prayer agency proved to be a very lucrative new profession, as described below, former mayors and those considered *lugyi* (*lujî*)[11] in the village entered this business. However, as the criteria for *lugyi* are vague and have nothing to do with ability or skill in prayer, the dissatisfaction of those who could not become prayer agents was clearly growing. The power to suppress this discontent may be the essence of the *lugyi*. In contrast, the right to open a *gadawbwe* shop was also originally on a first-come, first-served basis, but since 2016 it has been possible to open a shop by paying a deposit to the Board of Trustees. From 2019, the location of the shops, which determines the amount of sales, would be decided by lottery once a year. The right to set up a store is also limited to villagers, but from 2019 onwards, as long as they can pay a large deposit, they will be able to participate in this business, so the criteria are much clearer than for the right to become a prayer agent.

Most of the *gadawbwe*s placed around the stupa are sold off to the *gadawbwe* disposers in the evening. The *gadawbwe*s are then dismantled and the bananas go to wholesalers and then to retailers. Sometimes the coconuts are given to the banana vendors for free, but sometimes they are given to the village restaurants and to villagers. The *gadawbwe* disposers are all villagers, while the wholesalers and retailers are all outsiders. The income of the *gadawbwe* disposers can be regarded as a second order spillover effect, as the worshippers purchase *gadawbwe*s at the shops, and the *gadawbwe*s then pass on to the disposers via the Board of Trustees in the evening.

Based on the above, I will estimate now how much revenue was generated through the *gadawbwe*s for one year in 2016, as the *gadawbwe*s passed through the hands of the villagers from the shops to the Paya to the Board of Trustees to the *gadawbwe* disposers.

According to the books of the Board of Trustees, the revenue from selling bananas from disposed *gadawbwe*s was 205.47 million kyats in 2016 (see Table 5.1). The Paya's set disposal price was 500 kyats per banana bunch. The Paya's revenue would thus correspond to 410,940 banana bunches, or 136,980 *gadawbwe*s, if assuming three bunches per set. The *gadawbwe* disposers sold bananas at 700 kyats per bunch, so they could make 200 kyats per bunch just by distributing bananas from right to left with the permission of the Board of Trustees. In other words, the total annual

[11] As mentioned above, the word *lujî* means "elder, community leader, important person, respected person". While the majority of prayer agents fall into this category, there are some who do not. The criteria for selection are extremely vague, despite the fact that this is a position bringing in substantial income for a few minutes of incantation.

revenue of the 20 *gadawbwe* disposers was 82,188,000 kyats, and they collectively paid only 1,000,000 kyats in 2016 to the Board of Trustees as shown in Table 5.2, so the average monthly revenue per person would have been about 338,000 kyats. In comparison, the monthly income of agricultural workers was 80,000 kyats and that of plasterers 120,000 kyats in the same year, indicating that the *gadawbwe* disposers had an easy and lucrative job.

Of the *gadawbwe*s offered at the Paya, about 10 sets were donated to monasteries and Sangha schools a day, and the rest were disposed of as mentioned above. Therefore, the annual sales volume of *gadawbwe* shops was 146,630 sets, which is the sum of 136,980 sets to be disposed of and 3650 sets to be donated. The fixed price for a set of three bunches of *gadawbwe* was 3500 kyats, so the total turnover of the 10 *gadawbwe* shops amounts to 492.2 million kyats. After deducting the cost of materials such as bananas and coconuts, the labour cost of salesclerks, and the cost of purchasing bottled water, it was said that 30% of the total revenue was left, which was 147.66 million kyats. Subtracting the store opening fee of 2.95 million kyats, shown in Table 5.2, the total net revenue of the 10 stores was 144.71 million kyats, and the average monthly revenue per store was about 1.2 million kyats. This is 15 times the income of an agricultural labourer and 10 times that of a plasterer.

The income of prayer agents is independent of the number of *gadawbwe*s sold. They are hired if the worshippers who buy *gadawbwe*s think that prayer agents are necessary, otherwise they are not. Their income depends on a variety of factors such as the skill of the prayer, the urgency of the client's wish, and the relationship between the worshippers and the agents. Because the donation is made in good faith by each client, the prayer agents do not count the amount, and there are few agents who count the amount for each day. According to the seven prayer agents who were able to tell me their approximate incomes, there was a wide range of incomes: from 400,000 kyats per month for the lowest to 1.5 million kyats per month for the highest. The number of clients was more important for monthly income than the above income determinants. What mattered was not only the popularity of the prayer agents but also how long they stayed in the Paya. Some prayer agents had other jobs, such as farming or being a member of the Board of Trustees, and some could not attend the Paya for a long time because of old age or poor health. Even if the unit price per client was low, the monthly income of prayer agents who earned by working frequently seems to have been relatively better. The seven prayer agents whom I interviewed also told me the income of the other agents. This is only an estimate, but based on these surveys and interviews with the Secretary General of the Board of Trustees, the average monthly income per prayer agent in 2016 was approximately 800,000 kyats, after paying 100,000 kyats per month to the Board of Trustees as a rent for place. This figure may be less than it actually is, as half of the prayer agents have built new *taik* houses or bought new cars, which are still few in the village. At the lowest possible estimate as above, they earn 10 times more than agricultural workers and 6.7 times more than plasterers.

So far, we have only discussed the numerical value of the *gadawbwe*s' ripple effect, but let us now look at the stories of two villagers who achieved economic success through this effect.

The first is the story of Ko Min Swe, an owner of a *gadawbwe* shop. I first met him in 1990, when he was a young man at age 25. He did not hold any farmland at all and had a small thatched-roof shop in front of the Paya, where he sold mainly fried food, cigarettes, juice, and candles. In 1994, he was still a poor man earning about 100 kyats (equivalent to one USD) a day to make ends meet. In 1995, just after the completion of the paved road from the national highway to the Paya, staying close to the Paya, he became aware of the demand for *gadawbwe*s and became the first to specialise in *gadawbwe* for sale. Along with the prosperity of the Paya, sales at his *gadawbwe* shop grew rapidly, and by 2016 it was generating monthly sales of 6 million kyats and net revenue of 1.7 million kyats. By then, he had become one of only four car owners in the village at the time and an extremely wealthy person with pre-emptive rights over eight banana orchards. By 2018, the number of car owners in the village increased to eight, and he also bought more four-wheel-drive sport utility vehicles in addition to his pickup truck.

Table 5.5 shows the years that new *gadawbwe* shops were opened, following Ko Min Swe's example, and the previous occupation of each owner. As we can see, Ko Min Swe was the exclusive seller of *gadawbwe*s until 1997. Until 2000, no farmer became a *gadawbwe* shopkeeper. All the shopkeepers instead came from occupations with lower incomes than farmers, such as a fried food vender, a side-car driver, a carpenter and a plasterer. Later, two farmers opened *gadawbwe* shops, and next, another two *gadawbwe* shopkeepers came from the lowest class of the village, agricultural labourers. Both of these agricultural labourers borrowed a large amount of money both inside and outside the village to open their shops, but they told me that they had repaid all these loans in about three years. Until 1995, farmland holdings and household income were positively correlated in Thindaunggyi Village (Takahashi, 2000: 287), but the emergence and prosperity of *gadawbwe* shops disrupted this correlation, allowing the poor without farmland to move up the economic ladder in the village. The economic impact of the Paya contributed to the de-agrarianisation of the village.

Table 5.5 Year of opening an offering shop and the owner's previous job (as of 2016)

Name of the owner	Year of opening	Previous job
Ko Min Swe	1995	Fried food peddler
Ko Yan Aung	1997	Side-car driver
Ko Hla Myint	1997	Carpenter
Ko Kyaw Oo	1997	Plasterer
Ko Win Naing	1997	Carpenter
Ko Tum Moe	2000	Farmer
Ko Sein Ya	2005	Farmer
Ko Nay Myo	2005	Agricultural labourer
Ko Nandar	2007	Agricultural labourer
Ko Ye Kyaw	2009	Grocer (parents)

Source According to the author's survey

The second story is of Ko Kyaw Thein, a prayer agent. He was not from Thindaunggyi Village, but married the daughter of an agricultural labourer in Thindaunggyi in 1995. Having first lived in the village where he was born, the couple moved to Thindaunggyi Village in 2005 to escape poverty. He has a primary school education. Luckily, he was liked by an elder (*lugyi*) who became the Secretary General of the Paya's Board of Trustees in 2007. Thus, Ko Kyaw Thein was appointed as an official member of the Board, as the Deputy Treasurer. As a member of the Board, he received no salary but was able to be a prayer agent, a position normally reserved for elders. At the time, he was the youngest person on the Board. In this way, even those who had come from other villages could join the ranks of influential people in the village. This is one way that Myanmar villages differ from Japanese villages.[12] Because Ko Kyaw Thein was acting as a prayer agent while doing chores under the Secretary General, his income was lower than that of other agents, but he could earn much more than agricultural labourers. He also pushed his wife into becoming a *gadawbwe* disposer, the couple earning a fair amount of money there as well. Thus, the couple were able to send their daughter to university and get her a job in a private bank in Kyaukse town. In 2018, he built a new *taik*, the symbol of the rich in the village, and bought his own car. As in the case of Ko Min Swe, the Paya has given poor landless workers an opportunity to move up the economic ladder. However, it is important to remember that the success stories of these men, while not exceptional, are in the privileged few among the many villagers who do not benefit.

These are the ripple effects of the *gadawbwe* business on the village economy. As shown in Fig. 5.2, in terms of the flow of money, the banana suppliers and producing farmers precede the *gadawbwe* shops, while the buyers of the disposed bananas, the wholesalers, and the retailers follow after the shops. All of these people are outside the village. Thus, the economy surrounding *gadawbwe*s has various ripple effects not only within the village but also outside the village.

As of 2016, in addition to the *gadawbwe* shops, 25 more shops operated in the shopping arcade rented from the Board of Trustees: seven restaurants, 16 souvenir shops and two lottery shops. All of these shops were owned by villagers. These shops have an average net revenue of 10,000 kyats per day. The average monthly revenue per shop was estimated to be 285,000 kyats, since these shops had an average net revenue of 10,000 kyats per day and paid a monthly stall fee of 15,000 kyats to the Board of Trustees. Two restaurant owners and five souvenir shopkeepers were farmers, while the others were people who had moved from non-farmer jobs, such as carpenters, plasterers, and agricultural labourers.

In addition to the shops installed by the Board of Trustees, such as the *gadawbwe* shops, restaurants, and souvenir shops, there were also stalls and tables that were not owned by the Board. Those shops were selling processed foods such as fried crab, boiled pork, and betels, products from nearby villages such as turmeric, onions, and

---

[12] See Takahashi (2012:105) for the story of another person, Ko Kyaung Ni, who came to Thindaunggyi Village without money or food and became a successful milker and influential figure in the village.

guavas, and shirts made in nearby factories. The number of stalls and tables varied depending on the day, from twenty on weekdays to nearly fifty on weekends and Sabbath Days. The number of stalls and tables also varied due to people having other works or health reasons. Among these shops, villagers owned the stalls selling agricultural products and shirts. Such stalls number about five on weekdays and about twenty on Sabbath Days and weekends. In contrast, most of the stalls and tables selling processed foods were owned or managed by people from outside the village. The daily sales of these stalls and tables varied greatly: from 5000 to 20,000 kyats. The net revenue was usually about half of the sales. Although the stalls and tables were not owned by the Board of Trustees, the shopkeepers had to pay 300 kyats a day to the Board. Since 2018, these stalls and tables have been cracked down on, and many have moved to selling in shops with higher rents that were extended by the Board. However, those wishing to save on stall fees and newcomers from outside the village have increasingly been setting up stalls and tables near the national road, well away from the Paya.

Although it was a considerably less attractive job than selling *gadawbwe*s, eight girls sold garlands like necklaces to offer to the paya for around 200 kyats each. The girls hung out at the motorcycle parking lots and at the entrances to the stairs to the paya. They were between 15 and 18 years old and had not graduated from primary school. They were the daughters of landless agricultural labourers and plasterers in the village. They told me that they dropped out of school because they had to earn money quickly. After deducting the purchase price of wreaths, their profit was 5000 kyats on weekdays and 8000 kyats on Sabbath Days and weekends, which was higher than their parents' income. From these earnings, they paid 300 kyats daily to the Board as a fee.

The above are the economic ripple effects benefiting the villagers, but people outside the village also enjoy the various economic opportunities created by the Paya.

Every day I saw women with large bamboo baskets on their heads, selling boiled quail eggs, fried sparrows and quails, milk balls,[13] and so on, not only along the roadside and in the shopping streets, but also in the restaurants. They came to Thindaunggyi Village every day by bus from Nyaungbin Village in Natogyi Township, about 80 km west of Thindaunggyi. Natogyi is known as a poor area due to poor farmland and few job opportunities in the non-agricultural sector. The women started coming to Thindaunggyi Village around 2013, their numbers increasing to 10 in 2014, 15 in 2016 and 20 in 2018. The average daily sales amount of these women was 7000 kyats, but after deducting 2000 kyats for the bus fare to and from the village and the cost of materials, there was not much left. Even so, they told me that it was better than earning nothing in Nyaungbin Village.

Near the entrance to the paya, there were girls talking to worshippers, with a metal birdcage full of sparrows. They wanted worshippers to buy three sparrows for 1000 kyats. It is said that if you release them into the sky, you will get merits. The girls

[13] A Myanmar sweet made by mixing milk with sugar, oil, and so on to make a solid. It is called *nwânòugê* in Burmese.

did not catch the sparrows by themselves but bought them for 200 kyats each. Their net revenue was 2000 kyats on weekdays and about 5000 kyats on weekends and Sabbath Days. These little girls came from Letpan Village, located across the national highway to the west. This village is inhabited by Indian Muslims. In the past, this village used to have a cattle market every five days, attracting Bamar people from the surrounding, and the children interacted with each other on a daily basis without distinction of religion. However, close contacts between the villages of Thindaunggyi and Letpan were cut off following a 2013 clash between Buddhists and Muslims in Meiktila, about 100 km south of Kyaukse Town. The sparrow-selling girls, who were instantly recognisable as being of Indian descent, did not approach the Paya and sold their sparrows in a reserved manner at a place where they could always flee back to their own village across the national highway if they were driven away. They said that no one came to collect any fees from them.

All of the above jobs require more or less investment, but there is one job that can be done with just a small bowl. That is begging. Most of the beggars around the Paya were widows, and all of them were old women. The largest number of beggars—ten—came from Pakokku Township, 170 km west of Thindaunggyi Village, across the Ayeyarwady River, followed by three from Mandalay and three from Kyaukse Township, for a total of 16. None of them were from within the village. As of 2016, they told me that they earned 2000 kyats on weekdays and 3000 kyats on weekends and Sabbath Days. However, in 2018 they were evicted from the immediate vicinity of the Paya to the west side of the Minye Canal and their income seems to have decreased considerably. This reduced the number of beggars to about ten, but seeing that they are still begging in this village, it is probably because they cannot earn enough to eat even if they returned to their place of origin.

Having discussed the new occupations that emerged as a result of the prosperity of the Paya and their ripple effects, let us now estimate the total value added in the village generated by the glory of the Paya for the year 2016. In the order described above, the net revenue was 81.19 million kyats for *gadawbwe* disposers, 144.71 million kyats for *gadawbwe* shops, 134.40 million kyats for prayer agents, 85.50 million kyats for restaurants and souvenir shops, 30.76 million kyats for tables and stalls set up by villagers,[14] and 16.88 million kyats for flower sale girls.[15] Adding to these the revenues of the Board of Trustees of 1007.67 million kyats, the total value-added amounts to 1501.11 million kyats. This would be equivalent to the annual income of 1564 agricultural labourers or 1042 plasterers in the village. The number

[14] In 2016, there were 105 Saturdays and Sundays, 25 Sabbath Days, and 236 weekdays. As previously mentioned, 20 villagers set up stalls and tables on Sabbath Days and weekends, and 5 villagers set them up on weekdays, with a net revenue of 10,000 kyats per person on Sabbath Days and weekends, and 5000 kyats per person on weekdays. This figure is calculated by subtracting the fee of 300 kyats per day paid to the Board, then multiplying by the number of shops and the number of days each shop was open.

[15] It was estimated that there was a net revenue of 8000 kyats on Sabbath Days and weekends and 5000 kyats on weekdays, with each person paying 300 kyats per day for a place to the Board of Trustees.

of agricultural labourers and plasterers in Thindaunggyi Village in that year was 50–70 and 80–90 respectively, which shows how large this value-added amount is. In addition, the minimum wage in Myanmar was 3600 kyats per day, and in principle, no one could work more than eight hours a day or 48 h a week in 2016. If a worker worked to the maximum on this principle at the minimum wage, his or her annual income would be 1.12 million kyats. In that case, 1501.11 million kyats is equivalent to the annual income of 1336 workers. This means that the new occupations created by the Paya would be able to employ all villagers over the age of 18 at double the minimum wage, even if the 2013 population of 538 adults had increased slightly by 2016.

With the creation of these new occupations, de-agrarianisation accelerated dramatically in Thindaunggyi Village. As seen in Table 4.4, the number of households whose main occupations were running shops or restaurants increased rapidly, and the number of non-agricultural workers also increased, as explained in Table 4.12. There were many farmers who began employing labourers in agriculture and themselves became prayer agents, *gadawbwe* disposers, or souvenir shopkeepers. Similarly, many agricultural labourers gave up agricultural work to become clerks in *gadawbwe* shops or Paya employees. As a result, although the number of farm households did not change significantly, the number of non-farm households with non-agricultural occupations increased (see Table 4.4), and more villagers became employed in the non-agricultural sector, even though they were members of farm households. De-agrarianisation—such as adjustment of employment, change of income source, and transformation of social identity—has been progressing. However, the spatial migration out of the village to work in the non-agricultural sector, which is seen in many villages in Myanmar (Takahashi, 2017: 417–422; 2018: 100–107, 158–160), was rarely seen in Thindaunggyi Village, except for plasterers who usually go out to work. Such rapid expansion of non-agricultural employment *within* the village is a special characteristic of Thindaunggyi Village.

In Thindaunggyi, as in other Myanmar villages, powerful farmers with large agricultural landholdings have traditionally dominated village administration and the Board of Trustees, but non-agricultural workers—who have accumulated wealth as *gadawbwe* shop keepers and prayer agents—have been rising. Thus, de-agrarianisation—in my expanded definition, which includes non-agricultural workers moving up the rural economic hierarchy—is taking place. De-agrarianisation, in the sense that those who are not of farmer origin start to hold power in the village, may also occur. The Paya has facilitated various kinds of de-agrarianisation in the village.

Nevertheless, the socioeconomic disparity within the village has not decreased. Rather, it has widened. Only residents considered to be elders (*lugyi*s) in the village could become paya trustees or prayer agents, and the selection process of *gadawbwe* shopkeepers with pioneer privileges and of paya officials was also ambiguous. The gap between those villagers who have access to the new occupations—which pay more than agricultural labouring and plastering, and which provide more stable incomes than agricultural work—and the many villagers who do not have such access has been widening, causing frustration among the left-behind. This frustration exploded in 2018 when the Board of Trustees was replaced. A villager named Ko Thein Lwin mobilised a group of disgruntled villagers, ousted the Chairman and Secretary General, and succeeded in taking control of the Board of Trustees by assuming the post of Vice Chairman. This *coup d'état* removed the pioneer privileges of the *gadawbwe* shops and reshuffled the prayer agents. However, the villagers who were kicked out, as well as those people who still could not join the privileged group, would remain frustrated. There is no guarantee that a counter-coup will not occur. Previously, the *lugyis*' lack of economic interests made them respected by the villagers as elders and gave them political influence. However, when the *lugyis*' position is combined with economic privileges, it seems that even they could not be at ease.

Although access to the huge concessions created by the Paya was limited to the villagers, it naturally did not go unnoticed by outsiders. The Kyaukse Township Administration and the Buddhist Sangha intervened in the 2018 *coup d'état* and subsequent chaos. Their rationale was that the new trustees were not capable of managing the ever-growing Paya's enormous income and wealth. The villagers used to maintain the Paya out of their passionate devotion, but its grace became too great. This has led to conflicts of interest within the village and interference from outside. How will the villagers' accumulated merit and virtue be evaluated in the afterlife?

Chapter 6
Villagers on the Move: Mixed Multi-ethnic Settlement in Zeepinwea Village

A "side-car" and a motorcycle taxi run through the village. The former is a traditional transportation business that has existed since the socialist era, while the latter is a new occupation that appeared around 2010. Reflecting this, middle-aged and older people tend to work in the former and younger people in the latter. In many cases, the sons of farmers and agricultural labourers who moved to this village from other villages started operating motorcycle taxis (Zeepinwea village, January 2014)

A. Takahashi, *Regime Changes and Socio-economic History of Rural Myanmar, 1986–2019*, Studies in Economic History,
https://doi.org/10.1007/978-981-99-3272-6_6

Introduction

Researchers have not paid enough attention to the issue of migration during the period of Burmese socialism. It used to be argued that the migration of population in the rural areas of Myanmar was very low due to the regime's strict rural management and limited employment opportunities in urban areas. In response to this argument, I developed a different theory based on data collected in my village surveys conducted in 1987 and 1994, suggesting that there may have been considerable population movements even during the socialist period (Takahashi, 1997: 2–3, 23–24). However, this was inter-rural migration from rural to rural areas, not from rural to urban areas. Moreover, both households and individuals kept moving a large number of times (Takahashi, 1997: 23). With limited access to cities and no information about the income that could be obtained in the cities, villagers moved from village to village in search of a small wage differential and livelihood security. Rather than moving because of the expected income gap between rural and urban areas, as the Harris-Todaro model suggests, they moved because they owned so few assets in their present village, such as houses and land, that they could sacrifice them at any time, and in some cases move with them.[1] In other words, because of the low opportunity cost of migration, they decided to move even if the difference in social and economic living standards between the source and destination villages was small. Such a characteristic is most pronounced among non-farm households without farmland. Therefore, I proposed a hypothesis that the asset effect on migration should be taken into account when the asset gap between households is large and inter-rural migration is dominant, as in rural Myanmar (Takahashi, 1997: 24).

After I did the above study in the late 1980s and mid-1990s, the conditions that used to constrain migration before were gradually relaxed. First, the restrictions on farmers eased. In the past, farmers and the rural areas where they lived were strictly controlled by the land nationalisation system, the procurement system, and the state's planned cultivation system. The state strictly controlled the rural areas because it did not want the farmers, who were responsible for the most important source of revenue—the provision of agricultural products—to run away. As discussed in Chap. 2, the controlled agricultural and rural systems and policies were later gradually abolished and the fetters that prevented farmers from moving were loosened. As a result, it became easier for agricultural labourers, who had already before been highly mobile, to move around in search of employment by farmers. Secondly, the commodification of farmland progressed. More and more people sold their farmland and left the village. Those who bought that farmland increasingly moved into the village. Thus, both farmers and agricultural labourers became more likely to be mobile. Third, not only in big cities like Yangon, but also in provincial towns like

[1] Households with low incomes lived in inexpensive houses that could be built for about 15 days' wages, with roofs thatched with leaves of nipa palms and other palm plants, walls enclosed with the same leaves or with bamboo, and floors made of bamboo, except for a few wooden posts, which could be dismantled and transported on ox carts. People often built such houses on unoccupied land in the village, and were able to obtain similar land at low cost in their destination village, too.

Hlegu,[2] the demand for labour force was increasing in the construction, commercial and service sectors, and new housing was being developed. Cities that had been inhospitable to rural migration were becoming cities that could absorb migrants. As described above, the constraints of state control of rural areas were eased and the previously scant employment opportunities in urban areas grew considerably (Takahashi, 1997: 23). In this chapter, we examine whether these changes in external conditions changed the population movement patterns in Zeepinwea Village.

However, it is difficult to capture the movement of individual villagers in a survey of a single village. For example, if an entire household has left the village, it is not possible to know which members of the household have gone where. At the very least, in the case of household migration—which is widespread in the villages in Myanmar's delta region—the village mayor or secretary usually knows the households that have left the village and remembers most of their occupations and destinations. If we surveyed all households, we could know the actual situation of each person's migration, but I did not have time to do so in 2014. I was, however, able to obtain information from the village mayor and secretary on the previous residence and occupation of all households that had entered Zeepinwea Village. Therefore, I will first analyse the entry and exit of each household in the village. I then examine the extent to which the children of households that were living in Zeepinwea Village at the time of my surveys have moved away from their parents' homes. This allows us to track the movement of individuals, though it is limited. I compare the seven years from 1987 to 1994 with the nineteen years from 1994 to 2013 in order to describe some changes in that quarter of a century both in terms of households moving in and out of villages and in terms of individuals' movements. Notably, the migration patterns from 1987 to 1994 had differences depending on whether the persons owned farmland or not, and whether they were engaged in own farming or not, including in agricultural labouring (Takahashi, 1997: 11–13). Therefore, this chapter also considers whether migration patterns varied by occupation and how those patterns changed.

In this chapter, we first examine why the number of households in the village increased. Second, I organise information on the occupations of households that had left the village, their destinations, their occupations at the destination, the reasons for migration, and the ages of the householders and their spouses. Third, we scrutinise the geographical spread of households moving into Zeepinwea Village, as well as their changing patterns, by sorting the previous residence of the households according to their occupation.[3] Fourth, I complement the analysis of household migration by

[2] The area of Hlegu Township is about 1789 square kilometres. Hlegu Town, which bordered Zeepinwea Village, was the township seat, but nonetheless a rural town with a small urban area. However, in the 2000s, a residential area was built and workers commuting to the foreign-capital factories in the Yangon suburbs began to live there.

[3] As in the case of the out-migrant households, Takahashi (1997) categorised the in-migrant households by listing their occupations before and after moving into Zeepinwea Village, their previous residence, their reason for moving into the village, and the ages of the householders and their spouses. However, my 2014 survey was a sampling survey of households that were already living in the village in 1994, so the same analysis cannot be conducted. Therefore, I use the village mayor's

describing the out-migration of adult children from households that were living in the village at the time of my survey, that is, migration on an individual basis. Through these considerations, it is possible to draw a picture of population migration in suburban villages.

This migration accompanied the economic prosperity and expansion of Yangon city. Thus, this picture cannot be generalised to all rural areas throughout Myanmar.

6.1 Factors of Increase and Decrease in the Number of Households

Table 6.1 shows the cross-tabulation of the number of households in Zeepinwea Village by occupation, with the increase in the number of households due to *oekhwe* (household division) and in-migration, and the decrease in the number of households due to moving out and vanishing. The left side of the table shows the increase and decrease from 1987 to 1994, and the right side from 1994 to 2013. As mentioned, *oekhwe* refers to the widespread practice of adult children building a separate house and setting up a household when they marry. In some cases, households moved out of the village after they married and set up their new households in other villages, in which case they were classified as moving out rather than as *oekhwe*. In other words, the term *oekhwe*, in this chapter, is used only for cases where the children's households stayed in the village after marriage and independence from their parents.

Let us first try to classify the households that moved into or out of Zeepinwea Village by occupation. Of the 64 households that did their own (self-employed) farming (see Table 4.3) as of 1987, six households moved out and an equal number of six households moved into Zeepinwea by 1994. All the incoming householders were born in Zeepinwea, but had left the village once, and returned to the village to settle down (Takahashi, 1997: 10). In other words, from 1987 to 1994, only those who were born in the village could become farmers, after returning to the village. This is probably related to the system in which children and grandchildren were allowed to be *le'shìle'gou'* (currently cultivating the land), as described in Chap. 2. However, the picture was much different between 1994 and 2013: only three of the 13 new farming households in 2013 were returnees to the village, while the remaining 10 were people from outside the village who had bought farmland around Zeepinwea and moved into the village. As mentioned earlier, some ethnic-minority farmers came from as far away as Mon and Chin States. The sale and purchase of farmland (or more precisely, of cultivation right), which had been strictly regulated during the socialist period, became more active, and the farmers began to move their households along

---

and secretary's information. By asking the village mayor and secretary about the previous residences and occupations of all households moving into the village, I obtained the source villages and occupational changes of all households that moved into Zeepinwea Village after 1994. In addition, I interviewed 15 households out of the 69 households that had entered the village individually about their timing of migration, purpose, occupation, family structure, and changes in income.

Table 6.1 Occupations of Zeepinwea Village's *oekhwe* (divided) households, and of households moved in, moved out, and vanished

Occupation	Increased and decreased factors							
	1987 → 1994				1994 → 2013			
	Oekhwe	Moved in	Moved out	Vanished	*Oekhwe*	Moved in	Moved out	Vanished
Own farming	11	6	6		10	13	12	
Agricultural labourer								
Sayinnga	8	6	9	1	4	10	5	
Kyaban	2	7	4		32	21	5	
Vegetable gardening	3	2	1		0	0		
Carpenter, plasterer	2	2	1		2	1	1	
Small shop owner					2	0		
Peddler, street vendor	1				19	11	1	
Side-car driver		2			9	1	1	
Motorcycle taxi driver					8	3		
Car driver/assistant	1				9	1		
Cargo handling					5	1		
Public servant, company employee		4	2		2	3	2	
Factory worker					2	2		
Other jobs	2	1	3	1	2	2		2
Total number of households increased	30	30	−26	−2	106	69	−27	−2
Total number of households in the village		138 → 170				170 → 316		

Note Occupation is listed according to the occupation after *oekhwe* or moving in, and before moving out or vanishing
Source According to the author's survey

with the selling and buying. However, out-migrant farmers and in-migrant farmers numbered around the same, both in 1987–1994 and in 1994–2013. Thus, the number of new farm households increased mostly only through *oekhwe*. Even then, the total number of farm households in the village did not increase, because some existing farmers became non-farmers, as described in Chap. 4.

From 1987 to 1994, less than a tenth of all the farm households moved out: 6 out of the 64 households in 1987 had moved out by 1994. Similarly, out of the 66 farm households in 1994, only 6 had moved in after 1987. In the case of *non-farm* households, however, out of a total of 74 in 1987, 20 had moved out by 1994. Out of the 104 non-farm households in 1994, 24 had moved in after 1987. This gives an out-migration ratio of 27.0% (20/74) and an in-migration ratio of 23.1% (24/104), indicating that non-farm households such as agricultural labourers and company employees were clearly more mobile than farm households. The reason is that non-farmers, who were free in the double sense of not being controlled by the state and not holding cultivation rights of farmland, could change their residence more freely than farmers, reflecting the situation at that time when farmland holdings and its sale were strictly regulated by the state.

From 1994 to 2013, 12 out of the 66 *farm* households in 1994 moved out, and 13 out of the 55 farm households in 2013 had moved in. In other words, the out-migration ratio of farm households during this period was 18.2% and the in-migration ratio was 23.6%. Both ratios are significantly higher than the 1987–94 out-migration and in-migration ratios. On the other hand, for *non-farm* households, from 1994 to 2013, 15 out of the 104 non-farm households in 1994 moved out, and 56 out of the 261 non-farm households in 2013 had moved in. In other words, the out-migration and in-migration ratios of non-farm households during this period were 14.4% and 21.5%, respectively. In contrast to the 1987–1994 period, the out-migration and in-migration rates of farm households now exceeded those of non-farm households. The reason for this increase in farm households migrating out was that six out of the twelve out-migrant households moved their residences to Hlegu Town and surrounding residential areas, while keeping their farmlands intact. In contrast, the reason for the increase in farm household migrating in was that people outside the village purchased the cultivation rights of the farmland around the village and moved in, as mentioned above. The reason for the large decrease in the out-migration ratio of non-farmers is that non-farm employment in Hlegu Town increased and a number of foreign-owned factories started operating between Yangon City and Hlegu Town. More and more people began to commute from the village to these workplaces, eliminating the need to relocate entire households. The reason for the slight decrease in the ratio of non-farm households moving into the village is that the overall number of non-farm households increased substantially due to the *oekhwe* within the village, that is, the denominator grew. In other words, the number of households that had moved in itself had actually increased.

The second row from the bottom of Table 6.1 shows how the total number of households in Zeepinwea changed. The numbers of *oekhwe* households and moved-in households are positive, while the numbers of households that moved out and households that had vanished[4] are negative. We can calculate the "natural" increase in the number of households by subtracting the number of households that vanished from the number of households created by *oekhwe* household division. Thus, the natural increase in the number of households from 1987 to 1994 was 28. In contrast, the "social" increase, calculated by subtracting the number of out-migrating households from the number of in-migrating households, was only 4 households in 1987–1994, suggesting that the increase in the number of households in the village during that period was mostly due to natural increase. This does not mean that population movements were small (Takahashi, 1997: 2). Rather, the numbers of households moving in and out of the village were quite large, but they just happened to balance each other out. Using the same calculation method for the period between 1994 and 2013, the natural increase in the number of households was 104 and the social increase was 42. Thus, although the natural increase was large, the social increase had also become considerable.

The number of households in the village was noticeably increased by natural increase due to the practice of *oekhwe* (household division), but tracing the entry and exit of whole households into and out of the village shows that a large number of households moved in or out of the village. Nothing definitive can be said about these Burmese socialist era migrations because no studies have been conducted on them. However, by analogy with the situation in the early years of the following military regime from 1987 to 1994—when agricultural and rural policies were similar to those of the socialist period and urban population absorption capacity was not yet large—it is likely that there was considerable movement of whole households during the socialist period as well. The reason for such household mobility is not the disparity in expected income between rural and urban areas as in the Harris-Todaro model, but the low opportunity cost of mobility, such as the simple house and the open village social structure that is not closed but easy to enter and exit (Takahashi, 2012: 176–182; 2018: 195–197). Even if the development of a market economy and increased employment opportunities in urban areas later led to a surge in population movement to the cities, this was simply because villagers who had originally moved from rural areas to rural areas now moved to cities.

6.2 Households that Moved Out of the Village

From 1987 to 1994, 26 households, and from 1994 to 2013, 27 households *left* Zeepinwea Village. What occupations were these households engaged in? Why did they leave the village? Where did they move to, and what new occupations did they

[4] Two households "vanished" between 1987 and 1994, and another two households between 1994 and 2013, respectively. Namely, in 1987–1994, one elderly person who lived alone died—and thus that person's household vanished—and one young couple and their two children died of an epidemic. In 1994–2013, two elderly persons who lived alone died.

take up? How did the villagers' movement pattern change between these two time periods?

As mentioned earlier, the number of *farm* households that left the village between 1987 and 1994 was small. As shown in Table 6.2, three of the six farm households that left the village continued to farm in Hlegu Township, even though their farmland location changed (reference numbers 1–3).[5] The remaining three farm households disposed of their farmland and moved elsewhere (reference numbers 4–6). One household's destination was unknown, but the other two stayed in Hlegu Township.

The largest number of *non-farm* households that moved out of the village were the nine households of *sayinnga* (season-based agricultural labourer) (reference numbers 7–15). Six of these households left the village to work in other villages, and three left because the householder who worked as a *sayinnga* died. Of these three households, one moved because its son-in-law was employed as a *sayinnga* in another village (reference number 13), and one household moved because its son worked as a *kyaban* (daily or percentage-based agricultural labourer) in another village. As mentioned earlier, a *sayinnga* is employed on a seasonal or annual basis. In some cases, the employment period ends after one cropping season or year and is not renewed, but in other cases, the employment continues for several years. In terms of the principle of contract and in terms of the actual situation, this is by no means stable employment, as long-term employment is not guaranteed. If there is no employment in the village, it is their fate to migrate outside the village in search of employment. Because a *kyaban* (reference numbers 15–20) is a daily worker, his/her employment is even more unstable. Peddlers and fishermen are also susceptible to minor changes in the weather and the market. When employment opportunities decrease in a village, people have no choice but to move to other villages in search of similar jobs. From this perspective, we find that the *occupations* of non-farmers—including those who moved not only for employment purposes but also due to unexpected events such as the death of the householder—usually did not change after leaving the village. In other words, their income and employment security did not change much after leaving the village. There is no way to estimate their expected new income, but they probably did not make the decision to move based on expecting a higher income, because they do not expect to change their occupation as they would when moving to a large city. Their occupation is not stable enough in the first place to calculate an expected income.

When we trace the destinations of the above-mentioned moved-out households, their overwhelming majority, both farmers and non-farmers, remained in Hlegu Township. The exceptions included two households whose main occupation was river fishermen. They travelled around where they could catch fish and relied on distant relatives to reach their new villages in 1983 and 1985, respectively, moving to the Delta. Another household whose householder became a civil servant moved to

[5] It should be noted that I did not follow the households that left the village to their current addresses in 1994, but only interviewed the village mayors, village secretaries, and relatives and acquaintances of these households. However, with the exception of one peddler household and two fisherman households, their relatives were still living in the village, so there is not a large margin of error with respect to the matters described in this book. The same is true for my 2014 survey.

Table 6.2 Occupations and destinations of households that moved *out* of Zeepinwea Village in 1987–1994

Reference number	Former occupation	New occupation	Destination	Reason for moving out	Husband's age	Wife's age	Number of household members
1	Own farming	Own farming	In Hlegu T/S	Death of wife, remarriage	48		6
2	Own farming	Own farming	In Hlegu T/S	Compound transferred to sibling	35	32	6
3	Own farming	Own farming	In Hlegu T/S	To wife's home village	30	28	5
4	Own farming	*Kyaban*	In Hlegu T/S	Sale of agricultural land	47	26	5
5	Own farming	None	Hlegu Town	Sale of agricultural land		59	2
6	Own farming	Unknown	Unknown	Death of the male householder	31	31	2
7	*Sayinnga*	*Sayinnga*	In Hlegu T/S	Working in another village	24	24	4
8	*Sayinnga*	*Sayinnga*	In Hlegu T/S	Working in another village	26	19	2
9	*Sayinnga*	*Sayinnga*	In Hlegu T/S	Working in another village	42	33	5
10	*Sayinnga*	*Sayinnga*	In Hlegu T/S	Working in another village	42	37	8
11	*Sayinnga*	*Sayinnga*	In Hlegu T/S	Working in another village	26	23	3
12	*Sayinnga*	*Sayinnga*	In Hlegu T/S	Working in another village	35	35	5
13	*Sayinnga*	*Sayinnga*	In Hlegu T/S	Death of the male householder		35	2

(continued)

Table 6.2 (continued)

Reference number	Former occupation	New occupation	Destination	Reason for moving out	Husband's age	Wife's age	Number of household members
14	*Sayinnga*	*Kyaban*	In Hlegu T/S	Death of the male householder		33	9
15	*Sayinnga*	Unknown	Unknown	Death of the male householder		27	1
16	*Kyaban*	*Kyaban*	In Hlegu T/S	To wife's home village	33	30	3
17	*Kyaban*	*Kyaban*	In Hlegu T/S	Working in another village	30	36	2
18	*Kyaban*	*Kyaban*	In Hlegu T/S	Working in another village	38	36	6
19	*Kyaban*	Public Servant	Yangon	Transferred	38	34	8
20	*Kyaban*	*Kyaban*	Yangon	Death of the male householder	37	25	4
21	Carpenter	Carpenter	In Hlegu T/S	Working in another village	34	29	5
22	Public servant	Public servant	In Hlegu T/S	Transferred	37	31	5
23	Peddler	Peddler	In Hlegu T/S	Traveling as peddler		57	1
24	Vegetable gardening	*Sayinnga*	In Hlegu T/S	Working in another village	45	40	8
25	Fishery	Fishery	Delta region	Went where the fish are	35	25	6
26	Fishery	Fishery	Delta region	Went where the fish are	40	38	7
				Average →	*35.9*	*32.9*	*4.6*

Note Ages are as of 1987. If the householder was female, only the wife's age is entered in the column. If the householder died and the adult children left the village, the ages of the children and their spouses are entered as the ages of the "husband" and "wife"
Source Based on a survey conducted by the author in 1994

Yangon city due to a job transfer. Finally, one household lost their male householder and moved to Yangon where the widow was born. All the other households stayed in Hlegu Township. They all moved to other villages in Hlegu Township, except for one household that retired and bought a house in Hlegu town. Even in places where the cost of migration to Yangon was not so high, such as in Zeepinwea village, only a few households moved to the capital (Takahashi, 1997: 11). Migration in the Zeepinwea area was usually households moving between nearby villages, that is, rural to rural migration.

Households had diverse reasons for leaving the villages. These can be divided into economic reasons, such as "selling farmland", "working in another village", "transferring as a public servant", "peddling elsewhere" or "going where the fish are caught", and social reasons, such as "death of the householder", "moving to the wife's village" or "remarriage". Even if households moved for a "social" reason, they still needed to secure their family income, so it can be said that all the reasons are "economic", and some economic reasons included social backgrounds, such as having to dispose of farmland at the time of inheritance or being called as a *sayinnga* by relatives in other villages. It is noteworthy here that none of the given reasons indicate a motivation to move out of the village for economic betterment. The main motive for leaving the village seems to have been to secure a livelihood in the same occupation, even if the income was low and unstable. Nevertheless, since many of the households consisted of relatively young couples, it is not to say that they did not wish to improve their livelihoods in their new destination.

Households leaving villages from 1994 to 2013 showed a slight change in pattern, although the number of households was almost the same. As shown in Table 6.3, the number of farm households that left the village in 1994 to 2013 was 12. However, seven of these households continued farming their old farmland, moving only their dwellings to Hlegu Town (reference numbers 1–4) or Kyungalay Village which is connected to Hlegu Town along the old National Highway 1 (reference numbers 5–7). These were all farm households in Ywalay hamlet (area III in Fig. 4.3). This hamlet is the farthest from Hlegu Town in Zeepinwea Village, and its residential area is prone to flooding due to the overflow of Ngamoeyeik River. Originally, the hamlet was a cluster of shanties in the paddy fields, and only shabby houses on stilts were built. However, there were many farmers who owned relatively large farmlands in the Zeepinwea Village, and the post-socialist decontrol of paddy and rice sales sharply increased their income. For the sake of their children's education and the health of their elderly parents, they decided to buy a plot of land in the new residential area of Hlegu Town, build a modern house, and move out of their shoddy dwellings. They left their farm equipment and draught cattle in the old residential area of Ywalay, and began commuting there regularly by motorcycle from their new residences. This is a new type of farm household that has emerged in the twenty-first century. Apart from these households, the number of farmers who left the village was only five in 19 years, which is very small compared to the six households that left in the 7 years from 1987 to 1994. Of the five households that left the village after quitting their own farming, four households remained in Hlegu Township, while one household moved to Yenangyaung Township, which is more than 500 km away, engaging in oil drilling (reference number 8). There were 17 households in the 33 samples that changed from farm households to non-farm households over the past 19 years, but all of these households remained in the village even after becoming non-farm households. There appears to be no relationship between becoming a non-farm household and moving out of the village.

The trend during 1987–1994, when *sayinnga* and *kyaban* agricultural workers moved within Hlegu Township without changing their occupation, remained unchanged during 1994–2013. However, household mobility, which had before 1994 been confined to the township, expanded outside the township to some extent. Since 26 households left the village in the seven years between 1987 and 1994 and 27 households left the village in the 19 years between 1994 and 2013, the speed of moving out slowed down considerably. The number of households that left the village for social reasons, such as "death of the householder," "to the wife's home village," "remarriage," and "for children or parents," was 8 households between 1987 and 1994 and 20 households between 1994 and 2013, including those that moved only their residence. Thus, many households left the village mainly because of social factors, but the economic factor of earning a living may be inseparable from these factors.

6.3 Households that Moved into the Village

This section will discuss the characteristics of households that moved *into* Zeepinwea Village. In my 2014 survey, I did not run an exhaustive survey of households that had moved into Zeepinwea between 1994 and 2013 but conducted a sample survey of those households that had resided in the village already in 1987 and 1994. Therefore, information on household members and their reasons for moving was available in the case of households that had moved *out* of the village, but this information was missing for households that had moved *into* the village. In other words, we can explore merely the household occupations and previous residences, comparing the households entering the village in 1987–1994 with the households entering in 1994–2013. We will use information from the records of village mayors and secretaries on the occupations and previous residences of all the households that had entered the village. Additionally, I carried out a door-to-door survey of 15 out of the 69 households that had entered the village since 1995. I will insert information from these interview records as appropriate.

The number of households that moved into Zeepinwea Village in 1987–1994 was 30, as shown in the second row from the bottom of Table 6.1 and in the lower right corner of Table 6.4. Among them, 23 households, or more than three-fourths, moved in from Hlegu Township, which includes Hlegu Town. Table 6.4 includes a large number of farm households and agricultural (hired) labour households because these households made up the majority of the occupational structure of the village (see Table 4.3). One farm household coming from outside the township was a returning Army soldier born in the village, and one *sayinnga* was a retired Air Force soldier who moved into the village with his wife who was born in the village. Another

Table 6.3 Occupations and destinations of households that moved *out* of Zeepinwea Village in 1994–2013

Reference number	Former occupation	New occupation	Destination	Reason for moving out	Husband's age	Wife's age	Number of household members
1	Own farming	Own farming	Hlegu Town	Move residence only	31	33	4
2	Own farming	Own farming	Hlegu Town	Move residence only	41	39	3
3	Own farming	Own farming	Hlegu Town	Move residence only	43	36	7
4	Own farming	Own farming	Hlegu Town	Move residence only		57	3
5	Own farming	Own farming	In Hlegu T/S	Move residence only	26	21	3
6	Own farming	Own farming	In Hlegu T/S	Move residence only	27	33	3
7	Own farming	Own farming	In Hlegu T/S	Move residence only	33	33	5
8	Own farming	Oil rig worker	Out of Hlegu T/S	Working in another village	38	29	5
9	Own farming	Car driver	Hlegu Town	Working in another village	34	34	3
10	Own farming	Dependent	Hlegu Town	Death of the male householder		40	8
11	Own farming	Peddler	In Hlegu T/S	Death of the male householder		38	4
12	Own farming (tenant)	Unknown	In Hlegu T/S	Death of the male householder		27	4
13	*Sayinnga*	*Sayinnga*	In Hlegu T/S	To husband's home village	30	32	4

(continued)

Table 6.3 (continued)

Reference number	Former occupation	New occupation	Destination	Reason for moving out	Husband's age	Wife's age	Number of household members
14	*Sayinnga*	*Sayinnga*	In Hlegu T/S	To wife's home village	27	24	4
15	*Sayinnga*	*Kyaban*	In Hlegu T/S	Death of wife	33		4
16	*Sayinnga*	Cargo handling	Hlegu Town	Working in another village	32	25	3
17	*Sayinnga*	Peddler	Out of Hlegu T/S	Death of the male householder	35	24	2
18	*Kyaban*	*Kyaban*	In the township	To wife's home village	26	24	3
19	*Kyaban*	*Kyaban*	Out of Hlegu T/S	To wife's home village	42	32	6
20	*Kyaban*	*Kyaban*	In Hlegu T/S	Working in another village	25		3
21	*Kyaban*	*Kyaban*	In Hlegu T/S	To wife's home village	39	33	6
22	*Kyaban*	*Kyaban*	In Hlegu T/S	Working in another village	52	43	6
23	Public servant	Unknown	In Hlegu T/S	Death of the male householder		50	2
24	Company employee	Company employee	Hlegu Town	Working in another village	32	33	4
25	Side-car driver	Unknown	Out of Hlegu T/S	Death of the male householder		30	7
26	Peddler	Unknown	In Hlegu T/S	Death of the male householder		49	5

(continued)

Table 6.3 (continued)

Reference number	Former occupation	New occupation	Destination	Reason for moving out	Husband's age	Wife's age	Number of household members
27	Carpenter	Car driver	Hlegu Town	Working in another village	30	32	3
				Average →	*33.8*	*34.0*	*4.2*

Note Ages are as of 1994. If the householder was female, only the wife's age is entered in the column. If the householder died and the adult children left the village, the ages of the children and their spouses are entered as the ages of the "husband" and "wife"
Source Based on a survey conducted by the author in 2014

sayinnga household from outside the township relied on a network of ethnic Karen Christians, who moved into Paukkoung hamlet from the Ayeyarwady Region. One *kyaban* household, whose main occupation had been street vendor in Yangon, moved to the village on the advice of his sister who had married there. Another *kyaban* household came from Daik-U Township, about 100 km to the northeast, relying on his brother. The carpenter household came from Shwegyin Township, another 50 km north of Dai-U, and the side-car driver's household came from Tantabin Township, about 50 km to the west from Zeepinwea Village, relying on their siblings to come to the village. These results indicate that the most distant source of migration was 150 km from the village and that most of the migrants came from villages in Hlegu Township. All of them were ethnic Bamar or Karen, and no other ethnic groups moved into the village.

Similarly to the previous table, Table 6.5 summarises the entry of households into Zeepinwea in 1994–2013 by cross-tabulating household occupation and the source of the move. A clear difference from the 1987–1994 in-migration was that the proportion of households moving from within Hlegu Township decreased. The number of households that moved from within the Township, including those that moved from the huts in the paddy fields, was 29, which accounted for 42.0% of the 69 households that moved into the village, a significant decrease from the 76.7% in 1987–1994. In other words, the number of people moving in from more distant areas soared. Kayan Township, from which the next largest number of households moved into the village, is included in the same Yangon Region as Hlegu Township, but is far away across the Bago River. The third largest number of households that moved into the village was from Mon State, the capital of which is about 270 km from Zeepinwea Village by road. Some households have moved from even further away villages in Mon State. They are ethnic Mon, and when I interviewed them, I found that they spoke Burmese with a very strong accent.

The occupation of the moved-in households in the village was largely agricultural labourers, such as *sayinnga*s and *kyaban*s, reflecting the fact that many households in the village as a whole had these occupations as their main occupation, as

Table 6.4 Occupations and previous residences of households that moved into Zeepinwea Village in 1987–1994

Occupation\From	Hlegu Town	In Hlegu T/S	Out of Hlegu T/S	Yangon	Total
Own farming		5	1		6
Agricultural labourer		(9)	(3)	(1)	(13)
Sayinnga		4	2		6
Kyaban		5	1	1	7
Vegetable gardening		2			2
Carpenter, plasterer	1		1		2
Small shop owner					0
Peddler, street vendor					0
Side-car driver	1		1		2
Motorcycle taxi driver					0
Car driver/assistant					0
Cargo handling					0
Public servant, company employee	1				1
Factory worker					0
Other jobs	2	2			4
Without an occupation					0
Total number of households	5	18	6	1	30

Source Based on a survey conducted by the author in 1994

also in the 1987–1994 period. The number of households with peddlers and street vendors increased conspicuously, but six of these households moved into the village as *kyabans*, and their wives started street vending when their husbands died or were no longer able to work, so the mobility of peddlers and street vendors cannot be considered particularly high.

Interestingly, although the number of farm households decreased from 66 to 55 from 1994 to 2013 (see Table 4.3), the number of farm households that moved into the village increased from 6 to 13. Likely, the sale and purchase of farmland cultivation rights became active well before the enactment of the Farmland Law in 2012, stimulating the movement of farmers. In other words, it can be said that there were aspects of the 2012 Farmland Law that merely followed the existing reality. This phenomenon is inextricably linked to the de-agrarianisation of Zeepinwea Village, where an increasing number of villagers have been disposing of their farmland and commuting to offices and factories in Yangon city and its suburbs. The overwhelming majority of the new arrivals who bought this farmland around Zeepinwea Village were not from within Hlegu Township, but from distant areas such as Kayan Township and Mon State. Almost the same number of *sayinnga*s employed by these moved-in farmers moved from the same area with their employers. Already in 1987–1994, there

Table 6.5 Occupations and previous residences of households that moved into Zeepinwea Village in 1994–2013

Occupation\From	Hut in the paddy field	Hlegu Town	In Hlegu T/S	Yangon City	Kayan T/S	Kawhmu T/S	Kawa T/S	Ayeyarwady Region	Mon State	Chin State	Total
Own farming	1	1	1		5				4	1	13
Agricultural labourer	(1)	(4)	(10)		(12)		(2)		(2)		(31)
Sayinnga			2		6				2		10
Kyaban	1	4	8		6		2				21
Vegetable gardening											0
Carpenter, plasterer					1						1
Small shop owner											0
Peddler, street vendor			4		2		2	3			11
Side-car driver			1								1
Motorcycle taxi driver		2			1						3
Car driver/assistant					1						1
Cargo handling		1									1
Public servant, company employee			1	1				1			3
Factory worker		1				1					2
Other jobs		1						1			2
Without an occupation											0

(continued)

Table 6.5 (continued)

Occupation\From	Hut in the paddy field	Hlegu Town	In Hlegu T/S	Yangon City	Kayan T/S	Kawhmu T/S	Kawa T/S	Ayeyarwady Region	Mon State	Chin State	Total
Total number of households	2	10	17	1	22	1	4	5	6	1	69

Note 1 Yangon City, Kayan Township and Kawhmu Township belong to Yangon Region. Kawa Township belongs to Bago Region
Note 2 The road distance from Hlegu Town to Kayan Town is about 73 km. The distance to Kawhmu Town is about 79 km, to Kawa town it is about 36 km, to Pathein, the capital of Ayeyarwady Region, about 214 km, and to Mawlamyine, the capital of Mon State, about 287 km
Source Based on a survey conducted by the author in 2014

was already considerable inter-village migration of farmers and agricultural labourers from village to village, as well as out-migration and in-migration. However, in 1994–2013, all this migration became more distant and more extensive, probably due to the development of transportation and information networks.

For example, Ko Thein Win, who moved to Zeepinwea from a village in Yangon Region's Kayan Township with his family in 1996, told me: "I sold 20 acres of paddy field for 200,000 kyats and bought 14 acres of paddy field near Zeepinwea Village for 210,000 kyats. The farmland in the village of Kayan was not stable in rice production due to seawater coming in. From 1998 to 2006, I made a large profit of 200,000 kyats per acre a year by green gram cultivation because of good production and high prices. After that, it rained more often during the dry season and pests and diseases increased, resulting in a loss of 800,000 kyats in 2012. My son who came with me got a bachelor's degree, so I want to quit farming and live with him in a city". Ko Min Zaw, from another village also in Kayan Township, purchased 20 acres of paddy fields and moved into the village with his family, but died in 2008, and his wife, daughter, and son-in-law continued to farm. These two resettled farm households became some of the largest farmers in Zeepinwea Village and each came accompanied by a family of *sayinnga*s.

Ko Yin Htwe, an ethnic Mon, moved to Zeepinwea in 2008 from Mudon Township, Mon State, 296 km from Hlegu Town. (The four farm households who came to Zeepinwea from Mon State all came from different villages). Since the farmland price in Mudon was five times higher than in Zeepinwea Village, Ko Yin Htwe disposed of 7 acres of paddy fields and bought 32 acres near Zeepinwea Village. Three other Mon households also purchased 25–30 acres of paddy fields. Thus, these Mon migrants became among the largest farmers in the village.

Ko Fachun, an ethnic Chin, moved to Paukkoung hamlet with his wife and two children in 2004 from Paletwa Town, Chin State, a distance of 1000 km by road. With money sent by his brother in the United States, he purchased 18 acres of paddy fields near Zeepinwea Village between 2004 and 2006. The villagers in Paukkoung are Karen Baptists, but Ko Fachun is a Chin Anglican and has no connection to Paukkoung. Nevertheless, he was accepted by the people of the area because he is a fellow Christian. His brother also owns 7 acres of paddy fields, managed by Ko Fachun.

As described above, since my 1994 survey, new farm households, including ethnic minorities such as Mon and Chin, moved into the village from quite far away, and most of these households became large farmers belonging to the upper layer of Zeepinwea Village in terms of the size of their holdings. In addition, the vast compound of U Kala,[6] who had been the mayor of Zeepinwea Village for a long time since the Burmese socialist period, was sold to an ethnic Shan trader. U Kala's son-in-law, Ko We Kyaw, who followed him as the mayor in the early years of the military regime, sold his large *ûyin* (garden) to an ethnic Karen man who was a driver at the United States Embassy in Yangon. In this way, Zeepinwea Village, which had been divided into two ethnic areas—with Karen people living in Paukkoung hamlet

[6] For a history of the rise and fall of the U Kala family, see Takahashi (2018: 88–94).

and Bamar people living in Ywagyi and Ywalay hamlets—was transformed into a mixed multi-ethnic settlement with several ethnic groups living together. It could be seen as a return to the Zeepinwea Village of the colonial period, where farmers and agricultural labourers of diverse origins, including Indians, came and went.

6.4 Migrations of Individual Villagers

So far, we have discussed the relationship between household migration and occupation, which is key to population migration in rural Myanmar. However, I have withheld analysis of *individual* migration, which is the main focus of population movement studies. This is because even village mayors and secretaries do not know each former villager who left the village. In cases where the person has no relatives remaining in the village, door-to-door surveys alone could not give a complete picture of the destination, occupation, number of people, and so on. So, as a second-best measure, I decided to investigate changes in the migration patterns of individual villagers by surveying the occupation of each household and the destination of their adult children away from[7] their parents' home, in cases where at least one parent still lived in the village.

Table 6.6 shows the average number of "separated" adult children per household in Zeepinwea Village in 1987, 1994, and 2013. The table further divides these numbers by the children's occupation. The reason for using an average per household is that the number of households surveyed in 1987, 1994 and 2013 was different, so simply adding up the number of separated children alone does not allow for a comparison of these three time points on the same basis. However, between 1987 and 2013, the average number of household members decreased by more than one person, from 5.46 to 4.45, so even Table 6.6 cannot compare the three points as they are. Therefore, Table 6.7 corrects the average numbers per household in 1994 and 2013 by assuming that the average size of households in these two years is the same as in 1987. In the following discussion, we will refer to Table 6.7, which was processed in this way.

In 1987, at the end of the Burmese socialist period, the adult children's destinations remained within the village or the township. In other words, even if the view that there was little population movement during the socialist period is rejected (Takahashi, 1997:21), the extent of this movement was within a narrow area around the village. By 1994, there was little change in the migration pattern. In other words, adult children's migration during the socialist period and in the early years of direct military rule was rural-to-rural, not rural-to-urban, just as it was for household migration. Social mobility by marriage, rather than economic incentives, was the main cause of migration.

[7] In this chapter, "away from" or "separated" means separating one's livelihood or dividing one's household from that of one's parents—regardless of one's place of residence inside or outside the village. In contrast, the term "move out" is used only when a person who is "separated from" a parental household moves out of the village.

Table 6.6 Average number of separated adult children per household by their household occupation in Zeepinwea Village

Destination	In the Village			In Hlegu T/S			Out of Hlegu T/S			Yangon city			Number of out-migrants			Out-migration ratio		
Occupation	Male	Female	Total	Male	Female	Total	Male	Female	Total	Male	Female	Total	Male	Female	Total	Male	Female	Total
In 1987 (Number of surveyed households: 136; Average household size: 5.46 persons)																		
Own farming	0.30	0.27	0.56	0.25	0.23	0.48	0.02	0.03	0.05	0.02	0.05	0.06	0.28	0.31	0.59	0.95	1.18	1.06
Agricultural labour	0.11	0.11	0.23	0.11	0.11	0.23	0.00	0.07	0.07	0.02	0.00	0.02	0.14	0.18	0.32	1.20	1.60	1.40
Non-agriculture	0.39	0.18	0.57	0.21	0.07	0.29	0.00	0.00	0.00	0.00	0.04	0.04	0.21	0.11	0.32	0.55	0.60	0.56
Average	0.26	0.20	0.46	0.20	0.16	0.36	0.01	0.04	0.04	0.01	0.03	0.04	0.22	0.23	*0.45*	0.86	1.15	0.98
In 1994 (Number of surveyed households: 170; Average household size: 4.88 persons)																		
Own farming	0.27	0.38	0.65	0.27	0.14	0.41	0.03	0.05	0.08	0.00	0.05	0.05	0.30	0.23	0.53	1.11	0.60	0.81
Agricultural labour	0.13	0.13	0.27	0.08	0.23	0.31	0.02	0.02	0.04	0.04	0.10	**0.13**	0.13	0.35	0.48	1.00	**2.57**	1.79
Non-agriculture	0.21	0.25	0.46	0.17	0.12	0.29	0.04	0.04	0.08	0.04	0.10	0.13	0.25	0.25	0.50	1.18	1.00	1.08
Average	0.21	0.26	0.48	0.18	0.16	0.34	0.03	0.04	0.06	0.02	0.08	0.10	0.24	0.27	*0.51*	1.11	1.02	1.06
In 2013 (Number of surveyed households: 56; Average household size: 4.45 persons)																		
Own farming	0.26	0.21	0.47	0.00	0.00	0.00	0.05	0.05	0.11	0.05	0.05	0.11	0.11	0.11	0.21	0.40	0.50	0.44
Agricultural labour	**0.60**	**0.60**	**1.20**	0.00	0.20	0.20	**0.40**	0.00	**0.40**	0.00	0.00	0.00	0.40	0.20	0.60	0.67	0.33	0.50

(continued)

Table 6.6 (continued)

Destination	In the Village			In Hlegu T/S			Out of Hlegu T/S			Yangon city			Number of out-migrants			Out-migration ratio		
Occupation	Male	Female	Total	Male	Female	Total	Male	Female	Total	Male	Female	Total	Male	Female	Total	Male	Female	Total
Non-agriculture	0.53	0.56	1.09	0.09	0.16	0.25	**0.13**	0.03	0.16	**0.25**	0.25	**0.50**	0.47	0.44	0.91	0.88	0.78	0.83
Average	0.45	0.45	0.89	0.05	0.11	0.16	0.13	0.04	0.16	0.16	0.16	0.32	0.34	0.30	*0.64*	0.76	0.68	0.72

Note 1 "Separate" or "away from" means to live away from one's parent's home. As this does not necessarily mean leaving the village, some "separated" adult children live within the village

Note 2 The number of out-migrants is the total number of out-migrants living in Hlegu Township (T/S), outside of the Hlegu T/S (excluding Yangon City), and in Yangon City

Note 3 The "out-migration ratio" is the ratio of the number of adult children who left the village to the number of children who stayed in the village but separated from their parents' home

Note 4 Figures in the table are rounded off to the first two decimal places

Note 5 The average number of adult children leaving the village is shown in italics, and figures with large increases are shown in bold

Note 6 Figures in bold indicate particularly large increase

Source Author's surveys in 1987, 1994, and 2014

Table 6.7 Number of separated adult children per household by their household occupation in Zeepinwea Village (Corrected)

Destination	In the Village			In Hlegu T/S			Out of Hlegu T/S			Yangon city			Number of out-migrants			Out-migration ratio		
Occupation	Male	Female	Total	Male	Female	Total	Male	Female	Total	Male	Female	Total	Male	Female	Total	Male	Female	Total
In 1987																		
Own farming	0.30	0.27	0.56	0.25	0.23	0.48	0.02	0.03	0.05	0.02	0.05	0.06	0.28	0.31	0.59	0.95	1.18	1.06
Agricultural labour	0.11	0.11	0.23	0.11	0.11	0.23	0.00	0.07	0.07	0.02	0.00	0.02	0.14	0.18	0.32	1.20	1.60	1.40
Non-agriculture	0.39	0.18	0.57	0.21	0.07	0.29	0.00	0.00	0.00	0.00	0.04	0.04	0.21	0.11	0.32	0.55	0.60	0.56
Average	0.26	0.20	0.46	0.20	0.16	0.36	0.01	0.04	0.04	0.01	0.03	0.04	0.22	0.23	*0.45*	0.86	1.15	0.98
In 1994																		
Own farming	0.31	0.42	0.73	0.31	0.15	0.46	0.03	0.05	0.08	0.00	0.05	0.05	0.34	0.25	0.59	1.11	0.60	0.81
Agricultural labour	0.15	0.15	0.30	0.09	0.26	0.34	0.02	0.02	0.04	0.04	**0.11**	**0.15**	0.15	0.39	0.54	1.00	**2.57**	1.79
Non-agriculture	0.24	0.28	0.52	0.19	0.13	0.32	0.04	0.04	0.09	0.04	**0.11**	0.15	0.28	0.28	0.56	1.18	1.00	1.08
Average	0.24	0.30	0.53	0.20	0.18	0.38	0.03	0.04	0.07	0.03	0.09	0.11	0.26	0.30	*0.57*	1.11	1.02	1.06
In 2013																		
Own farming	0.32	0.26	0.58	0.00	0.00	0.00	0.06	0.06	0.13	0.06	0.06	0.13	0.13	0.13	*0.26*	0.40	0.50	0.44
Agricultural labour	**0.74**	**0.74**	**1.48**	0.00	0.25	0.25	**0.49**	0.00	**0.49**	0.00	0.00	0.00	0.49	0.25	**0.74**	0.67	0.33	0.50
Non-agriculture	0.65	0.69	1.35	0.12	0.19	0.31	**0.15**	0.04	0.19	**0.31**	**0.31**	**0.61**	0.58	0.54	**1.11**	0.88	0.78	0.83
Average	0.55	0.55	1.10	0.07	0.13	0.20	0.15	0.04	0.20	0.20	0.20	0.40	0.42	0.37	*0.79*	0.76	0.68	0.72

Note 1 The average number of household members in 1994 and 2013 is assumed to be the same as that in 1987, and each figure in both years is corrected
Note 2 Other notes are the same as in Table 6.6
Source Author's surveys in 1987, 1994, and 2014

By 2013, this trend had changed. Migration out of Hlegu Township, including to Yangon City, became more prominent. The most likely to move out of the township were the sons of agricultural labourer households and non-agricultural households,[8] that is, the non-farm households. More men went to work in the construction and transportation industries—for which demand increased with the market economy—than to work in the agricultural occupations in distant villages. Some daughters moved to Yangon already in 1994. They were ethnic Karen women who lived and worked as maids for foreign families stationed in Yangon. They included daughters from agricultural labourer households, but by 2013 all these households became classified as non-agricultural households because their parents became old and unemployed. There were also a few sons who left for Yangon in 2013. They lived and worked in breweries, furniture makers, and goldsmith's workshops. With the market economy in full swing and with more employment opportunities outside the agricultural sector, it seems that village youths began moving farther away from home, not for marriage but for economic motives.

Looking at the out-migration trends by *occupation*[9] shows that the number of farmers leaving was the same in 1987 and 1994 (0.59) but halved to 0.26 by 2013. However, this does not necessarily imply that the children of farmers became self-employed in agriculture in the village, because non-agricultural employment opportunities were increasing both inside and outside the village, and the adult children of farmers did not always choose to work in agriculture. The number of adult children from agricultural labourer households leaving the village increased from 0.32 in 1987 to 0.54 in 1994, and to 0.74 in 2013; similarly, the number of adult children from non-agricultural households leaving the village rose from 0.32, to 0.56 and then to 1.11. However, since the number of children remaining in the village increased more than that, we cannot assume that the tendency of children of non-farm households to leave the village expanded.

That is why we should compare the number of children who *left* the village with the number of children who separated from their parents' households but *remained* in the village. The ratio of the former to the latter can be used to calculate the out-migration ratio.[10] The overall out-migration ratio increased from 0.98 to 1.06 between 1987 and 1994, but this difference is small. In 1987, farm households and agricultural labourer households had higher out-migration ratios for both men and women than did non-agricultural households which are often assumed to be more mobile. This is due to social reasons, such as whether a person marries a fellow villager or an outsider. In 1994, the out-migration ratio of daughters of agricultural labourer households soared irregularly, and the out-migration ratio of male and female children of non-agricultural households also increased. This was due to the emergence of ethnic Karen daughters who worked in Yangon city and sons of non-farm households who moved out of the township, including to Yangon, as mentioned earlier. This trend

[8] For the definition of "non-agricultural household", see footnote 2 in Chap. 3.

[9] In Table 6.7, the total number of out-migration includes "In Hlegu Township (T/S)", "Out of Hlegu T/S" and to "Yangon city".

[10] From this definition, the out-migration ratio in Tables 6.6 and 6.7 are equal.

continued, and in 2013, there was a significant increase in the outflow of the adult children of non-farm households (agricultural labourer and non-agricultural households) to places outside of Hlegu Township, including to Yangon city. Despite this, the child out-migration ratio for all households surveyed decreased significantly: from 1.06 in 1994 to 0.72 in 2013. Comparing these two years, the out-migration ratio of farm households lessened by half, from 0.81 to 0.44, that of agricultural labourer households declined by less than one-third, from 1.79 to 0.50, and that of non-agricultural households dropped by about a fifth, from 1.08 to 0.83. The farm household out-migration ratio decreased because the number of people who left the village halved from 0.59 to 0.26. In contrast, the reason for the downturn in the non-farm household out-migration ratio was that the number of *oekhwe* within the village rose considerably, even more than the significant increase in the number of out-migration. The reasons for non-farm households to remain in the village are, first, an increase in employment opportunities in the non-agricultural sector in the village, such as peddlers, street vendors, small shop keepers, drivers of side-cars, motorcycle taxis and trucks, and cargo handlers, and, second, an upsurge in the number of young people commuting to factories and commercial facilities in and around Yangon City. This is a consequence of the de-agrarianisation.

As Zeepinwea Village is located in the special geographical conditions of Yangon's suburbs, benefiting from the economic development of Yangon city due to the market economy and the consequent urbanisation of Hlegu Town as a metropolitan suburb, young people are becoming de-agrarianised while living in the village, either by commuting from the village or by engaging in transport and commercial activities linking the village to Yangon city and Hlegu town. This may be a 21st-century form of development for rural areas in the suburbs of large cities such as Yangon and Mandalay.

Chapter 7
Myanmar Village Society: Comparing with Japan and Thailand

Monks reading sutras and preaching to funeral attendees. Unlike in Japan, they do not do this to the dead. Bodies are buried in a random part of the cemetery, where it is not known who else's bones would turn up, and small wooden grave markers are placed. People who came from far away and died in this village are also laid to rest in this cemetery, without ever returning home. (January 2016, Zeepinwea Village)

A. Takahashi, *Regime Changes and Socio-economic History of Rural Myanmar, 1986–2019*, Studies in Economic History,
https://doi.org/10.1007/978-981-99-3272-6_7

Introduction

For more than 30 years, I have walked around many villages across Myanmar, but I have always felt that there are no "villages" in Myanmar, or, more precisely, that there is a big difference between Myanmar and Japanese villages. For my family, who were full-time farmers in a Japanese village, the village always provided a norm of life and guaranteed agricultural production of a smallholder, but at the same time it enforced a way of behaviour and a sense of ethics that were valid only within the village. The village was always hanging over my head. However, even under the repressive socialist and military regimes, the villagers of Myanmar appeared to me to be surprisingly independent and free, as if they were not bound by the village. Of course, Myanmar also has objective and subjective village societies, but the residents' perceptions of the village, and the relationship between the village society and the people within that society, seem to be quite different from those in Japan. This led me to the idea of comparing village societies in Japan and Myanmar, using the perspectives of individual independence and village society as a guiding thread.

The purpose of this chapter is to clarify what kind of society the villages in Myanmar have. However, such a question is too vague. Therefore, I will describe the characteristics of Myanmar village society by comparing it with villages in other regions. There are two ways of comparing: contrasting opposites and juxtaposing similar objects. I chose a Japanese village as an example of the former and a Thai village as an example of the latter. This is because I have accumulated my own life experiences and learning about Japanese villages, and the same can be said about Thai villages, although not to the same extent as in Japan. Nevertheless, the question remains as to the angle from which to make comparisons. In this chapter, I would like to think about villages from the perspective of what kind of "cohesion" they have, what the cohesiveness derives from, and how it regulates villagers. First, I consider the village as an "objective group". In other words, we examine the village from the perspective of what kind of groups and organisations[1] exist in the village, how they accumulate, and how they relate to the village. Second, I consider the village as an object of "subjective cognition" of its members, or as a sense of belonging. Third, I assume that a broader "political power" has shaped the village. Namely, both the composition of groups and the formation of cognitive domains relate to the external environment—such as the political, administrative and economic regimes, which I refer to collectively as "political power". From these three points of view,

[1] In this and the next chapter, I define a "group" as an aggregate of people who have common goals and interests (joint goals), some sense of belonging (proactive communality), and some continuous interaction (communication). In contrast, I define an "organisation" as a structured group, that is, a group in which everyone's status and roles are differentiated, clarified, and institutionalised, and which also has a sustained system of command. An "organisation" is more than the sum of individuals (members)—it shows unique emergent properties that cannot be reduced to individual characteristics. Having said that, the difference between a "group" and an "organisation" is often ambiguous in Myanmar villages, so in this and the next chapter, if there is no particular need to separate them, I do not distinguish between a group and an organisation but treat them collectively as "groups and/or organisations".

the purpose of this chapter is to consider what kind of "cohesion" the village has, that is, the unity or communality of the village, and to inquire into the mechanism by which such "cohesion" is generated and reproduced.

The main theme of this chapter is the contrast between Myanmar villages and Japanese villages, whereas the Thai villages are the intermediate term connecting the two and will be described less. Unless otherwise mentioned, I use the term "village" to refer, in Japan, to a *kyūson* (old village), *ōaza*, or *buraku*, rather than to an administrative village,[2] and in Myanmar, to a village (*cêiywa*), not a village tract (*cêiywa ou'sù*), which otherwise is the administrative end in Myanmar.[3] In the case of Thailand, a village is built by peasants for the purpose of living freely from administrative and political control (Kitahara, 1990: 22), which may or may not overlap with administrative villages. In Myanmar, the following descriptions focus mainly on the villages of ethnic Bamar people in the central plains (Upper Myanmar), of ethnic Bamar and Karen people in the delta region (Lower Myanmar), and of ethnic Shan, Palaung, and Chin people in the mountainous areas. In Thailand, the descriptions focus on the villages of the Thai and Lao peoples in the northern, north-eastern, and central regions.[4]

Let use first explore different scholarly theories on Japanese, Thai, and Myanmar village societies. I will first discuss Japan, then Thailand, and finally, Myanmar.

7.1 Genealogies of Village Society Theories

7.1.1 Japan

First, let us look at the "*Shizen-son* (Common Village)"[5] theory. Scholars have often referred to the communal nature of Japanese villages through the term "common village". This is the argument that Eitaro Suzuki developed in his book *Principles of Japanese Village Sociology*, published in 1940 (Suzuki, 1968 (1940)). Suzuki tried to identify the "extent" of the village by the degree of accumulation of social groups

---

[2] *Kyūson* (old village) expanded through amalgamations from the Meiji era onwards, forming administrative villages. *Kyūson* and *ōaza* correspond roughly to the early modern villages in the feudal domain during the Edo period, but not necessarily to *buraku*. Therefore, in this and the next chapters, the geographic and social area called *ōaza*, *buraku*, or village, which corresponds to the common village described below, is called "village" in Japan.

[3] For definitions and legislations on villages, village tracts, and townships, see Chap. 2.

[4] Needless to say, there are many case studies that have led to these theories of village societies in Japan and Thailand. In the case of Myanmar, in order to construct the theory of village society in this chapter, I will take up cases of villages that are diverse in terms of region and period, both in my own case studies and in the literature cited. In other words, my theory of village society does not apply to only one village at one point in time. However, this is not to deny the possibility that this theory has a certain regional or historical character.

[5] The literal translation of "*shizen-son*" is "natural village", but as we shall see, it cannot necessarily be said to be a naturally formed village. Therefore, it is translated as "common village".

and social relations. He examined the ranges (or districts) where social groups and relations accumulated, from the smallest to the largest, with *koaza* or *kumi* (small village quarter or group) as the first range, *ōaza* or *buraku* (synonymous with "village" in this and the next chapter) as the second range, and administrative villages—after the amalgamation of towns and villages in 1889—as the third range. He then scrutinised ten different groups—administrative, economic, religious, kinship, neighbourhood, and so on—to see which groups were made up of members of which ranges, and which ranges had dense social relations between individuals that were not mediated by a group. As a result, he found that the range with the highest accumulation of autonomous groups and the highest degree of social unity was the second range, and named this community[6] the "common village" (Suzuki, 1968: 101–107).

Moreover, the common village has a "village spirit". According to Suzuki, the social unity of a common village is not merely the accumulation of groups and social relations, but an autonomous social consciousness, a systematic principle of behaviour, and something that could be called the "spirit of the village". The wills and relations of individuals do not create the village, but the spirit of the village shapes the wills and relations of individuals (Suzuki, 1968: 106–107). The villagers perceive this spirit, live by it as a code of conduct, and reproduce it. The *ujigami* (guardian god) represents the spirit of the village and protects the common village itself, and the *Shinto* shrine deifies it (Suzuki, 1968: 332).

A second theory about Japanese village society is the "*Ie-rengō* (Household Alliance)" theory. Kizaemon Aruga thought of the Japanese village as an extension of the alliances of households, without assuming ranges in advance as Suzuki did. For Aruga, a household is a unit of securing livelihood through organising labour. Because a household is a very small group (community), it would have difficulty surviving in a village on its own. It must therefore have livelihood relationships with other households to secure its survival. This is why some form of "*ie-rengō* (household alliance)" always arises when multiple households co-exist. In Japan, there are two types of household alliances: *dōzoku*, in which households are connected to each other in a hierarchical relationship, and *kumi*, in which households are linked to each other in an equal relationship. Both *dōzoku* and *kumi* are robust groups that continue for generations. The household alliances then become densely packed into a village (Aruga, 1969: 175–177). In this way, Aruga adopted the method of approaching the actual situation or essence of villages by analysing the structure of household alliances: first, the individual or family, then the household as its living community, then the household alliance, and finally the village as a complex of these. He doubted the idea that household alliances have an external frame from the beginning, such as a village or a *buraku*, and that they are compounded or accumulated within that frame (Aruga, 1971: 129). Therefore, as described below, he disagreed with Suzuki's

[6] The term "community" used in this chapter refers to a local society formed on the basis of regionalities and communal feelings, in which members have a sense of shared values and belonging and are subject to certain regulations. I believe that "collective" like Japanese "village society" and "community" have different social structures. In this chapter, I do not distinguish between "collective" and "community", but in the next chapter, I will make a distinction between them to further clarify the characteristics of Myanmar village society.

argument. However, Aruga agreed with the definition of a "common village" as a village that has formed as a result of gathering household alliances (Aruga, 1971: 170).

Third is the "*Jichi-sonraku* (Autonomous Village)" theory. Hitoshi Saito suggested that the Japanese "*jichi-sonraku* (autonomous village)" is neither a simple *dōzoku* (hierarchical household alliance) organisation nor a simple rural community. Instead, it is a *buraku* (village) that exercises a kind of administrative and judicial authority over a specific territory and its people (members), and has its own financial and property rights.[7] The *buraku* was formed in the midst of both opposition to and subordination to the rule of feudal power under the early modern feudal system, and has survived to the present day because it is an indispensable organisation for the subsistence of peasants (Saito, 1989: 32). In this sense, it is not a super-historical communal relationship, but a social relationship with a certain historical definiteness (Saito, 1989: v). Thus, the village community must be viewed from the perspective of the history of its relationship with "political power".

7.1.2 Thailand

First, let us look at the "Loosely Structured Society" theory. Thai village society was conceptualised as a "loosely structured society" by the anthropologist John Fee Embree (1950). According to Embree, the *Japanese* village has a social unity with a tight social structure in which the behaviour of people conforms closely to the formal social patterns of human relations. In the Japanese village, it is difficult for individuals to deviate, and reciprocal rights and duties are clearly marked and carried out. In contrast, the social structure of Thai villages is loose. A Thai village also has its own identity, and the members also have rights and duties, but they are less clearly defined and less strictly enforced. Individuals are allowed to act according to their own will, with less social pressure (Embree, 1950: 184–185).

Steven Isaac Piker, who surveyed villages in central Thailand, summarised the looseness of Thai village society as follows: (1) Villages do not operate as social units. For example, local temples and schools draw their clients from a number of surrounding villages, nor do all villagers from any given village worship only at one temple. (2) Villagers' loyalty to or identification with the village is remarkably weak. (3) Economic cooperation[8] normally rests upon *ad hoc* dyadic ties and implies no

[7] A particularly important point to be discussed about the traditional Japanese village is that it is a society with autonomous rights, such as administrative rights exercised through village gatherings, judicial rights as seen in *murahachibu* (village ostracism), the right to levy non-statutory taxes such as *buraku* fees, and property rights such as the total ownership of membership land. Therefore, it should be called an "autonomous village" (Saito, 1989: ii).

[8] Cooperation can be defined as "two or more persons combining their efforts". In this book, cooperation is divided into two types: cooperation between two people is called "dyadic cooperation", and that of more than two people is called "general cooperation".

lasting relationship between individuals or families. (4) Participation in and disengagement from a group is a matter of individual voluntariness, because there are no formal sanctions forbidding disengagement (Piker, 1969: 62–63). In other words, loose society is a society that is patterned through dyadic relations. However, the questions of why and how groups are created amid *ad hoc* dyadic ties, what kind of groups are created, and what is the relationship between the generated group and the village, which is also a group, remain open. In this chapter, I try to clarify these issues.

Second, there is the "Multi-household Compound" theory. Koichi Mizuno (1981) argued that there is a collective relationship in Thai rural society. According to Mizuno, even if children separate their households after marriage, their parents still control the farmland and thus joint relations in terms of agricultural production arise. The children and their spouses live in or next to their parents' compounds, forming a family form called a "multi-household compound" (Mizuno, 1981: 109).

Mizuno's theory of "multi-household compound" was deftly elaborated by Atsushi Kitahara as follows: (1) There is a kind of joint family that combines the independent households of parents and children, while the parent household is the centre. (2) The basis of the bond is the undivided land between the parent and child. (3) The households are linked by a joint function that consists mainly of living together in the compound and temporarily renting farmland. (4) When parents die and the equal inheritance of compound and farmland is completed, the joint function is significantly weakened, even if siblings live close to each other, and the joint family is basically dissolved. (5) Households that remain close to each other even after the death of their parents may be called a "proximity household group", to distinguish them from a "multi-household compound". (6) Village society is a complex of small communities, centred on "multi-household compounds" and including "proximity household groups" and non-kinship households (Kitahara, 1990: 130). Thus, Kitahara extended Mizuno's theory of the multi-household compound to broader Thai village society. This passage is in line with how Aruga, discussed above, extended a theory of household alliances to a broader theory of Japanese villages. Incidentally, while Mizuno argues that all these Thai groups are formed by the accumulation of the "logic of interpersonal relationships" and thus do not go beyond the individual (Mizuno, 1981: 110), Kitahara emphasises their function as groups (Kitahara, 1990: 119).

The third is the "Family Circle" theory. In contrast to Kitahara's emphasis on the group, this theory rejects the idea of the group and emphasises the accumulation of dyadic relationships. The "family circle" is defined as a complex of relational cognitions or an accumulation of dyadic relationships centring on each individual (*ego*) that emerges from birth, adoption, or marriage, and the boundary of the family is fixed only when it is recognised as a group living and residing together (Tsubouchi and Maeda, 1977: 22–23). This is an argument that originally emerged from Malaysian village studies, but Kuchiba and Takemura (1983) argue that the "family circle" theory also applies to Don Daeng Village in north-eastern Thailand, where Mizuno conceived the theory of "multi-household compound", and that the multi-household compound is only one part of the case (Kitahara, 1990: 128). The term "family circle" was envisioned in order to avoid the concept of a group, but it was also intended to indicate that there was still a subjective social sphere, rather than an objectively identifiable bilateral relationship such as a dyad or a network (Tachimoto, 2000: 207). However, the correlation between this social sphere and the village is unclear. In this chapter, I will try to investigate the moment when the subjective social sphere is demarcated by the objective boundary of the village.

Shigetomi (1992, 1996) elucidated the process of how groups form from dyadic relationships. Shigetomi argues that Thai village society is changing from a loose to a tight society. When various resources become scarce due to population pressure and commercialisation, villagers start to form collective cooperative organisations rather than continue *ad hoc* cooperation based on dyadic relationships (Shigetomi, 1996: 107–169). Cooperative organisations with clear rules and penalties are formed (Shigetomi, 1992: 166–176), such as joint management organisations for land shortages, labour exchange groups for labour shortages, and rice banks and cooperative shops for capital shortages (Shigetomi, 1992: 166–176). Thus, the village containing these groups and organisations is transformed into a tight society (Shigetomi, 1992: 165). Thus, Shigetomi's analysis follows the above-discussed Suzuki's way of depicting the changes in society by detecting the accumulation of groups and organisations. In the case of Myanmar, however, groups and organisations can be formed as an extension of the dyadic relationships, *without* the village society becoming tight. Let us explore these processes and principles next.

7.1.3 Myanmar

Although no discussion of Myanmar village society has led to a "theory" as with Japan and Thailand, I will examine different views on Myanmar village society by reviewing some articles that touch on village society.

Regarding Upper Burma (Upper Myanmar) during the dynastic period, that is, before 1885, John S. Furnivall, a British administrator, stated that villagers "all had common interests and common obligations" and tried to make the village "a pleasant place to live in", through mutually assisting in agriculture, maintaining wells, tanks, and paths, repairing the village fence, and keeping watch by turns at the village gate (Furnivall, 1957 (1931): 37). Thus, "a village in Upper Burma resembled a large family". Teruko Saito similarly suggested that "in a village in Upper Burma, as symbolised by the hedges surrounding the living space, the residence of the village leader provided a place for mobilising labour, allocating tax burdens, and arbitrating disputes, and the existence of the monastery provided a source of identity for the village" (Saito, 2008: 41). In contrast, Toshikatsu Ito argues that "since all the inhabitants of a village or hamlet were not under the same system of rule, the interests of the villagers did not coincide with each other, and although they may have cooperated in various aspects of daily life, they rarely engaged in political matters as a whole, and therefore there was no such thing as village unity or discipline" (Ito, 2013: 23–24).

After the British colonisation of Upper Burma, the commercialisation of agriculture progressed and the number of people leaving for Lower Burma (Lower Myanmar) increased rapidly, but the nature of the village in Upper Burma did not change significantly (Furnivall, 1957: 82–83). In Lower Burma, which was colonised earlier, in 1852, people were not bound to the village where they resided and readily migrated from one village to another[9] (Furnivall, 1957: 65). Over large parts of Lower Burma there were "villages but no village life" (Furnivall, 1957: 80).

Manning Nash described the villages of Upper Burma after independence in 1948 as follows. As a social unit, the village was a fenced settlement composed of persons with responsibilities to keep the fence intact. As a political unit, the village was composed of an elected headman and a council of four, through whom people paid taxes. Single family households are both the ideal and the statistical norm. Beyond family, the only perdurable groups are based on religious and ceremonial activities; otherwise relationships tend to be contractual, dyadic, and fleeting (Nash, 1965: 319–320). These characteristics of Myanmar villages are very similar to those of Thailand as described by Piker.

Discussing the villages of Upper Burma during the Burmese socialist period (1962–1988), Katsumi Tamura asserted the cohesiveness of the village. Tamura stated: "The village is distinguished from the surrounding cultivated land (*taw*) by a series of fences surrounding the compound, there is a *nat* (*na'*) that protects the village, and religious rituals such as the rituals for chanting protective sutras during the New Year and during epidemics, rain-making rituals and the village pagoda festival are held in the village as a unit. In other words, the village, as a cohesive local community, has concrete or socially clear boundaries" (Tamura, 1981: 42). However, according to my field research, the fences of the village are managed by individual households (Takahashi, 2012: 178), and not all villagers participate in the management of the *nat* shrine or the paya (pagoda) festival (Takahashi, 2012: 162–168). It is not possible to judge the communal nature of a village solely on the basis of visual impressions.

Saito's general impression of the villages in Lower Burma during the same period was that they are open, with people free to enter and leave, and that although they did not originally form close-knit communities, they have begun having loose communal ties based on residential areas. As examples, she cites *thaye naye athin* (congratulation and condolence associations) and monasteries (Saito, 1986: 150). However, it should not be overlooked that not all villagers participate in either the congratulation and condolence association or the monastery. Indeed, both organisations can even lead to the division of the village (Takahashi, 2012: 163; 2018: 186–188). Thus, the existence of groups and organisations in a village does not itself necessarily lead to a strengthening of the communal character of the village. Like Suzuki and Shigetomi, we need to examine the process of formation of groups/organisations and their contents. I will approach the relationship between groups or organisations and village cohesiveness in Myanmar from this point of view.

---

[9] The frequent migration of households around Zeepinwea Village, described in Chap. 6, may be considered a residue of this movement.

7.1.4 Two Genealogies of Theories on Village Society

The Japanese scholars' debate on Thai village society was basically bringing an existing debate from Japan studies into Thai studies. Namely, Mizuno's theory of the Thai "multi-household compound" corresponds to Aruga's theory of the Japanese "household alliance". Tsubouchi and Maeda's theory of the Malaysian and Thai "family circle" resembles Suzuki's theory of the Japanese "village spirit".

Aruga's theory of "household alliance" and Mizuno's theory of "multi-household compound" are "objective" analyses of the structure of group formation, in which individuals form households, households form household alliances or multi-household compounds, and these groups come together to form villages. Suzuki's theory of the "accumulation of groups" is probably related to this. Let us call this the "genealogy of *group* theory".

In contrast, Suzuki's theory of the "village spirit" and Tsubouchi and Maeda's theory of the "family circle" emphasise "subjectivity". In other words, no matter how many groups are objectively united or aggregated, that alone will not form a village or a certain social sphere. Instead, there must be a social consciousness that recognises the village or sphere as such. I will call this the "genealogy of *cognitive* theory".

These two genealogies—of group theory and of cognitive theory—are often in conflict. Aruga criticised the idea of the "common village" governed by the "spirit of the village," saying that "it is impossible to understand how the social unity Suzuki refers to arose without linking it to the character of the political structure of the time, and that it was extremely vulnerable to domination and interference from above, even if it appeared to be unique" (Aruga, 1971: 169). The family circle theory also argued against the theory of the multi-household compound: "The fact that houses for the parents' households and houses for the children's households are built in the same compound does not mean that there is a rule that this should be the case, but only that such a grouping is recognised in the village for economic considerations" (Tsubouchi & Maeda, 1977: 36). In response, Kitahara claimed that "the family circle theory cannot explain the superiority of the parent–child relationship in terms of data on joint cultivation and management of land and living together on the same compound", and again advocated the validity of the multi-household compound theory (Kitahara, 1990: 128). In this chapter, I attempt to combine the opposing "genealogy of group theory" and "genealogy of cognitive theory", because I believe that the social structure of Myanmar villages can be better understood by such a method.

Before that, I will start with a comparative study of the history of agricultural and rural policies and village social structure in Japan and Myanmar, bearing in mind Aruga's point that village structure must be viewed in relation to the political structure that defines it (Aruga, 1956: 44) and Saito's "autonomous village" theory. Then I will move on to the group theory and cognitive theory.

7.2 Myanmar Villages from the Viewpoint of Group Formation

7.2.1 Land and Water Management and the Villages

In Japan, the effects of historical "village demarcation" and "village contract" have continued for a long time (Takahashi, 2012: 138–150). Villages in early modern Japan (17th to 18th century) were constrained by a political structure based on "*kura-mai chigyo* (fiefdom on the rice tribute)" (Aruga, 1956: 45).[10] "*Muragiri* (village demarcation)" by "*kenchi* (feudal land cadastral survey)" established a village territory where villagers, residential areas and arable land were integrated. Thus, the village became "the subject of land occupation". At the same time, the "*murauke* (village contract)" system—whereby the village as itself took full obligation for the collection of the (brown) rice tribute—was introduced, while the village was also responsible for water management (Kimura, 1980: 73–74, 152–153). Thus, the feudal village became a unit of land occupation, tax collection and water use. According to Aruga, the "common village" of Suzuki was formed historically and politically in this way. At present, the land improvement district is responsible for the management of farmland and water. Thus, individuals belong to a multi-layered group that consists of the "household", "village", and "land improvement district". In addition, villages have carried out Japan's rice procurement since World War II, as well as, since the 1970s, the acreage-reduction policy—whereby villages allocate the amount of reduced procurement and adjust the area reduction per individual households. Thus, as Saito says, the Japanese "common village" has continued to the present day, although it has changed its name and form (such as *ōaza* or *buraku*).

In Myanmar, on the other hand, the colonial period's settlement surveys, which were similar to *kenchi* in Japan, were based on the *kwin* (*kwîn*)—cultivated area of a certain size—that had nothing to do with villages. Moreover, villages have not been the units for land tax collection (Takahashi, 2012: 139). Neither "*muragiri* (village demarcation)" nor "*murauke* (village contract)" was done. Water supply management is to be carried out only by interested parties. A village has multiple waterways and farmers from multiple villages are involved in water management. Moreover, they follow the orders and guidance of the Irrigation Department. Thus, the village does not take the lead in water management (Takahashi, 1993: 52–56).

In Japan, most of the common villages have a common land under collective ownership. It has been both a source of livelihood but as well as an indispensable part of the agricultural production. In other words, a Japanese village (*buraku*) has maintained strong cohesion through the experience of "*muragiri*", "*murauke*", the basic unit of water use, the existence of common land, and the various communal

[10] However, even before the early modern period, Japanese villages had a sense of cohesion in the form of communal living, collective cultivation, and the management of village halls (Fujiki 2010: 54–57, 68). In the early modern period, these spontaneous villages were overtaken by the shogunate's domain system, which developed nationwide, forming the villages of the early modern period.

labour associated with these (Takahashi, 2012: 151). Thus, the villages, which have maintained a certain degree of autonomy despite being regulated by political power, are "autonomous villages".[11]

In Myanmar, there are forests and marshes that are equivalent to common lands, called *amyâbain myei* ("land for all"). However, since anyone can enter this land and take trees or fish, a so-called tragedy of the commons (open access) may occur, in which finite resources will eventually be depleted. In such a case, the land will be managed by the state, or the state will lease or sell the land to individuals. The village will not become the managing entity. On the other hand, there are some closed village lands called "*ywa myei*" (village lands). These include lakes and swamps next to the village, unowned paddy fields, grassland, wasteland, and swidden land. However, although there is a notion that the village owns these lands, there are few examples of joint management by villagers. Even when joint management does occur, it is for a short period of time and the management is ultimately left to the individual (Takahashi, 2012: 152–161). It is often the case that village-owned wasteland is converted into residential land and sold to individuals. In other words, whether open or closed, common land is managed either by the state or by individuals in Myanmar. Specific groups within a village may manage various resources within and outside the village, but the village itself rarely takes the lead in management, and even when it does, it is only for a short time.

7.2.2 Religion and the Villages

Eitaro Suzuki states that the territory of the Japanese common village coincides with the sphere of the *ujiko* group, group of people who worship the *ujigami* of a *buraku* or *kyuson* (old village). The *ujigami* is the Shinto guardian shrine of the common village, and represents the communality of the social consciousness of the common village. The communal maintenance of the shrine unites the village members into a strong cohesive group (Suzuki, 1968: 332–334). In contrast, Suzuki says that the Buddhist temple is almost indifferent to the geographic scope of the community or the regional group. While the *ujiko* groups are local groups that collectively worship and maintain shrines, the *danka*—temple worshipper—groups are interconnected only by each individual's connection to the temple. Thus, the temple worshippers' groups are much less cohesive and united than the shrine worshippers' groups (Suzuki 1968: 337). Thus, Suzuki contrasts shrines and temples and concludes that shrines are the symbol of the common villages, while temples are not.

[11] As the theory of "autonomous village" emphasises, there is no doubt that the character of the Japanese village was defined by its historical relationship with upper political power. However, the response to power has always been at the village level probably because the village has also been a unit of livelihood, complementing the productive activities. Note that village meetings and village levies can also be seen in Myanmar villages, so it cannot be entirely ruled out that Myanmar villages can be autonomous villages.

Religious institutions in Myanmar villages can be considered as the equivalent of temples in Japanese villages. In Myanmar, the villages of the Bamar and Shan ethnic groups usually have Buddhist monasteries and payas, while the villages of ethnic Chin and Karen Christians have churches. For example, Zeepinwea village in Lower Myanmar—discussed in previous chapters—had two Buddhist monasteries as of 1986, and the village was divided into two groups of believers. The division was based on geography: an eastern and a western section. The two sections did not get along well, and intermarriages between them were extremely rare, compared to marriages within the sections (Takahashi, 1992: 42–43). As described in Chap. 4, the farmland around the village was later developed and three new monasteries were built, and a large number of believers from the village shifted to following these new monasteries. Upper Myanmar's Thindaunggyi Village—the other village discussed in previous chapters—had two monasteries, with two more monasteries in Taunghlwe Village, which forms an adjoining village tract. There, Buddhists in each village went to the monastery of their choice, regardless of whether they lived inside or outside the village. In some cases, parents and children in the same household attended different monasteries. In 2013–2014, I visited 54 households in Thindaunggyi and 56 households in Zeepinwea, respectively, and asked them which monastery's monks they serve the morning meal to. It turned out that more than half of the households in both villages were providing food offerings to more than one monastery per household. Each monastery organises a group of villagers called *Neikpanso Apwe*, which prepares the morning meals for monks. In Zeepinwea Village, a member of this "food offering group" went around the village to invite people to join the group, while in Thindaunggyi Village, a duty roster of donors was posted on the walls of the monastery. Let us compare this to a Christian village. Hnyalone Village in Chin State had 202 households (as of 2005), all of whom were Christians. The village had four congregations, called *athindaw*. These were each organised separately by the villagers (Takahashi, 2012: 165). This is an example of how, in Myanmar, not only Buddhist villages but also Christian villages have several congregations within a village, and religion does not enhance the cohesion of the village. Neither Buddhism nor Christianity assumes a group or regional character in principle, since both are based on a one-to-one bilateral relationship between the person and God or Buddha, whereby the individual believer is saved by believing in the doctrines and scriptures of a certain denomination. Suzuki states that Buddhism in Japan is completely indifferent to the geographical extent of regional societies (Suzuki, 1968: 335), and the same can be said of Buddhism and Christianity in Myanmar (Takahashi, 2012: 165).

In Myanmar, a *nat* (*na'*) spirit is equivalent to the *ujigami* in Japanese villages in the sense that, unlike Buddhism, the *nat* has a territorial nature and is an autogenous belief. The equivalent of an *ujigami* shrine is the *nat sinn*, or shrine of the *nat*. The *nat* has a certain territory to protect, such as paddy fields, houses, and weirs, in contrast to the Christian God and Buddhist Buddha, which do not have a territory. A village *nat* (*ywa zàun na'*)[12] protects the territory of the village. However, since the social

[12] The word *sàun*, which means "to protect", becomes *zàun* depending on the word before it. This is called "euphonic change of unvoiced to voiced sound".

hierarchy in this religion is, first, monk, then man, then *nat*, and, only finally, woman, it is mostly the women, especially the elderly, who pray to the *nat* and maintain the *nat sinn*. Moreover, some villages have more than one area deity—area *nat* (*ne sàun na'*)—including a village *nat*. Finally, in Lower Myanmar, the *nat* is retracted into each household to become a household *nat* (*ein zàun na'*), and there is no village *nat* to protect the village. Thus, the *ujigami* of Japan—where each village has only one shrine, which protects the territory of the village and symbolises the ethics and spirit of the village—is quite different from the Myanmar village *nat* (Takahashi, 2012: 166–168).

7.2.3 Groups and Organisations Within the Villages

In Myanmar, the role of the village in basic production activities, such as land and water management, is very small. Moreover, as discussed below, there is no collective commodity production activity that would assume or promote village cohesion.

Then, does Myanmar have no such thing as cooperative labour? This is not so. First of all, as a non-monetary exchange of labour, the practice of *le'sâ alai'* is known. In Thindaunggyi Village, this practice was done between owners of cattle, for ploughing and hallowing paddy fields. In another example, I observed how, in a village near Pathein town, two agricultural labourers who had been contracted to harvest rice exchanged labour among themselves. In other words, exchange of labour tends to take place only within a certain class of people with similar economic status, such as those who owned cattle or those who did not hold cultivation rights. This is also the case in the villages of Myanmar's non-Bamar peoples. For example, in a village near Namhkam (Nanhkan) town, where many tea-growing Ta'ang (Palaung) people live, this kind of labour exchange is called *kawe*, and a bit to the south, in a Ta'ang village near Namhsan (Nam San), it is called *karuwee-go*. This exchange is observed in weeding tea fields in the dry season and in picking tea in the rainy season. Both exchanges take place between tea farmers of similar size. Among Chin people in the suburbs of Hakha, there is a labour exchange called *flawbun*, which involves cutting trees and grass in preparation for swidden agriculture. It is carried out between swidden cultivators of the same size. All of the above labour exchanges are carried out on a one-to-one dyadic basis, in contrast to the *yui* (tie) in Japan, where neighbourhoods and relatives form groups and make labour contributions to these groups, that is, labour exchanges take place in the context of an individual-to-group relationship. Moreover, in Myanmar villages, these exchanges are done only within a limited range of the village, in terms of the number of households, area, and class, and the exchanges easily cross the boundary of the village by following the bilateral relationship, in contrast to Japanese villages (Takahashi, 2012: 115–119).

A group that looks similar to the Japanese *yui*, a women's rice-transplanting group called *kau'sai'si*, is found in villages in Upper Myanmar (see the photo on the first page of Chap. 1). However, while the *yui* is an organisation that exchanges labour internally, the *kau'sai'si* is an organisation that earns money externally and pays its members a percentage wage (Takahashi, 2012: 114–115). The "head of the group" called "*si gâunhsâun*" organises women by paying them wages in advance and sends them to the paddy fields to plant rice, in principle in groups of 10–15. The head gets one person's wage and the interest on the advance wages. The organisation consists of a dyadic relationship between the head and the individual transplanter, and there is no unity among the members. In this case, too, there is no principle that the members of the *kau'sai'si* are limited to women in the village. Instead, women from several villages may form a single *kau'sai'si*.

As mentioned above, in Myanmar, the concept of village farmland is weak, and the scope of labour exchange can easily extend beyond the village boundary, unlike in Japan, but the boundary of the village residential area is clear and villagers do have a sense of "our village". In this context, villages have autonomous associations, such as Congratulation and Condolence Association (*thayêi nayêi athîn*), Board of Trustees (*gôpàkà aphwè*), Drinking Water Use Committee (*yei komiti*), Security Association (*lounjounyêi aphwè*), and so on, and official groups, such as Firefighters' Association (*mîtha' aphwè*), Women's Association (*amyôudhamî yêiya*), Child and Mother Association (*kalêi mìgin yêiya*), Parent–Teacher Association (*mìbà hsaya athîn*), and so on. However, these groups or organisations are not for "production" but just for "consumption" or "life" not including commodity production.[13] The villagers in Myanmar do not necessarily need to cooperate with each other in "production", but they do need to help each other in daily "life", in order to live in the village. In fact, it may be easier to establish such organisations in Myanmar than in Japan. However, they also disappear quickly. In order to show this, I will examine the mechanism of forming groups and organisations in Myanmar and this mechanism's relationship to the village.

7.3 The Village as an Object of Cognition and as a Subjective Social Sphere

7.3.1 Myanmar Type Multi-household Compound

In Burmese language, a house as a structure is called *ein*, a home is termed *eindaun*, and the aggregate of a home's members—a household—is named *eindaundhâzù* or *eindaunzù* (Takahashi, 1992: 51). A family is called the *mìdhâzù*, meaning a "group of mother and children". The household is composed mainly of family members. Table 7.1 shows what kind of families lived in a household in six sample villages. In

[13] As Suzuki and Aruga say, in Japan, the cooperative nature of "life" encompasses all aspects of community, including production, consumption, political economy, religion, and so on. In this chapter and next chapter, I distinguish between "production" and "life". "Production" here refers to activities to produce goods and services as commodities. "Life" refers to the activity of producing non-commodity goods and services to be consumed in the community, and the activity of consuming the goods and services provided by this activity or "production".

all six villages, nuclear family households or quasi-nuclear family households (that is, fatherless or motherless families) accounted for more than half of all households in each village.[14] Table 7.2 shows the place of origin of the couple in each household. The table shows that, in three villages, the majority of marriages were within the village, and that, in the other three villages, the number of intra-village marriages was also considerably high.[15] The table also indicates that there is no rule on which village the husband and wife should live in. A few households have both husband and wife coming from outside the village.

As discussed above, the main form of village household in Myanmar is the nuclear family household, but each household does not necessarily own a separate compound or residential land. Similarly to Thailand, the custom of married children living in separate houses on land owned by their parents is also found in Myanmar. Multi-household compounds are widespread. They have a few households living together, each with their own house, in a single compound under the ownership of a single person.

In 1987, in Zeepinwea Village, out of a total of 136 households (138 households minus 2 non-surveyed households), 120 had houses in private compounds. 51 of these households were in altogether 21 multi-household compounds. Figure 7.1 illustrates the kinship relationships between households in Zeepinwea Village. Each circled number is a household. An ellipse around a few households represents a multi-household compound. The kinship relationships in these multi-household compounds were as follows: owner of the compound and daughter in 4 cases, owner and son in 9, owner and sibling (including in-laws) in 8, owner and nephew-or-niece in 6, and others in 3 cases (Takahashi, 1992: 135–137).

In 1994, 83 out of the 156 Thindaunggyi Village households lived on 30 plots of multi-household compound, as shown in the ovals on the village map on Fig. 7.2. Most multi-household compounds included two or three households, but there were also compounds of six or nine households living together. The relationship of kinship among these households was as follows: owner of the compound and daughter in 15 cases, owner and son in 16, owner and sibling in 8, owner and nephew-or-niece in 5, and others in 3 cases.[16]

In both Figs. 7.1 and 7.2, independent households appear to be interspersed among multi-household compounds. In both villages, although the majority of compounds were co-habituated by the households of parents and the households of their adult children, there were also many cases where the owner and their siblings, nephews and nieces lived together, and in rare cases, households of non-relatives moved into multi-household compounds. In other words, Myanmar's multi-household compounds are not a kind of joint family in which the independent households of parents and children

[14] For the geographical conditions and ethnic composition of each village, see Takahashi (2000: 60–73).

[15] As mentioned in the section on adult children's migration in Chap. 6, it is presumed that the intermarriage zone is gradually expanding among the younger generation and that intra-village marriages are declining accordingly.

[16] In both villages, the number of compounds and the simple total number of kinship relations do not match because some multi-households compounds have more than two households living together.

Table 7.1 Family structures of households

	Zeepinwea		Thindaunggyi		Kanthalay		Gukine		South Tande		Aingshe		West Phayekyun	
Family structure	Number of households	%	Number of households	%	Number of households	%	Number of households	%	Number of households	%	Number of households	%	Number of households	%
(a) Nuclear family	104	61.2	95	60.9	29	58.0	21	52.5	22	57.9	20	40.0	27	54.0
(b) Fatherless family	15	8.8	14	9.0	4	8.0	4	10.0	1	2.6	7	14.0	2	4.0
(c) Motherless family	5	2.9	3	1.9	1	2.0	3	7.5	1	2.6	2	4.0	2	4.0
(d) Semi-extended family	16	9.4	19	12.2	5	10.0	8	20.0	6	15.8	12	24.0	7	14.0
(e) Extended family	12	7.1	9	5.8	6	12.0	1	2.5	3	7.9	1	2.0	5	10.0
Others	18	10.6	16	10.2	5	10.0	3	7.5	5	13.2	8	16.0	7	14.0
Total	170		156		50		40		38		50		50	

Note (a) A family consisting of a married couple and children, or a married couple only
(b) A nuclear family lacking a father
(c) A nuclear family lacking a mother
(d) Nuclear family + single parents or grandchildren or siblings
(e) Families including two-generation couples
Source Takahashi, 2000, p. 98

Table 7.2 Birthplace of husband and wife

Place of birth of husband/wife	Zeepinwea		Thindaunggyi		Kanthale		Gukine		South Tande		Aingshe		West Phayekyun	
	Pairs	%	Pairs	%	Pairs	%	Pairs	%	Pairs	%	Pairs	%	Pairs	%
Both husband and wife are from the village	56	36.6	56	41.8	25	51.0	10	31.3	9	25.8	24	66.7	26	60.5
Husband from the village; Wife from outside	57	37.2	35	26.1	16	32.7	15	46.8	13	37.1	9	25.0	9	20.9
Wife from the village; Husband from outside	29	19.0	37	27.6	6	12.2	6	18.8	13	37.1	3	8.3	8	18.6
Both husband and wife are from outside the village	11	7.2	6	4.5	2	4.1	1	3.1	0	0.0	0	0.0	0	0.0
Total	153		134		49		32		35		36		43	

Note All couples in which both husband and wife are alive and are still married were counted. Therefore, more than one couple may be counted in one household
Source Takahashi, 2000, p. 99

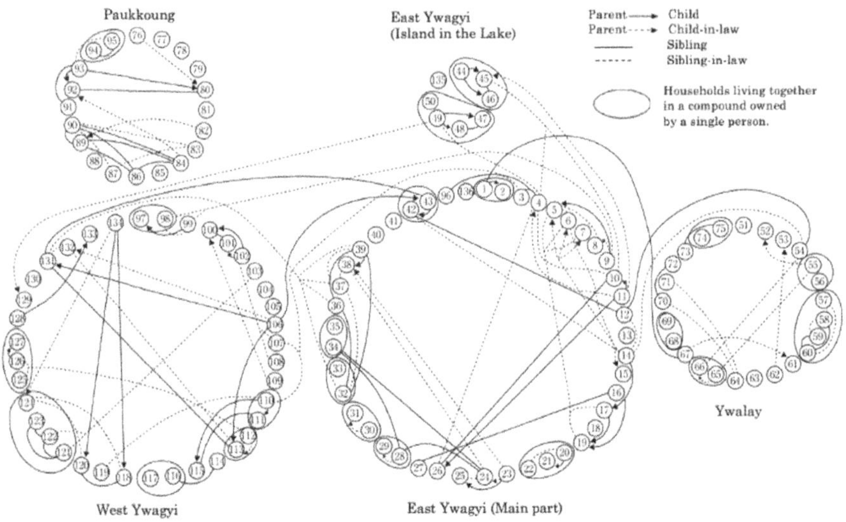

Fig. 7.1 Kinship (of the household head only) and multi-household compounds in Zeepinwea Village in 1987. *Source* Takahashi, 2000, p. 57

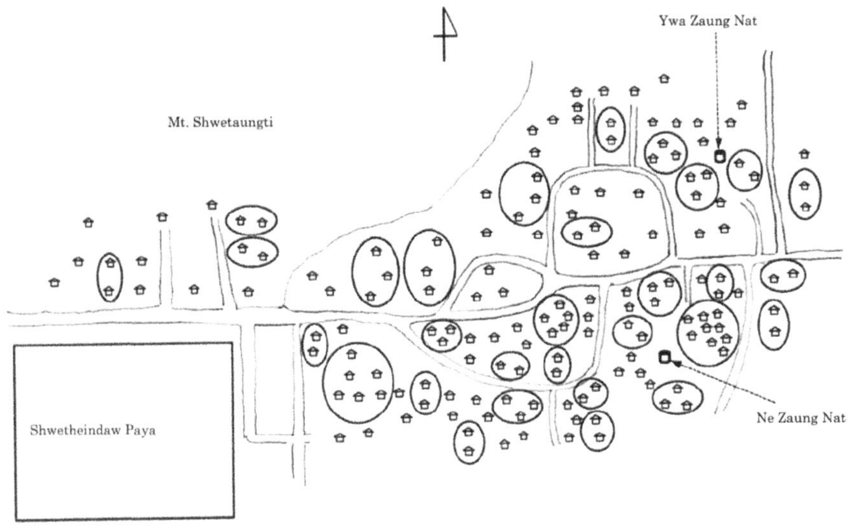

Fig. 7.2 Abbreviated map of Thindaunggyi Village and its multi-household compounds in 1994. *Source* Takahashi, 2015, p. 19

are united, as Kitahara describes, nor are they cooperate in terms of production as in Thailand. Depending on the size of the compound, the relationship between parents and their offspring, the financial situation of both sides and the preferences of the offspring couple, some offspring couple households choose to live together with their parent households, in separate buildings on the same plot. There are no clear norms for living together.

Nevertheless, it is often relatives who actually live together in the compound. Moreover, the practice of dividing the compound[17] upon the death of a parent, grandparent, aunt or uncle is largely the same as in Thailand. Thus, close relatives will live in close proximity. Similar to Kitahara's depiction of Thai village society, a Myanmar village is also a complex of small settlements, centred on "multi-household compounds" and intermingled with "proximity household groups" who are related by blood, with the addition of non-blood-related households.

7.3.2 The "Logic of Interpersonal Relationship", the "Logic of Frequent Contact", and the "Relatives of the Place"

Parents, children, and sibling tend to live in close proximity to each other even when outside the oval-encircled multi-household compounds in Figs. 7.1 and 7.2, and similar kinship networks also exist throughout the village even among households that are far apart. For Zeepinwea Village, this can be seen in Fig. 7.1, where the adjoining circled numbers indicate that the households are adjacent to each other and where lines drawn between households show many kin relations between distantly located households. This figure shows only the kinship relationships between the heads of households, so if other kinship relationships between households would be included, the kinship network would become even denser. This is also the case in Thindaunggyi Village, where dense kinship networks have developed outside of the multi-household compounds shown in Fig. 7.2. This is partly because of the expansion of proximity living, derived from the multi-household compounds, and partly because of the many intra-village marriages, shown in Table 7.2.

Within a Myanmar household, parents call their children "son" and "daughter". This is unlike in Japan, where parents address their children "elder brother" and "elder sister" to indicate the children's status within the family from the perspective of the youngest child. In Myanmar, even within a small group of households, the *ego* (self) calls others son (*thâ*), daughter (*thamî*), father (*apei*), mother (*amei*), elder brother (*akou*), elder sister (*amà*), younger brother (*nyi*), and younger sister (*nyimà*), and so on, with the *ego* (self) at the centre, without being conscious of its

[17] Myanmar does not have such a clear custom as in Thailand that all offspring households should inherit both compound and farmland equally after the death of parents. Although compounds are often divided after the death of the both parents, their boundaries are mostly ill-defined. Farmland is often divided and handed over by parents during their lifetime, and there are a handful of cases where residential lots are not divided after the death of a parent.

status within the household. These intra-household forms of address radiate outward, centring on the *ego*, extending not only to relatives such as uncle, aunt, and cousin, but also to non-relatives (Takahashi, 2012: 171–172). These relationships are one-to-one dyadic relationships between the *ego* and others. The principle or ethic of emotional mutuality that governs such dyadic relationships, which stem from kinship, is what Mizuno termed the "logic of interpersonal relations" (Mizuno, 1981: 203–204).

Following this "logic of interpersonal relationships", villagers frequently go back and forth between households. It is not only for specific purposes—such as leaving the child in the care of the parents, bringing meals to the parents, going to the grandparents' house to help out, or asking for pocket money—but also for small talk or just on the way to somewhere else. As shown in Fig. 7.2, many of the houses in the village do not face public roads, and people often have to pass through other people's compounds to get to their own houses. In other words, even if ownership is divided, people do not exclude others from using their housing lots for passing. As an extension of that, it is a daily occurrence for people to walk into other people's homes without greeting. This phenomenon is not limited to Zeepinwea and Thindaunggyi villages but can be seen in any village in Myanmar. In addition, there are many opportunities for villagers to get together: the aforementioned *le'sâ alai'*, the *kau'sai'si*, the employment relationship between farmers and agricultural labourers, food offering rituals at monasteries and homes, road building and canal cleaning on the orders of the township or district, and so on. In this book, I will term these frequent meetings of villagers as "frequent contact". The "frequent contact" also enables villagers to form a dense social network and strengthen emotional bonds of mutual attachment and sympathy. Since the amount of frequent contact is strongly determined by people's physical distance, the dyadic network naturally becomes denser within the village than outside of the village. This I define as the "logic of frequent contact".

Myanmar villages are filled with terms used in kinship relationships. In addition to the terms for consanguinity and affinity, people often use terms, which are rare in Japan, such as *khamî khàme'*, which refers to the relationship between *ego*'s parent and the spouse's parent, and *màyâ nyiàkou* and *lîn nyiàmà*, which describe relationships between the siblings' spouses. And for those relationships that still cannot be described, the term "*ya'hswei ya'myôu*" is applied. *Hswei myôu* means "relative" and *ya'* signifies place, so "*ya'hswei ya'myôu*" is the "relatives of the place". The outer edge of kinship is defined here, and the villagers are encompassed in the "relatives of the place". In fact, even strangers call each other "brother" and "sister". Perhaps this is what Furnivall meant when he said that the village resembled a large family (Furnivall, 1957: 30). A social network of dyadic relationships, connected by the "interpersonal relationship" and strengthened by the "logic of frequent contact", becomes aware of a common "place", and through this, the social sphere of the "village" is recognised.

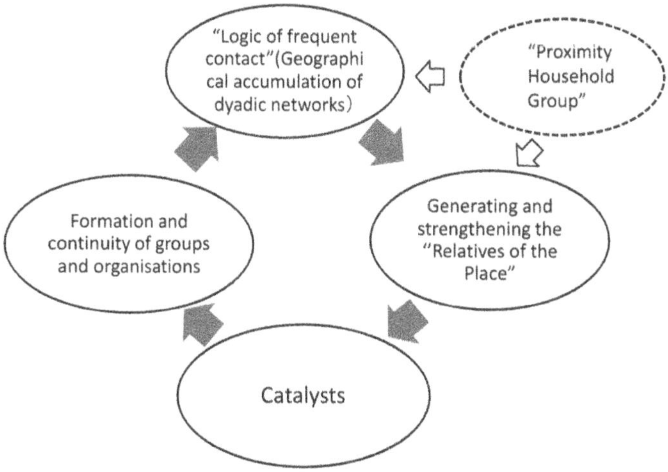

Fig. 7.3 Cycle of recognition and group-making in Myanmar villages. *Source* Takahashi, 2015, p. 20

7.3.3 The Cyclical Structure of Forming Groups and Recognising in Myanmar Villages

Finally, let me try to articulate the "genealogy of group theory" and the "genealogy of cognitive theory" in the context of Myanmar village society. Figure 7.3 is the conceptual diagram for my articulation.

"Multi-household compounds" are repeatedly formed and divided at various moments—such as at marriage, division of households or death of parents—thus creating "proximity household groups" (top right-hand corner of Fig. 7.3) in various parts of the village. However, the relationship between households in these "proximity household groups" is not inherited from generation to generation, unlike in the Japanese "*kumi*" (small village quarter). Moreover, the boundaries of these groups are unclear, and there is no collective or organisational activity based on household groups. It is nothing more than an accumulation of dyadic relationship backed by the "logic of interpersonal relationship" that can be simulated by kinship names seen from the perspective of the *ego*. These dyadic networks are further widened and complicated by intra-village marriages and household movements, as well as by various gatherings and by frequent visits by household members to each other, as mentioned above. These "frequent contacts" strengthen the sense of intimacy and trust among the members. Since the amount of "frequent contacts" is a dependent variable of physical distance, the village—which is an agglomeration of the "proximity household groups"—is conceived of as the "place" of frequent contacts. Thus, the village is recognised as the sphere of the "relatives of the place", as an extension of the "logic of interpersonal relationship".

Village groups and organisations are formed through the action of various "catalysts" on these cumulative dyadic relationships. For example, funerals and marriages act as a catalyst to form a Congratulation and Condolence Association; paya functions act as a catalyst to found a Board of Trustees; monasteries act as a catalyst to set up a group to offer meals for monks; frequent fires and cattle rustling act as a catalyst to organise a Security Committee; the donation of fire engines act as a catalyst to form a Fire Fighting Committee; and the donation of water lifting pumps from international organisations act as a catalyst to establish a Drinking Water Use Committee. If life comes to a standstill, this could be the catalyst for a collective rebellion or a social movement to reclaim the right to cultivate farmland. After 2012, such movements became prominent with the promulgation of the new Farmland Law. The discourse or thought whereby there was a tight structured community in the past can also be a catalyst. Attractive leadership and abundant funds can be catalysts. In recent years, small-scale financial organisations and community forestry groups have emerged, catalysed by government and NGO initiatives (Takahashi, 2012: 174–175).

Through the activities within these groups and organisations, the "logic of frequent contact" is activated, and a new cycle begins again, as shown in Fig. 7.3. So, groups and organisations are positioned as part of this cycle, in which dyadic relations based on the "logic of interpersonal relationship" are accumulated through frequent contacts within a village. Catalysts from inside and outside of the village act to create groups with specific objectives, which in turn strengthen dyadic relations. In Myanmar, the village society does not have to be "tight" like in Thailand, but people can form as many groups and organisations as they want, while remaining "loose". It is a characteristic of Myanmar villages that groups are formed through substantial relationships between individuals in this way. However, since these groups, which are made through the "logic of interpersonal relationship", are based on dyadic bonds between individuals, the outer shell of the group is fragile and not as strong as that of Japanese village groups, which are regulated by the ethic of the *buraku* (old village) (Takahashi, 2012: 175). If dyadic relationships, particularly with superiors or leaders, become uncomfortable or the "catalyst" becomes unattractive, individuals easily leave the group. As the number of departures increases, the group or organisation itself becomes merely titular and follows the path to extinction. Cooperative societies set up under the Ministry, as well as the state-led Women's Associations and Child and Mother Associations, are good examples of this.

In Myanmar, there is a high degree of independence of individuals from groups and organisations, and a high degree of freedom to leave. The multiple layers of dyadic networks make it easy to create as many groups as there are attractive catalysts, but if you do not like a group, you can easily leave, switch to another network and belong to another group or create a new one. However, this does not mean that the activity and emergence of groups and organisations in Myanmar would be low. The activity level is high because the group is made up of like-minded people, while the emergence level is high because the members are autonomous. The performance of groups and organisations is not related to whether the structures of village society are "tight" or "loose".

In this chapter, I examined the cohesion or communality in Myanmar village society, and the mechanisms of its creation and reproduction through the "objective group theory" and the "subjective cognition theory". The character and formation process of groups in Myanmar, as well as the mechanism by which villagers perceive what a village is, are very different from the Japanese "common village". In Myanmar, a social sphere of cognition, which I call the "relatives of the place", arises from groups such as "multi-household compounds" and "proximity household groups". This sphere defines the ambiguous unity of the village. Within this sphere, various groups come about from the accumulation of dyadic relations and the input of catalysts. This is quite different from the Japanese village, which has a solid cohesion to begin with and where groups and organisations can be formed within this unity. The nature of Myanmar village groups led me to the conclusion that the Myanmar village is a community for life, not for production. We should not deny the possibility that a community of production may be formed, depending on the type of the catalyst, but as long as that community is based on the principles of group formation described in this chapter, it is likely to be fragile.

Chapter 8
A Myanmar Village is a Community of Life

Souvenir shops along the gateway to Shwetheindaw Paya. The "*gandakudi*" of the Paya can be seen in the background. The day was a weekday, so there were few worshippers, but on Sundays and on Sabbath Days, the area is crowded with many visitors. Only the owners of stores and restaurants that receive daily income are eligible to participate in the village's Mutual Financing Association. There have been no cases of farmers or agricultural labourers becoming members of the Association. (Thindaunggyi Village, January 2016)

A. Takahashi, *Regime Changes and Socio-economic History of Rural Myanmar, 1986–2019*, Studies in Economic History,
https://doi.org/10.1007/978-981-99-3272-6_8

Introduction

For a thousand years, or even longer, the people living in a Japanese village[1] have maintained and worshipped the *ujigami* (guardian god), and maintained and used the forests (Suzuki, 1968: 103). Since the *Edo* period, they have managed farmland and water on a village basis; since the *Meiji* period, they have formed cooperatives, youth groups, and fire brigades. These groups and organisations have survived through the Meiji Restoration, the First and Second World Wars, post-war democracy, and other major regime changes in the country. Whether they are good or bad, Japanese village groups and organisations are enduring, and once established, they are difficult to dismantle. In contrast, Myanmar village groups and organisations are like bubbles, easily formed but quickly disappearing (Takahashi, 2018: 186–188). In Myanmar villages, there are many groups such as the Congratulation and Condolence Association, Board of Trustees of the Paya, Meal Offering Group, and Rice Transplanting Group, but all of them take the stance that only those who want to join will do so. Unlike in Japan, there is no compulsion for all villagers to join. Once people join, they can easily quit if they do not like the way of management or if their personal relations deteriorate. In extreme cases, a new organisation of the same type may be formed, and it is not uncommon for it to disappear again in a short time. In the case of governmental organisations such as school boards, youth groups, fire brigades, women's associations and cooperatives, villagers are only involved while the "catalyst" that benefits them as "consumers" is functioning, rather than due to any motivation to contribute to these organisations. Therefore, as soon as the budgets and instructions are lost, the organisations become merely nominal, so that it is difficult to know who the members are. The reason for this contrast between Japan and Myanmar is that the Japanese village is not just a "community" but a "collective (*kyōdōtai*)", while the Myanmar village is not a "collective" but just a "community". In the previous chapter, I have lumped both Japanese and Myanmar villages together as "communities". However, in this chapter, I strictly divide "collective" and "community". To elaborate on Embree's argument, a "collective" is like a tightly structured society, while a "community" is like a loosely structured society, but this is not all. Using this framework, this chapter explores the social characteristics of Myanmar villages, while contrasting Myanmar villages with Japanese villages.

[1] In this chapter, as in the previous chapter, when I use the term "village" or "hamlet", I do not mean an administrative village in Japan, but a *kyūson* (old village), *ōaza*, or *buraku* from before the merger of towns and villages in 1889. In Myanmar, "village" means not a village tract (*cêiywa ou'sù*), which is the country's smallest administrative unit, but a village (*cêiywa*) which is a component of a tract (see Chap. 2). In practice, however, there are many exceptions. In many cases, the Japanese *ōaza* is directly called a *buraku* and becomes a "common village"; in other cases, there are several *buraku*s within the *ōaza* and each of them forms a "common village", or several *buraku*s unite to make up a "common village". What is important is that there is a (*sonraku*) *kyōdōtai* or "(village) collective" somewhere in these villages. In contrast, in Myanmar, a single village may be geographically divided into three districts, as in the case of Zeepinwea Village, and there may be villages with different religions and ethnic groups, as in the case of Paukkoung Hamlet, or several small villages may come together to form a single residential area. What is important here is that there is no such thing as a *kyōdōtai* or "collective" in any of these groups or clusters of settlements in Myanmar.

The fundamental importance in the life (and production) of a Japanese *buraku*[2] is that the village should be united in everything, and for this purpose, voluntary obedience or self-restriction is inevitable (Kida, 1967: 8). In contrast, Myanmar villagers do not willingly obey or restrict themselves for such unity. If they do, it is to maintain good dyadic relationships, and if they exceed the limit of their endurance, they simply break the relations and switch to other dyadic relationships. To move into a village in Japan, a person must be accompanied by the village head or a mentor, bring souvenir gifts for key persons, and go around the village while being instructed on whom to socialise with and how to deal with them (Kida, 1967: 39–40). To marry, a bride must go door to door in bridal costume to each household belonging to the *kumi* (village quarter) (Takahashi, 2012: 99). In Myanmar, however, people can live anywhere in the village with the permission of the village mayor, and they do not need to bring any souvenirs or go around to greet villagers. Even if both spouses have no connection to the village, they can marry and immediately take up residence in the village (Takahashi, 2012: 101–102). The creation of a network of dyadic relationships comes later. Japan's Agricultural Fundamentalism (*Nōhonshugi*) Movement, which was radicalised during the Showa Depression of 1929–1931, was supported by "fascism from below" (Teruoka, 1981: 170)—using the traditional *ōaza* (*buraku* or *kyūson*) unit and exploiting the Five-person Association (*gonin-gumi*) system[3] (Watanabe, 1985: 2). In Myanmar, too, during the Burmese socialist period and the following military regime, a system of surveillance by villages and neighbourhood associations was established. However, it did not function, and movements to support socialism and military rule from below did not arise. This is because the Myanmar village is a "community" composed of independent and free villagers, while the Japanese village is a village "collective" that forces people to limit themselves for the sake of harmony and cohesion.

The discussion in this chapter will proceed towards the thesis that a village in Myanmar is a "community of life", while a village in Japan is a "collective of production".[4] The contrast between these two can be divided into two parts: first, "collective" *versus* "community", and second, "production" *versus* "life". I begin with a general discussion of the collective and the community in the first part, and then move on to specific examples of various groups and organisations in villages in Japan and

[2] Kida says that a "village" is a demarcation for control by the state, while a *buraku*, unlike a village, is a natural group (Kida, 1967: 9–10). In that case, a "village" would mean an administrative village. In this book, *buraku* as the common village is the "village".

[3] The terminal and minimal administrative structure in villages and towns in the Edo period. The five peasants also provided mutual assistance in daily life as fellow peasants, but it was more of an organisation for controlling and monitoring the peasants by mutual surveillance. In 1940, the *gonin-gumi* reappeared as the *tonari-gumi* (Neighbourhood Association) system, which was abolished in 1947.

[4] The definition of "production" and "life" is the same as in the previous chapter. I have already argued in the previous chapter that the Japanese village is a community of both "production" and "life", while the Myanmar village is a community of "life" without commodity "production". In this chapter, I will simplify it and say that a "community of production" naturally includes life, while a "community of life" simply includes daily livelihood, without commodity production and related activities.

Myanmar, to examine the nature of their "communality" and to distinguish whether they are related to "production" or to "life". I will then move on to discussing "production" *versus* "life". Finally, using "collective failure" or "failure of the collective" as a framing concept, I will try to find answers to questions such as the following: Why could Myanmar villages not sustain groups and organisations for a long period of time, despite often creating them so easily? Why did the repressive regimes of Burmese socialism and military dictatorship fail to truly infiltrate the rural areas, despite their long-lasting rule?

8.1 Defining "Collective" and "Community"

In comparing the collective and the community, I first define their spatial domains. In Japanese language, the word for "collective"—*kyōdōtai*—sometimes implies "local society", while international solidarity and internet gatherings are also referred to as *kyōdōtai*. In this chapter, I will refer to the Japanese village local community, that is, a "common village", as a "village collective (*sonraku kyōdōtai*)" or simply a "collective (*kyōdōtai*)". Regarding the concept of "community", the sociologist Robert M. MacIver, who has been a major authority on community studies, and Charles H. Page said: "The bases of community are locality and community sentiment" (MacIver & Page, 1950: 9). In line with this, this chapter defines the "community" as a social space that corresponds to a village collective.

The Japanese word "*kyōdōtai*", which is translated into English as "collective" in this book, consists of two words: "*kyōdō*" and "*tai*". According to Moto Miho (1994), *kyōdō* is defined in the *Nihon Daijiten* (Dictionary of Japan) of 1892 as "a Chinese word, coming together to do things", and in the *Genkai* (A Sea of Languages) of 1904 as "doing things jointly". Derivatively, it means to "cooperate" (Miho, 1994: 50–51). According to the Seventh Edition of the *Kojien* dictionary, the word "*tai*" means "a thing with a form," so the word "*kyōdōtai*" means "a group of people who do things together". However, the socioeconomic meaning of this word is more complicated. According to Hisao Otsuka, the material basis of the *kyōdōtai* (in German language, *Gemeinde*) is the land. The collective is the entity that occupies this land. Its social basis is an organisation (in German, *Gemeinwesen*). As long as the basis of social relations is in the form of a collective, the "collective mode" (*Gemeinschaft*), which is the ancient prototype of kinship organisations, survives in some form of "collective organisation" and forms the basic external frame of collectivity (Otsuka, 1955: 25–28). In other words, the "collective mode" is the principle of collectivity—which does not encompass territorial limitation—but if it reaches the stage of occupying land, it becomes a "collective" (Nagashima, 1997: 64). If the subject of the occupation is a village, the territory is limited and becomes a "village collective". However, according to Otsuka, the collective disappeared with the advent of industrial capitalism, and what remains is only a "remnant".

In the same way as Otsuka, based on a Marxian view of history, Ferdinand Tönnies called a group formed by people's mutually positive relations "*eine Verbindung*"—an "association" or a "union"—and divided it into *Gemeinschaft* and *Gesellschaft* (Tönnies, 1957, Book 1: 34–35).[5] Whereas the *Gemeinschaft*'s union of members is based on an existential and natural "intrinsic will", the *Gesellschaft*'s union is, by contrast, based on an ideational and artificial "selective will" (Maniwa, 1978: 23). In *Gemeinschaft*, people stay together in spite of everything that separates them; in *Gesellschaft* they remain separate in spite of everything that unites them (Tönnies, 2001: 52). The binding principle of *Gemeinschaft* is "mutual understanding" or "consensus", derived from an *a priori* and pre-determined unity. This is a special social force that unites "people as parts of one whole" (Tönnies, 1957, Book 1: 59; Tönnies, 2001: 32–33). This is exactly the characteristic not found in community, but found in collective. In contrast, the simple expression of the general will of *Gesellschaft* is a "convention" or "agreement" made on the basis of a new conception of freedom, which must be artificially imagined and invented (Tönnies, 1957, Book 1: 111; Tönnies, 2001: 63). This argument by Tönnies shows that the collective belongs among *Gemeinschaft*s. Tönnies also suggested that the age of the *Gemeinschaft* was followed by the age of the *Gesellschaft*, and that the former is disappearing but still forms the substance of social life (Tönnies, 1957, Book 2: 207–210). Both Otsuka and Tönnies share the view on history whereby the collective or the *Gemeinschaft* is pre-modern or early social relations. After the modern era, only their relics remain.[6]

In his early research, MacIver, who explored the concept of "community," defined community as "any area of common life", including "village, or town, or district, or country, or even wider area" (MacIver, 1920: 21). For him, the word "community" had two senses: "local society", meaning villages and towns, and "the whole world", signifying national society and the world of humanity. The latter meaning—of the whole world—was dominant in MacIver's early papers (Ogasawara, 1976: 109). In MacIver's later writings, the bases of community are "locality" and "community sentiment" (MacIver & Page, 1950: 9–10), thus adding a subjective basis to the community and limiting its objective basis to the locale (Ogasawara, 1976:109).

According to George A. Hillery, 69 out of 94 different definitions of community include three points that are commonly found in community life: social interaction, area, and common ties (Hillery, 1955: 118). In other words, if we read Hillery's social interaction and common ties as communality, we can find that the minimum common denominator in the various definitions of community is "locality" and "communality". In the case of "locality," if we limit the community to the village, we can say that the collective also has this feature. The specific content of "communality" is "community sentiment" such as common values, sense of belonging, and obligations and responsibilities (MacIver & Page, 1950: 291–294), which is also applicable

[5] The original is in German; English translations are also available such as Tönnies, 2001. However, this chapter refers mainly to the Japanese translation (Tönnies, 1957).

[6] Both Otsuka's theory of collective and Tönnies' theory of *Gemeinschaft* are viewpoints on history, rather than proven "historical facts" (Takahashi, 2012: 132–133).

Table 8.1 Collective and community

	(Village) Collective	Community
Communality	(Locality and communal feelings) (Shared value, Sense of belonging, Duty)	
Historicity	Pre-modern, "relic"	Ahistorical
Totality	Something more than the sum total	Individual synthesis only
Individuality	Oppressive to individuality	Respect and development of individuality
Spontaneity	Automatic compulsory joining	Formed by individual will
Relationships	Individual *versus* group; Affiliation	Dyadic relationships; network
Assistance	Collective responsibility	Individual's will; Reciprocal
Openness	Closed	Open

to collective. The minimum common denominator of a community—"locality" and "communality"—exists in a collective as well (Table 8.1: Communality).

However, in a context where "collective" and "community" are used distinctly, they still carry a special intention. The differences between the two are summarised in Table 8.1.

As mentioned above, MacIver and Otsuka consider community to be transhistorical (MacIver, 1920: 169–170) and collective to be pre-modern. Tadashi Fukutake stated that a community is never a historical concept, but a local society characterised by area characteristics and local social sentiment (Fukutake, 1956: 5). Hitoshi Saito argued that the Japanese village collective, which is an autonomous village, is not a supra-historical communal relationship, but a social relationship with a certain historical definiteness (Saito, 1989: v). That is, "community" is a supra-historical concept, while "collective" is a notion with historical definiteness (Table 8.1: Historicity). From the discussion so far, we can say that historically and locally, a collective is a proper subset of a community. This chapter therefore redefines the complementary set of collective as community, and contrasts the "collective" with the redefined "community".

A community is not more than the mere sum of its members (MacIver, 1920: 90–91). In contrast, a collective is neither the sum of individuals nor reducible to individual relations, but more than that (Iwatani, 2004: 68) (Table 8.1: Totality). Socially, a collective is a single, supra-individual social consciousness that defines the behaviour of individuals (Suzuki, 1968: 97–107). Economically, because the subject of land occupation is the village collective, the whole of it (beyond the individual) is defined by material conditions and does not allow internal members to act freely and individually (Furushima, 1963: vii-viii). In this way, the collective works against individuality in a repressive way, whereas community is nothing more than a mere association of similar individuals and in this sociality the individuality of its members can be demonstrated and developed (Maniwa, 1978: 25) (Table 8.1: Individuality). When the Japanese word "*komyuniti*" is used as a translation of "community" instead of "*kyōdōtai* (collective)", it carries with it the desire to create independent, proactive, democratic social solidarity (Fukutake, 1978: 187). In other words, a community is something that is actively formed by the intention of each individual, while a collective is something where one belongs passively regardless of the will of each individual (Table 8.1: Spontaneity). Therefore, as shown in Chap. 7 in the example of how one calls other household members, *ego* in the collective is positioned in the group or organisation and is forced to identify with the rules and norms of the collective. In contrast, the *ego* in a community can autonomously form a network of bilateral relationships with the self as the centre (Table 8.1: Relationships). The gratuitous collaboration that arises from this is collective and semi-obligatory assistance in the case of a collective, and reciprocal and voluntary assistance through dyadic relationships in the case of a community (Table 8.1: Assistance).

There is a difference in the degree of openness between a collective and a community. A collective is estranged from the outside world and is dominated by a kind of blockade. However, a community is inherently open to the outside world (Table 8.1: Openness). This is because community is an intermediate group that exists in a multi-layered manner between individuals and society, and has not only internal but also external relations from the outset (Hiroi, 2009: 24–25).

As summarised in Table 8.1, I have discussed the contrasts between collectives and communities in terms of their historicity, totality, individuality, spontaneity, relationships, assistance, and openness. However, actual local village societies cannot be classified according to such an extreme dichotomy. In the next and subsequent sections, I will compare the compositional principles of groups and organisations in villages in Japan and in Myanmar from the above perspectives. For example, I will explore the historicity and spontaneity of the groups and organisations, examine the relationships of these groups and organisations to the villages, and investigate differences in the social structure of Myanmar and Japanese villages.

8.2 Political Power, the Village, and Groups and Organisations for Production

A collective is a social relation with historical definiteness; if we add territorial limitation, it is also a local social group. Then, what is historical definiteness? In this chapter, I define it as the history of the relationship between the superstructure—such as political regime, administrative institutions, and economic system—and the villages and villagers. Most of the social groups and organisations in the village have been historically formed in relation to these superstructures. Based on this, I discuss how the differences in the interrelationships between political power and villages have brought about similarities and differences in the histories of Japan and Myanmar.

8.2.1 Farmland Management and the Villages

As mentioned in the previous chapter, in early-modern Japanese villages, the "*muragiri* (village demarcation)" by "*kenchi* (feudal land cadastral survey)" established the village territory, where villagers, their residential areas and arable land were combined. Thus, the village became the "subject of land occupation", laying the foundations for the village collectives that have continued to the present day. In contrast, in Myanmar, such integration of village residence and cultivated land never happened. In the Settlement Operation of the colonial period under the British Empire, which is similar to the cadastral survey in Japan, an appropriate area of *kwin* (*kwîn*)—cultivated area of a certain size—was determined by the settlement authority based on the geographical conditions, regardless of the residence of the farmland's holder. Moreover, the cultivator's farmland was assessed on a holding (*ûpain*) basis. Thus, in contrast to Japan, a village territory that would include farmland as a means of production, was never determined in Myanmar. The concept of "village farmland", as in Japan, has not been established until now (Table 8.2: Land Management).

Thus, Myanmar villages have never been "the subject of land occupation", which is a necessary condition of a collective, and this has an influence on modern agricultural land management. In Japanese villages, it is natural to give priority to transactions between co-villagers when borrowing and selling farmland (Takahashi, 2012: 138–139). And in Japan's current policy of farmland liquidation, *buraku* (= village) is fully involved. In contrast, around Zeepinwea Village there are five *kwins*, which are cultivated by farmers from 15 different villages, while in Thindaunggyi Village, farmland is held by farmers from 10 different villages in three *kwins*. Unlike in Japan, the residents of the village and the agricultural land holdings around the village do not coincide at all. The village mayor has to collect land tax from the scattered farmers, but the transaction cost of collecting the tax is higher than the small amount of tax collection, which is ridiculously lower than the cost of paper for receipts (Takahashi, 2012: 143). So, in both Zeepinwea and Thindaunggyi villages, the mayors paid the land tax in one lump sum with their own pocket money. Since the village is not involved in any sale, purchase, or lease of farmland, farmland has been liquidated across villages, as described in Chap. 4, resulting in phenomena such as land speculation by ethnic Chinese businesspeople and mixed multi-ethnic settlement in a village.

8.2.2 Taxation in Kind and the Villages

In both Japan and Myanmar, the purpose of cadastral surveys is to levy and collect land tax. In early modern Japan, land tax in kind, that is, annual tribute (*nengu*) paid in brown rice, was levied at the village level. Thus, a village responsibility system (*murauke*) was established in which the village as a whole was jointly responsible

Table 8.2 Comparing village groups for production, life, and religion in Japan and in Myanmar

	Japan	Myanmar
1. *Political power, the village, and groups and organisations for production*		
Land management	*Kenchi* → *Muragiri*	Settlement → *Kwin*
Taxation in kind	Village-based contract	Direct contract between farmers and the state
Maintenance of irrigation and drainage	The village as a unit	By each canal
Cooperatives	In every village (production)	In administrative village (production → consumption → extinction)
Common land	Indivisible collective ownership and management	Ownership unclear, management by individuals
Agricultural production	No agriculture without village	Agriculture and villages are unrelated
Labour exchange/collaboration	*Yui* (labour contributions to the group)	Personal and dyadic relations
2. *Groups and organisations for life*		
Village common fund	Spontaneous. Collected from all households. Multi-purpose. Continual	Enacted by law. With unpaid households. By purpose. Temporary
Mutual financing association	Territorially related. Poor relief. Long term	Dyadic and non-territorial relationships. Financing for moneylenders. Short term
Congratulation and condolence association	*Kumi* or *Dōzoku*	Intra-village, but there may be more than one
3. *Religion and the village*		
Buddhist temples/monasteries	No domain. Personal faith	No domain. Personal faith
Ujigami versus *Nat*	Believers are all villagers. Spirit of the whole village	Spirit with domain, but not the whole village

for paying the tax in kind. This system was made possible by the broader system whereby villages and farmland were integrated (*muragiri*). This system ended in the Edo period (1603–1868), but its legacy has continued to the present day, as evidenced by the fact that the brown rice procurement system that began during World War II and the production adjustment policies that followed were implemented on a *buraku* (that is, village) basis. Although it was much later than the Edo period in Japan, in Myanmar, too, a system similar to the tribute system of offering paddy in kind, which is called the paddy procurement system, was enforced during the period of Burmese socialism and the military regime that followed. However, because the integrity of the farmland and the village was not as strong as in Japan, the village contract system was tried without success in Myanmar. As a result, individual farmers were forced to make deliveries directly to government agencies (Table 8.2: Taxation in Kind). In the case of Japan, the mutual monitoring of farmers arising from the system of collective responsibility allowed the tribute receivers to keep transaction costs down. In Myanmar, in contrast, since the monitoring function among farmers did not work, it was difficult for the state to secure the amount of tribute as planned because of the rampant cheating around measurement and quality and the bribery of officials by cleverly using *nalehmu* (Takahashi, 2012: 78–79).

8.2.3 Irrigation and Drainage Management and the Villages

In Japan, because of the *muragiri* and *murauke* systems, each village, as a unit, has been responsible for acquiring and managing the water needed for rice cultivation. Since the village and the farmland were inseparable, and the entire village had to take responsibility for any drought damage suffered by an individual, it was natural for the village to take the lead in water management. Moreover, if one farmer neglected to manage waterways or wasted water, it could reduce the production of the entire arable land in the village, so the village monitored and enforced the work of individuals. Villages were not mere "settlements," but had the character of basic unit organisations that jointly acquired, allocated, and managed water, a scarce resource essential for production and livelihood (Tamaki, 1983: 12–13). This is basically unchanged to this day.

In contrast, a village in Myanmar is not involved in water management. The small irrigation canals, watercourses and field channels, which are stretched like sewing through the paddy fields around the village, have been managed by groups of farmers who use them. Since there are a number of canals in the paddy fields, even farmers living in the same village will be involved in managing different canals. In addition, as mentioned earlier, farmers from multiple villages cultivate their land in a single *kwin*, so farmers from different villages are often involved with one canal. The management of the canal is not a joint responsibility of the village as one, but a canal head (*myâun gâun*) is appointed by the Irrigation Department, which is a government agency, and that person is fully responsible for the management (Table 8.2: Maintenance of Irrigation and Drainage). The canal head has the right to call the beneficiary farmers for canal maintenance, but he often instead collects money from the farmers in order to hire labourers. Some farmers do not even weed or dredge the canals as a form of labour service but send agricultural labourers to those tasks (Takahashi, 1993: 52–56). No matter how one looks at it, it is clear that the village does not take the lead in managing irrigation and drainage in Myanmar.

In Japan, the village became the unit of production and related systems, such as land management, tax collection, and irrigation and drainage conservation, as a result of political power forcing it and each village's response to it. In contrast, in Myanmar, where political power did not create institutional frameworks such as *muragiri*, *murauke*, or village-based watercourse management, there was no external push for forming a collective of production.

8.2.4 Cooperatives and the Villages

In Japan, various small cooperatives such as farm household cooperatives, agricultural cooperatives, agricultural improvement cooperatives, and so on, were established on the basis of *oaza* or *buraku* (village) in the latter half of the Meiji period. The functions of these cooperatives were mainly to improve agricultural production technology. Some of them also engaged in joint work, joint purchasing, joint sales, and savings. With the enactment of the Agricultural Association Law in 1899 and the Industrial Association Act in 1900, these spontaneous small cooperatives were organised as the end-units of the government, agricultural associations, and industry associations (Tanahashi, 1955: 1, 4, 12, 23–24). The *buraku* (village) created such agricultural cooperatives as a natural response to the commercial economy. Indeed, agricultural cooperatives could not have been established without the *buraku* in the first place (Saito, 1989: 35). During the Showa Depression (1929–1933), village-based small cooperatives were incorporated as agricultural execution cooperatives under the Five-Year Plan for the Expansion of Industry Associations in 1933, and all farmers were consolidated at the village level into nationwide organisations called Industry Associations. The village level also became the unit of supply, rationing and policy coordination in the controlled economy of the wartime regime (Noda, 1998: 4). As a part of the post-war democratisation, agricultural associations and industry associations were dismantled, and agricultural cooperatives were born, but these were also based on village organisations such as the agricultural execution cooperatives (Hokkaido Central Association of Agricultural Cooperatives, 2016: 21). Later, various village-based organisations such as agricultural machinery use cooperatives, agricultural product marketing cooperatives, farming cooperatives, and land use adjustment cooperatives, and so on, emerged and have continued to the present. In this way, village-based production organisations are ubiquitous in Japan and have been active for a long time.

The first cooperative society in Myanmar was organised in 1904 during the British colonial period, the same year that the Department of Cooperatives was also established. In 1924–1925, among 5563 cooperatives, 5349 worked as agricultural cooperatives and 4211 worked as credit cooperatives (MaSaLa, 1974, (I): 241). However, when the central organisation was dissolved in 1932, only 152 credit cooperatives remained in 1936 (MaSaLa, 1974, (I): 285). Like this, the cooperatives in the colonial period were basically Raiffeisen-type credit unions. The 1947 Constitution included a provision that the state would give priority to cooperatives when distributing agricultural land and other goods (Articles 30 and 42), which promoted the cooperative movement, but as in the colonial period, this was organised from above. The 1956 Cooperative Societies Act, which is based on the 1947 Constitution, did not contain the word "village (*ywa*)" and the relationship between villages and cooperatives is unclear. In 1957, out of 14,183 cooperatives, 6966 were agricultural cooperatives (including credit business) and 5129 were consumer cooperatives (MaSaLa, 1974, (I): 421). However, the establishment of village-level cooperatives did not progress during this period due to the civil war. When security stabilised during the Burmese socialist period, the Village Cooperative Societies Rule of 1971, which was one of the rules of the Cooperative Societies Act of 1970, was enacted. As expected of a socialist organisation, Article 4 of the Rule stipulated that cooperatives shall be formed in each village tract, not each village, to jointly manage and cultivate agricultural land, jointly purchase and use agricultural machinery, jointly store and sell agricultural products, jointly raise and repay agricultural funds and jointly purchase consumer goods. In 1972, 14,589 cooperatives were organised, of which 10,750 were village tract cooperatives (MaSaLa, 1974, (II): 429). By the end of socialism, however, only the name of "cooperatives" remained. As mentioned earlier, irrigation and drainage management, an important part of farmland management, was consistently under the control of the Irrigation Department. As for communal cultivation, cultivation rights were held by individual farmers and all management and cultivation of farmland was done by them, without any collaboration of any kind. While unowned land and wasteland were regarded as common land, villagers usually used them individually (Takahashi, 2012: 152–154). Although there may have been some joint use of agricultural machinery, the system was replaced by a rental service provided by the Department of Agricultural Mechanisation. The Ministry of Cooperatives also provided agricultural funds, but loans from the Ministry of Agriculture were more common. Storage and sale of agricultural products were mainly carried out by the state agricultural marketing agencies. There was a time when the village tract cooperatives acted as subordinate agencies to collect the procured paddy and distribute it to non-farmers in the village, but this did not last long. In some cases, rice, salt, oil, and soap were distributed at low prices through cooperatives, but the distribution did not reach the end villages (Table 8.2: Cooperatives). The villagers thought that the cooperatives were governmental institutions headed by the Minister of Cooperatives, and that they were no different from the Burma Socialist Programme Party and the police. The Burmese word for a cooperative is "*thàmàwàyàmà*", a word derived from the Pali language, which means to get together and make efforts. However, the cooperatives were distrusted to the extent that they were ironically referred to as "*thâwà mayâwà*", that is, "the sons and wives [of cooperative officials] get fat" (Takahashi, 2012: 151). Thus, the history of Myanmar's cooperatives, which began in 1904, is one of organising from the top down. The reason for the failure of the cooperatives is not only the corruption of the management, but also the lack of collective and communal relations, which are the foundation of cooperatives, in the villages themselves. The Ministry of Cooperatives, with its long history, was downgraded to a department within the Ministry of Agriculture, Livestock and Irrigation in 2016. Since then, villagers have joined cooperatives if they can get low-interest loans, otherwise they do not.

8.2.5 Common Land and the Villages

Japanese villages have property rights, which cannot be given to individuals. A typical example is the land owned by the *buraku* (village) as a whole, such as the common forest and grass land. This land has been used not only for the villagers' daily life, such as logging for building materials and firewood, but also for production, such as collecting fertiliser for arable land (green manure, compost) and fodder for livestock. Even today, when the common land is leased, or partially disposed of, and when the products of the land, such as mushrooms and timber, are sold, the profits are used to pay for various village-related expenses and for village savings. The right to manage and dispose of the village land belongs to the *buraku* (village), which is a collective body. The villagers, who are the individual members of the village, are given only the exclusive right to use and profit from this land. Village members do not have equity ownership of this land, nor can they demand its division. The village as a collective is the owner of the land, and any individual can exercise the right to use and profit from the land as long as they are a co-villager, but they lose all rights when they cease to be a co-villager.

There are some lands in Myanmar that may be equivalent to the common forest and grass lands of Japan. One of them is the forest and swampy land called *amyâbain myei*, or "the land owned by everyone". However, since "everyone" refers to an unspecified large number of people, if everyone enters this land and takes trees and fish, eventually the resources will be depleted, which may cause a so-called "tragedy of the commons (open access)". In such a case, instead of leaving the management of the land to village tracts or villages, the state tries to prevent the use of the land by introducing a system of protected forests and/or state land, and some of the land is sold by the state to individuals as logging and/or fishing rights (Takahashi, 2012: 152). The other is *ywa myei*, that is, village land, or *boun myei*, that is, common land. The Oxbow Lake in Zeepinwea Village, mentioned in Chap. 4, is also called *ywa myei*. However, only the owners of land that faces the lake can cultivate water spinach (*gazunywe'*) here. In addition, fish are also caught here, but villagers do not fish communally; instead, individuals who bid for fishing rights uproot the fish, and the tender is open to people from outside the village (Takahashi, 2012: 154). In some villages of Okpho Township in Central Myanmar, I saw grazing areas called *zaje'*, also called *ywa myei* or *boun myei*. However, this land was advantageous to wealthy farmers with many cattle, because there was no restriction on the number of cattle grazing. It was useless to households that did not own cattle, which accounted for more than half of the households in the village. In Hnyalone Village, Hakha Township, Chin State, there was a village forest where villagers collected firewood and charcoal. But wealthy people who owned horses and cattle grazed their livestock there. The animals ate the tree buds and young grasses, thus decreasing the productivity of firewood and charcoal significantly (Takahashi, 2012: 153). In this way, only a few wealthy people (generally influential people in the village) tend to benefit from the village land and common land in Myanmar villages, and their resource management is sloppy. Many villagers are alienated from these lands (Table 8.2: Common Land).

Japanese villages have some collective landholding, which the village as a whole has a legal right to in the form of property rights and which relates to production as well as life. In contrast, in Myanmar, there is no concept or substance of collective landholding as a property right. In Japanese villages, participation in the management activities of the common land, such as clearing undergrowth of forests, planting trees, repairing landslides and roads, is obligatory and compulsory, but there is no such obligation or compulsion in Myanmar villages. In this sense, too, the Japanese village as a collective is a subject of land occupation, while the Myanmar village is not.

8.2.6 Agricultural Production and the Villages

As mentioned earlier, the Japanese village is a collective in which farmland occupation, taxation, and irrigation management are integrated into the "production" of rice and other agricultural products. As long as the farmers are in the village, they are automatically incorporated into these production-related organisations and are under the supervision of other members, making it impossible for them to fully demonstrate their individuality. In feudal times, in order to supply sufficient irrigation water and complete the payment of tribute to the feudal lord under the village responsibility system (*murauke*), not only did the villagers have to monitor each other, but they also had to work together. Such collective assistance was self-generated in the village as a unit and was eventually utilised in cooperatives that spread across the country as a matter of policy, enabling villages to be more productive than the sum of their individual members.

In contrast, Myanmar villages have historically never formed such village-based organisations or groups that would be involved in production and to which all farmers would be forced to join. Agricultural land is controlled by the state agricultural land management authorities, which has nothing to do with the residential areas of the villages, and irrigation and drainage are under the control of the Irrigation Department, which is not involved in any way with the village. Villages are not jointly or severally responsible for the provision of agricultural products. Instead, individual farmers directly face the state's agricultural product collection agencies. Cooperatives are also state institutions, with very few horizontal links among members. Without orders or guidance from officials, villagers are not even aware of their membership in these cooperatives. There are no groups or organisations based on the village as a unit that would be involved in production and no communal elements are found. In Japan, individual farmers are dependent on the village to run their farming operations, whereas in Myanmar, the village and the individual farming operations are unrelated (Table 8.2: Agricultural Production).

8.2.7 Labour Exchange and Collaborative Labour in the Villages

Above, I discussed how Japan and Myanmar contrast in terms of where the village is involved as a whole or as a unit in the supply and demand for goods and services that relate to production, or in their management and operation. However, there are also groups and organisations that are involved in production whose members are not necessarily all the villagers or all the households in the village and which are formed independently of political power.

One of these is the custom of labour exchange without money. One Myanmar example is *le'sâ alai'*, mentioned in the previous chapter. It means "to respond when others offer a hand", that is, to return the amount of labour that corresponds to the amount of labour offered to oneself. As I have already mentioned, and as this name implies, any labour exchanges under this manner are one-to-one dyadic relationships. In contrast, in Japanese villages, there was an organisation for non-monetary exchange of labour called *yui*. This system allowed for an equal exchange of labour for a short period of time. Namely, in a *kumi*, (a group of neighbouring households in a village) or in an agricultural association consisting of several *kumi*s, the same number of people provided each other with the same amount of labour for the same number of days to carry out the same tasks, mainly rice planting and harvesting (Takahashi, 2012: 114). This is not an exchange of labour in a one-to-one bilateral relationship between individual farmers, but rather a contribution of labour to a small organisation—the *yui*—which differs in its organisational principle from that of the *le'sâ alai'*.

The other Myanmar example is the *kau'sai'si* (women's rice-transplanting group), which may seem to resemble the *yui*. But *kau'sai'si* is not a non-monetary exchange of labour. It is an organisation that earns money externally and pays wages to its members, while *yui* is an organisation that exchanges labour internally. There are several rice-transplanting groups in a village, and their members come from all over the village or from other villages. Unlike in Japan, the *kau'sai'si* is not based on the premise of neighbourly relations or household-based relations. The rice-transplanting group is an organisation formed by a bilateral wage contract between the *si gâunhsâun* (head of the group), who is the organiser, and each transplanter. There is no solidarity between the member transplanters, and they are free to come and go as they wish, belonging today and leaving tomorrow, which is a completely different constitutive principle from *yui* (Table 8.2: Labour Exchange and Collaboration).

Thus, the kind of collaboration and organisation for productive purposes that has formed in some *parts* of the village is also different in Japan and Myanmar. Japan has collective assistance and Myanmar has reciprocal assistance (Table 8.1: Assistance).

8.3 Groups and Organisations for Life

As I mentioned above, Myanmar villages have no such organisation for production where the whole or the social unity of the village would regulate the individual. However, there are many groups and organisations for *life*, although the principle of organisation is different from that in Japan. In Myanmar, villagers do not necessarily need to cooperate with others in the village in terms of production, but they do need to help each other in terms of life beyond production, in order to live in the village. Thus, villages have various groups and organisations for *life* (Takahashi, 2012: 176–177).

8.3.1 Village Common Funds and Finances

In Japan, each village has its own financial system, which is managed by the village itself. The sources of income are the proceeds from the aforementioned common lands, donations from influential people, subsidies from the government, and levies (*buraku* fees) collected from villagers. The expenditure items range widely: building and maintaining waste collection depots, cleaning gutters, street trees and common facilities, installing and maintaining security lights and signs, purchasing circulars and stationery, subsidising children's associations and neighbourhood associations, and organising shrine rituals, festivals, and other events. Villagers are obligated to pay *buraku* (village) fees, and if they refuse to pay, they may be ostracised. In most cases, the budget is managed by the village head or the treasurer. The head and treasurer are appointed on a rotating basis from among each household respectively, and all households are in charge.

In Myanmar, some villages have a fund called "*cêiywa yanboun ngwei*", or "village common fund". In 2015, in Zeepinwea Village, the mayor received payment from a successful bidder for the fishing rights of Oxbow Lake and turned this into a village fund. He then added his personal wealth to the fund to pay for the paving of the village road. According to the villagers, this is the first time that fishing rights revenue had been used for the benefit of the village since the 1990s, when the village primary school was repaired. Other than these two projects, it is unclear how the fund was spent. This may be an effect of the democratisation of the village where the mayor of the village became an elected position. Thindaunggyi Village and surrounding villages have a "*ywa win je*", or "village entry fee": When a man from another village marries a woman from the village, or when a man from the village marries a woman from another village, the groom pays money to the bride's village. This money is kept by the village chief[7] as a fund and is used mainly for celebrations and sometimes for condolences. In Taunglwe Village near Thindaunggyi, the village chief began to collect an electrification fund of 3 million kyats (about 300,000 yen) per household, which deepened the division among villagers (Takahashi, 2018: 38–39). In Kanthalay Village in central Myanmar, a drinking water utilisation committee was formed to collect 4.6 million kyats from each household to build a water supply system in the village. However, the households that could not pay the water fee were not supplied with water. In addition, the right to collect water fees was based on a bidding system—the successful bidder took over the management of the water supply and the collection of water fees (Takahashi, 2018: 81–82). The above cases have three common features: funds are created for specific purposes, such as celebrations, electricity, and water supply; not all villagers or all households have to pay;

[7] In this case, the village chief is not the mayor of the village tract. Sometimes, the village chief and the village tract mayor are the same person. See Chap. 2.

and the fund is managed by one or two influential people for a long period of time, rather than on a rotating basis like in Japan.[8]

In Zeepinwea and Thindaunggyi villages during the socialist era, all households were required to pay a contribution called *khwêdân*, as villagers told me during my survey in 1987. A farmer's monthly contribution was about one to two days' worth of milled rice equivalent, and a non-farmers' contribution was about half that amount. Even so, about one-third of all households reported that they did not pay the fee due to poverty.

Such a system of a village common fund is not autogenous in Myanmar. It was promoted as a state policy based on the "Law on Common Fund for Village Economic Development (*cêile' sîbwâyêi phùnphyôuhmùyan yanbounngwei e'ùbadei*)", enacted in 1960. After the enactment of this law, some villages called for all households to contribute, some tried to obtain funds from ponds and forests, some set short-term objectives for collecting money and solicited contributions, and some did nothing. In 1974, the Burmese socialist regime issued an "Order on the Establishment of the Village Development Project Monitoring Committee (*cêile' deithà phùnphyôuyêi lou'ngânbâinmyâ cîca' hmù komiti phwèsîjîn amèin*)", and in 1977, "Regulations on the Recording of Activities and Funds Relating to the Common Fund for Rural Development (*cêile' deithà phùnphyôuyêi yanboun ngwei hnìn pa'the'ywèi lou'ngânbâin hnìn ngweisayînbâin hsainya llou'htôunlou'nyî*)", and ordered the executive members of the Village Tract People's Councils to strengthen the common fund system. In November 2014, the 1960 Law on Common Fund for Village Economic Development was repealed.[9] Like cooperatives, village common funds were initiated by legislation from above, in contrast to Japan, where both systems emerged endogenously at the village level. However, even though the system was initially generated or activated by the catalyst of state orders and direction (such as the Common Fund Law and Regulations), funds for the purposes of congratulations and condolences, maintenance of village roads, repair of schools, electrification and laying of water supply and so on, were set up by the villagers themselves. Those funds' purpose itself would be the catalyst for money collection and enforcement, leaving aside the question of the funds' continuity. Even though the funds are also a system from above, they do not disappear like dew as the government-built organisations do.

---

[8] In the villages of Hakha Township, Chin State, each household contributes one-tenth of its income in the form of money, agricultural products, and livestock to the churches, which redistribute it to the poor. In this case, the village is not directly involved.

[9] The repeal of the Law appears to be related to the Microfinance Law, which was enacted in 2011 and came into effect in 2013. The conventional village common fund became less important as the Microfinance Law provided villages with a lump sum of money and the microcredit activities by NGOs increased as a result of democratisation. Moreover, new ways of raising and using the village common fund emerged, in which multiple households in a village receive individual loans from small-scale financial institutions to carry out village-wide projects, as in the case of the electrification project in Taunglwe Village and the water supply project in Kanthalay Village. These are due to new "catalysts" such as small-scale financial institutions and bidding systems. The feasibility and continuity of the projects depend on how effective the "catalysts" are and how long they remain effective.

As discussed above, the Japanese village financial system is autogenous, participatory, multi-purpose, and continuous. In contrast, Myanmar's village common funds are initiated by legislation, have some non-participating households, are purpose-specific, and are short-term (Table 8.2: Village Common Fund).

8.3.2 *Mutual Financing Associations and the Villages*

According to Motoi Kimura (1980), early-modern Japanese villages had various types of *kō* (fraternity), which could be roughly classified into three categories: (1) *kō* as a village organisation, (2) *kō* as a religious organisation, and (3) *kō* as an economic organisation. The first type, *kō* as a village organisation, is represented by the contract *kō*, which existed widely in the Tohoku region. It was a gathering of household heads and was the fundamental organisation of the village, responsible for village rituals, water use, and management of the forest. *Kō* as a religious organisation included village-based groups such as the *kō* dedicated to the mountain gods, paddy field gods, and water gods, and the *kō* praying for the health of children, as well as cross-village groups such as the *kō* of Ise Shrine worshippers and the *kō* worshipping mountains like Fuji, Daisen, and Minobu. As for *kō* as an economic organisation, the mutual financing associations *tanomoshi-kō* and *mujin-kō* are famous (Kimura, 1980: 143–147). The first historical record of a *tanomoshi-kō* is dated 1275 in the Kamakura period (1185–1333). Originally, it was a system of financing for the common people through small-scale self-management and operations based on territorial ties, blood ties, and a sense of community, with mutual relief as its essence. After the mid-Edo period, it became a tool for gambling and plundering by merchants and *samurai* (Shimizu, 1972: 177). However, in rural areas, *tanomoshi-kō* continued to be one of the various forms of collective association based on geographical affiliation (Izumida, 1992: 9–10). The basic mechanism has remained unchanged since the early days of the scheme: members pay contributions on a certain date, a certain amount of money is paid to the winner determined by lottery or bidding, and all the contributions are paid out to all members of the *kō* before the scheme matures. The first person to receive the contributions of all the members was called the "*kō-oya* (*kō* parent)", and since the needy often became the *kō-oya*, *tanomoshi-kō* was a financial association that jointly provided relief to the poor (Shimizu, 1972: 179).

The above scheme is called a rotating savings and credit association (ROSCA) in economics, and the number of this type of credit association is increasing rapidly in Myanmar due to the activities of the United Nations Development Programme (UNDP) and various NGOs. In contrast, autonomous credit associations, which are not encouraged by outside forces, are only occasionally seen among market traders and transporters in Myanmar towns. Surprisingly, one such association was born in Thindaunggyi Village, which was originally a farming village. In this village, it is called "*sù cêingwei aphwè*"[10] and was organised by a 27-year-old woman in 2009,

[10] In Burmese, "*sù*" means to collect, "*cêingwei*" means money, and "*aphwè*" means group.

with her as the "parent", called "*asùkain* (collector, or collection manager)" in the village. The association is often called *Ma Swe sù cêi* after her name, Ma Swe. Her purpose is to raise funds for her main business, moneylending. Every evening, she goes from shop to shop on her motorcycle to collect the day's contributions. Each 10 days, she delivers the entire 10-day contributions to one member, in an order that is predetermined by lottery. In 2009, there were 16 members, so it took 160 days to complete a round. All the members were owners of *gadawbwe* shops and restaurants, and none of them were farmers or agricultural labourers. As an organiser-and-collector, Ma Swe is entitled to receive the entire contributions of all members first. She lends these at a high interest rate of 10–15% over a 10-day period. There are no long-term ROSCAs in Myanmar, such as those in rural Japan, which would take 10 or 20 years to complete a round[11] (Embree, 1939: 142–143). Thus, farmers who do not earn a daily income or agricultural labourers who earn less than the daily contribution cannot join even if they wanted to. In other words, this Thindaunggyi Village *sù cêi* would not have arisen in the first place without the prosperity of the gateway town around the Paya. With the rise of the Paya, the association's members increased to 40 by 2019.

These credit associations are also organised on the basis of a bilateral relationship between the organiser and individual members, with very little mutual assistance, not to mention collective assistance across the village. The organisers or collectors are moneylenders, and the members are the rich, so it is far from helping the poor. The organisers take full responsibility for various risks, such as the theft or loss of contributions and the mid-course withdrawal of members. In other words, there is no need for trust among the members, and the formation and survival of the credit association depends solely on whether each member trusts the organiser. It is not an organisation in which all households or all members of a village participate, and it can easily cross the boundary of a village. When a credit association crosses a village or town boundary, its members often do not know each other (Takahashi, 2018: 123–125). The principle of the mutual financing association of Myanmar is also based on a dyadic relationship, which has nothing to do with the communality of the village (Table 8.2: Mutual Financing Association).

8.3.3 Congratulation and Condolence Associations

The "*buraku* (village)" where my birthplace is located is administratively called a "*ku* (ward)", and within that ward there are several "*kumi*" or "neighbouring households' groups". The group to which my birthplace belongs consists of eight households. This group held the *obisha* banquet, a well-known ritual in Chiba Prefecture. Households

[11] In Myanmar, there are no social relations like those in Japanese villages where household-to-household relations continue for many generations over a long period of time and a collective monitoring function works. Thus, mutual financing associations lasting more than ten years, as in Japan, are unlikely to be established in rural Myanmar.

belonging to this group were also the ones to which the bride went door to door on her wedding day, accompanied by a mediator (Takahashi, 2012: 99–100). At the funeral of my parents, it was the members of this group who attended the funeral as a duty. Before funeral companies took charge of funerals, funerals were held in the household's house. In addition, not only at funerals but also at Buddhist memorial services, the women of the group always attended and chanted Buddhist hymns. In the *buraku* where I was born, until at least the 1980s, a part of all Shinto rituals and celebratory and condolence events were collectively managed by the *kumi*, which is an alliance of households based on geographical ties.

In the villages of Upper Myanmar, too, there are congratulation and condolence associations. They are called *thayêi nayêi athîn*, as mentioned in the previous chapter. In Thindaunggyi Village, it is called *luhmùyêi athîn*, or "social obligation association". This association uses the "village entry fee", mentioned above, to buy and store dishes, chairs, tables, and other items for weddings and funerals held in the village. However, this is not enough, so some villagers provide plates, spoons and other tableware on a case-by-case basis. Each item of the tableware, no matter how small, is inscribed with the name of the owner. Even those who have never contributed money to the village, or who do not provide dishes, or who are not villagers, can use this equipment free of charge if they hold a celebration or condolence event in the village. In other words, the *athîn*'s activities are not based on a system in which the providers and beneficiaries of goods and services would remain the same in the long run due to geographical ties, as is the case with Japanese groups. The *athîn*'s activities are guided by the ambiguous tacit understanding that if someone is in trouble, everyone would help each other.

In 2012, another congratulation and condolence association was established in Thindaunggyi Village. The name is *seidanashin luhmù kuniyêi athîn*, or "social service association with sincerity", and it mainly deals with mourning. The reason given for making this new association was that using the same tables, dishes, and so on, for both mourning and for celebration is bad luck, but this is only an excuse, because the villagers have always done so and other villages still use the same items for both. This *athîn* is led by the village elders and well-liked people, but the actual organiser and manager is Ko Thein, a man in his 30s who married a Thindaunggyi woman and came to live in the village. It is said that his ambition is to use the new organisation to become a powerful figure in the village. He has collected a large amount of donations from inside and outside the village, and through his energy he has turned it into an organisation that owns a hearse. Those who are dissatisfied with this association have not joined it, of course, but many villagers join both *athîns* to enjoy the benefits of both. They participate as "consumers" rather than as "members," and are ready to leave the association if it is not useful to them. In other words, unlike the case in Japan, villagers can join several congratulation and condolence associations and leave them at any time.

In contrast, there is no congratulation or condolence association in Zeepinwea Village. None of the more than a hundred Lower Myanmar villages that I have visited had such an association. Perhaps only very few villages in Lower Myanmar have it . However, even without such an association, many villagers and non-villagers congregate through the tight-knit dyadic networks described in the previous chapter, bringing gifts for weddings and offerings for funerals, and without a clear allocation of roles, they cook, set up the venue, carry coffins, and so on. In times of celebration or mourning, a permanent association may not always be necessary, as the networked "relatives of the place" will be there to assist on each occasion.

8.3.4 Governmental Organisations and Autogenous Organisations

There are also governmental groups and organisations for daily life. For example, each village in Japan has a firefighting organisation called "*bundan* (branch)" or "*bu* (part)". It is a governmental organisation based on the Fire Brigades Regulations of 1894, the Fire and Disaster Management Organisation Act of 1947, and so on, and has a history of more than 100 years. The end unit in the village is a "volunteer" organisation in which all the young men in the village are obligated to participate. Some of these organisations have become inactive in recent years due to the ageing of the villagers. Yet, 50 years ago, as a junior high school student, I was trained to march in formation and to handle fire hoses. In Myanmar, too, each village tract has a fire brigade, called *mîtha' aphwè*. However, in most villages, the brigade is merely nominal and people often do not know who is a member or are not even aware that they are a member. In Zeepinwea Village, there was a fire brigade headed by a side-car driver, Ko Maung Cho, with two members, but when he died of an epidemic, the brigade disappeared. In a village in Pakokku Township, a fire brigade was formed with the donation of a used fire engine from Japan and was active, but there were always problems about who would pay for repairs and who would spend money for gasoline, and when the engine broke down, the fire brigade became a mere name. Similarly, in the 2010s, with the donation of a large number of agricultural tractors from the Indian government, tractor cooperatives were organised one after another in many villages in Lower Myanmar, but they also disappeared one after another due to problems such as repair costs and rent. In the case of Zeepinwea Village, the catalyst for forming a fire brigade was a motivated leader, and in the case of the Pakokku Township village, the catalyst was the donation of a second-hand fire engine, but when the catalyst disappeared or became a burden, the activity went downhill. The tractors donated to villages in the Delta suffered a similar fate.

In Japan, during the Meiji (1868–1912) and Taisho (1912–1926) periods, the Ministry of Education and the Ministry of Home Affairs encouraged the formation of organisations such as youth groups and women's associations in villages throughout the country. Their activity continues even now with the principle that all relevant persons in the village participate. In Myanmar, too, some villages have government-mandated organisations such as the *amyôudhamî yêiya* (women's association), the *kalêi mìgin yêiya* (mother and child association) and the *lungwe aphwè* (youth group).

Similarly to the above-discussed cooperatives, these government-mandated organisations have repeatedly been made and disappeared, and made again, since the Burmese socialist era. They emerge when there is a catalyst—such as strong local government guidance and mandate, spirited women or youth, or external funding—for the formation and operation of the organisation, but fizzle out when the effects of these catalysts fade.

The village Security Association (*lounjounyêi apwè*) has a similar name to the village tract Security and Administration Committee (*lounjounyêi hnìn ou'chou'yêi komiti*), which was created by the Revolutionary Government in 1962, as mentioned in Chap. 2, but it is neither official nor autogenous. Their relationship to the colonial Village Act and the Revolutionary Government is unclear. However, even after the disappearance of the village tract Security and Administration Committee, the village Security Associations are still in place in many villages to the present day. This is because there is no end to the catalysts that continue, such as theft of livestock, robberies, burglaries, fires, and various violent crimes.

As mentioned in the previous chapter, some villages also have a Board of Trustees (*gôpàkà aphwè*) or a Drinking Water Use Committee (*yei komiti*). These are organised by a small percentage of the village population, with the paya or drinking water pump as the catalyst, and the rest of the villagers participate only as consumers of services. If the paya or pump becomes unattractive because another prestigious paya is erected or the pump breaks down, the organisation disappears.

8.4 Faith-Related Groups and Organisations and the Villages

Let us examine the correlation between faith-related groups and the village. I compare Japan and Myanmar, not in terms of the content or the piety of beliefs, but in terms of the relationship between religion and village cohesiveness. In view of the similarities between Japan and Myanmar, I contrast territorial deities and Buddhism in both countries.

According to Eitaro Suzuki, the Shinto shrine of the *ujigami* (guardian god) is the symbol of the Japanese common village. The social consciousness existing in the village requires, first and foremost, that every villager be an *ujiko* (child of *ujigami*) of the same *ujigami*, as a minimum form of expressing that each shares the same social consciousness (Suzuki, 1968: 421). Social consciousness is a systematic norm in all aspects of life in a common village (Suzuki, 1968: 437). In other words, as mentioned in the previous chapter, the *ujigami* who is deified in the shrines is a symbol of the social unity of the villagers, and it is a territorial deity representing the "spirit of the village" that governs the domain of the village.

In Myanmar, too, there are cases where a single spiritual symbol provides some kind of norm for the ethics of life in a particular area. This is the case with the belief in *nat* (*na'*) spirits. Numerous *nat*s protecting[12] specific domains, such as houses, paddy fields, weirs and forests, can be seen throughout Myanmar. For example, the *einzàun na'* guarding houses and compounds, the *lezàun na'* protecting paddy fields, the *sezàun na'* securing weirs, and the *tôzàun na'* preserving forests are well known. There are also *nezàun na'* who protect specific *ne* (territories), indicating that a Myanmar *nat* (*na'*) is indeed a territorial deity. There is also a *nat* called *ywazàun na'*, which protects the village (*ywa*) from bad luck. The corner of the village has a *na'sin*, a small shrine to the deity. Inside the shrine is a deity that protects the area of the village, as the village god does in Japan. However, unlike in Japan, the shrine is not a symbol of the social unity of the villagers. First of all, there is no village social consciousness that would differ beyond the village boundary in Myanmar, thus, of course an *ywazàun na'* does not represent that. As mentioned in the previous chapter, it is almost exclusively the elderly women who comfort and pray to the *nat*, and many men do not pay attention to it. The *ywazàun na'* has survived quietly, overshadowed by major world religions such as Buddhism and Christianity. It is found only in the villages of the ethnic Bamar people in Upper Myanmar and in the villages of other ethnic groups in the mountains, but it is rarely seen in the delta region of Lower Myanmar. The existence of *ywazàun na'* in Myanmar is quite different from Japan, where *ujigami* deities are universally present and symbolise the social unity of the village.

Myanmar villagers' life ethics are not guided by *nat* beliefs, but by world religions such as Buddhism and Christianity. Buddhism, in particular, is the core religion followed by 90% of the population, including the ethnic Bamar, who account for close to 70% of the population, as well as other major ethnic nationalities such as the Shan and Karen. While villagers do not go to the *na'sin*, they visit the paya and monasteries on a daily basis to pay homage to Buddha images and monks. The monks provide the villagers with sermons on life and ethics. When a village is isolated, such as in the mountains or in the deep delta, and there is only one monastery in the village, it appears as if the monastery, like a shrine in Japan, defines the ethics of life in the village community, and that Buddhism is the religion of the community. But if there is a monastery outside the village, and a villager likes the monk there better, the villager will not become a believer in the village monastery but in that monastery outside the village. The cases of Zeepinwea and Thindaunggyi described in the previous chapter illustrate this point. The same is true not only of Buddhism but also of Christianity, which is not necessarily one church per village, as mentioned in the previous chapter. In Japan, as well, there are cases where there is only one Buddhist temple in a village and all the inhabitants are its members, but this is rather unusual, and even in such cases it is common for some of the villagers to be members of temples in other villages (Suzuki, 1968: 335). Even in the Edo period (1603–1868), when not only Christianity but also some sects of Buddhism were forbidden, it was common to have a mixture

[12] Although they are called protective *nat* (*saun na'*), most *nat*s are not mere guardian deities, but spirits that can bring disasters if not treated properly. In other words, by worshipping and consoling the *nat*, one can avoid disasters. Belief in *nat*s is more about praying for them not to bring misfortune than about asking them to protect something.

of Zen and Shin Buddhism believers living in one village (Suzuki, 1968: 336). As mentioned in the previous chapter, both Buddhism and Christianity are based on a dyadic relationship between God or Buddha and oneself. In the case of Myanmar in particular, compared to Japan, individuals are not bound by their family's tradition of Buddhism, so they can decide on their own which monk they believe in, and deepen the dyadic bond between themselves and the monk concerned, regardless of their family or village. Of course, members of a monastery may link together laterally to support the monastery, but this is a secondary religious community that transcends a particular territory and is different from a village community. Neither in Myanmar nor in Japan does Buddhism enhance the cohesion or communality of the village sphere.

8.5 A Myanmar Village is a Community of Life

In the above, we have compared the reality and character of the various groups and organisations that exist in villages in Japan and Myanmar. I will now return to the contrast between collectives and communities (Table 8.1) and try to reframe the collective nature of Japanese villages and the community nature of Myanmar villages.

As Suzuki puts it, the Japanese "spirit of the village" takes precedence over the free will of the individual, as it moulds the will and relations of individuals, rather than the will and relations of individuals creating the village (Suzuki, 1968: 107). Japanese villages have forced individuals to obey voluntarily or to limit themselves for the sake of village cohesion and survival (Kida, 1967: 8). Japanese villages do not favour the individual and have always oppressed it (Murata, 1978: 67). In the Myanmar village, there is no morality or ethic of life that would bind the individual in this way. In other words, the village is not repressive to the individual (Table 8.1: Individuality).

These Japanese village norms that constrain and mould individual intentions and actions are due to the collective nature of production, which is defined by Japan's historical condition that the productive capacity is low and people cannot make a living without mutual dependence, as already mentioned. For example, in the case of the village-contract system of rice tribute, if a peasant fails to pay the annual tribute, other villagers have to make up the difference. The irrigation system managed by the village also needs to be monitored because if someone neglects to maintain the system, downstream people will be inconvenienced and the rice production in the village will be affected. In contrast, in Myanmar, the village never became a unit of in-kind taxation or water management and lacked the historical conditions for a village to become a village collective (Table 8.1: Historicity).

As long as you are born in a Japanese village, you are automatically a member of the *ujiko* (children of the god), as you are born within the area protected by the *ujigami* (guardian god). When you grow up, you must automatically become a member of local associations, such as congratulatory and condolence association, mutual financing association, youth group, fire brigade, and so on. In contrast, in Myanmar villages, there is no group or organisation other than the family that one would automatically become a member of. Buddhism and *nat* belief are individual choices, as are labour exchange and congratulation and condolence associations (Table 8.1: Spontaneity).

The fundamental necessity of village life in Japan is that the village should be united in all matters (Kida, 1967: 8), and the concept of immersion in the collective (= village) is dominant. In the village, the individual is positioned in relation to the group or organisation. In Myanmar, in contrast, the individual is located in dyadic networks and in bilateral relationships centred on the self (*ego*) (Table 8.1: Relationships).

The system of labour exchange that emerges from these relationships takes the form of labour provision to groups and organisations such as *yui*s and agricultural associations in the case of Japan, as already mentioned, whereas in Myanmar the pattern is one-to-one labour exchange on an individual basis. The former can be called collective assistance and the latter reciprocal assistance (Table 8.1: Assistance).

On the basis of this collective assistance embedded in the Japanese village, a financing association can bring large sums of money that cannot be saved by individuals equally to its members. A mechanised association can create economies of scale in small, dispersed farmland holdings. An agricultural products sales cooperative can have price bargaining power that is unattainable by individuals. In this way, Japanese villages have achieved a performance that is more than just the sum of the individuals. Myanmar villages' dyadic network society can also function as collective assistance as long as there are effective catalysts. However, since social relations in rural Myanmar are basically a one-to-one dyadic network, village society is no more than a synthesis of individuals (Table 8.1: Totality).

According to Hisamoto Horikoshi, old Japanese villages had a "function" that if a villager could not afford to make a living, everyone would work together to make sure that this villager could earn a livelihood. This was a "village function", not because the villagers were on good terms with each other, but because it was their "duty" to do so as long as they lived in the village, no matter how badly they got along (Horikoshi, 1979: 206). The farmers who introduced new crops and varieties to the village and spread new technologies to all the villagers, so-called "*tokunō* (practical farmers)" and "*rōnō* (exemplary farmers)", emerged as a result of this "village function". In Myanmar villages, there are elders (*lugyî*) who are loved by villagers and have a certain influence on village religion and politics, but there are few *tokunō* or *rōnō*. This is because there is no "village function" in Myanmar that would try to raise the level of life or production of the entire village by helping villagers who are struggling to make a living or by raising the level of agriculture in the village as a whole. If there is such a person, it is because of his or her individual qualities, not because of the communal principle that is at work in Japanese villages.

The Japanese village has a clear boundary. It is the range within which the "spirit of the village" regulates the ethics of life of the villagers. It is also the range of land and water managed by the village as the "subject of land occupation". In addition to these geographical boundaries, the boundaries of the village are socially closed to the outside world (Murata, 1978: 29). The village is a country, and entrants must greet the natives politely. When entering a village, a newcomer usually serves liquor and greets people (Suzuki, 1968: 454). Minoru Kida, who had assumed that "Japanese citizens and foreigners alike could live in rented houses anywhere in Japan as long as the landlord was aware", found it necessary to be taken around the village by the headman and mentor, carrying souvenirs and being instructed on how and with whom to socialise (Kida, 1967: 3–4). My wife had to wear a bridal gown and go door to door to greet each household belonging to the "*kumi*" to which my birth family belongs, even though she had no relation to those households and did not live there. She had to do it simply because of becoming the wife of an eldest son (Takahashi, 2012: 99). In the past, Japanese villages had a ritual called "*mushi-oi* (insect expulsion)", to prevent agricultural pests from entering the village or to drive them out of the village (Suzuki, 1968: 425). It is a ritual that symbolises the closed nature of the village, where people do not care what happens to other villages as long as their own village is fine. The village cemetery is also closed to the outside world. For new people coming to live in the village, it remains difficult for one or two generations to build a grave in the village cemetery.

Compared to the closed nature of Japanese villages, Myanmar villages are much more open. As mentioned earlier, there are boundaries between villages as living areas, but there are no such boundaries for land related to production, such as paddy fields, upland fields, and irrigation canals. The boundary of residential land is also ambiguous. To become a resident of a village, it is enough to build a house or rent a house or room in the village. There is no need to take into account geographical ties. Even a couple with no connection to the village can quickly become residents of the village (Takahashi, 2012: 101–102). In Zeepinwea Village cemetery, there are many graves of people who came to the village as labourers or patients of the East Monastery. The area of the cemetery is limited, but anyone, anywhere, and any number of people can be buried in the village cemetery because the corpses are buried in random places, where bones have already been buried and dug up many times. In Myanmar, we often hear the word "*wâin kunyide*", which means to help villagers who are in need. However, this is not a duty as a villager, but a dyadic relationship—of compassion as a Buddhist and of closeness to those in need. Therefore, it extends beyond the borders of the village and even to foreigners like me. The Myanmar village is a society with a high degree of openness (Table 8.1: Openness).

In summary, the Japanese village has a strong collective character, while the Myanmar village has a strong community character. As mentioned earlier, Japanese villages have functioned not only as the subject of production-related activities such as irrigation control, village responsibility system, collective ownership of common land, cooperatives, and so on, but also as a unit of communal activities in daily life such as financial management, mutual financing associations, shrine festivals, marriage and funeral rites, children's and youth associations, and others. In other words, the Japanese village is a "collective of production and life", while the Myanmar village is a "community of life" that lacks communality in production.

8.6 Collective Failure

In a market economy, a situation can arise where the allocation of resources is not Pareto-optimal, that is, economic efficiency is not achieved, leading to "market failure". Examples include imperfect competition, externalities, public goods, increasing returns to scale, and information asymmetries. Failures can also occur when governments intervene in market transactions and try to correct such market failures. This is "government failure". Examples include "pork barrel" (the use of government funds for projects designed to please voters or legislators and win votes), "crowding-out" (massive issuance of government bonds for public investment and tax reduction in order to achieve popular policies), and inefficient management of public enterprises. Therefore, in Development Economics, the *community* has been attracting attention as a system to mitigate these two failures. Communities are expected to play a role in providing local public goods, such as mutually supportive safety nets, shared resource management, and enforcement of contractual transactions. When lending money to villagers, if banks or the state lend directly, they have to send someone out frequently to find out about the borrower's financial situation and to remind them if they are in arrears, but if villagers form groups and monitor each other, transaction costs are lower. If the forest is managed by the village, the transaction costs are lower than if the state sends civil servants, and if villagers monitor the forest 24 hours a day, they can prevent the market failure of overcutting by individuals. The village contract system and village water management also save transaction costs for tribute procurement. And indeed, through communal monitoring and regulation, Japanese villages have achieved economic efficiency in the management of common land, procurement and production adjustment, various cooperatives and village farming, institutional finance, and joint use of agricultural machinery and large-scale facilities. The "communal advantages" described above are more clearly and effectively demonstrated in a "collective" rather than in a "community".

Yet, this type of collective management or collective-based organisation may impose transaction costs on villagers, in the form of "constraints", or prevent them from maximising their economic benefits. These costs include not only costs that can be converted into prices in terms of opportunity costs—such as daily socialising, weddings, funerals, and various communal activities—but also those that cannot be easily converted into prices, such as mental or ethical inconvenience. When leasing or selling farmland, if there is an implicit regulation that villagers have to do it among themselves (Takahashi, 2012: 138), the rents or selling prices of farmland will diverge from market prices. When villagers have to return from the city to the village for collective work or for neighbourhood rituals, their cost of doing so will also be a cost for maintaining the collective.[13] I have seen villagers who have suffered physical and mental disorders due to the tremendous peer pressure of the village collective.[14]

Let us call such inefficient price formation, transaction costs for maintaining the collective, personal and ethical constraints, and so on, a "collective (*kyōdōtai*) failure". The stronger the binding power of the *kyōdōtai*, the better it will be able to cooperate in agricultural production, manage common property, and provide mutual aid and joint work, as in Japanese villages. However, mutual restrictions not only prevent individuals from becoming independent, but they can also lead to excesses or outbursts, such as the "village ostracism (*mura-hachibu*)," village-wide election fraud, and the arbitrary disposal of common property by powerful individuals. In recent development economics, it has been argued that communities—but in the context of this book, collectives—must be re-emphasised, especially in developing countries where market failures and government failures are evident. Yet, "collective failure" such as economic inefficiency and personality restraints should also be taken into account form the Japanese experience. Just as there are failures in markets and governments, there are failures in collectives.

In comparison with the Japanese village, the Myanmar village is a society with significantly less "collective failure". There is no "village spirit" that would regulate the ethics of individual life in Myanmar villages. The villagers are free to join or leave any group or organisation in the village, and they can act autonomously without being constrained by the village. As mentioned in Chap. 4, the former mayor of Thindaunggyi Village sold his farmland to outsiders at extraordinary prices. He would not have been able to repay his sons' debts if there had been a regulation that farmland in the village should be sold only to co-villagers. The Myanmar village does not inhibit the orientation towards economic efficiency. The household migration and the mixed multi-ethnic settlement of the village described in Chap. 6 also indicate not only the openness of villages but also the weakness of village regulations on individual behaviour. Examples of this happening in Zeepinwea Village include outsiders buying farmland and quickly becoming large farmers, a household from a different ethnic group, such as Shan or Karen, suddenly building a large mansion in the centre of the village, and a Korean Christian mission building a church in a Buddhist village.

The low incidence of "collective failure" in Myanmar villages is partly related to the fact that the villages are communities of life lacking the communal nature

[13] In August 2020, I received a letter from the Buddhist temple where my parental home was a parishioner. My parental home had become vacant after my parents passed away. A bill for 250,000 yen per parishioner for the restoration of the building was sent to my present address. This bill to me, who has been out of the village for decades, means that those who were born in the village collective must continue to pay for the maintenance of the collective even if they leave the village. This is another good example of the strong binding power of the collective.

[14] In my previously published book, I wrote: "When I see not only my father, but also several of my classmates in the *buraku*, whom there are only seven, become mentally ill and two young people commit suicide within a three-minute walk of my birthplace, the mental pressure that the village exerts on the villagers feels hard to ignore (Takahashi, 2012: 109)". I received comments from my acquaintances who read this sentence, saying that such a thing had happened also in their birthplaces.

of production. In a village that is a community of production, withdrawal or expulsion from productive groups and organisations such as cooperatives and water users' associations are fatal for individuals and households living in the village. If they are removed from the community, their source of income is cut off at once, and they cannot make a living. Therefore, individuals must be willing to accept unreasonable constraints and coercion from the community. Thus arises "collective failure" (Takahashi, 2012: 138). In contrast, a village that is merely a community of life bonds individuals more weakly. Security associations and fire brigades are high in externalities, so you do not need to be a member to be protected from theft or fire, and the probability of theft or fire does not decrease just because you are a member. The drinking water utilisation committee allows anyone to use the water as long as they pay for it. In other words, there is little risk of losing their livelihood even if they leave the committee. Even if they do, it is not a big problem because they can join any group for life as soon as they move to another village. The individual can pursue economic rationality without worrying about the village. The groups and organisations are less binding on members leaving. Even if a few members leave, it is not a big burden for the remaining members, and it is easy to add new members because the threshold of the group is low. If a large number of members leave the group, the group becomes unsustainable, but if the group disappears, the constraints on individuals become meaningless (Takahashi, 2012: 180–181). There is very little room for "collective failure" to occur in Myanmar villages.

As we argued in the previous chapter, dyadic networks of bilateral relations accumulate thickly in the Myanmar village through the "logic of frequent contact", and various catalysts work on that logic to create various groups and organisations. Then, frequent contacts occur again to strengthen the organisations and to promote the emergence of new groups. It is a characteristic of Myanmar villages that groups and organisations are formed through substantive interactions between individuals. Thus, the mechanism of formation is different from that in Japan, where there is a framework of villages and various groups are moulded on the village (*buraku*) basis through formalised interactions. Groups and organisations based on actual interaction can be organised more quickly and easily than those based on formal interactions. However, since these groups and organisations are based on connections between individuals, the outer shell of the group is fragile and not as strong as that of Japanese village groups, which are regulated by villages (Takahashi, 2012: 175). If the dyadic relationship becomes strained, or if the "catalyst" loses its influence, individuals will easily leave the group or organisation. As the number of defectors increases, the group or organisation itself becomes merely nominal, and follows the path to extinction. Groups and organisations in Myanmar villages are like dreams or bubbles that easily form and disappear (Takahashi, 2018: 188).

In a dyadic network centred on the *ego* (self), the more threads there are, the lower the risk of isolation. There is no need to fear collective alienation, such as being ostracised. There is no need to be upset if one or two threads are broken. There are plenty of other threads. Individuals in the accumulation of dyadic relationships have the "freedom of severance" to cut the threads (Takahashi, 2012: 181). This high potential for severance is the backbone of the freedom and self-reliance of Myanmar's villagers, helping them to avoid "collective failure".

This social structure, with its low incidence of "collective failure," has been a factor in the long continuance of repressive regimes such as Burmese socialism and military rule. As I have repeatedly mentioned, Myanmar's coercive rule has been based on orders and surveillance from above. However, once it entered the village, it was unable to utilise communal horizontal linkages. The threads of bilateral relationships connect vertically, horizontally, and diagonally, but they break and connect, making them unsuitable for continuous mutual surveillance, and the regime could not provide the "catalysts" that would sustain a community of surveillance that transcends the dyadic relationships. The villagers also had the "freedom of severance" from the neighbourhood group surveillance system[15] promoted under the Burmese socialist regime.

Myanmar's harsh and repressive agricultural and rural institutions and their enforcement systems, which I described in Chap. 2, lacked thoroughness and were eventually undermined by *nalehmu*, bribery and bilateral intimacies (Takahashi, 1992: 104–105; 2012: 77–82). The dyadic network principle allowed for flexible and complex relationships and organisations—invisible to the power—to accumulate within the village, and to absorb and dissipate rigid policies. Thus, dissatisfaction and frustration with the regime rarely reached an extreme state within the village, and outbursts were small and rare.[16] Even under the brutal and coercive regime, the villagers lived a surprisingly free and independent life. The "absence of village collective" became a means of unconscious resistance to strong authority, which at the same time contributed to the longevity of oppressive regimes such as Burmese socialism and the broader military rule.

[15] This system of surveillance by "neighbourhood groups" stemmed from the Japanese military period which introduced to Myanmar the *tonari-gumi* (Neighbourhood Association) system, a symbol of Japanese rural fascism.

[16] However, "explosions" such as the Peasant Rebellion of 1930–31, the refusal of paddy offerings at the end of the socialist period and the subsequent struggle for democracy in 1988, and the anti-military movements since February 2021 can occur. Even in such cases, "catalysts" such as the livelihood crisis, Sayar San (the symbolic leader of the Peasant Rebellion), Aung San Suu Kyi, and the *coup d'état* were necessary.

Chapter 9
Conclusion: Change and Continuity in the Social Economy of Rural Myanmar

A. Takahashi, *Regime Changes and Socio-economic History of Rural Myanmar, 1986–2019*, Studies in Economic History,
https://doi.org/10.1007/978-981-99-3272-6_9

The trampling and threshing by cattle (above photo, taken in August 1994), which had been done in Myanmar villages for a long time, disappeared after threshing machines were introduced in 2008 (lower photo, taken in August 2013). Around 2016, those machines were replaced by combine harvesters. Some wealthy farmers in this village had planned to earn extra income by renting out threshing machines, but were disappointed. (A side-note: the roofing material of the house in the background of the cattle is *wakat*). (Thindaunggyi Village)

This book has covered 33 years of Myanmar's socio-economic history up to 2019, starting in 1986 with the last stage of the Burmese socialist regime led by Ne Win, followed by the military regimes of Soe Maung and Than Shwe from 1988 to 2011, the Thein Sein regime that promoted democratisation and liberalisation despite being born out of the military regime in 2011, and the Aung San Suu Kyi regime that was established in 2016 with the support of the people. The book's narrative focused on agriculture and rural areas, which form the core of Myanmar's economy and society. In the first part of the book, I described the changes in agriculture and the transformation of village society through the keyword "de-agrarianisation". In the second part, in contrast, I discussed the *core* of Myanmar villages—or, the socio-economic characteristics of rural Myanmar, which have remained largely unchanged from at least 1986 to the present. I developed a theory of the "absence of village collective", by comparing Myanmar and Japan.

The book's introduction divided the modern history of Myanmar, which gained independence after the Second World War, into four periods: the post-independence civil administration period (1948–1962), the Burmese socialist period (1962–1988), the military regime period (1988–2011), and the democratisation period (2011–2021). The political system and economic institutions of each period were then examined. The political system was divided into democracy and dictatorship. Notably, the economic systems did not correspond to the political systems. Thus, I added the indicator of whether the economy is open or closed, to make the differences between the four time periods become clearer. In addition, the period of Burmese socialism can be divided into two, and the democratisation period from 2011 can be divided into two periods as well.

In Chap. 2, I discussed the agricultural system and rural policies after Myanmar's independence, considering agriculture and rural villages as two different categories. The agricultural history of modern Myanmar is characterised by three systems: the state ownership of farmland, the procurement system, and the planned cultivation system. By examining how these three systems were established and implemented, this book highlighted Myanmar's unique transitions of agricultural policies and administrations. Although the book focused on these three systems, it covered the entire range of agricultural policy and administration, including the agrarian system in general, the irrigation system, the cooperatives policy, and the agricultural extension.

We explored each of these three agricultural systems through time. The system of agricultural land nationalisation was stipulated by the 1947 Constitution and the 1953 Land Nationalisation Act. The Constitution remained in force until 1974, while the Land Nationalisation Act was in effect until 2012. The State Agricultural Marketing Board Act, which supported the procurement system, was enacted in 1950, and repealed only in 2013. The planned cultivation system was enshrined in the 1953 Land Nationalisation Act, so its duration was the same as that of the Act—until 2012. In short, if we look only at the laws, the above division of Myanmar's modern history into four periods does not make sense. It remains necessary to examine the three systems from the perspective of the content of the law, but it is more important to explore the process of implementation and the effectiveness of each system. Then, the periodisation becomes clearer. In the post-independence civil administration period, these three systems were implemented separately, and except for the procurement system, they were not effective. In the Burmese socialist period, however, the three systems, while using the same law as during the previous period, came to function in conjunction with each other as the three pillars of agricultural policy, not only supporting agriculture but also becoming the backbone of the national economy and severely restricting the free economic activities of the people. During the following post-socialist military period, the three systems continued to regulate agriculture in Myanmar as a trinity, though the content and scope of the policies to which the laws applied changed. The three systems of agricultural administration, which were enacted during the post-independence civilian period in order to restore the country's economy to the hands of the Myanmar people, were used by the subsequent socialist and military regimes as a means to control the peasants and became fetters for the development of agriculture. The liberalisation of peasant agriculture had to wait for the 2010s' democratisation period, when the Land Nationalisation Act and the State Agricultural Marketing Board Act were abolished.

In terms of rural and village policy, the basic law, the "Burma Village Act", was enacted in 1907 during the pre-independence colonial period and governed rural areas for 105 years, whether nominally or practically, until it was repealed in 2012. Its focus was on two points: maintaining village security and sanitation, with no provisions guaranteeing the rights of villagers or their participation in village self-governance. During the post-independence civilian period, the security situation in rural areas was not stable and the enforcement of the law was limited. In contrast, during the following socialist period, a new system descended to the villages through the Village Tract Security and Administration Committee and, later, the Village Tract People's Council. The system went far beyond the provisions of the law, controlling villages from above and severely restricting villagers' freedom. During the post-socialist military regime, although not as detailed as during the socialist period, village governance continued to be based on the 1907 Village Act, which enforced security, sanitation, and subordination to the military government. So, both the socialist and later military regimes tried to subordinate the village to the centre and control the villagers on the basis of the Village Act enacted during the colonial period. However, the social structure of Myanmar's villages, as described in Chaps. 7 and 8, is such that while villages accept the restrictive and repressive rural management policies, it dissipates the effects of these policies. In 2012, during the democratisation period, the Village Act was finally abolished, and the Town and Village Tract Administration Law was newly enacted. The law added new sections on villagers' rights and welfare, including democratic mayor election procedures, resource management within village tracts and poverty reduction. In addition, as described in Chap. 8, semi-mandatory attempts to make villagers collect village funds—such as the "Law on Common Fund for Village Economic Development" (promulgated in 1960 during the end of the post-independence civil administration period) and the "Regulations on the Recording of Activities and Funds Relating to the Common Fund for Rural Development" (issued in 1977 during the socialist period—had throughout failed and were abolished in 2011. These were replaced by the Microfinance Law, which was not necessarily bound by village territories.

Thus, the laws and regulations on agriculture and rural areas that were enacted democratically during the post-independence civilian period were skilfully used by the autocratic regime to constrain agricultural growth and suppress the rural areas for 50 years. However, they were finally abolished at the beginning of the partial democratic period.

In Chap. 3, I discussed the position of agriculture and rural areas in the national economy. Myanmar's agricultural land area is around 12.5 million ha, which is the third largest among ASEAN countries after Indonesia and Thailand, but not much different from the Philippines and Vietnam. The share of farmland in the country's total land area is about 18%, which is less than that of Thailand, Vietnam, and the Philippines, where farmland is more than 30%, and Indonesia, Cambodia, and Malaysia, where farmland is more than 20%. At least, these figures do *not* give us an image of Myanmar being an especially agricultural country.

Although paddy fields (*le*) account for the largest share of the total farmland area by far, their share has been decreasing. Instead, the shares of upland fileds (*ya*) for growing beans and perennial croplands classified as gardens (*ûyin*) for planting rubber and oil palm, both of which are promising commodity crops, have been increasing. In proportion to the decline in the share of paddy fields, the ratio of rice acreage to the total acreage has also fallen. This does not mean that the area of paddy fields and rice cropping itself has decreased, but rather that much of the uncultivated land that was developed during the military regime was converted into upland fields and gardens rather than into paddy fields. The weight of paddy fields and areas sown with rice has decreased due to the rapid increase in the planting of beans and rubber.

In the first half of the socialist period, the share of the agricultural sector in the gross domestic product, measured by *constant* prices, was less than 30%, but in the 1990s it reached nearly 40%, a trend that was maintained in the first half of the post-socialist military period. However, in the latter half of the 2000s, the ratio began to decline and returned to the level of the 1960s when socialism had begun. During the democratisation period, the agricultural sector's share of GDP decreased further to an unprecedentedly low level of 17.7% in Fiscal Year (FY) 2017/18.

The drop in the GDP share of the agricultural sector, measured in *current* prices, was even larger. In the latter half of the socialist period and in the first half of the following military period, the ratio of agriculture to GDP was increasing. Its share exceeded 50% in FY 1992/93. The share of agricultural GDP was larger in current prices than in real prices because Myanmar's agricultural prices, which had been controlled during the socialist period, were suddenly decontrolled in the beginning of the following military period, while the terms of trade for the manufacturing sector and the commercial and service sectors improved. In other words, these figures show that the farmers became relatively richer in the first half of the military period. In the period of democratisation, the share in current prices declined to less than 20%. By FY 2017/18, it was only 15.4%, lower than the share of real GDP. The transition to a market economy after the collapse of socialism initially impacted farmers positively, but this was only temporary. Whether measured by constant prices or current prices, the receding trend in agriculture's share of GDP has been clear.

Turning from agriculture to the farm households who manage it, the number of *farm* households—meaning the households that hold cultivation rights of farmland and manage agriculture, not the many landless labourers who work in agriculture—is on average less than half of the total number of rural households, as shown in Table 3.6. In other words, more than half of rural households in Myanmar are non-farm households. However, the sum of farm households and agricultural labourer households, that is, the number of households engaged in agriculture, accounts for two-thirds of the total number of households. Non-agricultural households, that is, households not engaged in agriculture, constitute a third of rural households. Thus, the average rural village in Myanmar cannot be described as a "purely agricultural village" because not even half of the households are farm households and a third of the households have nothing to do with agriculture. The proportion of farm households is particularly low in the plain areas, where rice cultivation is more prevalent.

In order to explore the trend of the agricultural working population at the individual level rather than at the household level, I compared the results of two censuses, 1983 and 2014. In 1983, 75.2% of Myanmar's total population lived in rural areas and

80.4% of their labour force was engaged in agriculture, forestry or fisheries, but by 2014, the rural resident population had decreased to 70.4% of the total population and the proportion of the rural population involved in agriculture, forestry or fisheries had declined to 68.7%. As the number of forestry and fisheries workers is very small, this can be regarded as a trend in the *agricultural* working population. In other words, both the number of households engaged in agriculture, as well as the number of individuals working in agriculture, is about two-thirds of the total rural population. When including urban areas, in 1983, the agriculture, forestry and fisheries workers accounted for 64.6% of all workers in Myanmar, but by 2014 they had fallen to 52.4%. The agricultural sector's share of GDP has declined further, so that already in 1983, the average income of agricultural sector workers was only two thirds of the average income of all workers and by 2014 it was only two fifths. This is a macroeconomic factor that drives de-agrarianisation.

Comparing the consumption structure in rural and urban areas, the total consumption expenditure of rural households is only two-thirds of that in urban areas. This disparity probably reflects the lower income in rural areas. Rice is the only item which rural households spend more money on than do urban households. In particular, spending on education is much lower, leading to high levels of child labour and low literacy rates in rural areas. This may induce people to move to urban areas in search of education and employment opportunities.

Chapter 4 described the socio-economic history of two villages: Zeepinwea Village in Lower Myanmar and Thindaunggyi Village in Upper Myanmar. I have been doing research in these two villages almost every year for more than 30 years since 1986. This chapter was written based on my field surveys about livelihoods in these villages in 1987, 1994, and 2013.

Zeepinwea Village is located in the tropical monsoon climate zone, with an annual rainfall of around 2700 mm concentrated in the rainy season from May to October. Starting from November, the dry season has almost no rainfall. The first inhabitants of the village were of Mon ethnicity, and it is thought that the Bamar ethnic group moved into the village during the British colonial period, giving rise to the present Burmese language name of the village, which is relatively new. In 1987, the population was 753 people and the number of households 138, almost the same as seven decades earlier. However, the number of households soon increased rapidly—from 170 in 1994 to 316 in 2013.

In terms of household occupation, *farm* households accounted for 46.4% of all households in the village in 1987, falling to 38.8% by 1994 and to 17.4% by 2013. Nevertheless, when adding to this the agricultural labourer households—whose main occupation is agricultural hired labour—it is possible to say that, in 2013, half of the households in the village were still engaged in agriculture. Yet, this ratio had decreased significantly compared to 1987, when 80% of the households in the village were engaged in agriculture. Moreover, among households engaged in agricultural hired labour, the number of *kyaban* (*càbân*) households—which work merely on a daily or piece-rate basis—had increased. In contrast, the number of households that were *not* engaged in agriculture had increased rapidly. They mainly worked as peddlers or street vendors. Thus, with the shift to a market economy, more and more households had begun earning a living on the fluctuating daily wages of *kyabans* and street vendors.

Examining the changes in the employment situation of each villager individually, rather than as households, revealed the following three things about Zeepinwea Village. Firstly, the number of self-employed "land-holding" farmers had decreased significantly. Secondly, the number of female agricultural labourers had decreased dramatically. Female rice transplanters had instead become street vendors, selling vegetables and other goods on the roadsides around the central market of Hlegu Town. This was because although the daily income from street vending may be less than from rice transplanting labour, the work is available throughout the year rather than only seasonally. In addition, some women who would formerly have become agricultural labourers went to high school or college and found work as seamstresses or clerks in garment factories. Thirdly, among the village men, the number of agricultural labourers as well as self-employed farmers decreased, while the number of non-farm workers increased. Young men especially tended to work as motorcycle taxi drivers, followed by long-distance cargo drivers and assistants, while middle-aged and older men tended to work as "side-car" bicycle taxi drivers.

The average size of farmland holdings among my 39 sample households in Zeepinwea declined by nearly half, from 10.25 acres in 1987 to 5.38 acres in 2013. Especially all the large farmers who in 1987 held more than 14 acres of paddy fields reduced their holdings. The main reason for selling farmland was to pay for treatment of illnesses. A notable number of households disposed of their farmland when a family member suffered from malaria, cancer, or stroke. Most of the purchasers of farmland in Zeepinwea Village came from outside the village and migrated to the village to do agriculture. For this reason, despite the fact that many former farm households sold their farmland by 2013 and thus became non-farm households, the total number of farm households in the village decreased only slightly. Not only sales and purchases, but also leases, that is, tenancy, increased. Although both the sale and lease of farmland were prohibited by the Land Nationalisation Act, the illegal transfer of farmland had been increasing long before the law was repealed in 2012. It could be said that the pressure of market economy turned the Land Nationalisation Act into a so-called dead letter, already before it was abolished.

At the time of my surveys in 1987 and 1994, Zeepinwea Village was a traditional rice monoculture village. However, in 1996, canal irrigation was introduced to some of its paddy fields, allowing for double cropping paddy rice. At about the same time, the use of walking tractors (cultivators) began to replace cattle ploughing. This was because it was impossible to plough the hardened paddy soil in the dry season with animal power. The introduction of the walking tractors was followed by threshing machines, and in the 2010s, harvesting by combine harvesters began.

Only traditional varieties of rice were planted in Zeepinwea until 1980, after which the regime enforced the planting of high-yielding varieties. Thus, the proportion of traditional varieties plummeted to only 16.4% at the time of my 1987 survey. However, it increased again to 54.4% in 1994, and in the 2013 rainy season, 95.7% of the paddy fields were planted with traditional varieties, while high-yielding rice varieties were almost absent. Traditional varieties require less fertiliser and sell at a higher price, although their yield is lower. The market economy encouraged a return to traditional rice varieties. In addition, while the only rice that could be grown in the dry season was thought to be the non-photosensitive high-yielding varieties, more and more farmers have been growing traditional varieties of glutinous rice for brewing.

As for the dry season cropping—that is, the after-crop to wet-season rice cultivation—only a small amount of groundnut cropping using residual soil water used to be practised. The introduction of irrigation was a major change to these farming methods. Not only dry-season rice cultivation, but also green gram cultivation spread, with prices soaring due to the demand from overseas, which led to the emergence of green gram *nouveau riche*. However, from around 2008, diseases and insect pests began to occur constantly, and even with the use of pesticides, yields decreased. By 2017, green gram cultivation had disappeared. Instead, groundnut cultivation was revived. The new groundnut had a higher yield than the previous variety, and more and more farmers begun growing it again.

From 1987 to the present, the price of farmland in Zeepinwea Village has been increasing continuously. From 1987 to 1994, the rate of increase in the price of paddy rice was much higher than the rate of increase in the price of paddy field. This led some farmers to purchase more farmland for cultivating paddy rice. However, from 1994 to 2013, the rate of increase in farmland prices was much higher than the rate of increase in paddy rice prices. The price of farmland has been increasing since 2008 because of speculative purchases due to the expectation that Yangon City and Hlegu Town will be expanding. Thus, farmlands in Zeepinwea have been sold to outsiders one after another.

The concept of *dadounghton*—which is "the area that a nuclear family could cultivate with its own labour and a yoke of draught cattle, and earn a living", the traditional unit of arable land in Myanmar and the unit of allocation during Myanmar's agrarian reform—became a mere fiction as the price of farmland rocketed. In 1987, the price of *dadounghton*, which is around 10 to 12 acres of paddy field in Zeepinwea Village, was slightly higher than the price of a bullock in Zeepinwea. It was possible for one child to inherit the paddy field in *dadounghton* and the other children to inherit the cattle and precious metals. Although the price rose to two or three oxen by 1994, it was still possible for only one child to inherit the paddy field while keeping *dadounghton*. However, by 2013, 10 acres was equivalent to 10 to 50 oxen, and it was impossible to give this many bullocks to one child while the number of oxen was decreasing. As a result, the cultivation right of farmland was divided and inherited, and *dadounghton* was relegated to oblivion.

The second village where I have worked since 1986—Thindaunggyi Village—is located in the savannah climate zone. In Thindaunggyi Village, the distinction between the wet and dry seasons is as clear as in Zeepinwea, but the rainfall in the wet season is around 800 mm, which is less than one third of that of Zeepinwea. Thindaunggyi Village is said to be one of the oldest villages in Myanmar, as its history dates back to the eleventh century. In contrast to Zeepinwea, the number of households and population in the Thindaung Village Tract—which includes Thindaunggyi Village—increased significantly during the 66 years from 1921 to 1987, which includes the time of Myanmar's independence in 1948. My surveys showed that both the population and the number of households in Thindaunggyi Village continued to increase until at least 2013. However, the size of households has decreased, as in Zeepinwea Village, due to the practice of *oekhwe*.

In Thindaunggyi Village, farm households accounted for only half of the total households between 1987 and 1994. However, when adding the agricultural labourer households, the households engaged in agriculture accounted for 73.8% of all households in 1987 and 67.9% in 1994, or three-quarters to two-thirds of all households in the village. By 2013, however, farm households accounted for less than one-third of all households, and even together with the agricultural labourer households, the households engaged in agriculture accounted for less than half of all households. In inverse proportion to this, the number of plasterers and shop keepers had been increasing. Plastering is Thindaunggyi's special "village occupation" that is said to date back to the dynastic period, and although it declined during the British colonial period, it was revived after independence. Riding the crest of the construction boom during the military regime, just over a quarter of the total number of households in the village did plastering as a household occupation at the time of my 2013 survey. The rapid increase in the number of households with shop management as their main occupation is attributable to the expansion of the gateway town of Shwetheindaw Paya where new occupations emerged, such as selling souvenirs and providing food and drink to visitors.

Changes in the employment status of individual villagers in Thindaunggyi can be summarised as follows. First, although the number of farm households did not decrease, unlike in Zeepinwea Village, the number of men and women engaged in self-employed own farming declined sharply, as in Zeepinwea. This was because parents continued to farm but their children, the new workforce, were no longer farming. However, these new non-agricultural workers included no factory workers like those in Zeepinwea Village. This is not to say that they could not access foreign-funded factories, but the Paya offered better employment opportunities in the village. Second, the number of female agricultural workers decreased between 1987 and 1994, but not since then, unlike in Zeepinwea Village. This is because double cropping is common in Thindaunggyi Village, meaning that there are almost constant opportunities for agricultural employment throughout the year, especially for female labourers. In contrast, the sons of agricultural labourer households were more likely to work as plasterers, and the proportion of male agricultural labourers decreased considerably. Third, while the overall number of non-agricultural workers increased sharply in both villages between 1994 and 2013, the ratio of non-agricultural workers to the total number of workers increased from 24.2 to 61.2% in Zeepinwea Village, but from 25.4% to only 47.7% in Thindaunggyi Village. This is because the number of farm households in Zeepinwea Village decreased and the female agricultural labour force shifted to the non-agricultural sector in large numbers, while this did not happen in Thindaunggyi Village. Thindaunggyi's number of farm households did not decline because land prices were high thanks to high farmland productivity. This allowed farmers to cope with sudden shocks, such as needing to pay to treat a serious illness, without having to sell all of their farmland. Despite such differences, there is no doubt that *de-agrarianisation* is progressing in both villages.

In Zeepinwea Village, the collapse of farm households with large holdings has led to a levelling off downwards of farm holdings in the village as a whole, with the average size halving. In contrast, there was no significant change in the average holding acreage in any stratum in Thindaunggyi Village. The reason for this small fluctuation was that the farmland in the village had long been irrigated, allowing for double cropping. Thus, farmland prices in Thindaunggyi have been higher than in Zeepinwea, which has non-irrigated and paddy rice monoculture, and the acreage inherited or sold at one time has been smaller. In addition, because Thindaunggyi has the practice of mortgage tenancy, which does not exist in Zeepinwea Village, it is easier to obtain a large amount of cash and people do not need to sell all of their farmland to recover from illness and thus become landless. However, the acreage of farm households with large holdings decreased, while the acreage of middle-sized holdings remained almost the same and the acreage of the households with smallest holdings increased. In other words, the averaging to medium-sized farmers has progressed in Thindaunggyi Village over the 26 years from 1987 to 2013.

Although precipitation in Thindaunggyi Village is so low that rain-fed rice cultivation is almost impossible, paddy rice has been cultivated in two seasons a year and various double cropping systems have been practised by artificial irrigation using a canal, which was completed around the 12th or 13th century. In the case of double cropping, non-photosensitive, high-yielding rice varieties were planted since the 1980s as the *mojoe* crop—the crop that is planted before the rainy season—while traditional rice varieties were planted as the *kaukkyi* crop—which is planted during the rainy season. The rainy-season *kaukkyi* rice was used for home consumption. However, since the 1990s, high-yielding rice varieties became the mainstream in the *kaukkyi* cropping season, too, which contrasts with Zeepinwea Village, where farmers have reverted to traditional varieties. Kyaukse is one of the rare areas in Myanmar where high-yielding varieties of rice have been established as the rice for home consumption. A variety of double cropping systems have been developed in this village, such as *mojoe* rice to *kaukkyi* rice, sesame to *kaukkyi* rice, sesame to onion or garlic, *mojoe* rice or *kaukkyi* rice to pepper, and *kaukkyi* rice to onion or garlic. As a result, since the socialist era, Thindaunggyi has been richer economically than a paddy-rice monoculture village like Zeepinwea. However, as the market economy developed, the focus shifted to the production of highly profitable agricultural products, and sesame, pepper and garlic cultivation disappeared, leaving only onions. In Zeepinwea Village, irrigation was introduced in the 1990s to enable double cropping, so the gap in agricultural income between the two villages has narrowed.

These decades saw big changes in farming technologies. The farming villages in Upper Myanmar, including Thindaunggyi, began using winnowing machines in the socialist era. By contrast, the villages in the delta region, including Zeepinwea, were using a bamboo basket hung under the apex of a *sinn—a sinn* is made up of several metres of wood or bamboo in the shape of a triangular pyramid—and the winnowing machine was introduced only during the post-socialist military regime. Thindaunggyi was also much earlier than Zeepinwea in introducing walking tractors (cultivators), but Zeepinwea was five years ahead of Thindaunggyi in the use of threshers. The integrated process of carrying bundles of rice from the paddy fields to the compound, threshing by oxen, and winnowing with a winnowing machine had been a long-established practice in Thindaunggyi. So, it lagged behind Zeepinwea, which had to introduce the thresher to cope with dry-season rice cultivation. Later, both villages shifted to combine harvesters at about the same time, and the thresher quickly became useless.

In Thindaunggyi Village, agrarian reform based on the Land Nationalisation Act was never implemented, and *dadounghton* existed from the beginning only in name but not in reality. The price of farmland equivalent to *dadounghton* was already four to six times higher than the price of a yoke of draught cattle in 1987, because the profitability per acre was much higher than that of the rice monoculture areas in the Delta, even during the socialist period. Therefore, the inheritance method of giving *dadounghton* as it is to only one child, as was the case in Zeepinwea village, was not adopted in Thindaunggyi. Instead, divided succession became the norm. Although the steep rise in Thindaunggyi farmland prices was evident from the early stages of the transition to a market economy between 1987 and 1994, the purpose of buying farmland was, as also in Zeepinwea, to practise agriculture. From 1994 to 2013, paddy fields in the lower price range continued to be sold for agricultural purposes, such as onion cultivation, but paddy fields along the then National Highway were sold for non-agricultural purposes, such as for restaurants and gas stations. The price jumped to the equivalent of 200 years of agricultural profits.

Thus, although the two villages had some different patterns, they also experienced plenty of common phenomena that indicated de-agrarianisation. These included a decreased proportion of farm households in the village, a decline in the share of agricultural workers in total employment, a waning in the value of farmland as a means of agricultural production, a diminution in the importance of agriculture as a source of income, and an increase in the number of workers working outside the village.

Finally, the consumer life in both villages was changing along the same vector, albeit with some temporal differences. In this chapter, I highlighted four changes. First, in terms of transportation, motorcycles have been replacing bicycles since around the turn of the century. As of 2013, 14% of all households in Zeepinwea and 70% in Thindaunggyi owned a motorcycle. This has given rise to new professions such as motorcycle taxi and *tawlaji* transportation.

The second change in consumer life is electrification. The number of households with watt-hour metres, that is, access to electricity, in Zeepinwea was 0 in 1987, 7 out of 170 households in 1994, and 114 out of 316 in 2013, while in Thindaunggyi, the number was 4 out of 126 households in 1987, 27 out of 156 households in 1994, and 165 out of 236 in 2013. In both villages, electrification progressed in an off-and-on manner, starting with the richer households and leaving the poorer households out of the electrification process. In Myanmar villages in general, electricity is not supplied to all households at the same time, but watt-hour metres are installed gradually over a period of years, starting from the households that can afford the installation cost of materials and labour. This is one of the realities that represents rural Myanmar where economic disparity is large.

Third, along with electrification, the method of obtaining water for drinking, bathing, and washing has also changed. The traditional method of getting water for domestic use was to fetch it with buckets from ponds or public wells and to bring it to individual dwellings. Affluent households have been gradually shifting to digging their own wells and using electric pumps to lift the underground water. As a result, the maintenance and management of ponds and public wells, which had been the responsibility of the wealthy, must now be carried out by the relatively poor, and these facilities will increasingly deteriorate. Those who cannot afford individual wells are forced to rely on relations with well owners or to use water from rivers and irrigation canals. The shift from the common to the private is quite general in rural Myanmar, and the villagers respond to this trend by using the social networks that they have accumulated.

The fourth change has been the spread of smartphones, which leapfrogged fixed-line and mobile phones, similarly to how combine harvesters were introduced in Myanmar. Both fixed-line phones and SIM cards for mobile phones used to be prohibitively expensive for villagers at the regulated price set by the government. There was a sense that mobile phones were out of reach for ordinary people. However, in 2013, the price of SIM cards was lowered to less than one-hundredth of the former official price, which is less than the daily wage of an agricultural labourer, and inexpensive Chinese-made smartphones with these SIMs inserted quickly spread to rural areas. One can easily ask a nearby household for electricity to charge one's smartphones. Thus, around 2017, even households without electricity metres, such as daily farm workers and impoverished street vendors, also came to own smartphones. While there are large disparities between the rich and the poor in the diffusion of traditional infrastructure—such as transportation, electricity, and water—the disparities seem to be much smaller in the new infrastructure of information.

Chapter 5 described the prosperity of the village economy in Thindaunggyi Village, owing to the great development of the Shwetheindaw Paya, which is said to have been built in the eleventh century. When I first visited this village in 1987, the Paya was already famous for being built by King Anawrahta, the first king of the Bamar, but its fame was spread only in the local Kyaukse District at most. However, with the transition from the socialist period to the new capitalist military regime, military politicians and military cronies came to worship at the Paya, and the fame of the temple spread, starting from the Mandalay Region and expanding to the Sagaing Region, Bago Region, and Yangon Region. As the number of worshippers increased sharply, donations to the Paya skyrocketed, and the Board of Trustees of the Paya used these donations to construct a *gandakudi*, *danmayoung*, and *zayat*. This project had a backward linkage effect in Mandalay City and Kyaukse Town on the building constructors, Buddhist artisans, and goldsmiths.

What was brought to the village economy was a huge forward linkage effect. As a result of the Board of Trustees' decision, the agricultural land around the Paya was reclaimed one after another for the construction of not only religious facilities, such as a lecture hall and a resting place for worshippers, but also a worship route and a shopping street, and thus the gateway town expanded. These surrounding facilities provided new employment opportunities for the people of Thindaunggyi Village. A number of new occupations have been created that were not previously available, including Paya employees, prayer agents, *gadawbwe* dealers, *gadawbwe* disposers, staff of restaurants, souvenir shops, and various stalls, and flower sellers. These new jobs were almost exclusively occupied by the villagers of Thindaunggyi, but outsiders were also able to enter the new, less lucrative jobs, such as supplying bananas to *gadawbwe* shops, selling fried food at stands, peddling live sparrows, setting up street stalls outside the compound of the paya, and begging.

In 2016, the total value added generated from the donations to the Paya and the new occupations in which Thindaunggyi villagers were employed was about 1.5 billion kyats. This money could potentially employ all villagers over the age of 18 at double the minimum wage. The Paya created new non-agricultural employment opportunities for the villagers. It also made it possible for those non-farmers who had emerged as beneficiaries of the Paya to enter village politics, which had traditionally been dominated only by rich farmers. In many respects, the Paya promoted the de-agrarianisation of the village.

Chapter 6 discussed the relationship between people's migration and the transformation of the political and economic system in the rural areas of Myanmar's delta region, using the case of Zeepinwea Village. The discussion was divided into four parts. First, we examined the factors that make the number of households in a village increase or decrease. We divided the factors into "natural" factors, such as *oekhwe* (household division), and "social" factors, such as moving in and out of the village. The numbers of households moving out and households moving in were relatively equal during 1987–1994. Thus, the number of Zeepinwea Village households increased almost only through household division. There were "social" population movements, but in-migration and out-migration seem to have balanced each other, and thus the village population size did not change much. Both out-migration and in-migration ratios were higher for non-farm households than for farm households, indicating that non-farm households who were free from repressive agricultural policies were more likely to move. During 1994–2013, the number of households moving into the village greatly exceeded the number of households moving out, while the number of household divisions also increased, so that the total number of households in the village nearly doubled in these two decades. The propensities to move during this period were reversed, with farm households having a higher propensity to move than non-farm households. It seems that this relates to the relaxation of strict agricultural land administration policies.

Second, discussing the *out*-migrant households that left the village, we focused on the relationship between people's reasons for leaving the village, the occupations of their households, and their destinations. From 1987 to 1994, 3 out of the 6 farm households that left the village remained farmers, while 17 out of the 20 non-farm households that left continued their old occupation at their destinations. Only two households moved to Yangon city, while the rest moved to rural villages, more than three quarters of which were in Hlegu Township, which Zeepinwea Village belongs to. Such nearby rural-to-rural migration was a feature of this period. Between 1994 and 2013, a series of farm households moved their homes to the nearby town but continued farming on their original farmland in the village. They began commuting by motorcycles or staying in huts in the paddy fields only during the busy farming season. There was a tendency for relatively wealthy farm households to leave the village to pursue modern lifestyles and education for their children. This is also de-agrarianisation in the sense that they have left the agricultural village, even though they have not stopped farming. As for the out-migration of non-farm households, the agricultural labourer households—*sayinnga* and *kyaban*—made up the majority and continued to move within Hlegu Township without changing their occupation. Their trend of moving to nearby rural villages remained. However, compared to 1987–1994, the pace of out-migration of both farm and non-farm households clearly decreased. This is because with the development of the market economy and the expansion of Yangon city, the number of job opportunities in commuting distance from the village increased.

Third, we analysed the relationship between households moving *into* the village, their occupations, and sources of migration. From 1987 to 1994, the overwhelming majority of households that moved into the village were farm households and agricultural labourer households. Many of them also moved in from within Hlegu Township. Thus, the phenomenon of inter-rural migration in a vicinity was the same both for moving in and for moving out. However, this situation changed between 1994 and 2013. It became noticeable that farmers from far away—hundreds of kilometres away—purchased farmland in Zeepinwea Village and moved in. Local villagers who held cultivation rights over farmlands were disposing of their lands and becoming non-farmers, leading to more and more people from far away buying these lands and moving in to become farmers in Zeepinwea. In addition, agricultural labourer households often migrated into the village together with these newly arrived farmers, coming to work for the farmer. In households where the male agricultural labourer died, the wife often became a street vendor. Some urban residents bought farmland and residential land in the village not only for farming but also for speculation and recreational purposes, and some of them moved into the village. In addition to the Bamar and Karen ethnic groups that originally inhabited the village, other ethnic nationalities such as Mon, Shan, and Chin also moved into the village, making Zeepinwea an increasingly multi-ethnic village.

Fourth, we examined the migration of individuals apart from household migration. Due to survey constraints, I restricted my analysis only to the migration of the adult children of household heads who were resident in the village at the time of my earlier surveys. Both in 1987 and 1994, the offspring who left their parents' households tended to stay in the village or within Hlegu Township. In the socialist period and the early years of the following military regime, the migration of adult children was not from rural to urban areas but from village to village, as was the case with household migration. By 2013, the situation was different: the adult children of non-farm households were increasingly moving out of Hlegu Township, including to Yangon city. Their motivation for moving out also changed, from social mobility due to marriage to an economic purpose. However, when we calculate the out-migration ratio—the ratio of the number of adult children who left the village to the number of all adult children who were living in the village after having separated from their parents' home—the ratio was the smallest in 2013. The number of people engaged in agriculture, both of farm households and of agricultural labourer households, has decreased, so that the number of people who remain in the village and do agriculture has declined sharply. The increase in the number of villagers working in the non-farm sector, such as peddlers, street vendors, small shopkeepers, drivers of "side-cars" (bicycle taxis), motorbike taxis and trucks, and cargo handlers, as well as young villagers commuting to factories and commercial facilities in and around Yangon, is the reason for the decrease in the out-migration ratio, despite the deepening de-agrarianisation.

Although de-agrarianisation has been steadily progressing in both Thindaunggyi and Zeepinwea villages, the spatial relocation—that is, population movement by leaving villages—is not as pronounced as I observed in Chin State (Takahashi, 2007: 418–419), Shan State (Takahashi, 2018: 159–160) and Karen State (Takahashi, 2018: 104–107). However, various de-agrarianisation phenomena defined in Chap. 2—such as occupational adjustment, income-earning reorientation, transformation of social identification, decline in the relative value of farmland in agriculture, increase in the socioeconomic status of non-farm workers, and urbanisation of the rural land-scape—have deepened in both villages. These socio-economic transformations in both villages represent the major aspects of de-agrarianisation that are occurring in various forms across rural Myanmar.

In Chap. 7, I developed a theory of Myanmar village society, asking what kind of society Myanmar villages are, and more specifically, what kind of cohesion they have and where this cohesion derives from. I did this in three steps. First, based on previous studies of Japan, Thailand, and Malaysia, I organised the scholarly theories on village society into two genealogies: "objective group theories" and "subjective cognition theories". I combined these two often conflicting genealogies, in order to create a theoretical framework for understanding Myanmar village society.

Second, I summarised the "objective group" theories. The first was the "theory of the accumulation of groups", which emphasises the accumulation of administrative, economic, religious, blood, neighbourhood and other groups, as well as their autonomy and social unity in the Japanese villages. The second was the "theory of the household alliance", in which the smallest living group, the household, is federated to form a Japanese *kumi* or *dōzoku*, and several of these are aggregated to form a village. These two theories consider the Japanese village as an accumulation of groups and/or organisations. These theories have been applied and extended to theories on Thai village societies in the form of the "multi-household compound theory" and the "proximity household group theory". I have found multi-household compounds and proximity household groups in many villages in Myanmar and discussed the differences between them and those in Thailand in this chapter.

Third, I compared Japanese and Myanmar villages from the perspective of "subjective cognition" theories, which examine how individual villagers (the *ego*s) perceive themselves within the groups or organisations of the village. In the Japanese village, there is an autonomous social consciousness that can be called the "village spirit" which configures the will and relationships of individuals. Individuals recognise themselves on the basis of the village as a unit. This is the "village spirit theory". In contrast, the "family circle theory", which has been advocated in Malaysian and Thai village studies emphasises the accumulation of dyadic relationships centred on the self. This theory also applies to the Myanmar villagers, who recognise themselves in one-to-one dyadic relationship between *ego* and others. Households and villages merely provide a "place" where self-centred dyadic networks are formed. The village does not mould the will and the relationships of individuals.

This chapter concluded with my theory of Myanmar village society, elucidating the principles of how groups and organisations are formed in rural Myanmar, for which I combined "objective group theories" and "subjective cognition theories". In Myanmar villages, multi-household compounds are repeatedly formed and divided at various junctures, such as marriage, division of households and death of parents, creating "proximity household groups" in various parts of the village. The dyadic networks, underpinned by the "logic of interpersonal relationships"—which people simulate in the Burmese language by using the *ego*'s kinship names—expand to include households, multi-household compounds, and proximity household groups. These dyadic networks become more extensive and complex with intra-village marriages and movements of households within the village. These networks are strengthened by frequent mutual visits between households and the "logic of frequent contact" at various gatherings. This deepens the sense of mutual closeness and trust. Since the repetition of "frequent contacts" is a dependent variable of physical distance, the village is formed as a "place" for frequent contacts. This I defined as the "logic of frequent contacts". In this way, the village is recognised as a sphere of "relatives of the place" through the "logic of frequent contacts", which is an extension of the "logic of interpersonal relationship". Groups and organisations are formed when various "catalysts" act on such cumulative dyadic relationships. Various "things and affairs" can be catalysts, ranging from concrete things such as water, land, funerals, fires, or thieves to abstract things such as history, coercion, or leadership. In other words, groups and organisations are positioned as part of a cycle in which dyadic relations based on the logic of interpersonal relationships are accumulated through the logic of frequent contacts within a certain territory, such as a village, and then catalysts from inside and outside of the village act to form groups and organisations with specific purposes, which in turn strengthen the dyadic relations. However, since these groups and organisations are based on personal ties, if the dyadic relationships, especially with the leader, become strained, or if the "catalyst" becomes less attractive, individuals will easily leave the group or organisation. Furthermore, if the number of seceders increases, the group or organisation itself will become insignificant and follow the path to extinction. The coercive rule of socialist and military regimes, as well as microfinance and community forestry promoted by national and international organisations and NGOs, can easily be organised in a very short time on the basis of the accumulation of a close dyadic network within the village, if there are catalysts such as coercion, guidance, funds, or supervisors. However, if the catalyst ceases to function, the organisation can easily weaken and eventually disappear in a short period of time. Thus, Myanmar's village organisations are like bubbles that are easily created and tend to disappear quickly.

In Chap. 8, I discussed the "absence of a village collective (*kyōdōtai*)" in rural Myanmar. In the previous chapter, I had not distinguished between community and collective. In this chapter, after confining a collective to a "village collective" and a community to a "local community", I distinguished between community and collective to highlight the characteristics of Myanmar village society in comparison with Japanese village society. First, as an analytical framework, I outlined the contrast between community and collective in terms of historicity, totality, individuality, spontaneity, relationships, assistance, and openness. Next, I compared Japanese and Myanmar villages in terms of the groups and organisations for production, such as for land and water management, taxation in kind, cooperatives, common land, and labour exchange; groups and organisations for daily life, such as for the village fund, mutual financing associations, congratulation and condolence associations, fire brigades, and women's associations; and groups and organisations for religion, such as for Buddhism and spirit worship. I then explored the differences between the two countries through an analytical framework of contrasts between community and collective, leading to the conclusion that the Japanese village is a "collective of production (and life)" and the Myanmar village is a "community of life" (it lacks the communal nature of production). The absence of a village collective means that mutual and communal surveillance through close horizontal ties cannot function. Thus, strong-arm rule becomes undermined and weakened on the ground level, paradoxically allowing for a long-lasting rigid policy. The villagers in Myanmar were able to avoid the "collective failure" that is common in Japanese villages, and could live relatively free and autonomous lives even under very repressive regimes. The villages of Myanmar have self-sustaining "individuals" who do not relate to the dichotomy of the independent "individuals" of Western "modern society" *versus* Asia where the establishment of civil society was delayed due to the absence of such "individuals".

Finally, how should we think about the relationship between the socio-economic transformation—the de-agrarianisation—of rural Myanmar (depicted in Chaps. 3–6) and the immutable core—the "absence of collective"—of Myanmar rural society (discussed in Chaps. 7 and 8)? Since the "absence of collective" preceded de-agrarianisation, it is not the case that de-agrarianisation promoted the loosening of the collectivity. Moreover, since de-agrarianisation has progressed even in villages where collectives are (or were) strong, as in Japan, we cannot assume that the absence of collectives is a trigger for de-agrarianisation. In other words, the two are unrelated at the starting point. However, it is possible that de-agrarianisation is faster in the absence of the constraints of the collective. Some catalysts for creating village groups and organisations may become less effective because the network of dyadic relationships that has accumulated within the village has also spread outside the village. Nonetheless, de-agrarianisation and the absence of collective do not seem to be closely related in the recent socioeconomic history of Myanmar. This is because the absence of collective is stipulated by the historical background or the superstructure, but de-agrarianisation mirrors the changes in the base. Nevertheless, since both are historical processes, they do intersect and strongly influence each other somewhere along the time axis. Currently, the groups and organisations formed in the cities by people who left their villages in the process of de-agrarianisation are likely based on networks of dyadic relationships. Thus, at least in their initial stage, such groups and organisations are likely to reflect the structure of rural communities.

Epilogue

As promised in the preface, I should say something about trends in Myanmar's rural areas since the catastrophe of February 2021.

The peasants' "everyday resistance" was the background to the 1988 pro-democracy movement. The farmers, who were forced to offer their produce to the state at low prices, resisted by means of *nalehmu*—bribing officials to silently accept paddy mixed with rubbish and pebbles or to bulk up the weighing—which led to the abolition of the procurement system in 1987. This triggered inflation in urban areas, which developed into the struggle for democracy the following year. The mass movement of citizens for democratisation gained momentum, similarly to the current post-coup situation, but did not extend beyond the urban movement. Although there were some anti-government movements in rural areas, such as refusal of procurements and raids on agricultural establishments, they were sporadic and there was little linkage with urban areas. At that time, the military successfully carried out the coup by overrunning the urban areas. The military regime, which emerged after the armed suppression of the democratisation movement, suppressed and pacified the anti-military movement in rural areas by relaxing the system whereby farmers had to offer agricultural products to the state at low prices and by increasing the amount that farmers could freely sell in the market. The following rise in agricultural commodity prices, which led to favourable agricultural terms of trade and temporary and relative rural affluence, did not help the anti-military movement in rural areas, where 75% of the total population lived at the time.

In contrast, the current anti-military movement has spread far and wide into rural areas. At the turn of the twenty-first century, Chinese motorbikes began to proliferate in villages. Since the Thein Sein government's liberalisation policy that began in 2011, smartphones have become widespread in rural areas, and car and motorcycle owners have also increased rapidly. Villagers have been able to easily obtain national and international information and keep in touch with people in the cities. In addition, the number of universities has increased from about 20 in 1988 to 168 in 2015, and many university graduates and university students can now be found in the village,

A. Takahashi, *Regime Changes and Socio-economic History of Rural Myanmar, 1986–2019*, Studies in Economic History,
https://doi.org/10.1007/978-981-99-3272-6

whereas in the past there were very few. Thus, villagers have kept in touch with urban populations by telephone and social networking sites, used modern means of transport and joined the urban anti-military movement in droves. The core of this group were university graduates and current university students coming from or living in the village. It can be argued that the development of communication and transport networks expanded the network between urban and rural areas, and that the movement was catalysed by students from the villages who had received higher education.

These are only the means and processes by which the villagers are linked to the anti-military movement, but more important would be their motives. All agricultural land in Myanmar is state-owned, and the former military regime confiscated agricultural land for next to nothing in compensation, using this system as a means of intimidation to prevent the free use and disposal of agricultural land. This was changed by the 2012 Farmland Law, which guarantees the right to cultivate farmland and liberalises the leasing and sale of the right. Furthermore, in 2018, the Land Acquisition, Resettlement and Rehabilitation Law was enacted to ensure that adequate reparation and compensation is provided for land expropriation. Also in 2012, the Ward or Village Tract Administration Law came into force, allowing villagers to vote for the administrative head of their village ward, albeit indirectly, and since 2016 they could elect the head more directly. This experience of liberalisation and democratisation is what motivates villagers to support the anti-military movement *en masse*. It could be argued that liberalisation and democratisation are the catalysts.

Meanwhile, the income gap between rural and urban areas has been widening. Using the 1983 and 2014 population censuses and gross domestic product statistics, we can divide the agricultural sector's share of GDP by the share of agricultural workers in each year. This gives 63.5% in 1983 and 39.2% in 2014. In other words, in 1983, the average income of agricultural sector workers was around two-thirds of the average income of all workers, but by 2014 it was around two-fifths. Unless a regime's agricultural and rural policies, whether military-dominated or democratic, aim and achieve democratisation politically and liberalisation and inequality reduction economically, it will not have the support of the villagers. If so, everyday and tacit resistance will continue, even if there is no longer explicit resistance.

Bibliography

[English Literature]

Adas, M. (1974). *The Burma delta: Economic development and social change on an Asian rice frontier, 1852–1941*. University of Wisconsin Press.
Bryceson, D. F. & Jamal, V. (1997). *Farewell to farms: De-agrarianisation and employment in Africa. Research Series No.1997/10*. Ashgate.
Central Statistical Organisation (CSO, Myanmar). *Statistical yearbook*. Each year edition.
Central Statistical Organisation. *Agricultural statistics*. Each year edition.
Embree, J. F. (1939). *Suye Mura: A Japanese village*. University of Chicago Press.
Embree, J. F. (1950). Thailand—A loosely structured social system. *American Anthropologist, 52*(12), 181–193.
Furnivall, J. S. (1957). *An introduction to the political economy of Burma* (3rd ed.). People's Literature Committee & House.
Government of India. (1926). *The Burma village manual*. Superintendent Government Printing and Stationery.
Government of India. *Census of India, Burma. 1891, 1901, 1911, 1921, 1931*. Office of the Superintendent of Government Printing, Burma.
Government of the Union of Myanmar. (2016). *Formulation and operationalization of national action plan for poverty alleviation and rural development through agriculture (NAPA) (working paper-7): Rural cooperative*. Food and Agriculture Organization of the United Nations.
Hillery, G. A., Jr. (1955). Definition of community: Areas of agreement. *Rural Sociology, 20*(2), 111–123.
Luce, G. H. (1959a). Geography of Burma under the Pagan Dynasty. *Journal of the Burma Research Society, 42*(1), 32–51.
Luce, G. H. (1959b). Old Kyaukse and the coming of the Burmans. *Journal of the Burma Research Society, 42*(1), 75–112.
Luce, G. H. (1969). *Old Burma-early Pagán Vol.1 text*. J. J. Augustin Publisher.
MacIver, R. M. (1920). *Community: A sociological study*. Macmillan.
MacIver, R. M., & Page, C. H. (1950). *Society: An introductory analysis*. Macmillan.
Nash, M. (1965). *The golden road to modernity: Village life in contemporary Burma*. John Wiley & Sons.
Piker, S. (1969). 'Loose structure' and the analysis of Thai social organization. In H.-D. Evers (Ed.), *Loosely structured social systems: Thailand in comparative perspective* (pp. 61–76). Yale University, Southeast Asian Studies.

A. Takahashi, *Regime Changes and Socio-economic History of Rural Myanmar, 1986–2019*, Studies in Economic History,
https://doi.org/10.1007/978-981-99-3272-6

Republic of the Union of Myanmar, Ministry of Immigration and Population. (2015). *The 2014 Myanmar population and housing census*. Department of Population.

Rigg, J. (2001). *More than the soil: Rural change in Southeast Asia*. Pearson Education.

Scott, J. C. (1998). *Seeing like a state: How certain schemes to improve the human condition have failed*. Yale University Press.

Shigetomi, S. (1992). From 'loosely' to 'tightly' structured social organization: The changing aspects of cooperation and village community in Rural Thailand. *Developing Economies, 30*(2), 154–178.

Socialist Republic of the Union of Burma, Ministry of Home & Religious Affairs. (1986). *1983 Burma population census*. Immigration and Manpower Department.

Stewart, J. A. (1925). *Burma Gazetteer, Kyaukse District. Volume A, B*. Superintendent Government Printing and Stationery.

Than, M., & Nishizawa, N. (1990). Agricultural policy reforms and agricultural development in Myanmar. In M. Than & J.L.H. Tan (Eds.), *Myanmar dilemmas and options: The challenge of economic transition in the 1990s* (pp. 89–116). Institute of Southeast Asian Studies.

The Burma Research Group. (1987). *Burma and Japan: Basic studies on their cultural and social structure*. Burma Research Group.

Taylor, R. H. (1987). *The state in Burma*. C. Hurst & Company.

Tönnies, F. (2001). *Community and civil society* (J. Harris & M. Hollis, Trans.). Cambridge University Press (Original work published 1887)

United Nations. (2022). *2021 Demographic yearbook*. United Nations Publication.

University of Rangoon. (1933). *Inscriptions of Burma, Portfolio I, 493–599 B.E. (1131–1237 A.D.)*. Oxford University Press.

[Burmese Literature]

Bahou lounjounyêi hnìn ou'chou'yêi komiti (BaLaKa, Central Security and Administration Committee). (1973). *cêiywaou'sù lounjounyêi hnìn ou'chou'yêi komiti phwèsîboun, lou'ngântawun, lou'paingwìn hnìn ahtau'ahtâpyùmì ùbadei hnìn lou'ngânhsethwehmûsani' (Organisation, duties and authorities, relevant laws and regulations, and methods of communication of the village tract security and administration committee)*. bahou lounjounyêi hnìn ou'chou'yêi komiti.

Myanmà hsousheli' lânzin pati pati sîyôunyêi bahou komiti htanàjou' (MaSaLa, Burma (Myanmar) Socialist Programme Party Central Organising Committee Headquarter). (1971a). *myanmà leyamyei thamâin I, II (Myanmar Farmland History I, II)*. Myanmà hsousheli' lânzin pati (MaSaLa).

Myanmà hsousheli' lânzin pati pati sîyôunyêi bahou komiti htanàjou' (MaSaLa, Burma (Myanmar) Socialist Programme Party Central Organising Committee Headquarter). (1971b). *myanmà hsousheli' lânzin pati ì taundhu ledhamâ yêiya ahma' 3 (Farmers' Affairs of the Burma Socialist Programme Party, Vol. 3)*. Myanmà hsousheli' lânzin pati.

Myanmà hsousheli' lânzin pati pati sîyôunyêi bahou komiti htanàjou' (MaSaLa, Burma (Myanmar) Socialist Programme Party Central Organising Committee Headquarter). (1974). *myanma nain-ngan thàmàwàyàmà atwê I, II (Cooperatives in Myanmar, Vols 1, 2)*. Myanmà hsousheli' lânzin pati.

Myanmà hsousheli' lânzin pati pati sîyôunyêi bahou komiti htanàjou' (MaSaLa, Burma (Myanmar) Socialist Programme Party Central Organising Committee Headquarter). (1985). *myanmà hsousheli' lânzin pati ou'kahtajî ì khi'pyâun tauhlanyêi thamâinwin mèingûn bâunjou' (Collection of Speeches on the History of the Social Revolution by the Chairman of the Burma Socialist Programme Party)*. Myanmà hsousheli' lânzin pati.

Myanmà hsousheli' lânzin pati pati sîyôunyêi bahou komiti htanàjou' (MaSaLa, Burma (Myanmar) Socialist Programme Party Central Organising Committee Headquarter). (1987). *myanma nainngan zabâ sai'pyôu htou'lou' yâunhcàhmù (Paddy Rice Production and Distribution in Myanmar)*. Myanmà hsousheli' lânzin pati.

Nyunt, N. (2002). *Maha shweitheindo mya'swa phayâ thamâin (History of the Great Shwetheindaw Paya)*. Thânhtai' yadana pounhnei'tai'.

Pyancâyêi htanà (Ministry of Information). (1964a). *bamà taundhu ledhamâ khi'pâun hswêinwêibwê thamâin asà ôundô hswêinwêibwê (Ondaw Conference as a First Landmark Meeting in the History of Burmese Farmers)*. Pyancâyêi htanà (Ministry of Information).

Pyancâyêi htanà (Ministry of Information). (1964b). *Pou'pâ hswêinwêibwè (Popa Conference)*. Sapebei'man pounhnei'tai' (Sapebei'man Printing Office).

Pyidaunzù myanma nainngan tohlanyêi asôuyà (Revolutionary Government of the Union of Burma). (1966). *1953 kùhni' leyamyei nainnganbain pyùlou'yêi e'ùbadei (Land Nationalisation Act of 1953)*. Bahou pounhnei'tai' (Central Printing Department).

Pyidaunzù myanma nainngan tohlanyêi asôuyà bahou myeiya komiti (BaMaKa, Central Agricultural Land Committee, Revolutionary Government of the Union of Burma). (1964). *thîzâ hcàhâyêi hnìn taundhu ledhamâ ahkwìnayêi kagwedhì ùbadeimyâ shîndân (Commentary on Tenancy Act and Protection of Farmers' Rights Act)*. Tohlanyêi asôuyà bahou myeiya komiti (Central Agricultural Land Committee, Revolutionary Government).

Pyidaunzù myanma nainngan tohlanyêi asôuyà bahou myeiya komiti (BaMaKa, Central Agricultural Land Committee, Revolutionary Government of the Union of Burma). (1972). *bahou myeiya komiti hnyuncâje'myâ (Collection of Directives of the Central Agricultural Land Committee)*. Zamani pounhnei'tai' (Zamani Publishing).

Pyidaunzù myanma nainngan tohlanyêi asôuyà bahou myeiya komiti (BaMaKa, Central Agricultural Land Committee, Revolutionary Government of the Union of Burma). (1973). *taundhu ledhamâdâin thìthìndhì myeiyakei'sàhnìn pa'the'dô ache'myâ thindân sazaun (Educational Pamphlet on Agrarian Issues that Every Farmer Should Know)*. Bahou myeiya komiti (Central Agricultural Land Committee).

Pyidaunzù myanma nainngando asôuyà leyasai'pyôyêi hnìn thi'tôyêi wunjî htanà (Ministry of Agriculture and Forestry, Government of the Union of Burma). (1948). *1948 kùhni' leyamyei nainnganbain pyùlou'yêi e'ùbadei (Land Nationalisation Act of 1948)*. Pyidaunzù myanma nainngando asôuyà sapounhnei'tai' (Union of Burma, Government Printing Department).

Pyidaunzù myanma nainngando nyeinwu' pipyâhmù tihsau'yêiaphwèyôun (NaWaTa, Secretariat of the State Law and Order Restoration Council of the Union of Myanmar). (1989). *cêiywaou'sù nyeinwu' pipyâhmù tihsau'yêiaphwèmyâ ì lou'ngântawunmyâ hnìn lou'ngânhsaunywe'hmùsani' (Responsibilities and Practices of the Activities of the Village Tract Law and Order Reconstruction Council)*. Myanma nainngando nyeinwu' pipyâhmù tihsau'yêiaphwèyôun.

Pyidêyêiwunjîhtanà ahtweidwei ou'chou' yêi ûsîhtanà (htwei ou', General Administration Department, Ministry of Home Affairs). (1977). *cêile' deithà phùnphyôuyêi yanbounngwei hnìn pa'the'ywèi lou'ngânbâin hnìn ngweisayînbâin hsainya lou'htôunlou'nyî (Procedures on Activities and Accounting Related to the Rural Development Fund)*. Pyidêyêiwunjîhtanà.

Pyidêyêiwunjîhtanà ahtweidwei ou'chou' yêi ûsîhtanà (htwei ou', General Administration Department, Ministry of Home Affairs). (1995). *myòu hnìn cêiywa e'ùbadei le'swêsaun (Instructions on the Town and Village Act)*. Pyidêyêiwunjîhtanà.

Sandáthìrì. (1956). *shweitheindo (9) khayain thamâin hnìn thanbou'dei pânbâunsoun phayâshìkhôu thamâin (Shwetheindaw 9 Kayain and the History of Obeisance to the Paya with Full Sambodhi)*. Htândôcâun.

Thein, L., & Tun, A. Z. (2019). Nainnganbain sîbwâyêi lou'ngân kôuhkù ca' biliyan 260co ashôun pomi. (Nine state-owned enterprises with losses in excess of 260 billion Kyats.) *7 Day Daily*. August 22. https://www.7daydaily.com/story/164472

[Japanese Literature]

Aruga, K. (1956). Sonraku kyōdōtai to ie (Village Collectives and Households). In Sonraku Shakai Kenkyūkai (Village Society Research Group) (Ed.), *Sonraku kyōdōtai no kōzō bunseki (Structural analysis of village collectives)* (pp. 21–49). Jichōsha.

Aruga, K. (1969). Toshi-shakaigaku no kadai (Issues of Urban Sociology), (Aruga Kizaemon chosakushū VIII). In *Minzokugaku·shakaigaku hōhōron (Methodologies of folklore and sociology)* (pp. 151–203). Miraisha.

Aruga, K. (1971). Sonraku shakai no riron (Theory of Village Societies), (Aruga Kizaemon chosakushū X). In *Dōzoku to sonraku (Clans and villages)* (pp. 79–179). Miraisha.

Ba Maw. (1973). *Biruma no yoake (Breakthrough in Burma)* (Y. Yokobori, Trans.). Taiyo Shuppan (Original work published 1968).

Fujiki, H. (2010). *Chūsei minshū no sekai—Mura no seikatsu to okite (The world of the medieval peoples: Village life and rules).* Iwanami Shoten.

Fukutake, T. (1956). Gendai nihon ni okeru sonraku kyōdōtai no sonzai keitai (Existence forms of village collectives in contemporary Japan), In Sonraku Shakai Kenkyūkai (Village Society Research Group) (Ed.), *Sonraku kyōdōtai no kōzō bunseki (Structural analysis of village collectives)* (pp. 1–20). Jichōsha.

Fukutake, T. (1978). *Nihon no nōson, dai 2 han (Japanese Villages, second edition).* Tokyo Daigaku Shuppankai.

Furushima, T. (1963). *Kyōdōtai no kenkyū (Studies of collectives)*, (Furushima Toshio chosakushu dai 7 kan). Sanyosha.

Goto, Y. (1985). Kenichichō (Cadastral survey book). In *Kokushi daijiten 6 (Dictionary of national history Vol. 6)* (pp. 197–198). Yoshikawakobunkan.

Hiroi, Y. (2009). *Komyunitī o toinaosu—Tsunagari · toshi · nihonshakai no mirai (Reconsidering communities: Connections, cities, the future of Japanese society).* Chikumashobo.

Horikoshi, H. (1979). *Mura no nakade mura o kangaeru (Considering villages in a village).* Nipponhoso Shuppankyokai.

Ito, T. (2013). Konbaun ōchō zenki ni okeru sonraku komyunitī ni tsuite (About the Village Communities in the Early Konbaung Dynasty). In B*ungaku ronsō (Literary Symposium)* (Aichi Daigaku Bungakusha) (Vol. 148, pp. 1–30).

Iwatani, N. (2004). Shohyō (Book review): Uchiyama, Masao. Gendai chūgoku nōson to 'kyōdōtai'—Tenkanki chūgoku kahoku nōson ni okeru shakai kōzō to nōmin (Modern Chinese villages and 'collectives': The social structure and farmers of the villages in North China at the turning point). *Ajia Keizai (Asian Economy)*, *45*(1), 65–70.

Izumida, Y. (1992). Nōson kinyū no hatten to kaitengata chochiku shinyōkō (ROSCAs)—Nihon ni okeru kō no yakuwari (Development of the rural finance and rotating saving and credit associations (ROSCAs): The roles of mutual financing associations in Japan). *Utsunomiya Daigaku Nōgakubu Gakujutsu Hōkoku (Bulletin of the Faculty of Agriculture, Utsunomiya University)*, *15*(1), 1–18.

Kida, M. (1967). *Nippon buraku (A Japanese Village), (Iwanami shinsho 623).* Iwanami Shoten.

Kimura, M. (1980). *Kinsei no mura (Villages of Early Modern Period), (Kyoikusha rekishi shinsho 105).* Kyoikusha.

Kitahara, A. (1990). *Tai nōson shakairon (Theory of Thai Rural Societies).* Keiso Shobo.

Klimko, G. N. (1966). *Dokuritsu Biruma no nōgyō mondai (Agricultural problems in independent Burma)* (I. Nakayama, Trans.). Ajia Keizai Kenkyujo (Original work published 1964)

Kotani, H. (1982). *Kyōdōtai to kindai (Communities and modernity).* Aoki Shoten.

Kuchiba, M. & Takemura, T. (1983). 'Yashikichi kyōjū shūdan' saikō—Tōhoku Tai-Dondēn mura no tsuiseki chōsa (chūkan hōkoku) (A reconsideration of "multihousehold compound": In Don Daeng Village, Northeast Thailand (Interim Report). *Tōnan ajia kenkyū (Japanese Journal of Southeast Asian Studies)*, *21*(3), 288–308.

Kudo, T. (2015). Posuto gunsei no Myanmā—Kaikaku wa dokomade susunda ka (Myanmar in the Post-Military Regime: How far have the reforms progressed?) In T. Kudo (Ed.), *Posuto gunsei no Myanmā—Kaikaku no jitsuzō (Myanmar in the post-military regime: The realities of the reforms)* (pp. 1–23). Ajia Keizai Kenkyujo.

Kuramoto, R. (2014). *Sezoku wo ikiru shukkesha tachi—Jōzabukkyōto shakai Myanmā ni okeru shukke seikatsu no minzokushi (The ordained living in the secular world: Ethnography of ordained lives in Myanmar, a Theravada Buddhist society)*. Hozokan.

Maniwa, M. (1978). *Kyōdōtai no shakaigaku: Ningensei no jubaku to kaihō (Sociology of collectives: The curse and liberation of human nature)*. Sekaishisosha.

Miho, M. (1994). Kyōdōtai to mura—Nihongo no naka no komyunitī to kyōdōtai (Collectives and villages: Communities and collectives in the Japanese language). *Shakai Kagaku Jānaru (The Journal of Social Science), 32*, 43–56.

Mizuno, K. (1981). *Tai nōson no shakai soshiki (Social organizations of the villages in Thailand)*. Sobunsha.

Murata, N. (1978). *Mura wa horobu (Village will be collapsed)*. Nihon Keizai Hyouronsha.

Nagashima, T. (1997). Otsuka Hisao no kyōdōtairon (Otsuka Hisao's theory of collectives). In Y. Iwamoto & K. Kunikata (Eds.), *Ie to kyōdōtai—Nichiō hikaku no shiten kara (Household and collective: A comparative perspective on Europe and Japan)* (pp. 60–76). Hosei Daigaku Shuppankyoku.

Noda, K. (1998). Senzenki nōka shōkumiai no keitai to kinō: Nihon nōgyō · nōson ni okeru 'ko to shūdan' no rekishiteki bunseki (Configuration and function of farmers' small associations in the pre-war period: Historical analysis of 'individuals and groups' in Japanese agriculture and villages). *Kyoto Daigaku Seibutsu Shigen Keizai Kenkyū (The Natural Resource Economic Review, Kyoto University), 4*, 1–20.

Nōgyōkyōdōkumiai · Hokkaido Nōgyōkyōdōkumiai Chūōkai (JA: Japan Agricultural Cooperatives-JA Hokkaido Central Association). (2016). *JA no shikumi—Kyōdōkumiai o Manabu (How JA works: Learn about cooperatives)*. Nōgyōkyōdōkumiai · Hokkaido Nōgyōkyōdōkumiai Chūōkai

Ogasawara, S. (1976). Amerika shakaigakushi no issetsu—R. M. MacIver Kenkyū (A view of the history of American sociology: A study on R. M. MacIver). *Nara Kyōiku Daigaku kiyō (Bulletin of Nara University of Education) 25*(1), 101–120.

Ogiwara, H., Wada, H., & Ikuta, S. (1973). *Tōnan Ajia Gendaishi IV Biruma · Tai (Contemporary history of Southeast Asia 4: Burma and Thailand), Sekai Gendaishi 8 (Modern World History 8)*. Yamakawa Shuppansha.

Otsuka, H. (1955). *Kyōdōtai no kiso riron (Basic theory of collectives)*. Iwanami Shoten.

Saito, H. (1989). *Nōgyō mondai no tenkai to jichi sonraku (Development of agricultural issues and autonomous villages)*. Nihon Keizai Hyoronsha.

Saito, K. (1963). Biruma no bēkokukeizai to nōsanbutsu hanbaichō (Rice economy and agricultural marketing board in Burma). *Ajia Keizai (Asian Economy), 4*(8), 2–22.

Saito, T. (1980). Shimo-Biruma bēsakuson no nōgyō rōdōsha—Chungarē-mura ni okreru sono jittai (Agricultural labourers in a rice cultivating village, Lower Burma: The actual situation in Kyungale Village). *Ajia Keizai (Asian Economy), 21*(11), 76–91.

Saito, T. (1982). Biruma ni okeru nōgyō rōdōsha kaisō no keisei (The formation of an agricultural labourer class in Burma). In T. Takigawa (Ed.), *Tōnan Ajia nōson no teishotoku kaisō (Low-income strata in rural Southeast Asia)* (pp. 235–264). Ajia Keizai Kenkyujo.

Saito, T. (1986). Birumashiki shakaishugika no nōson shakai (Rural society under Burmese Socialism). In Ajia Teikaihatsu Chiiki Nōgyō Mondai Kenkyūkai (Study Group on Agricultural Problems in Underdeveloped Areas in Asia) (Ed.), *Daisan-sekai nōgyō no henbō (Transformation of Third World Agriculture)* (pp. 123–151). Keiso Shobo.

Saito, T. (2008). *Tōnan Ajia no nōson shakai (Rural society in Southeast Asia)*. Yamakawa Shuppansha.

Sato, J. (1962). *Sekai no kome 9: Biruma no kome (Rice of the world Vol. 9: Rice of Burma)*, (Shōhin keizai sōsho dai 19 go). Nōrin-suisangyō Seisansei Kōjō Kaigi.

Shigetomi, S. (1996). *Tai nōson no kaihatsu to jūmin soshiki (Village organization for rural development in Thailand)*. Ajia Keizai Kenkyujo.

Shimizu, K. (1972). Tanomoshi ni tsuite—sono rekishiteki na keika to genzai no jōtai (About mutual financing association: Its historical course and current situation). *Nara Kyōiku Daigaku Kiyō (bulletin of Nara University of Education), 21*(1), 177–191.

Suzuki, E. (1968). *Nihon nōson shakaigaku genri jo ·ge (Principles of Japanese rural sociology Vol. 1, 2)*, (Suzuki Eitaro chosakushū dai 1,2 kan). Miraisha (Original work published 1940)

Tachimoto, N. (2000). *Kazokuken to chiiki kenkū (Family circle and area studies)*. Kyoto Daigaku Gakujutsu Shuppankai.

Takahashi, A. (1988). Kome no kuni Biruma ni asu wa aruka: Dokuji no shakaishugi wo hatan saseta nōgyō no shippai (Is there a tomorrow for Burma, the land of rice?: Agricultural failure that ruined its own socialism). *Ekonomisuto (economist), 66*(50), 68–73.

Takahashi, A. (1991). Kami-Biruma kangaison ni okeru nōchi hoyū to nōsanbutsu no shōhinka—Shimo-Biruma nōson tono hikaku (Farmland tenure and commodification of agricultural products in an irrigated village in Upper Burma: Comparison with a village in Lower Burma). In H. Umehara (Ed.), *Tōnan Ajia no tochi seido to nōgyō henka (Agrarian systems and agricultural changes in Southeast Asia)* (pp.149–188). Ajia Keizai Kenkyujo.

Takahashi, A. (1992). *Biruma deruta no beisakuson—'Shakaishugi' taiseika no nōson keizai (A rice village in the Burma delta: Village economy under the rule of 'socialism')*. Ajia Keizai Kenkyujo.

Takahashi, A. (1993). Kami-Biruma ·Chausē chihō no kasen kangai to nōgyō (Canal irrigation and agriculture in Kyaukse District of Upper Burma). *Ajia Keizai (Asian Economy), 34*(12), 33–64.

Takahashi, A. (1995). Kami-Biruma nōson no nōgaishūgyō to kaisō kōzō—Shakaishugi makki no ichi kangaison o jirei to shite (Off-farm employment and socio-economic strata in a rural village in Upper Burma: A case study of an irrigated village in the late socialist period). In K. Mizuno (Ed.), *Tōnan Ajia nōson no shūgyō kōzō (Employment structure in rural Southeast Asia)* (pp. 51–78). Ajia Keizai Kenkyujo.

Takahashi, A. (1997). Myanmā ni okeru nōsonkan setai idō to shokugyō kaiso (Rural-to-rural household migrations and occupational hierarchy in Myanmar). *Ajia Keizai (Asian Economy), 38*(11), 2–24.

Takahashi, A. (1998). Biruma ni okeru nōchi hōsei no tenkai to nōmin no 'shoyūken'—Nōchi kokuyūkahō to Nēwin no 'nōchi seido kakumei' o chūshin ni (Agricultural land policy and the "tenure" of farmers in Burma during the "U Nu" and "Ne Win" Era: Focusing on the land nationalisation act and the 'revolution in the agrarian system'). In K. Mizuno (Ed.), *Tōnan Ajia nōgyō hatten no shutai to soshiki—Kindai Nihon tono hikaku kara (Actors and organisations of rural development in Southeast Asia: In comparison with the Japanese case)* (pp. 29–60). Ajia Keizai Kenkyujo.

Takahashi, A. (1999). Myanmā—Konnan na sijō keizai eno ikō (Myanmar: Difficult transition to a market economy). In Y. Hara (Ed.), *Ajia keizairon (Asian economic theory)* (pp. 295–323). NTT Shuppan.

Takahashi, A. (2000). *Gendai Myanmā no nōson keizai—Ikō keizaika no nōmin to hi-nōmin (Myanmar's village economy in transition: Farmers and non-farmers under the market-oriented economy)*. Tokyo Daigaku Shuppankai.

Takahashi, A. (2002). Biruma—Gun ni yoru 'kaihatsu' no teitai (Burma: Stagnated 'development' by the military). In A. Suehiro (Ed.), 'Kaihatsu' no jidai to 'mosaku' no jidai—1960 nendai - genzai (The Era of 'Development' and the Era of 'Fumble': 1960s to present), (Iwanami Kōza Tōnan Ajiashi 9) (pp. 205–230). Iwanami Shoten.

Takahashi, A. (2004). Tōhoku Myanmā (Biruma) sankanchi ni okeru tanada no keizaiteki sonritu kōzō to shigen kanri (Economic sustainability of rice terraces and forest resource management in the mountainous area of Northeast Myanmar (Burma)). *Tokyo Daigaku Tōyōbunka Kenkyūjo Kiyō (The Memoirs of the Institute of Oriental Culture, Tokyo, University of Tokyo), 146*, 309–352.

Takahashi, A. (2007). Yakihata, tanada, Marē ·konekushon—Myanmā ·Chin kyūryō ni okeru shigen riyō to keizai kaisō (Swiddens, rice terraces, and Malay connections: Resource use and socio-economic strata in the Chin Hills, Myanmar). *Tōnan ajia kenkyū (Japanese Journal of Southeast Asian Studies), 45*(3), 404–427.

Takahashi, A. (2008a). Biruma kome yushutsu toukei no saikentō to 'kokunai', kokkyo, kaigai yushutsuryō no hensen (A review of the rice export statistics of Burma (Myanmar): Time series variation in volume of 'inland', border and foreign trade.). *Tōyōbunka (Oriental Culture), 88*, 49–67.

Takahashi, A. (2008b). Fānibaru (Furnivall). In S. Momoki (Ed.), *'Shimpan' Tōnan Ajia o shiru jiten (New cyclopaedia of Southeast Asia)* (Vol. 369). Heibonsha.

Takahashi, A. (2012). *Myanmā no kuni to tami—Nichimen hikaku sonraku shakairon no kokoromi (State and people of Myanmar: Toward a theoretical comparison of village societies in Japan and Myanmar)*. Akashishoten.

Takahashi, A. (2013). 'Sakoku' to keizai seisai—Shūkai okure no kaihatsu shugi (Isolation and economic sanctions: Developmentalism one lap behind). In *Myanmā o shiru tameno 60 shō (60 chapters to learn about Myanmar)* (pp. 299–303). Akashishoten.

Takahashi, A. (2015). Hikaku no naka no Myanmā sonraku shakairon—Nihon, Tai, soshite Myanmā (Comparative study of Myanmar village society: Japan, Thailand, and Myanmar). *Tōnan Ajia rekishi to bunka (Southeast Asian History and Culture), Tōnan Ajia gakkaishi (Journal of Japan society for Southeast Asian Studies), 44*, 5–26.

Takahashi, A. (2016). Taisei tankan to Myanmā nōson shakai no shakai keizai henyō (Regime change and the socioeconomic transformation of Myanmar's village society). In H. Nagai, H. Tanabe & K. Nemoto (Eds.), *'Aunsansūchī seiken' no Myanmā: Minshuka no yukue to aratana hatten moderu (Myanmar under the 'Aung San Suu Kyi Administration': The future of democratisation and new models of development)* (pp. 111–150). Akashishoten.

Takahashi, A. (2018). *Sōsei no Myanmā—Nōson no kurashi kara mita, henbō suru kuni (Myanmar of the people: A country in transition, seen through the life in rural villages)*. Akashishoten.

Tamaki, A. (1983). *Mizushakai no kōzō (Structure of the water society)*. Ronsosha.

Tamura, K. (1981). Kami-Biruma no sonraku no kōzō to chitsujo (Structure and order of a village in Upper Burma). *Kagoshima Daigaku Kyōyōbu Shigakuka Hōkoku (Historical Science Reports of Kagoshima University), 30*, 35–47.

Tanahashi, H. (1955). *Nōka shōkumiai no kenkyū (Study on farmers' small associations)*. Sangyotosho.

Teruoka, S. (1981). Shōwa kyōkōki no nōson taisaku (Policies for village collectives during the showa depression). *Kansai Daigaku Keizaironshū (The Economic Review of Kansai University), 31*(2), 151–203.

Tönnies, F. (1957). *Gemainshafuto to gezerushafuto: Junsui shakaigaku no kihon gainen jo ·ge (Gemeinschaft and Gesellschaft: Basic concepts of pure sociology)*. (J. Suginohara, Trans.). Iwanami Shoten (Original work published 1887).

Tsubouchi, Y. & Maeda, N. (1977). *Kakukazoku saikō (Reconsideration of nuclear families)*. Koubundou.

Watanabe, A. (1985). Nihon fashizumu to uyoku nōmin undō: Chibaken kōkoku nōmin jichirenmei o jirei to shite (Japanese fascism and the right-wing peasant movement: The case of the imperial farmers' self-governing federation of Chiba prefecture). *Tochiseidosigaku (Historiography of Land Systems), 27*(3), 1–17.

Index

A. Takahashi, *Regime Changes and Socio-economic History of Rural Myanmar, 1986–2019*, Studies in Economic History,
https://doi.org/10.1007/978-981-99-3272-6

R

S

T

U

SPRINGER NATURE

GPSR Compliance

The European Union's (EU) General Product Safety Regulation (GPSR) is a set of rules that requires consumer products to be safe and our obligations to ensure this.

If you have any concerns about our products, you can contact us on ProductSafety@springernature.com

In case Publisher is established outside the EU, the EU authorized representative is:

Springer Nature Customer Service Center GmbH
Europaplatz 3
69115 Heidelberg, Germany

The manufacturer's authorised representative in the EU is Springer
Nature Customer Service Centre GmbH, Europaplatz 3, 69115 Heidelberg,
Germany. If you have any concerns regarding our products, please
contact ProductSafety@springernature.com

Printed and bound by CPI Group (UK) Ltd, Croydon, CR0 4YY
30/09/2026
02225324-0008